A History of Old English Literature

BLACKWELL HISTORIES OF LITERATURE

General editor: Peter Brown, University of Kent at Canterbury

This series aims to be comprehensive and succinct, and to recognize that to write literary history involves more than placing texts in chronological sequence. Thus the emphasis within each volume falls both on plotting the significant literary developments of a given period and on the wider cultural contexts within which they occurred. "Cultural history" is construed in broad terms and authors address such issues as politics, society, the arts, ideologies, varieties of literary production and consumption, and dominant genres and modes. Each volume evaluates the lasting effects of the literary period under discussion, incorporating such topics as critical reception and modern reputations. The effect of each volume is to give the reader a sense of possessing a crucial sector of literary terrain, of understanding the forces that give a period its distinctive cast, and of seeing how writing of a given period impacts on, and is shaped by, its cultural circumstances. Each volume recommends itself as providing an authoritative and up-to-date entrée to texts and issues, and their historical implications, and will therefore interest students, teachers and the general reader alike. The series as a whole will be attractive to libraries as a work that renews and redefines a familiar form.

A HISTORY OF OLD ENGLISH LITERATURE

R. D. Fulk
and
Christopher M. Cain

with a chapter on saints' legends by
Rachel S. Anderson

Blackwell
Publishing

350 Main Street, Malden, MA 02148-5018, USA
108 Cowley Road, Oxford OX4 1JF, UK
550 Swanston Street, Carlton South, Victoria 3053, Australia
Kurfürstendamm 57, 10707 Berlin, Germany

First published 2003 by Blackwell Publishers Ltd, a Blackwell Publishing company

Library of Congress Cataloguing-in-Publication Data

Fulk, R. D. (Robert Dennis)
 A history of Old English Literature / R.D. Fulk and Christopher M. Cain ;
with a chapter on saints' legends by Rachel S. Anderson.
  p.   cm. — (Blackwell histories of literature)
 Includes bibliographical references and index.
 ISBN 0–631–22397–5 (HB)
  1. English literature—Old English, ca. 450–1100—History and criticism.
 2. Hagiography.   I. Cain, Christopher M.   II. Anderson, Rachel S.   III. Title.
 IV. Series.

PR173 .F85 2002
829.09—dc21

2002020896

A catalogue record for this title is available from the British Library.

Set in 10.5 on 13 pt Galliard
by Ace Filmsetting Ltd, Frome, Somerset
Printed and bound in Great Britain
by TJ International, Padstow, Cornwall

For further information on
Blackwell Publishing, visit our website:
www.blackwellpublishing.com

Contents

Illustrations

Map

Plates

Preface

With this study we hope to serve the needs of those students and teachers who feel particularly committed to the changes that have characterized our field in recent years. The renewed emphasis on historicism and the decline of formalist aestheticism in medieval studies have rendered it desirable to have a literary history that attends more singularly to the material and social contexts and uses of Old English texts. Although the need is greater than this volume can really satisfy, we hope that the present study will nonetheless prove useful to those who, like us, see literature's relation to history and culture as our field's area of chief pedagogical interest, and the respect in which it has most to offer literary studies at large.

The Anglo-Latin context is of particular concern. Michael Lapidge has put the matter succinctly: "We should always remember that works in Latin and the vernacular were copied together in Anglo-Saxon scriptoria, and were arguably composed together in Anglo-Saxon schools. What is needed, therefore, is an integrated literary history which treats Latin and vernacular production together as two facets of the one culture, not as isolated phenomena" (1991: 951–2 n. 1). It may be an obstacle to the compilation of such a history that, as he says, "No adequate history of Anglo-Latin literature of the later period has yet been written," but the insights furnished by his own prodigious contributions to Anglo-Latin studies take us close to the goal. Still, it would not have been possible to produce so thoroughly an integrative study in a volume of this size. Although we have attempted throughout to sketch briefly the Latin background against which Old English texts ought to be viewed, we have in no sense aimed for a balanced treatment of Latin and English texts, but we have attended to the former only to the extent that they contribute to our understanding of the latter. Also, because of length limitations, we have not been able to treat every known text in Old English; yet in our effort to cover a wider range of material than has been usual in Old English literary histories we have been obliged to treat fairly briefly some of the texts, particularly poetic ones, that have, primarily on aesthetic grounds, historically received a disproportional share of critical attention.

Although we have tried to emulate one respect in which prior histories have been most useful – in their bibliographical guidance – we have laid special emphasis on scholarly studies of the past 15 years, because students may generally find references to earlier works in these and in prior histories. Naturally, many studies of real value are not cited here, since our bibliographical coverage has been highly selective.

It is a pleasant duty to acknowledge the debt of thanks we have incurred in the compilation of this volume. Alfred David very generously read the manuscript and offered countless invaluable suggestions. Michael Lapidge provided timely copies of material in press, and Stefan Jurasinski furnished expert advice on legal literature. The staff of the Indiana University Libraries came to our rescue continually. Leanda Shrimpton oversaw the production of the illustrations, and Anna Oxbury's copyediting improved the manuscript immensely. We are especially indebted to Andrew McNeillie, who conceived this project and guided it from start to finish with care and understanding. To all of these generous souls we wish to express our gratitude.

R. D. F., C. M. C.
Bloomington

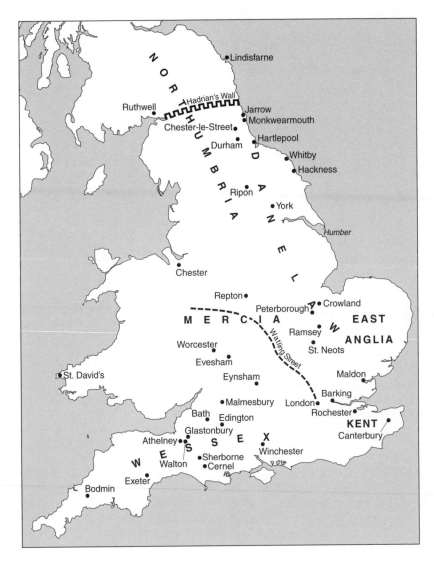

Some places mentioned in the text

Introduction

Anglo-Saxon England and Its Literature: A Social History

I Cultural Difference and Cultural Change

One of the aims of literary studies in recent years has been to defamiliarize the most natural-seeming aspects of our own culture, to promote awareness of how our way of life is neither natural nor inevitable. The importance of culture studies in current literary scholarship thus arises in part from the role that an awareness of alterity has come to play, since nothing illuminates the contingencies of contemporary attitudes and ideas as much as the study of cultural difference. Within the field of English, then, Old English studies afford unique opportunities, since no literature in English is as culturally remote as that of the Anglo-Saxons, and the differences expose clearly some of the otherwise invisible assumptions on which modernity, as we perceive it, is based. To cite just one example, the very act of reading a book, such as this one, differs fundamentally from the early medieval experience, and in a variety of ways. Even when reading was a private activity, readers commonly pointed to the words and spoke them aloud;[1] but more often reading was a communal activity in which many "readers" never actually saw the page. In a modern classroom the text is a physical object: usually each student has an identical copy, and when instructed to do so, all turn to a particular page. But no two copies of a medieval book were alike, and in any case books were precious objects, the product of weeks of painstaking labor, from the preparation of the animal skins of which they were made to the copying, letter by letter, of the text, and thus they were too valuable for wholesale distribution to students in the early period. Naturally, studying a text is a different and slower process under such circumstances. Reading aloud in groups differs from silent reading in that it is not a method well suited to the study of complex philosophical writing, such as the products of scholasticism that arose only in the twelfth and thirteenth centuries, when silent reading became the norm in academic settings. The method of reading thus affected the very nature of early medieval texts (Saenger 1982: 385–6; 1997: 83–99). Even so fundamental a matter as word division is different: designed for oral delivery, Old English texts of this period organize syllables not into words but into groups arranged around a primary stress. When even so seemingly straightforward a process as reading differs in significant ways, one should expect the literature of the Anglo-Saxons to reflect some enormous material and conceptual differences in regard to matters we take for granted. One purpose of this introduction is to highlight a few of those differences, the ones most necessary to an understanding of Old English literature.

For literary purposes the defining characteristic of Anglo-Saxon culture is its fusion of two contrasting strains, the military culture of the Germanic peoples who invaded Britain in the fifth century and the Mediterranean learning introduced by Christian missionaries from the end of the sixth.[2] With its emphasis on heroic legend, the native literature of the Anglo-Saxon invaders reflected the martial basis of their society. The literate products of Mediterranean learning are of a sort more familiar to us: prose predominates, and genres are diverse, including sacred narratives, homilies, histories, annals, works of philosophy, and many other sorts, some of purely liturgical, legal, or administrative use. In the surviving literature of the Anglo-Saxons these two cultural strands are woven into a single fabric, often in ways that seem startling to us. Nowhere is the tension between the two deployed more effectively than in the preeminent work of Old English literature, *Beowulf*, which tells of clearly ancient heroic deeds from a contemporized perspective, attributing to the hero some of the qualities of a good Christian. This fusion of cultural strains characterizes a variety of texts and artifacts, including saints' lives recast in the terms of heroic poetry; King Alfred's translation of Boethius' *Consolation of Philosophy*, into which Weland the smith of Germanic myth is introduced; the Old English Orosius, in which the Germanic conquerors of the Roman Empire are portrayed more sympathetically than in the Latin original; the Anglo-Saxon Chronicle, which contains passages in prose and verse that call to mind heroic legend; and the Franks (or Auzon, or Clermont) Casket, a box of carved whalebone on which are depicted scenes from early Germanic legend side by side with the adoration of the magi and the destruction of Jerusalem by the soon-to-be Emperor Titus in AD 70 (see chapter 1 and plate 4).

A hindrance to a concise description of Anglo-Saxon culture is the length of the historical period, which lasted from the invasions of the fifth century beyond the arrival of the Normans in 1066, as Old English texts continued to be copied for another century and a half. Naturally the society underwent some profound changes over the course of so many centuries; and yet the literature does not always reflect those changes, especially the poetry, since it is steeped in tradition and often seems to reflect a long-outmoded way of life. The culture that the invaders brought with them in the fifth century certainly had much in common with that of the (mostly) Germanic tribes described by Cornelius Tacitus in his *Germania* (ed. Winterbottom 1975, trans. Rives 1999), completed in AD 98. At times Tacitus is frankly moralizing, chastening his fellow Romans by portraying the admirable qualities and customs of peoples they considered barbaric; at other times he is disapproving of Germanic practices, and so we need not assume that he has distorted the general outline of the societies he describes for the sake of portraying the Germans uniformly as noble savages. Caution is advisable in generalizing about the invaders of Britain from Tacitus' account, as contact with Rome was just beginning to produce in his day important changes among the Germans, particularly in regard to the growth of private property and the rise of new kinds of military organization and technology. But the comparison is nonetheless instructive, especially in regard to *Beowulf*, which depicts a world that has more in common with the tribal culture described by Tacitus than with Anglo-Saxon society of about 1000, when the manuscript was copied.[3]

Tacitus' Germany is a collection of some 70 nations perennially at war with their neighbors and among themselves. Each is ruled by a king, who is supported by his *comitatus*, or war-band of retainers. He provides them with horses, arms, and plentiful feasts; they in turn contribute cattle or grain and serve him in battle. It is the duty of the *comitatus* to glorify their lord by their deeds, and it is lifelong infamy to survive one's chief and return from battle if he has fallen. So eager for martial exploits are the young men that in times of peace, those of noble family will often seek out other nations in pursuit of opportunities to fight. At their feasts it is not unusual for the men from morning to night to consume a fermented drink made from barley or wheat – Tacitus' Roman audience naturally was unfamiliar with beer and ale – and as a consequence, dangerous quarrels frequently arise, and blood is not uncommonly spilt. The feuds ensuing from such manslaughter are a matter of intense honor to the family of the slain. However, vengeance in like kind is not their only option, as the killer may pay compensation, if that is acceptable to all.

To what extent Tacitus' observations still held true for the Anglo-Saxon invaders of Britain is difficult to say, but certainly the world he describes differs surprisingly little from that of *Beowulf* and the other surviving scraps of heroic verse in Old English, in which most of these same features are evident. Nonetheless, Old English society has already evolved a considerable distance from this model by the time the first manuscript records appear, and long before the time of the Norman invasion the last remnants of tribal society are a distant recollection. In the early period the English were divided into a number of kingdoms, as often at war with one another as with the Britons. By the end of the period we find instead an English proto-nation under a centralized government, with a complex economy supported by well-regulated trade and taxation. While Tacitus describes a world in which there is no urban life, just villages of scattered wooden structures, by the time of the Venerable Bede, writing in the early eighth century, York was already an urban center, and in the eleventh century its inhabitants numbered probably as many as 10,000.[4] London was no doubt larger, and from an early date. Even the fundamental unit of society, the *comitatus*, grew outmoded early on: the Old English word for such a group, *gedryht*, has fallen out of general use by the time of the earliest records, and it is preserved only as a poetic term.

Yet several aspects of the Germanic society that Tacitus describes continue to be relevant in the Anglo-Saxon world, albeit in altered form. The duty to vengeance remained an imperative to the end of the period, and though the Church discouraged feuds, assigning identical penances for homicides and for killings performed in vengeance, the only method of dealing with homicide in Anglo-Saxon law until the Norman Conquest was through the action of kindred (Whitelock 1951: 13–17). The law codes continued to regulate the degree and division of compensation (called *wergild*, lit. 'man-payment') till the end of the period. Payment was originally measured in livestock, the native currency (OE *feoh*, becoming ModE *fee*, and cognate with Latin *pecu* 'sheep, flocks; money'), and its acceptance was no doubt viewed not as a mercenary act but both as the killer's admission of wrongdoing and as reaffirmation of the honor of the victim and his family.[5] Yet wergild assumed new functions and forms as the society evolved. It may at first have been simply a device for putting an end to feuds, which might otherwise continue indefinitely, killing following upon killing, as sometimes happens in the Icelandic sagas. In the historical period, though, wergild is a measure of social status, since every man and woman bears a wergild, valued on a scale from monarch to slave. Social rank determines the amount to be paid not just in cases of homicide but in offenses of various kinds, and wergild functions, it seems, less as a means to end feuds than as a deterrent to personal injury. This was particularly important to the Church, since its members could not rely on family to exact vengeance when a churchman was killed. In a society in which there was nothing like a constabulary, the only very reliable source of personal security was the threat of vengeance posed by one's kinsmen or lord. This is why the lone and lordless exile is portrayed as the most pitiful of figures in Old English verse. Wergild payable to the king thus served to protect those without the support of family, such as clergy and foreign merchants. It also, however, came to serve the function of extending the power and wealth of the monarchy, as in the later period the laws provide for the payment of wergilds to the king for all sorts of infractions.

The larger point to be drawn is that if the social conditions described in verse seem to resemble more closely those of Tacitus' *Germania* than the complex society that England had become by the tenth century, this may be taken as a reflection of the way that the ancient traditions of verse archaize and rebuild on a heroic scale every variety of matter they touch. This is true of native traditions like those of *Beowulf*, but also of biblical narrative and saints' lives, in which patriarchs and saints are recast as God's heroic champions, and Christ's apostles play the role of his *comitatus*. This transformative habit is in turn a reflection of the continually fruitful tension, mentioned above as pervading Old English literature, between native and Mediterranean influences. References in the literature show that the Anglo-Saxons were keenly aware of both their past among the Germanic nations of the Continent and their present status as the bulwark of Christian civilization among the unconverted nations of the north. That they retained a sense of community with the rest of the Germanic world, even as the form of English society grew ever more different from it, is shown in a variety of ways, but most clearly in the fact that even as late as the dawn of the eleventh century, heroic verse dealing with legends set in Scandinavia and on the Continent, like *Beowulf*, with no explicit connection to England, continued to be copied into English manuscripts.

2 Gender and Authority

The world that Tacitus describes is obviously very much a male-centered
one, and it might be expected that in a society so dedicated to warfare,
women would play decidedly secondary roles. Certainly there was nothing like equality of the sexes, and yet Tacitus admiringly portrays Germanic women as both responsible and respected members of the society
– though it should be remembered that his aim in doing so is to draw
pointed contrasts with Roman women, whose behavior he held in particularly low esteem. Germanic women, he says, are close at hand in
warfare, and their presence serves to deter cowardice, making men conscious of their honor. The men are said to seek women's advice and to
act upon it, crediting women with prescience – a quality attributed to
Germanic women in some other sources, including Caesar's *De bello
Gallico*. To insure peace, young women taken from noble families make
the best hostages (hostages being treated not as prisoners but as members of the court, playing a diplomatic role), as the men are more concerned for their women's safety than for their own. The husband brings
a dowry to the wife, the opposite of the Roman custom. Tacitus is
emphatic about the wife's role as partner in toil and danger, suffering
and daring with her husband in peace and war alike; but such remarks
must be weighed against his observation that the men, when they are
not fighting or hunting, simply sleep and eat and do nothing, relegating care of the house and fields to the women, the old men, and the
weakest members of the family.

Certain of these observations resonate in the poetic records of Old
English. One poet tells us that a wife should be generous with gifts,
kind to those under her care, cheerful, trustworthy with secrets, and
courteous in the distribution of mead, and she should advise her husband well (*Maxims I* 82–92). *Beowulf* indeed shows us Wealhtheow,
the queen of Denmark, distributing drink to the *comitatus* at a feast,
rewarding Beowulf's valor with rich gifts, and offering her husband
advice on affairs of state. A term applied twice to women in verse (and
once to an angel) is *freoðu-webbe* 'peace-weaver'. This has been interpreted to refer to noblewomen's role in diplomatic marriages arranged
to secure peace between hostile nations, the metaphor alluding to medieval women's chief occupation, the weaving of cloth. It may, however,
have wider reference, in accordance with the level-headed and peace-
able sorts of qualities attributed above to a good wife. This, in any case,

is what is implied by the *Beowulf* poet's remark that the pride and cruelty of the princess (Mod-)Thryth were not qualities appropriate to a *freoðu-webbe* (lines 1940–3). Certainly, though, diplomatic marriages were of great strategic importance (despite Beowulf's doubts about their efficacy, lines 2029–31), as, for example, Æthelberht I of Kent's marriage to Bertha, a Christian Frankish princess, no doubt played a significant role in the first Roman missionaries' success in converting him.

It has often been said that women are severely marginalized in *Beowulf* and similar heroic verse. Certainly males are at center stage, as one might expect in poetry about feats of arms. Yet it would be rash to suppose that martial deeds are the sole measure of true worth in the world that Old English heroic poetry portrays; and even if they were, the ferocity and devotion to the duty of vengeance shown by Grendel's mother would serve to challenge the underlying assumption about gender and heroic accomplishments. But the *Beowulf* poet develops the hero's humane qualities and diplomatic skills in some detail (see chapter 9), and so there is no reason to suppose that the portrayal of some of the same qualities in Wealhtheow and the explicit reverence expressed for her are not just what they appear to be – marks of her genuine importance. In actuality, only the character of Beowulf himself is developed extensively, and thus it may be asked whether any of the remaining characters except for Hrothgar and Grendel is accorded more real attention than Wealhtheow and Grendel's mother. So, too, though the two fragments of *Waldere*, another heroic poem, are brief, the speaker of one of them is a woman, Hildegyth – though she is hardly a *freoðu-webbe* but one who incites her male companions to battle. In the related heroic traditions of Scandinavia, both in the poetic edda and in some of the sagas, women are often the central figures, in part because they bring the greatest psychological complexity to heroic legends: owing loyalty both to their own and to their husband's families, they are often required to choose between courses of action that will produce equally tragic results (see Phillpotts 1928).

When we turn to religious verse, in their agency the female characters contrast markedly with those of later literature. Cynewulf's Elene, as the emperor's viceroy in Jersualem, is that poem's central figure of authority and heroic action against God's enemies; in his poem on St. Juliana, the martyr converts the seemingly passive virtue of chastity into a literal wrestling match in which she overpowers the devil; and Judith in the poem by that name is, like Beowulf, the beheader of her enemy.[6] When we consider how infrequently, in the period from the

Norman Conquest until the rise of the novel, narratives were again to center on such prominent female protagonists in English literature, the portrayal of women in Old English heroic literature seems quite remarkable.

The poetry, which is an amalgam of artificial conventions, represents an idealized view. Yet history records the memory of Anglo-Saxon women who did hold positions of authority and public esteem, doing the same work as men. Three about whom we know something are Hild, Hygeburg, and Æthelflæd. Hild (614–80) was a grandniece of Edwin, the first Christian king of Northumbria, and she converted with him in 627. She presided as abbess first at Hartlepool and then at Whitby, which she founded; she also organized a monastery at Hackness. So successful was her foundation at Whitby, the Venerable Bede tells us, writing in 731, that by his day the house had produced five bishops. In her own day, too, her success can be measured by the fact that Whitby was chosen as the site of the great synod of 664, at which it was decided that the Anglo-Saxon Church would follow Roman rather than Celtic practice in determining the date of Easter – a seemingly trivial question, but one which masked larger issues, particularly those of the subjection of insular Christianity to Roman authority and its integration with the Church on the Continent.[7] It was at Whitby also that Cædmon lived (see chapter 6). Behr (2000: 51–2) finds in the archaeological record evidence that the authority of noblewomen like Hild in religion and politics in the Conversion Age was a tradition inherited from pre-Christian times.

In the two centuries after the Conversion, about a dozen pioneering English abbots and missionaries were memorialized in Latin accounts of their lives, some of them produced by the leading scholars of the day, including Bede and Alcuin (see below). Two brothers from Walton who participated in the Bonifatian mission, Willibald and Wynnebald, were thus memorialized by Hygeburg, an English nun at Heidenheim in what is now Germany, in highly wrought Latin prose (ed. Holder-Egger 1887: 80–117; partial trans. Talbot 1954: 153–77). That Hygeburg is not an unusual case in her Latinity is shown by the number of women who corresponded with Aldhelm and the missionary Boniface (see below), and by Aldhelm's description of the wide reading of the nuns at Barking for whom he composed his prose *De virginitate*.[8] Hygeburg's lives of Willibald and Wynnebald illustrate that at least in the pre-viking period there was women's scholarship to rival men's. Work such as this hints at a remarkable set of conditions in education of the day, conditions to which there was no parallel in England in the following centuries until the Early Modern period.

Æthelflæd (d. 918) was *hlæfdige* 'lady' of the Mercians, a status roughly equivalent to the earlier status of queen, except that Mercia was in the process of permanently losing its independence, and she was thus ultimately subject to the rule of her younger brother, Edward the Elder, king of Wessex. She rallied the Mercians against the vikings of the Danelaw, the area of viking control that included all of England east of Watling Street, and perfecting a policy devised by her father, King Alfred the Great, she built and garrisoned fortifications that proved highly effective at ending Danish depredations in Mercia. Then, in 917–18, she and Edward, acting in close concert, launched an offensive that led ultimately to the recapture of the Danelaw and the end of all Danish control of England south of the Humber. There are indications, as well, that her military strategies were effective at securing Mercia against renewed viking attacks from the north (see Wainwright 1959). In her day she dominated the political scene in the midlands and the north, and her military accomplishments enabled the unification of England for the first time under a single king of the royal house of Wessex.

Such case histories suggest that Anglo-Saxon women enjoyed opportunities of an extraordinary nature by comparison with later eras. There is in fact evidence that their institutional rights were not inconsiderable, as documented by Fell (1984: 56–9). The payment of a dowry to the wife, observed by Tacitus among the Germans, is a fact of Anglo-Saxon society. Called in Old English the *morgen-gifu* 'morning-conveyance', it was usually a substantial amount, in some known cases amounting to five hundred or more acres of land, and it became the possession of the woman herself, not of her male kin, to dispose of as she pleased. Over and above this dowry a wife had other rights to property, as a married couple's estate was held jointly, and in the earliest laws, at least, a woman might leave her husband and still retain half the property if the children remained with her, much as in later Icelandic law. Women's wills testify to the amount of wealth they could accumulate and to their right to leave it to whichever inheritors they pleased. Conditions naturally varied from place to place over such a lengthy period, and it seems that women's authority and their opportunities, especially in the Church, declined at a rate inverse to that of the growth in the Church's power in England (see Dietrich 1979: 38, and Lees 1999: 133–7). Most of these rights were abrogated by the Normans, since the feudal system they brought with them was predicated on land tenure in exchange for military service, a system that disfavored women's control of land. There is thus justice in the conclusion of Doris Stenton that English women were in the Anglo-Saxon period "more nearly the equal companions of their husbands and brothers than at any other period before the modern age" (1957: 348). Such a conclusion challenges certain preconceptions of mainstream gender theory, which, as Lees (1997: 152) remarks, are often founded on presentist assumptions. Thus, as she observes, the study of Old English texts potentially has a singular contribution to make to the larger realm of feminist studies – a contribution, however, that is as yet almost entirely unrealized, as gender theory has rather dictated the nature of Old English feminist criticism than benefited from Anglo-Saxonists' awareness of historical difference.

3 Effects of Conversion

It is inevitable that Anglo-Saxon society as we encounter it in the earliest records should have differed markedly from the world that Tacitus describes, if for no better reason than that more than half a millennium elapsed between them. But doubtless the chief impetus for change in early English society was the conversion to Christianity. We know very little about the religious beliefs of the invaders. The names of some of their gods, preserved in the names of the days of the week, in royal pedigrees tracing the descent of monarchs from Woden and other gods, and in some other glancing contexts, are known to us, but what form worship of the gods took, and whether there was a systematic mythology about them, as there was much later in Scandinavia for some of the same gods, is not known (see Niles 1991a). The English were nonetheless slow to give them up. The work of conversion began in 597 with the arrival of Augustine, prior of St. Andrews in Rome, along with nearly 40 Roman monks, sent by Pope Gregory the Great; and yet the early successes of these Roman missionaries were largely obliterated by the deaths of the first converted kings, after which paganism returned to most areas. As a consequence, the last of the Anglo-Saxon areas to be converted, the Isle of Wight, did not adopt Christianity until 686, during Bede's lifetime.

Conversion represents a fundamental shift in the society, something far greater than simply a change of faith. It created a new class of citizens, churchmen who stood outside any family structure, under the direct protection of the king. Conversion of the king was all-important, as his consent enabled the imposition of tithes and fasts, which were voluntary at first, but which grew to be compulsory by the tenth century. The king's conversion also entailed the granting of authority to ecclesiastical law. To be sure, ecclesiastical authority was not immediately or wholly effective at obliterating Germanic customs disapproved by the Church, such as divorce, concubinage, and marriage within prohibited degrees of relation. But it should be clear that royal conversion amounted to the ceding of considerable power to the Church: conversion established an authority that would grow in time to challenge that of the monarchs themselves as the Church accumulated wealth and prestige through tithes and through bequests from the rich and powerful for the repose of their souls. Conversion also had the less tangible effect of producing a sense of community with Christian Europe, promoting the imitation of certain Continental practices. The most salient of these for the economy was the introduction of a system of coinage in Kent and East Anglia before the end of the seventh century, and in the other major kingdoms soon afterward.

The most important consequence of the Conversion, however, was the foundation of a literate culture on the Latin model. The early Germanic peoples had an alphabet (or *futhorc*, a name derived from the first six letters) consisting of runes, ultimately based on Mediterranean alphabets (see Elliott 1989, Page 1999). Shaped for carving on wood and other materials, runes were employed for short inscriptions, such as those on surviving Old English coins, weapons, and other implements (see plate 1), but the recording of texts of any substantial length had to await the introduction of writing on vellum. This innovation had consequences that were immediate and far-reaching for the society. It contributed immensely to the development of a uniform code of law by enabling laws to be recorded in a fixed state, and indeed, Æthelberht I of Kent, the first Anglo-Saxon king to be converted, recorded laws "after the models of the Romans," as Bede says – laws that are now known to be based, in part, on literate Continental models.[9] More important, churches and monasteries produced charters as an effective means of securing their land against seizure by competing claimants. The use of charters, writs, and wills subsequently spread to the laity, and they came to assume the first degree of importance in an economy based on land ownership, in which social status, as expressed in wergild, was measured by the extent of one's acreage.

Plate 1   Late ninth-century iron *seax* (long knife or short sword, 81.1 cm) found in the Thames at Battersea. Inlaid on the blade in wire are a *futhorc* and a man's name, BEAGNOÞ © British Museum.

4 Latinity of the Pre-Viking Age

The uses of writing in Anglo-Saxon England are in fact surprisingly varied when one considers that literacy in the modern sense of the word was for the better part of the period limited effectively to ecclesiastics, and thus its products should be expected to pertain to matters of religion and church governance. Indeed, few vernacular texts survive from the early period, when, as King Alfred observes, the language of written texts was normally Latin (see below). It is natural that Latin should have been the usual language of ecclesiastical written discourse in the early period because the Anglo-Saxon Church during the first centuries after the Conversion sought contact with the greater Christian community of Europe and inspiration in the patrology, both of which depended upon using the international language of the Church. As the faith became established in England and Christian scholarship flourished, the cultivation of Latin literacy enabled the English to produce native Latin literature modeled on what had been gathered from the Mediterranean world, and thus to assert England's inheritance of the mantle worn by the Church Fathers. Reading this literature, one imagines a feeling of wonder on the part of its creators as they contemplated their role as pioneers of the faith, living at a great moment in history, and given by God the responsibility of making themselves the new Fathers on the northern frontier. Their conception of their role as inheritors is evident even in the mechanics of early English book production: the Codex Amiatinus, for example, an important bible made at Monkwearmouth-Jarrow during Bede's lifetime, is so faithfully patterned after its Italian exemplars that it was not recognized until recently as English (see plate 2).

One of the chief occupations of early English ecclesiastics was thus the intensive study of Latin.[10] Indeed, knowledge of Latin was essential to understanding Scripture and to the proper functioning of monasteries, as monks were expected to participate in the Divine Office, the daily cycle of prayers around which monastic activities were structured. From the age of seven, oblates learned by heart the prayers included in the Divine Office (such as the Pater Noster and the Creed), the entire Latin Psalter, and significant portions of the Latin hymnal. Although beginners were given a general explanation of the meaning of such texts, only later, as they began to acquire the rudiments of Latin grammar, would they understand fully what they were reciting. Since monks were expected to speak Latin among themselves, in the later Anglo-Saxon period some of the first texts that the learner would have encountered were *colloquia*, Latin conversations generally among fictitious tradesmen, which imparted the vocabulary necessary for everyday transactions (see Lendinara 1991: 275). The linguistic fundamentals were learned from Latin grammars, and several Anglo-Saxon scholars produced these for their students; others produced elementary treatises on Latin meter and orthography (chapter 6), since these subjects were also taken up at this early stage in the novice's training. It would be difficult to improve upon Michael Lapidge's account of what came next (1996a: 2–3):

> After the novice had learned the rudiments of Latin grammar and metre, he proceeded to those Latin texts which constituted the medieval curriculum, a course lasting some ten years. The novices read the texts with

CODICIBVS SACRIS HOSTILI CLADE PERVSTIS
ESDRA DO FERVENS HOC REPARAVIT OPVS

Plate 2 The Codex Amiatinus (Florence, Biblioteca Medicea-Laurenziana, Amiatino 1), fol. v, showing Ezra in the library/scriptorium, with a fine classicizing majuscule inscription in the margin. This manuscript, the oldest extant complete Latin bible, is one of the three pandects that Bede tell us were made under the direction of Ceolfrith, abbot of Monkwearmouth-Jarrow, who died in 716. Photo SCALA.

minute attention: word for word, line for line. Probably the master dictated a passage and the students transcribed it onto wax tablets [see plate 3]; by class on the following day they had to learn the text thoroughly. They then erased the passage and replaced it with the next.

Lapidge further points out that the contents of the curriculum exerted an influence on the kinds of vernacular literature preserved in Old English manuscripts. The chief variety of text studied was a series of versifications of Scripture (such as Alcimus Avitus' *Poema de Mosaicae historiae gestis* and Juvencus' *Evangelia*), and indeed one of the four Old English poetic manuscripts, the Junius or "Cædmon" Manuscript, is a collection of vernacular works of this kind, including *Genesis, Exodus,* and *Daniel.* Another component of the curriculum made students familiar with poetic works of allegorical and typological significance, including Caelius Sedulus' *Carmen paschale* and Prudentius' *Psychomachia*; correspondingly, there are some Old English poetic allegories, chief of which is *The Phoenix* (chapter 6), a translation of the *De ave phoenice* attributed to Lactantius (itself a poem studied in some versions of the curriculum) that appends to the story of the phoenix's death and rebirth a versified allegorical explication. Early in the curriculum, learners also studied the moral maxims of the *Disticha Catonis* – another text that was translated into Old English – and although this text can hardly have given rise to the Anglo-Saxon predilection for the gnomic mode in verse (see chapter 8, section 1), certainly it fed a deep-rooted tradition in early Germanic poetry. It may even have inspired collections like the Old English *Precepts* and *Maxims I* and *II* – though these do have parallels in Old Icelandic verse. In some versions of the curriculum, learners studied the collections of *enigmata* 'mysteries' of the Late Latin poet Symphosius and of the Anglo-Saxons Aldhelm, Tatwine, Eusebius, and Boniface. These were doubtless the inspiration for the Old English riddles preserved in the Exeter Book (chapter 1), and indeed two of those riddles are translations from the curricular texts. Knowledge of the curriculum is in fact fundamental to an understanding of the composition of the Old English poetic corpus, a point that will be taken up again below (chapter 8). For now it is sufficient to note that Old English literature is preserved solely in manuscripts compiled by ecclesiastics, and the literary tastes of those compilers were formed by intensive and protracted study of Latin texts like these.

Within a century of the Conversion, English schools were producing scholars in the first rank of Latin learning. The chief cause of this was

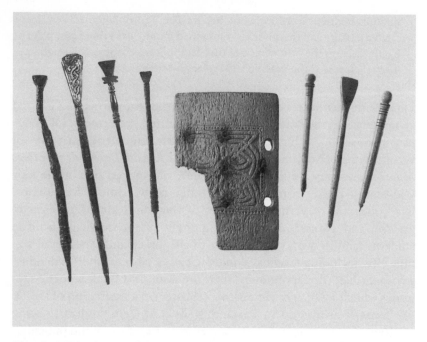

Plate 3 Tablet from Suffolk and styli found at Whitby, made ca. 800. A recessed area on the reverse of the tablet is designed to hold wax, on which students would write with a stylus. The lesson could then be erased by heating the tablet. © British Museum.

the guidance furnished by Theodore of Tarsus as archbishop of Canterbury (668–90).[11] A Cilician (Greek-speaking) monk in Rome when Pope Vitalian appointed him, Theodore, together with the African Hadrian, abbot of a monastery near Naples, was sent to bring order to an Anglo-Saxon Church in disarray when plague had carried off much of its administrative hierarchy. The school that Theodore and Hadrian established in Canterbury attracted students from everywhere in England and thus served as a model for monastic schools across the island. Theodore's immense scholarship was put entirely in the service of teaching. As a result, he wrote little himself, though at his instruction his students collected his teachings on penance (see chapter 6) and his commentary on books of the Bible and the patrology (reconstructed by Bischoff and Lapidge 1994). From his classroom also stems a significant body of glosses (chapter 1). Greek learning in Anglo-Saxon England is usually traced to Theodore (see Bodden 1988), and in recent years it has come to be recognized what an immense influence Theodore and Hadrian's school had on English letters, spawning the efflorescence of learning that began in the late seventh century and culminated a century later in the works of Alcuin.

At Theodore and Hadrian's school was educated the first great English scholar, Aldhelm (d. 709), a West Saxon of noble birth who was successively abbot of Malmesbury and bishop of Sherborne.[12] He is best known for his epistles (one of which includes his century of hexametrical *enigmata*: see chapter 1) and his treatises in prose and verse on the virtue of chastity, written for the nuns of Barking Abbey, near London (chapter 6). Aldhelm's schooling at Canterbury in recondite Latin verse is evident from his prose style, which is characterized by high obscurity of diction, gathering abstruse vocabulary from the least accessible portions of the Latin curriculum in a tour de force of erudition. A fairly typical example is the following sentence from his prose *De virginitate* (or *De laudibus virginitatis*, ed. Ehwald 1919: 236–7), explaining why the married state is acceptable even though virginity is superior:

> Numquid mala punica cittis granisque rubentibus referta et simplo librorum tegmine contecta contemptibilem naturae calumniam perpeti putantur, licet mellifluos palmeti dactilos et mulsum nectaris nicolaum longe inconparabiliter praestare credamus.
>
> Are pomegranates stuffed with pips and red seeds and protected with a single covering of rind, thought to suffer a contemptible calumny of nature, even though we believe that the juicy dates of the palm and the honey-sweet nectar of Nicolian dates are incomparably better by far? (Trans. Lapidge in Lapidge and Herren 1979: 65)

Because its impenetrable vocabulary is that of the glossaries (Greek ἑρμηνεύματα) compiled to guide students through the most obscure texts of the curriculum, such a style is called *hermeneutic*. As a result of their scholarly nature, Aldhelm's works entered the curriculum and their style was widely imitated throughout the Old English period – even by as late a figure as Byrhtferth of Ramsey (see below, section 5). It even finds a certain equivalent in vernacular verse of a macaronic nature (as remarked by Lendinara 1991: 276), most pertinently the poem *Aldhelm* (chapter 6).

The Venerable Bede (672/3–735), Aldhelm's younger Northumbrian contemporary, could scarcely have been more different in temperament and interests.[13] Given at the age of seven to the twin monastery

of Monkwearmouth and Jarrow, by his own account he spent the remainder of his life within that community, where his delight was always
in learning, teaching, and writing. His educational aims are expressed
in the relative simplicity of his style, which contrasts with the ornate-
ness of Aldhelm's. They are also expressed in the selection of topics on
which he chose to write. His treatises – on spelling, metrics, cosmology, computus (see chapter 7), and the interpretation of the Old and
New Testaments, among other matters – are for the most part works
with an educational purpose, and some of them remained the standard
textbooks on these topics in European schools throughout the Middle
Ages. Indeed, it was Bede who made his native Northumbria a site of
learning to compete with any other in Christendom.

Today it is primarily for his historical and narrative writings that Bede
is known, and preeminently for the great work of his last years, the
Historia ecclesiastica gentis Anglorum 'Ecclesiastical History of the English Nation'.[14] Following mainly chronological order, Bede traces in
five books the political history of Britain and the progress of the faith
among the Anglo-Saxons. Book I, after a description of the island of
Britain derived entirely from earlier authorities, covers the period from
the first, temporary occupation by Julius Caesar in 55–54 BC to the
period just before the death of Pope Gregory the Great (AD 604); Book
II extends from Gregory's death to the slaying of king Edwin of Northumbria (633) at the hands of the pagan king Penda of Mercia, resulting
in the apostasy of Northumbria; Book III concerns the replanting of
the faith in the north and the conversion of the midland kingdoms;
Book IV records the effects of Archbishop Theodore's reforms and the
lives of Ss. Wilfrid and Cuthbert (d. 687); and Book V brings the
history up to the year of its completion, 731. The most familiar passages are the story of Gregory the Great and the English boys for sale in
the Roman slave market (II, 1; see Frantzen 1997); at the conversion of
Northumbria, the pagan counsellor's comparison of life to the flight of a
sparrow through a hall (II, 13; see Toswell 2000); and the story of
Cædmon's miraculous gift of song (IV, 24).

Bede's history has been much admired both for its orthodoxy and its
historical method. In his dedicatory preface to king Ceolwulf of
Northumbria (reigned till 737) Bede lists his many sources and implies
that, wherever possible, in regard to both written and oral fonts of
information he has been careful to check his facts by recourse to more
than one source. Particularly valued by historians is Bede's frequent
habit of quoting verbatim and in its entirety the correspondence of

popes and bishops relating to the English mission, and other documents that shed light on Church history. The result is not exactly factual – the work is larded with accounts of miracles and deific visions, including those of Fursa, Adamnan, and Dryhthelm (see chapter 6) – but such supernatural matters are generally employed not for their sensational interest but as a form of evidence, proving the sanctity and divine favor of God's champions in England. When one considers how great were the obstacles in Bede's day to compiling and sifting such a vast volume of information from so many different, and often distant, sources, his history seems truly remarkable. The uniqueness of his accomplishment is demonstrated in no way better than in the acknowledgment that if we did not have this book, our knowledge of Anglo-Saxon history up to Bede's day would be pitifully meager. And yet our heavy reliance on Bede for knowledge of this period inevitably skews the historical picture in some ways. Bede's sources of information for the history of his native Northumbria were numerous and varied, in part because so much of the material for his history was gathered not from books but from those who either preserved oral traditions or were themselves witnesses to the events described – so young was the establishment of Christianity in England in Bede's day. The farther from home Bede ranges, the sparser his sources of intelligence. As a consequence, though it is true that Northumbria held a position of political and cultural preeminence at the beginning of the eighth century, certainly the relative sparseness of Bede's information on the other kingdoms, especially Kent and Mercia, distorts the picture of English culture of the time. It led some scholars of about a century ago, for instance, to assume that much of the anonymous corpus of Old English poetry was composed in Bede's Northumbria, since no other period or kingdom before the reign of Alfred the Great seemed to have produced a literate culture substantial enough to account for such a body of material.

While Bede's work demonstrates the heights to which the work of individual English scholars could attain in the pre-viking age, a sense of the breadth of English Latinity at this time may best be derived from an examination of the letters that passed to and from English missionaries on the Continent. Less than a century after the Conversion, the English had launched a concerted effort to introduce the faith to Germany and Frisia, as well as to reform the Frankish Church. The most distinguished of the missionaries was Boniface (ca. 675–754), a West Saxon whose English name was Wynfrith.[15] Before he took up his mission in 719 he proved himself a man of scholarly accomplishments, producing

an elementary Latin grammar of some ingenuity (chapter 7) and a particularly intricate set of metrical *enigmata* (chapter 1). After Boniface's
martyrdom in Frisia at the age of nearly 80, an unnamed associate collected the correspondence pertaining to his mission. It furnishes an
unparalleled view of the extent of literacy in Latin during this period,
among both men and women, in the high compositional quality of
Boniface's many English correspondents' writing, as well as in the variety of books that the letters describe as passing from English religious
houses to the Continent.

Among the remaining English scholars of this period who could be
named here, certainly the greatest was Alcuin (Old Northumbrian
Alhwine, ca. 735–804).[16] A Northumbrian educated at the cathedral
school of York, in 782 he was invited by Charlemagne (whom he met
en route from Rome) to direct his palace school. The practices he insti-
tuted there had inestimable consequences for the course of learning in
Europe, as they represented some of the chief accomplishments of the
Carolingian Renaissance, insuring the transmission of texts from antiquity to the later Middle Ages, even developing the script that was to
be adopted throughout the West, and on which modern roman type
like that of this book is based. Alcuin's *oeuvre* is immense, including
works on grammar, rhetoric, orthography, theology, Scripture, and hagiography. In addition, 311 letters are preserved, and some of his poems
are of exceptional interest for the affinities they bear to Old English
lyric verse (see chapter 8, section 2).

5 Literacy and Learning in the Viking Age

In the early period the rulers of the Anglo-Saxon kingdoms vied for
political and military predominance, and the contested overlordship
passed from kingdom to kingdom with the changing political circumstances. Northumbria seems to have dominated the political scene for
much of the seventh century, while the eighth belonged to Mercia under the long reigns of Æthelbald and his even greater successor Offa,
who claimed authority over all the Anglo-Saxon kingdoms (though his
control of Northumbria, if it was actual, was short lived). The ninth
century began as a period of West Saxon ascendancy, when King
Ecgberht conquered and annexed Mercia, gained control of all the kingdoms south of the Humber, and forced the nominal submission of
Northumbria to his overlordship. As the century progressed, though,

the political scene was gradually and permanently transformed by what was to be the turning point in Anglo-Saxon history, the arrival of the vikings.

When they sacked the monastery at Lindisfarne in 793, disastrous as this event was (it is lamented in a substantial poem by Alcuin, ed. Dümmler 1881: 229–35), it was a comparatively minor act of mayhem perpetrated by a raiding party typical of the first viking groups in England, which rarely comprised as many as 50 ships. Little more than half a century later the entire political scene had been transformed, as the raiders no longer came in independent parties but in vast armies under a central command. Not content as before to haul their plunder back to Scandinavia at the close of each summer, they now came bent on conquest, dividing the land among them in the north and the east and settling there permanently. Though political control of these areas would soon enough change hands, the populations would remain Scandinavian, with far-reaching consequences for the English language and for the subsequent history of the regions.

Northumbria fell to the invaders in 865, East Anglia in 867, and most of Mercia by 877. Wessex, the last remaining kingdom, was itself largely overrun in midwinter 878 by the forces of the Danish king Guthrum; but in the spring the West Saxon king Alfred, grandson of Ecgberht, rallied his forces and soundly defeated Guthrum at Edington, Wiltshire, obliging the Dane to agree to baptism and to a treaty confining his people to the Danelaw.[17] This treaty had the effect of awarding to Alfred ("the Great," as he has been styled since the sixteenth century) rule over all parts of England that were not under viking control, making him, in effect if not in name, the first of a long dynasty of kings of all England. He was able to retain control of his realm in the face of later viking attacks by developing a system of fortified towns and outposts, none farther than 20 miles from the next, along with a highly effective administrative system for manning them. This array of fortresses proved effective at compelling the invaders to commit themselves to a sustained war, at which they were not skilled, as opposed to the unexpected raids at which they had been so successful.

With the destruction of the churches and monasteries, all ecclesiastical structure in much of the north and east was annihilated; even in the south and west there ceased to be any monastic life (Knowles 1963: 36), though Alfred's biographer Asser is uncertain whether this is because of the vikings or English lack of discipline (cap. 93: see chapter 2). Religious communities in the eastern Danelaw are not in evidence again until the middle of the tenth century; the monasteries were not restored in Northumbria during the Anglo-Saxon period. In Wessex, King Alfred was obliged to bring ecclesiastics from abroad to tutor him and to staff the two religious houses he built for men and women. Not surprisingly, then, in the preface to his translation of Gregory the Great's *Regula pastoralis* (see chapter 2) he paints a sorry picture of the state of learning in the later ninth century, saying that there were few south of the Humber who could translate even a letter from Latin – not a single person, to his recollection, south of the Thames when he came to the throne – and, he adds wryly, probably not many beyond the Humber, either.[18] Yet he attributes such illiteracy to the carelessness of churchmen even before the ecclesiastical centers and their libraries were all plundered and burned. Whatever its cause, it is this Latin illiteracy that prompted Alfred to initiate his program of translation of what he saw as the most useful works (see chapter 2), amounting to what has been called the first great flowering of English prose.[19] In his preface Alfred also reveals his intent that the children of all freemen of sufficient wealth should be taught to read English, and some of them Latin as well. To modern readers accustomed to taking literacy for granted it may not be apparent what a radically new proposal this was, especially at a time when literacy was regarded as the province of religious persons and very few others.

Whether Alfred's educational plan was ever executed we have no way of knowing.[20] Certainly Latin literacy remained uncommon for many years: in the preface to his *Grammar* (ca. 993, ed. Zupitza 1880), Ælfric tells us that a few years earlier, before Dunstan and Æthelwold restored monastic life, no English priest could compose or fully understand a letter in Latin (p. 3). The evidence of lay literacy in the tenth and eleventh centuries, in the form of books bequeathed by the laywoman Wynflæd,[21] translations from Latin made at the request of lay persons, and even, astonishingly, composition of the ostentatiously hermeneutic Latin *Chronicle of Æthelweard* by a lay nobleman, is mostly contestable. The difficulty of gauging lay literacy at this time is aggravated by the probability that lay persons did not themselves read but had books and documents read to them by local churchmen or by the clergy customarily attached to the households of the nobility.[22] Yet even this must be regarded as a form of literacy, for it means that lay persons were versed in Christian learning, regardless of the means.[23] Whatever its possible ultimate effect on lay reading, certainly Alfred's program of translation had the consequence of dignifying the vernacular, legitimizing English

as a language of scholarship, which it had never been before. The promotion of vernacular reading no doubt detracted from the importance
attached to Latin; certainly, Anglo-Saxon Latinity never regained the
refinement that it had achieved in the pre-viking age. Anglo-Latin verse
is scarce after Alcuin's day; Alfred's practice of enlisting the help of
scholars from abroad to rebuild English letters never ceased to be a
necessity after his reign, with the result that the greater portion of Latin
prose pertaining to England, well into the eleventh century, was composed by non-natives; and Latin compositions of this period are often
of a debased nature, evincing barbarous syntax (like Æthelweard's
Chronicon) and the ostentatious display of hermeneutism, which so
often characterizes the work of students whose skills were actually quite
limited.[24] The concomitant of this decline in Latinity, however, is a rich
body of vernacular literature unparalleled on the Continent.

A more proximate impetus for rising lay literacy, even if less direct,
was the revival of learning in Benedictine houses under the reforms
introduced from the middle of the tenth century. Influenced by a movement in some monastic communities on the Continent, especially at
Fleury and Ghent, the reformers aimed to reestablish monastic houses
destroyed nearly a century earlier by the vikings, to wrest control of the
remainder from the secular canons who occupied them, and to impose
strict adherence to the Rule of St. Benedict, which prescribed a carefully regulated set of daily monastic duties in an austere way of life.[25]
Bolstered by royal support for the program, the three chief architects of
the reform managed to remake the Anglo-Saxon Church on the basis
of monastic life nearly a century after English monasticism had been
virtually obliterated by the vikings: they were Dunstan (ca. 909–88),
archbishop of Canterbury; Æthelwold (d. 984), bishop of Winchester;
and Oswald (d. 992), bishop of Worcester and, later, archbishop of
York.

The literary consequences of the reform were far-reaching. Beginning in the latter half of the tenth century we see an explosive growth in
book production that is responsible for the existence of all but a minuscule fraction of surviving Old English manuscripts. Even the language
in which texts were transmitted underwent change, as the Early West
Saxon dialect of Alfred and his contemporaries – the "standard" dialect
of most grammars of Old English – gave way to Late West Saxon, not
simply a later version of Alfred's language, but a national *Schriftsprache*
of a slightly different local character, and with a distinctive vocabulary, which was promulgated by Æthelwold and his students.[26] Most

important, though, the reimposition of monastic discipline spurred a renewal of literary production. Very little survives in either Latin or English that can be assigned with confidence to the former half of the tenth century; the years around and shortly after the millennium, on the other hand, represent the golden age of Old English prose composition, as it is reflected in the work of its greatest practitioners, Ælfric (fl. 989–ca. 1010), abbot of Eynsham; Wulfstan (d. 1023), archbishop of York and bishop of Worcester; and Byrhtferth (fl. ca. 993–ca. 1016), a Benedictine monk of Ramsey.

Most of the work of Ælfric, a student of Æthelwold, was written at the request of pious laymen, most prominently Æthelweard, *ealdormann* of western Wessex (and author of the chronicle mentioned above), and his son Æthelmær.[27] Not surprisingly, his writings are devoted to the instruction of both lay persons and monks. Thus, although he did compose, in addition to a pedagogically oriented *Colloquy* (chapter 7, section 3), two Latin saints' lives, of Ss. Swithun and Æthelwold, they are abridgments in simple prose of works composed by others in hermeneutic style, rendering them suitable to the generally low level of achievement among Latin learners in his day.[28] His much larger body of works in Old English is similarly popular in design – for example his homilies, which are generally translations of Latin texts with clarifying commentary for the unlearned, undertaken, he tells us in the preface to the first series (ed. Wilcox 1994: 107, 108), because of the paucity of Latin works available in translation and the many errors in English books that were mistaken for truth by the unlearned. Ælfric's style, too, reveals his popularizing aims, especially the alliterative style that he adopts for many of his homilies and saints' lives, for it imitates the alliterative patterns, though not the meter, of heroic verse (see chapter 3). Relatively little in Ælfric's *oeuvre*, then, amounts to original composition, as it was his stated aim to translate and interpret such works as were necessary to the education of those who looked to him for guidance in the faith. The effectiveness of his program of translation may be measured by the comparatively large number of surviving manuscripts of his works (e.g. 35 of the first series of *Catholic Homilies*, 29 of the second) and by the late date at which they continued to be copied and used – into the first part of the thirteenth century.

Wulfstan II of York is also best known as a homilist, though his accomplishments as a jurist are equally remarkable.[29] As an advisor to both Æthelred II (d. 1016) and Cnut (d. 1035), he compiled much of the surviving legislation from the first part of the eleventh century in both Old English and Latin. More than a dozen surviving manuscripts show signs of having been used by or prepared for him (see N. Ker 1957: 562 and Bethurum 1957: 2, 98–101). Several of his homilies are reworkings of Ælfrician material, and like Ælfric he composed with the aim of promoting clarity and effectiveness. Also like Ælfric he exhibits a distinctive style, though it is less like verse and more self-consciously oratorical (see chapter 3).

Byrhtferth would doubtless hold a more prominent place in English literary history if more of his work survived intact, if his canon could be more securely identified, and if more of it were in English.[30] In his characteristically hermeneutic style he composed Latin *vitae* of St. Ecgwine and the reformer Oswald, the latter a major source (though not always a reliable one) of information on the historical setting of the Benedictine reform, of which Byrhtferth was a passionate partisan. His best-known work, the *Enchiridion* (chapter 7, section 1), which alternates between Latin and English, is the most ambitious scientific work of the viking period, being mainly a commentary on his computus, but treating in some depth such diverse topics as Latin metrics, grammar, rhetoric, and number symbolism. A Latin historical compilation of his, extending from the conversion of King Æthelberht I of Kent to the death of Alfred, was incorporated into the twelfth-century *Historia regum* of Symeon of Durham (see Lapidge 1981); and various other medieval texts, especially John of Worcester's early twelfth-century *Chronicon ex chronicis*, show evidence of reliance on a lost chronicle of tenth-century history by Byrhtferth (Baker and Lapidge 1995: xxxii–xxxiii).

The newfound discipline in monastic life under the reforms and the ferment of scholarship it provoked seem to have elicited from many of the laity a sympathetic yearning for a life of piety and learning. We see this desire expressed in a variety of ways by some of the most powerful aristocrats of the day, for example in the generous patronage lent a variety of religious houses by Byrhtnoth, the hero of Maldon (chapter 9) and one of the most influential men of his day; in Ælfric's translation and interpretation of Latin texts for several lay patrons (see Lapidge 1996c: 89–90 for a list); and in the pious visions of Leofric (chapter 6), earl of Mercia and head of one of the two most powerful families in England in the eleventh century. It might even be argued that lay religious fervor put an end to Anglo-Saxon England, because the ascetic Edward the Confessor produced no heir, thus provoking the dispute over the succession that led to the Norman Conquest. Whether or not that is an accurate assessment, it is certainly true that in the tenth and eleventh centuries we see evidence of a religious fervor among the laity such as we do not encounter at any earlier period in England. The evidence of lay literacy at this period points to pious purposes as its chief motivation.

Ælfric, Wulfstan, and Byrhtferth wrote during some of the darkest days of the viking age, when England was again besieged after roughly half a century of relative tranquility. The policy of appeasement adopted after the battle of Maldon – paying off the invaders at exorbitant sums rather than fighting them – contributed to the unpopularity of King Æthelred "the Unready" (OE *unræd* 'shiftless' or 'ill-advised'), and it did not ultimately deter the vikings from conquering England and placing a Dane, Cnut, upon the throne in 1016. Yet for all the contempt that Æthelred's policy earned him, even from modern historians, it seems to have been effective in at least one significant respect: the devastation during this period was nothing like that during Alfred's day. Monastic life was not in danger of extinction. The middle of the century saw no native writers of distinction, but the production of books in English continued unabated, and it in fact did not flag until William the Conqueror and his successors filled the monasteries with Normans, who had little interest in English books.

6 The Nature of Old English Poetry

Less than 9 percent of the surviving corpus of Old English is in the form of verse – about 30,000 lines, chiefly in four manuscripts:[31] (1) the Junius or "Cædmon" Manuscript (Oxford, Bodleian Library, Junius 11), containing versified scriptural narratives (*Genesis A* and *B*, *Exodus*, *Daniel*) formerly attributed to Cædmon, plus *Christ and Satan*, which was added later;[32] (2) the Vercelli Book (Vercelli, Biblioteca Capitolare CXVII), a book of homilies among which are interspersed *Andreas*, *The Fates of the Apostles*, *Soul and Body I*, *Homiletic Fragment I*, *Dream of the Rood*, and *Elene*;[33] (3) the Exeter Book (Exeter, Cathedral 3501), an anthology of diverse poetic types, containing most of the surviving lyric poetry;[34] and (4) the *Beowulf* Manuscript or "Nowell Codex" (British Library, Cotton Vitellius A. xv, fols. 94–209), containing, in addition to *Beowulf* and *Judith*, three prose texts in English (*Life of St. Christopher*, *Wonders of the East*, *Letter of Alexander to Aristotle*).[35] A smaller body of verse is to be found scattered widely in manuscripts that are not primarily poetic.[36]

The survey above of the relations between the Latin curriculum and the contents of the Old English poetic manuscripts reveals that, aside from the small body of secular heroic verse that survives, there is little in the verse corpus that cannot reasonably be supposed to have been inspired by the sorts of Latin texts that were studied in Anglo-Saxon monasteries and minsters. Doubtless, various kinds of lore were always preserved in metrical form: compositions like *The Rune Poem* and *Maxims I* and *II* (chapter 8, section 1) have analogues elsewhere in the Germanic world; and *Widsith*, whose catalogue structure is paralleled in briefer form in some Icelandic poems (see chapter 9), is surely not based on a Latin model. Yet all but a small portion of Old English verse is in fact translated from Latin sources, and it finds analogues of varying proximity in the Latin curriculum. This conclusion explains a number of peculiar facts about the corpus of Old English poetry. The songs of the Germanic peoples before they were converted were very possibly concerned primarily with tribal history in the form of what we should call heroic legend and myth.[37] This is the only function that Tacitus ascribes to such songs, and given the way that heroic vocabulary permeates all Old English poetic genres, including such unheroic compositions as riddles, prayers, allegories, and homiletic pieces, heroic verse must at least have dominated the poetic repertoire in the days before the Conversion. Understanding the curricular inspiration for the bulk of the corpus should make it seem less peculiar that the Exeter Book and the Vercelli Book are such jumbled collections of seemingly mismatched genres. Had there existed such a variety of poetic genres in prehistoric times, we might have expected them to be organized in some comprehensible way. Instead we have a reflection of the Latin curriculum, with its wide-ranging scope and eclectic approach to textual types. Indeed, the curricular emphasis on poetic texts explains why, in the supremely practical business of constructing manuscripts, any appreciable space should have been devoted to vernacular songs, which we might have expected churchmen to regard as frivolous exercises by comparison to the sermons, translations, and liturgical, historical, and scientific texts that form the bulk of the surviving Old English corpus. Matter that might otherwise have seemed unpromising as poetic material was lent dignity and worth by its emulation of similar curricular poetic texts of a pious nature.

Yet a fundamental difference persisted between Latin and Old English composition in verse. Even after the introduction of book production, native literature remained mostly an oral medium. This is of no small importance to the study of Old English literature, since oral and literate compositions demand substantially different approaches. The fundamental fact of oral literature is that it is performative. While we tend to think of literary works as books, the earliest Germanic literature cannot be said to have had any existence except in performance. In this sense, then, all literature was popular literature, since only performed songs could be learned and transmitted. A consequence of performance is that the text of any given work had no fixed form. This observation highlights how oral literature differs from a performative medium like modern drama: dissimilarities in different performances of the same oral narrative are not to be regarded as deviations from a correct or original text; each performance *is* the text. Presumably, different performances of the "same" narrative material might differ profoundly, as when, for example, Hrothgar's court poet combines unrelated narratives about ancient heroes to form a nonce song in praise of Beowulf (*Beowulf* 867–915). Thus the roles of poet and performer are not differentiated: the Old English word *scop* (pronounced *shawp*) applies to both. In the light of these observations it should be clear that although we tend to speak of modern poetry as having been "written" (i.e. composed) and of being "read," these terms must usually be avoided in regard to Old English poetry, as they impose a modern model of production and reception that distorts our understanding of early medieval conditions. King Alfred, for example, almost certainly did not "write" the metrical preface to the *Pastoral Care* (see chapter 2), since it is unlikely that he could write (O'Brien O'Keeffe 1990: 84–5), writing being a menial and laborious activity reserved for scribes. Even the term "poems," though not yet stigmatized in Old English literary criticism, is prejudicial, as it seems that all such compositions were sung, or capable of being sung, to the accompaniment of a stringed instrument, a lyre or harp (see Boenig 1996); and "poem" and "song," though perhaps undifferentiated for Anglo-Saxons, have very different connotations for us.

The orality of the medium explains why even late into the eleventh century, nearly all verse in Old English is anonymous: authorship is a concept foreign to a literature in which ancient traditions are continually refashioned and there is no single correct or original text of a work. Even in nearly the only instance in which we find in manuscript a direct attribution outside of a vernacular poem to its maker, the expression is not one of authorship but of performative primacy: *Primo cantauit Caedmon istud carmen* 'Cædmon first sang this song'. For much the same reason it would not have occurred to the Anglo-Saxons to supply titles for their poetic works. Titles imply a textual stability that comes only with literacy, and thus the ones attached to Old English poetic texts are all modern. Two modern concepts dependent on fixed authorship and ideal texts are notions of authorial originality and individual style. Modern sensibilities favor what is new and different about literary works, so that a high value is placed on overturning literary traditions and producing works that are strikingly original; the entire purpose of a tradition-bound medium like oral poetry, on the other hand, is to keep old stories alive, each performance amounting to an act of recreating the tradition. In striving to produce something strikingly new, modern authors aim to develop a distinctive style. Old English poetry, on the other hand, is exceptionally uniform in style. Although a poet's habits in choice of vocabulary or syntax may differentiate one poem from another (see Schaefer 1997: 108), the differences are exceptionally subtle, and they are almost certainly not the product of a *scop*'s desire to express his individuality.

Oral literature tends to be poetic in form – and indeed, as remarked above, Tacitus says that their ancient songs were the only form of history and tradition among the Germani. In part this is because heroic literature is by nature archaizing, aiming to memorialize the deeds of ancestors, and archaized language belongs particularly to the realm of poetry. But it is also because stylized language is an aid to the composition of a literature preserved in memory alone. Since composition is *ex tempore*, traditional vocabulary and phrases allow the *scop* to satisfy the alliterative and metrical requirements of a line by furnishing him ready-made material that at the same time enhances the poetic authority of his narrative by its association with a long poetic tradition. Beginning in 1928, Milman Parry argued that the Homeric epics represent an oral mode of composition, containing traditional verse formulas like "swift-footed Achilles" and "rosy-fingered Dawn" that serve the dual purpose of filling out the epic meter and evoking heroic traditions. Parry and his student Albert Bates Lord tested this hypothesis in the 1930s by the extensive study of unlettered singers in the Balkans, who compose in a similar way.[38] These ideas were applied most extensively to Old English by Francis P. Magoun, Jr. (1953), who demonstrated the formulaic nature of Old English poetic composition, as the following brief passage illustrates:

> Ðonne eft gewāt   æðelinga helm,
> beorht blæd-gifa,   in bold ōðer,
> ðær him togēanes,   God herigende,
> tō ðām meðel-stede   manige cōmon. (*Andreas* 655–8)

Then once again the protector of princes, bright glory-giver, went into
another hall, where many, praising God, came toward him at the meeting-
place.

Most of the individual verses are repeated exactly, or nearly so, at other
places in the poetic corpus. Yet although *Ðonne eft gewāt* 'then once
again went' and *beorht blæd-gifa* 'bright glory-giver' are in that sense
equally formulaic, it is the latter that seems to belong particularly to the
traditions of poetic diction, being a useful, stylized epithet like "swift-
footed Achilles." The verse in fact serves a typically formulaic purpose
here, since it is not an essential element of the narrative but a mere
appositive, setting up the alliteration on *b* required by the second half
of the line, *in bold ōðer* 'into another hall', which is an indispensable
narrative element. The formula *tō ðām meðel-stede* 'at the meeting-place'
functions similarly, adding little information to *ðær him togēanes* 'there
toward him' but enabling the alliteration on *m* in the second half of the
line.

Magoun was convinced that formulism entailed orality. Yet many
Old English poems are apparently literate productions, translated from
Latin, and formulas are scattered as densely in these as in poems without Latin sources (see Benson 1966). It has thus proved more productive to think of orality and literacy in relative terms. Of course no surviving
Old English text is genuinely oral, but to a greater or lesser degree all
preserve features of oral style that set them apart from genuinely literate
productions. This is most clearly demonstrable from parallel texts. Few
vernacular poetic texts are preserved in more than one copy, but when
more than one does survive, copies may differ significantly – as, for
example, the two poems on the soul's address to the body do (see chapter
6). By contrast, scribes treated Latin texts as having a fixed form, and
they attempted to copy them faithfully. O'Brien O'Keeffe (1990) has
shown that this is most likely because the scribes brought to vernacular
poems attitudes associated with oral compositions, not attributing to
them a stable textual condition. Scribes might recompose vernacular
poetic texts as they copied because of the high stylization of poetic
diction: the formulaic language did not belong to any one poet but to
the entire culture, and such resistance to the idea of fixed authorship

naturally discouraged notions of textual integrity of the type that we hold.

The form of Old English poetry is more complex than it may at first seem. Even more than alliteration and meter, what distinguishes Old English verse from prose is its distinctive diction.[39] Words like *swāt* 'blood' and *dēor* 'bold' are not found in prose (for a list of poetic terms, see Griffith 1991: 183–5), presumably because they are archaic words that passed out of everyday use but are preserved in verse because of the traditions they evoke. Many poetic words are compounds, which are often nonce words, seemingly formed by the poet for the specific context, for example *brim-wylf* 'sea-wolf' and *āglǣc-wīf* 'adversary-woman' as applied to Grendel's mother.[40] The imaginative element in the creation of such *hapax legomena* is doubtless what lends them their poetic flavor. This imaginative quality is expressed in compounds in verse more than those in prose, in that they often have an elliptical nature, neither constituent denoting literally the compound's referent, as with *sāwel-hūs* 'soul-house', i.e. body, and *wæl-nett* 'battle-net', i.e. coat of mail. Such are called *kennings* (from the term *kenningar*, roughly 'paraphrases', applied to similar constructions in Icelandic), though a kenning may also be a phrase, as with *ganotes bæð* 'gannet's bath', i.e. sea.[41] Compounding also may serve the more mechanical function of fulfilling the formal requirements of alliteration. For example, *-dryhten* 'lord' may be combined with *frēo-* 'noble', *gum-* 'man', *sige-* 'triumph', *wine-* 'friend', and others, as the alliteration requires (see Niles 1983: 138–51).

Because its vocabulary is the chief distinctive characteristic of verse, poets composed in a manner suitable to maximize the density of poetic diction. This was accomplished by the fertile use of appositives. For example, in the passage from *Andreas* quoted above, the only poetic compounds appear in appositive phrases, *beorht blǣd-gifa* amplifying *æðelinga helm*, and *tō ðām meðel-stede* amplifying *in bold ōðer* and *him togēanes*. This process of varying poetic terms in appositive constructions is called *variation*, and it is what often gives Old English poetry a halting quality in translation.[42] In inferior compositions, variation tends to be aimless and the compounds entirely conventional. In the hands of a skilled poet, however, variation very often has a meaningful structure that lends rhetorical interest to a passage. A frequent deployment of variation of this sort is in a strategy of incremental amplification. Thus when the speaker of *The Wife's Lament* calls her husband *heard-sǣligne, hyge-geōmorne, / mōd-mīðendne, morðor-hycgendne* 'luckless, melancholic, secretive, intent on violence' (19–20), the aggregation of descriptors is arranged in a kind of order of increasingly dangerous and antisocial qualities, building to the final threat of violence.

Poetry is most commonly structured in both local and global ways by a strategy of *contrast*.[43] *Beowulf* shows this tendency at the macrostructural level in that it is made up entirely of two contrasting moments in the hero's life; and in *Juliana* we find a typical approach to characterization in the way that Cynewulf has flattened the characters, by comparison to his Latin source, in order to heighten the contrast between his protagonist and her opponents, in a practice referred to as *polarization*.[44] Local contrasts are frequent as well, as when, in a very common rhetorical strategy, the poet of *The Phoenix* lists the inclement kinds of weather that do *not* disturb the bird's home (*nē hægles hryre, nē hrīmes dryre* . . . 'nor the downpour of hail, nor the fall of frost . . .' (16)), then adds, *ac sē wong seomað / ēadig ond onsund* 'but the meadow remains pleasant and flourishing' (19–20). The common device of understatement called *litotes* or *meiosis* is often nothing more than the omission of the positive component of such a contrast, as when the dying Beowulf affirms the righteousness of his life, saying, *nē mē swōr fela / āða on unriht* 'I have not sworn many oaths wrongfully' (2738–9).[45] The ironic mode that pervades Old English verse is also a variety of contrast, pitting a false set of expectations against hard truth, as when, in *The Battle of Maldon*, Byrhtnoth responds to the vikings' demand for payment, saying that the weapons they desire as tribute will be turned against them in battle (46–8). Irony obviously serves the *scop*'s purpose of illustrating his subjects' grim resolve in the face of deadly trials. Another convention, the so-called beasts of battle type-scene or topos, serves a related purpose. Typically, the raven, the eagle, and the wolf are said to haunt the fringes of the field before a battle, in anticipation of having their fill of the slain – though there is much variation in both the elements and the contexts of the convention (see Griffith 1993 and Honegger 1998). Such conventions, along with other typical images (such as referring to stone ruins as the "old work of giants") illustrate the formulaic nature of verse not just in its diction but also in the very attitudes that it adopts toward human experience. The form and content of verse are thus so inseparably joined by heroic conventions that it is most likely not as the result of the poet's individual intentions that characters in religious poems like *Dream of the Rood* and the versified saints' lives seem to inhabit the same heroic world as Beowulf.

Another pervasive mode of Old English verse, in addition to the ironic, is the sententious.[46] Even if English poetry before the Conversion was primarily heroic in nature, aphoristic verse is most likely a native variety (see chapter 8, section 1) rather than a result of Latin influence, not only because of the analogous gnomic poems found in early Scandinavian texts (*Hávamál* and the Old Scandinavian rune poems being the closest parallels) but because there is an aphoristic strain that pervades disparate verse types. Appreciation of the pithy, epigrammatic statement is also evident in a favorite rhetorical device of the *scopas,* especially the *Beowulf* poet: the summarizing and syntactically independent lone verse that dramatically closes a passage in a longer work. For example, Beowulf finishes a speech expressing his resolve with the remark, *Gǣð ā wyrd swā hīo scel!* 'Fate will always go as it must!' (455); the narrator soberly punctuates his account of the burning of Beowulf's corpse on the pyre with the conclusion, *Heofon rēce swealg* 'Heaven swallowed the smoke' (3155b); and Moses, after the drowning of the Egyptians, ends an address revealing God's will for his chosen people, *Bið ēower blǣd micel!* 'Your renown will be great!' (*Exodus* 564).[47] The nature of gnomic verse is preservative, transmitting accumulated wisdom. Thus in function it is in fact close to verse that records ancient legends, and for that reason it might be expected to be an archaic type. Modern readers may be tempted to discount the importance of gnomic utterances, but a careful reading reveals that the sententious elements are often essential to a poet's aims, serving as palpable evidence of the value of hard experience (see chapter 8).

Because all but a small number of the surviving manuscripts were made as a result of the monastic reforms introduced in the tenth century, the language of the vast bulk of the corpus is Late West Saxon, the literary standard written in all parts of the country after Æthelwold's day. Scribes' facility with the standard varied, though, and often features of the scribe's own dialect, or of the dialect of his exemplar, are mixed into prose texts, helping us to identify their origins. Nearly the entire corpus of verse is also written in Late West Saxon, but with a distinct admixture of archaic and dialectal features, mostly of an Anglian nature. This is most likely because of Anglian cultural predominance at the time when native verse was first extensively recorded. (Indeed, even the prose of Alfred's reign shows the influence of Mercian spelling practices.) For example, in verse, OE *wealdend* 'ruler' is spelt much less frequently with the West Saxon diphthong *ea* than with the Anglian monophthong *a,* while *waldend* is comparatively infrequent in prose. Features like this one point to the existence of a poetic *koine,* or common literary dialect for verse. Yet some features of the language of verse cannot be explained convincingly this way, since they are not found in poems known to have been composed by non-Anglian poets. For example, the West Saxon verb *libban* 'live' is found only in the poetic works of King Alfred and in the poem *Genesis B* (translated from Old Saxon, in which the verb takes the form *libbian*), while everywhere else in verse the verb takes the Anglian form, *lif(i)gan* or *lifian*. A sizeable number of such features renders it very probable that the bulk of Old English verse was not originally composed in West Saxon but in one or another Anglian dialect.[48]

A few poems can be dated to a period of 30 years or less by what is known about the circumstances of their composition – for example, *Cædmon's Hymn*, the poems in the Anglo-Saxon Chronicle, the works of Alfred, and *The Battle of Maldon*. Most poems, though, are contextless, and currently there is little agreement about their dating. The example of datably early compositions like *Cædmon's Hymn* and *Bede's Death Song*, which are found in both early Northumbrian form and Late West Saxon, demonstrates that poems in manuscripts of the tenth and eleventh centuries may have been copied and Saxonized from much earlier exemplars – though the tendency of scribes to recompose vernacular verse as they copied (as explained above) complicates the assumption that a poem is early or late. Until about 20 years ago, although there was some dissent, there was a fairly broad consensus about the general outline of the chronology of undated poems. For example, *Beowulf* and the biblical narratives of the Junius Manuscript were thought to be early (no later than the eighth century, most likely the first half), Cynewulf and *Andreas* somewhat later, and *Judith* and *Christ and Satan* later still, in the post-Alfredian period. The issues have been discussed chiefly in controversy regarding the date of *Beowulf* (summarized by Bjork and Obermeier 1997), but they have broad application, and this chronology can no longer be called consensual.

Non-linguistic criteria produce widely different estimates of the age of poems (as among the contributors to Chase 1981). The linguistic evidence is less flexible, though it is far less certain than the evidence for the Anglian composition of most poems. This evidence is chiefly metrical, e.g. monosyllabic scansion of originally monosyllabic words like *tācen* 'sign' and *wuldor* 'glory' and dissyllabic scansion of contracted forms like *sēon* 'see' and *nīor* 'nearer'. In general, poems that scholars once for the most part agreed were early are rich in such metrical archaisms, while poems presumed to be later are not.[49] Clearly, evidence of this sort, though it is often the firmest we have, is quite imprecise. In this book we have not hesitated to offer opinions about the relative dating of poems when there is evidence of a sufficiently probable nature, but these should be recognized as conjectures rather than facts.

Many more Old English prose texts than poems can be associated with particular writers and thereby dated. For the remainder, relatively little anonymous prose is thought to antedate the monastic reforms of the tenth century. Anglo-Latin literature is the most narrowly datable of all, and in constructing a history of Old English literature it is Anglo-Latin texts that must provide the framework into which undated vernacular works may be tentatively inserted.

I

The Chronology and Varieties of Old English Literature

Histories of literary periods can generally rely on simple chronology to organize the material that they cover. There are significant obstacles to such an approach to Old English, the most obvious of which is that in the vernacular, much prose and all but a few lines of verse cannot be dated with any precision. Anglo-Latin works provide a broad framework of literary subperiods within the Anglo-Saxon era, since these are much more narrowly datable. Thus, as detailed above, the studied Latinity of the age of Aldhelm, Bede, and Alcuin (roughly the eighth century and the latter part of the seventh) is sharply distinguishable from the utilitarian vernacularity of the age of Alfred and his immediate successors (the end of the ninth century and the first half of the tenth); the latter in turn contrasts with the renewed (though circumscribed) Latinity of the immediately succeeding age of revived Benedictine monasticism (see Lapidge 1991c). Vernacular prose can be fitted roughly to this framework: before the Viking Age the normal language of extended prose was Latin; texts of the Alfredian period are mostly identified as such in the works of Asser, William of Malmesbury, and others; and thus nearly all the remaining Old English prose is generally assigned to the tenth and eleventh centuries. The assignment of most of the prose to the last hundred years of the period, then, does not contribute much to constructing a literary history based on chronology.[1]

The problems are more severe in regard to the poetry. Although there is reason to doubt whether Old English was much used for substantial prose compositions before Alfred's day (see n. 1), the case is clearly otherwise in regard to verse. We have no early poetic codex to prove the recording of substantial poems – such verifiably early scraps of verse as we have are preserved as marginalia or passing quotations in Latin texts – but we know that such existed, in view of Asser's tale of how Alfred, as a child, memorized such a volume (see chapter 2), and in view of the observation in the Old English Bede (but not the Latin) that Cædmon's late seventh-century compositions were taken down at dictation (ed. T. Miller 1890–8: 2.346). From canons issued in multiple years by councils at *Clofeshoh* forbidding the practice, we also may surmise that secular verse was sometimes used paraliturgically before 747 (see Remley 1996: 57), and one would suppose this was written. Thus it is not inherently implausible that even some of the lengthier surviving poems should be late copies of much earlier works. There is linguistic evidence to support this view.[2] Anglo-Saxonists are sharply divided about the dating of most poems, and since it makes a considerable difference whether, for example, *Beowulf* is viewed in the historical context of Bede's day or Æthelred the Unready's, until there is greater consensus about dating, too much conjecture will always attach to describing Old English poetry in developmental terms, except in regard to its formal properties (meter, alliteration, diction, and so forth).

A further obstacle is the considerable variety of literary types represented, each of which is better compared to similar types, regardless of chronology, than to unrelated but coeval texts. Ælfric's lives of saints do not make an uninteresting comparison to the roughly contemporary *Battle of Maldon*, but they may be compared more profitably to hagiographies of the age of Bede. For that reason the chapters that follow are organized by literary type rather than by period. The one exception is that works of the Alfredian period are discussed in ensemble, for together they shed light on the concerns of Alfred and his court at a particularly interesting historical juncture. The literary types around which the remaining chapters are organized are not all indisputably categories that the Anglo-Saxons themselves would have recognized. Certainly *passiones sanctorum* (chapter 4) and *sermones* (chapter 3) formed recognized subgenres, but the distinction between the two is not always definite, since homilies might concern the lives of saints rather than the daily lection from Scripture. Types like "legal literature" (chapter 7) and "biblical narrative" (chapter 5) may have no demonstrable historical validity, but the way such material is organized in manuscripts frequently suggests that such concepts do have more than present utility.

The manuscripts also reveal much about the uses of literacy, though to perceive this it is necessary to shed some modern preconceptions about literacy and literature. At a time when literacy was limited almost wholly to ecclesiastics, we should expect it to have served fairly limited purposes, preserving only such Church-related matter as was not suitable to memorial transmission. Indeed, being illiterate, lay persons would have had little reason to care about writing at all, were it not for the legal functions that writing assumed, particularly in the form of charters proving the right of religious houses and individuals to hold land (see chapter 7). Thus Alfred's proposal to extend literacy to the children of all the aristocracy (see section 5 of the introduction) must be seen not as an early example of Jeffersonian idealism about the virtue of universal education but as a calculated effort to fill the ranks of churchmen decimated by the viking invasions. After all, up to Alfred's day, with rare exceptions like the two seventh-century kings Sigeberht of East Anglia and Aldfrith of Northumbria, to think of an educated person was to think of an ecclesiastic: there was no secular scholarship.

Certain modern preconceptions about literature must also be shed, since the Anglo-Saxons naturally did not distinguish literature as art from other literate compositions in quite the way we do. The important distinction was not between literature and other writings but between prose and verse, the latter marked by its elevated diction and artificial conventions, as well as by metrical forms that, in the case of Latin verse, required prolonged study in the monastic schools. The privileged nature of verse is the likeliest explanation for the preservation of poems like *Beowulf, Deor,* and *Waldere,* which we might not otherwise have expected to be written down at all, since books were precious and difficult to produce, and such texts seem to have little to do with the religious and utilitarian purposes to which manuscripts were put. Given the Anglo-Saxons' own apparent attitude toward verse, and given the basis of modern Anglo-American literary studies in British aestheticism, it is not surprising that studies of Old English literature throughout the last century should have been devoted primarily to verse. Yet for the Anglo-Saxons the distinction between prose and verse seems at times one simply of form, for even the unlikeliest material could be versified, including a calendar of saints' feasts (*The Menologium*), the preface to a rule for canons (*Vainglory*), and the philosophical ruminations on God's foreknowledge and human free will in Boethius' *Consolatio philosophiae.* The poetry is thus quite diverse in subject: nearly every literary category treated in the chapters below includes examples of both prose and poetry.

So diverse were the uses to which literacy was put that the succeeding chapters cannot conveniently encompass all the textual types encountered. Indeed, the body of texts preserved in Old English is larger and more diverse than anything encountered elsewhere in Europe before the twelfth century (see Wormald 1991a: 1). Thus it may be useful briefly to describe here some of the more incidental varieties, especially as they are revealing about the uses of literacy. Perhaps the commonest writing preserved from the period is, in fact, the mass of glosses and glossaries encountered in so many manuscripts.[3] Glosses are closely tied to the Latin curriculum. They naturally were used as aids to the comprehension of texts in Latin, and their ultimate source was the authority of knowledgeable teachers. Hence it is not surprising that some glossaries used in England and on the Continent can be traced to the pedagogy of familiar scholars, including Theodore and Hadrian at Canterbury (to whom can be traced the origins of a family of glossaries of which the Leiden Glossary is the oldest surviving example: see Lapidge 1986b and Pheifer 1987) and Æthelwold and his circle at Glastonbury and Winchester (see Gretsch 1999). Glosses are found in both English and Latin (often together, often alternating randomly), in interlinear and marginal form, and in ink and drypoint (i.e. scratched into the parchment with a stylus). Usually they are simple synonyms; longer exegetical insertions are generally classed as scholia. Most commonly one encounters widely separated glosses on individual words ("occasional glosses"), though after the early tenth century it is by no means unusual to find interlinear, word-for-word glosses of entire texts ("continuous glosses," the earliest example being the Vespasian Psalter). Such continuous glosses are found to Latin psalters, gospels, the Benedictine Rule, the *Regularis concordia*, the *Liber Scintillarum* 'Book of Sparks' (an early eighth-century compilation from the Church Fathers by Defensor, a monk of Ligugé near Poitiers), and works by Abbo of St. Germain, Ælfric, Benedict of Aniane, Fulgentius, Isidore of Seville, Gildas, Prosper, Prudentius, and Popes Gregory the Great and Boniface IV.[4] All the glosses on a text, along with the words that they gloss (called *lemmata*, sg. *lemma*, usually Latin, rarely Greek or Hebrew) might then be copied sequentially into another manuscript to form a rudimentary glossary referred to by the term *glossae collectae*. An example is the glossary to the prose and verse texts of Aldhelm's *De virginitate* in British Library (abbr. BL), Cotton Cleopatra A. iii., fols. 92–117 (ed. Wright and Wülcker 1884: 485–535). Because they preserve the original order of the lemmata, it is frequently possible to identify the sources of such collections. That becomes more difficult when the glosses are rearranged alphabetically. Alphabetization was never complete, however: it might be that all words with the same first letter are listed together, or the first two letters; never more than three. Alphabetization naturally made glossaries more useful than *glossae collectae*, but alphabetization was not the only useful arrangement. As monks, when they spoke at all, were expected to speak only Latin, learners found it convenient to have listed together a variety of words belonging to the same semantic sphere, for example household implements, buildings and their parts, parts of the body, trees, and various plants. Ælfric's *Glossary* (ed. Zupitza 1880) is an example of such a so-called class-glossary. Some of the earliest manuscripts that preserve Old English are glossaries, including the Épinal and Corpus Glossaries; the former manuscript may have been written as early as ca. 700.[5] Glossaries thus provide important evidence for the early state of the language. Glosses and glossaries are also our chief witnesses to dialects other than West Saxon.

Catalogues are the sort of form one might expect to find in manuscripts devoted to preserving information that resists memorization, and the commonest sort in Old English includes royal genealogies and regnal lists, which tend to be found in manuscripts of laws and chronicles. Lists of kings exist for all the major Anglo-Saxon kingdoms. The purpose of the genealogies is generally taken to be more propagandistic than historical. Certainly the way that the genealogies have been repeatedly extended by the addition of names reaching ever further back into the remote and largely imaginary past, eventually leading to Adam, does suggest an effort to shore up the dignity of Anglo-Saxon dynasties, particularly of the house of Wessex.[6] Bishops, saints, and their resting places also have their lists, though the manuscript contexts in which these are found vary widely.[7] Historical works by and large tend to assume the form of lists of an annalistic nature, as with Orosius' history and the Anglo-Saxon Chronicle and related texts (chapter 2).

Narratives of the historical sort are usually in Latin and concern religious history. In addition to Bede's *Historia ecclesiastica* (see section 4 of the introduction), there is the so-called *Laterculus Malalianus* of Archbishop Theodore (ed. and trans. J. Stevenson 1995a). The *Laterculus* ('List', the title given it in modern times because of an imperial list from Augustus to Justinus that closes it) represents the most extensive of the surviving works from Theodore's own pen. It is a translation of John Malalas' *Chronographia*, a sixth-century chronicle of the world in Greek, to which is added an original typological history of the life of Christ.[8] Preparatory to his *Historia ecclesiastica* Bede composed a short *Historia abbatum,* on the founding of his monastery at Monkwearmouth-Jarrow and on its abbots Benedict Biscop and

Ceolfrith.[9] Alcuin's *Versus de patribus, regibus, et sanctis Euboricensis ecclesiae* 'Verses on the Fathers [i.e. Bishops], Kings, and Saints of the Church of York' (ed. and trans. Godman 1982), in 1658 hexameters, draws on myriad sources – particularly on Bede, and on Alcuin's own experience and that of his acquaintances – to recount the history of the northern see from Roman times to the archiepiscopacy of Alcuin's teacher Ælberht (767–8). Of particular interest is the list of authors available for reading at York (1536–62). Similar is the *De abbatibus* of one Aediluulf, a chronological account of the history of an unidentified cell of Lindisfarne, composed in the first quarter of the ninth century.[10] Both of these poems are as much hagiography as history, and the hagiography of the former in particular has a patriotic cast to it (see Bullough 1981). The purpose of Alcuin's poem in fact seems to be to provide York with an idealized picture of Northumbria's glorious past in order to spur present reform at a time when politics and morals in the north were in disarray (Godman 1982: xlvii–lx). In English there are two shorter historical texts of a religious nature. The first is an account of the monastic reforms during the reign of Edgar, which is appended to Æthelwold's translation of the Benedictine Rule, and which begins abruptly because the heading in the manuscript was never filled in (ed. Cockayne 1864–6: 3.432–4). The second (ed. Thorpe 1865: 445) is a brief account of St. Wulfstan, bishop of Worcester (d. 1095), though it has little in common with hagiography and much with cartularies, as it is chiefly a record of the estates that he secured for Worcester. It is in fact copied into Hemming's Cartulary (see chapter 7, section 1), where it is followed by a fuller Latin version. Mention should also be made of the *Encomium Emmae Reginae* 'Praise of Queen Emma' (ed. and trans. Campbell and Keynes 1998), composed by a monk or canon of Saint-Omer in Flanders on the commission of Queen Emma (Ælfgyfu) herself, the wife successively of Æthelred II and Cnut. It is a highly politicized account, in Latin, of the Danish conquest of England, which resembles nothing so much as secular hagiography. Its purpose was probably to promote the succession of Emma's son Harthacnut to the throne, against the claim of Edward the Confessor. A similar life of Edward, commissioned by his queen Edith from another Flemish monk, may have been intended to prepare the kingdom for the transfer of power to her family upon the king's death.[11] If so, the Conquest rendered it irrelevant.

One of the more interesting and peculiar categories of textual types is the range of brief notes encountered, mostly commonplaces and super-

stitions. They are often written in margins or on empty leaves, sometimes filling a blank space at the end of a longer text, though occasionally as part of a more formal series of miscellaneous texts, as in BL,
Cotton Tiberius A. iii. These reveal much about the preoccupations
and beliefs of English monks and canons both before and after the
Conquest. There are notes, for example, on the names of the days of
the week, the months, the winds, the letters of the alphabet, the nu-
merals, family relationships, on the age of Christ's mother at the time
of the Annunciation and of her death, on the size of Noah's ark and of
St. Peter's in Rome, on the 6 ages of the world, on the Anti-Christ, on
the 15 days preceding Doomsday, on the age of the world since creation, on cryptographic writing (e.g. substituting consonants for vowels), on lucky and unlucky days, on the prognostic significance of
sunshine, thunder, phases of the moon, dreams, the letters of the alphabet, the day of the week on which Christmas falls, and so forth.[12]

Of a related character are charms, of which there survive in Anglo-
Saxon manuscripts about a hundred examples, in Latin, English, and
gibberish.[13] A dozen are wholly or partly in a semi-metrical form (see
ASPR 6.116–28), and some contain letters of the Greek and runic alphabets (e.g. N. Ker 1957: no. 390.b). The charms are directed against
a wide array of maladies and misfortunes, including fevers, flux, dysen-
tery, nosebleed, wens, chicken-pox, a noxious dwarf, various wounds,
the theft of cattle or horses, evil spirits, the loss of a swarm of bees,
unfruitful land, and aches in the eyes, ears, stomach, and teeth. Thus
many of them have affinities with medical recipes, adding only prescribed rituals to the concoction of medicines, and some are actually
found in medical manuscripts (see Kieckhefer 1989: 56–90). Yet it is
more often difficult to distinguish between charms and prayers (see
Olsan 1992) – charms in fact often call for the recitation of prayers –
and indeed, many are preserved in rather pious contexts, such as the
Bosworth and Vitellius Psalters (Ker: nos. 129 and 224), and a copy of
the Benedictine Rule (no. 154B).[14] This may seem odd to readers who
think of Christian religion as antithetical to superstition, and of the
charms as therefore associated with pagan belief. To the contrary, aside
from an allusion to Woden in the *Nine Herbs Charm* (*ASPR* 6.119–21,
l. 32), the only very explicit reference to pagan belief has the ancient
gods (gen. pl. *Ēsa*, cognate with Old Icelandic *Æsir*) reduced to the
status of malevolent, disease-inducing bogies, along with elves and
witches.[15] Since the Church taught that the old gods were demons –
one word for pagan worship, for example, is *dēofolgield,* lit. 'sacrifice to

devils' – this variety of supernaturalism must have seemed, to some, of a piece with belief in angels, devils, the intercession of saints, and the efficacy of relics.[16] The views of an exceptionally orthodox thinker like Ælfric are instructive: he warns against setting dates of travel on the basis of prognostics, and drawing children through the earth at a crossroads, concocting love potions, and consulting witches about matters of health (*De auguriis*, ed. Skeat 1881–1900: 1.364–82). His objection, however, is simply that this is offensive to God: he freely admits that witches have knowledge of disease (though their knowledge comes from the devil) and that devils do cause poor health in humans and loss of cattle. That he felt obliged to preach against magical practices implies that they were familiar – some of the penitentials and canon collections also censure them – and the wide range of manuscripts in which prognostics and charms are found suggests that moral revulsion like Ælfric's may have been relatively uncommon in abbeys and minsters. Indeed, faith in charms and auguries is evident in some more substantial texts, such as the dialogues of Solomon and Saturn (see chapter 8, section 1), and even *Beowulf* (lines 204, 3051–75). In sum, the seeming marginality of charms and prognostics as textual types may be regarded as a product of the way religion, science, and superstition are sharply distinguished in contemporary academic discourse, and it thus highlights a significant difference between Anglo-Saxon and contemporary thought.

The riddles are also difficult to situate squarely in any of the succeeding chapters. In modern scholarship they are often treated as lyrics, perhaps because those in Old English are nearly all found exclusively in the Exeter Book, and perhaps because some are narrated in the first person. Yet the Exeter Book includes many short poems with no real lyrical content, and the riddles are distinguished from all other Old English verse by their frank humor. The riddle genre was established in England by Aldhelm, who wrote a century of Latin *enigmata* ('mysteries', ed. and trans. Glorie 1968; also trans. Stork 1990 and Lapidge in Lapidge and Rosier 1985: 61–101, the latter with an informative introduction) in imitation of the late Latin poet Symphosius. These were his best known verses, studied widely in the early Middle Ages as part of the monastic curriculum. They were also imitated both in England and abroad, notably by Tatwine (the Mercian archbishop of Canterbury 731–4) and Eusebius (possibly to be identified as Hwætberht, abbot of Monkwearmouth-Jarrow from 716 to sometime after 747, for Bede calls him by that name), who filled out Tatwine's collection of 40, arranged in an ingenious word puzzle, with another 60.[17] Boniface also composed *enigmata*, 20 in all, treating the vices and virtues in acrostic form;[18] Bede apparently composed some that are now lost (see Lapidge 1975); and a few scattered Anglo-Latin riddles by others survive.[19] The genre is thus a scholarly one (see especially Lapidge 1994d), and so it is not surprising that the riddles in Old English, in imitation of the Latin ones, are all in verse. Aldhelm's "mysteries" are sober contemplations of God's Creation, but Tatwine's and Eusebius' focus chiefly on classroom topics, everyday objects, and fantastic creatures. Thus while Aldhelm certainly was the model for several specific Exeter riddles (see Tupper 1910: xxxvii–xliv, and Williamson 1977, *passim*), Tatwine's and Eusebius' may have inspired the playful tone (though not the ribaldry) of many of the remaining vernacular riddles, which contrasts so strikingly with the somber dignity of other Old English verse.[20]

In the standard edition there are 91 riddles in the Exeter Book, though damage to the manuscript, along with disagreement about where some riddles begin and end, renders it impossible to be certain that there were not originally 100.[21] They are written out in three groups of 57, 2, and 33 in the latter part of the manuscript, though one of the middle two is simply another copy of no. 28. One is in Latin (86), though its solution depends upon an English pun. Two are translations: no. 38 renders Aldhelm's final riddle, "Creatura" ('Creation' or 'Nature'), and fairly faithfully, while no. 33 translates the corresponding number in Aldhelm's collection, "Lorica" ('Mail Coat'), and it is also found in a Northumbrian version called *The Leiden Riddle* after the location of the manuscript.[22] There is some reason to think that the riddles were culled from various sources (e.g., several seem to demand the same solution, such as "ship" and "sword"), though except for the translation of Aldhelm's "Creatura," the language and meter of the collection are notably cohesive (see Fulk 1992: 404–10). Spellings such as runic HIGORÆ 'magpie, jay' and non-runic *agof* (backward for *boga* 'bow', with mistaken scribal modernization of *-b* to *-f*) support the evidence for the relatively early and/or dialectal origins of at least some of the riddles (pp. 404–10).

No solutions are provided in the manuscript, though in blank spaces a rune was here and there written or scratched after the copying of the text, presumably the first letter of a guess at the solution. In one instance (no. 34) a solution in cryptography has been copied from the margin of the exemplar into the text of the poem. The solutions to many of the riddles are obvious, though quite a few are uncertain. They are almost all familiar objects (shield, cup of drink, horn, anchor, etc.) and animals (swan, nightingale, cuckoo, barnacle goose, ox, fox, etc.), occasionally larger forces of nature (wind, sun, constellation, moon and sun together, Creation). A few are absurdly obscure (Lot and his family, ten chickens, one-eyed seller of garlic). The device of *prosopopoeia*, or attribution of human characteristics to animals and objects, is frequent, so that the speaker is often the object itself. Obfuscation is enhanced in a variety of ways, the most obvious of which is the use of runes within the text, which may stand for letters or rune-names, and which may or may not be in the proper order. Less obvious, and more playful, is the use of *double entendres*, particularly salacious ones, as when an onion is described as standing tall in a bed, being hairy underneath, gripped by a peasant's daughter, and making her eyes water (no. 23), and when a key hanging by a man's thigh is described in terms that may make readers blush (no. 42). Naturally, the ribald suggestions are devised to lead the solver away from the true solution. If some describe the vernacular riddles as a popular form, rather than the learned one they certainly are, it is surely because of this playfulness, as well as the association with everyday life that their solutions lend them. It is also because they are the one literary type in which servants and peasants are significant actors (see Tupper 1910: li, and cf. Tanke 1994), with the result that the riddles seem a continual exercise in deflation, turning the heroic diction that they share with the rest of the native verse tradition into something like mock epic. The deflationary rhetoric is well suited to the form: the pleasure to be derived from riddles lies in discovering that things described so artificially and obscurely are actually quite familiar; the pleasure to be derived from mock epic is also in recognizing the familiar and ordinary behind artificial language.

Brief mention may be made of inscriptions, which are found in runic and non-runic form.[23] Most are memorials or marks of ownership or authorship of the objects on which they are found, but two present substantial texts: the inscriptions on the Ruthwell Cross (see chapter 6 and plate 7) and the Franks Casket (plate 4). The function of the latter object is mysterious, and all the more so because of its juxtaposition of scenes from religious history and Germanic legend carved in bone, with texts in runic and roman letters. Two of the panels contain verses, one describing the stranding of the whale out of which, presumably, the casket was made, the other seeming to allude to a Germanic legend that has not been identified conclusively, elements of which are also depicted graphically on the panel. Our puzzlement about this panel is probably not entirely unintended, for only here has the inscription been purposely obfuscated, most of the vowels having been replaced by symbols that are not actual runes, but which resemble the runes for the last letter in the runic name for each vowel, for example a rune resembling s to represent ı, since the runic name for ı is *īs* 'ice'.[24] This obfuscation has been thought by some to reflect a taboo against sinister pagan themes (e.g. Francovich Onesti 1998: 301), though it seems likelier to us that all is in play – that the scenes depicted may belong to a legend chosen expressly for its obscurity, and the runic puzzle then is simply part of the guessing game.

A text unparalleled in the Old English corpus is *Apollonius of Tyre* (ed. Goolden 1958), a translation of some unidentified version of the *Historia Apollonii regis Tyri*, itself probably rendered from an Alexandrian romance.[25] The story is in any case typical of this genre, with its shipwrecks, disguises, narrow escapes, concealed noble births, and coy *amours*, and thus the whimsy of *Apollonius* contrasts markedly with the sobriety of other Old English prose. It is even more peculiar that the text is found wedged between a selection from Wulfstan's *Institutes of Polity II* and a list of English saints in a manuscript that Wormald (1999c: 208) has described as "a manual for the drilling of a Christian society" on principles laid down by Wulfstan (Cambridge, Corpus Christi College (abbr. CCCC) 201). Nothing could be further from Wulfstan's high seriousness, especially because for the archbishop (as for Chaucer's Man of Law, *Prol.* 77–89) the theme of incestuous relations between father and daughter that plays a prominent role in *Apollonius* seems to have been especially repugnant (see chapter 3). It may be that *Apollonius* was seen as edifying literature because virtue is rewarded and vice punished (see Archibald 1991: 87–96), but it is no less a wild anomaly in Old English for that. Unfortunately, a quire is missing from the manuscript, and thus about half the Old English version has been lost.

In fine, the material conditions in which Old English literature is preserved have a significance that readers accustomed to print culture may at first find difficult to comprehend. The technology of print both (1) standardizes texts and (2) demotes the material value of books. This means that, correspondingly, (1) modern readers may not perceive that every Old English manuscript, unlike a printed book, is unique, or that its layout and scribal variants are designed to convey interpretive information that is not found in most printed books (see, e.g., Robinson 1980); and (2) modern readers may not perceive that the sheer fact of a text's preservation in a manuscript attests to its usefulness within ec-

Plate 4 The Franks Casket (eighth century?), front panel, depicting the Adoration of the Magi (right, with MAGI in runes in a cartouche) and scenes from the story of Weland (left), showing Weland in his smithy (with a murdered prince's corpse underfoot) and either Weland or his brother capturing birds to fashion wings for their escape. The verses in runes in the border may be translated (not uncontroversially), "The flood cast up a fish on a mountain; the sea grew brooding where it swam onto the sand. Whalebone." © British Museum.

clesiastical settings, given that manuscript space was too precious to be squandered on texts of no practical use. The latter point means that readers must work hard to discard modern assumptions about the inherent worth of "the literary" and strive rather to interpret texts like augural formulas, charms, and riddles in terms of the service they performed for the Anglo-Saxon Church. This utilitarian principle is of particular importance in regard to the interpretation of texts that may at first seem wholly unrelated to the work of God's servants, especially the heroic poems that are of so much interest to modern readers.

2

Literature of the Alfredian Period

Most of what we know about the life and character of King Alfred the Great (reigned 871–99) derives from the only known Latin work of any considerable length composed in the later ninth century, an unfinished life of the king (ed. W. Stevenson 1904; trans. Keynes and Lapidge 1983: 67–110) composed in 893 by Asser, a Welshman from St. David's, perhaps bishop there, whom Alfred had enlisted to assist him in his literary and educational plans.[1] Perhaps best described as secular hagiography, the work seems to have been inspired by Einhard's life of Charlemagne, which Asser quotes at several places, and so it is now widely viewed as political propaganda designed to elevate Alfred to the company of the Frankish emperor (see R. Davis 1971, but cf. Keynes and Lapidge 1983: 40 and n. 62). Asser is indeed prone to exaggeration, making Alfred preeminent at all he sets his hand to, a quality that may have served to recommend their new overlord to the Welsh churchmen who were (aside from the king himself) probably Asser's chief intended audience. But it tends to undermine his credibility as a biographer. The greater part of the work (cap. 1–86) is a Latin translation and expansion of a version of the Anglo-Saxon Chronicle (see below) for the years up to 887. The remainder is a paean to Alfred's accomplishments, especially in the face of persistent ailments, emphasized to mark the king's piety (according to Kershaw 2001). It is not surprising that particular attention and praise are reserved for Alfred's attainment, late in life, of literacy in Latin as well as English – not simply because of Asser's role in Alfred's education, but because literacy truly was an extraordinary accomplishment in a monarch before the tenth century. Woven into these two strands of the narrative are anecdotes of, among other matters, the king's youth, how Asser came to serve Alfred and was rewarded by him, and Alfred's persistent poor health. The most familiar of these anecdotes is the story of how Alfred won from his mother a book of English poems by memorizing its contents when they were read to him (cap. 23), a passage valued for the light it sheds on the lay use of books in the ninth century and the transmission of vernacular verse both in manuscript and in memory.[2] Also much cited, chiefly to nationalist ends, is the account, shared with the Chronicle, of the dramatic reversal of fortune for Alfred and Wessex (cap. 53–6) when he took refuge in a Somerset marsh, built fortifications at Athelney, rallied the people of Somerset, Wiltshire, and Hampshire, and won a decisive victory at Edington. He subsequently forced the viking invaders to agree to peace and to leave Wessex, and shortly thereafter the viking king Guthrum was baptized with Alfred as his sponsor.

Alfred's accomplishments hardly require the aggrandizement that Asser and the Chronicle accord them, as they are sufficiently impressive even in bare summary. In turning the tide of the early viking wars, achieving victory after very nearly seeing his kingdom annihilated, establishing a burghal system of defense that would keep the invaders in check for nearly a century, and laying the groundwork for the unification of England for the first time under a single king, Alfred left a brilliant military and political legacy. That in such troubled times he should have left a literary legacy of equal importance for the history of Old English literature is truly remarkable. These two achievements, however, are not unrelated. Alfred saw the task of rebuilding the country not simply as a matter of defeating the invaders but of restoring the glory it had seen in former days – a glory expressed to the world most manifestly in the Latin scholarship of Englishmen like Aldhelm, Bede, and Alcuin. Doubtless Alfred wished to create a common national, religious, and cultural identity in the face of the emerging pan-Scandinavian empire that would eventually come to dominate northern Europe (K. Davis 1998, Smyth 1998). But he tells us expressly in the letter prefaced to the *Pastoral Care* (see section 5 of the introduction) that the system of education he intended to establish for lay persons was for the purpose of revitalizing English literacy, so that learning might thrive again. His decision to promote literacy first in English thus created an immediate demand for English texts worthy of study, since Latin had until then been the language of scholarship. The translations that he and his circle undertook, which represent the first really significant extant body of prose in English – a body unparalleled in early medieval Europe – should thus be seen as an integral part of his plan for restoring England. The texts that he selected for translation should be expected to bear directly on that purpose (see Bately 1988b, 1990).

It is generally accepted that four of the surviving translations from this period are the work of the king himself: the *Pastoral Care*, the *Consolation of Philosophy*, the *Soliloquies*, and the prose psalms of the Paris Psalter.[3] The first of these translates Gregory the Great's *Regula* (or *Cura*) *pastoralis* or *Liber regulae pontificalis* (ed. Judic 1992; partial English trans. Leinenweber 1998), composed about 590 as a handbook for bishops, explaining the qualities requisite for spiritual leadership and cataloguing the variety of human characters a bishop is likely to encounter. Gregory was the first monk to occupy the papal throne, and he composed this work shortly before he assumed the duties of the pontificate, at a time when he was reluctant to abandon his life as an abbot. Thus the work also examines the conflict between the attraction of private, devotional intellectualism and the stress of public service – a theme that surely appealed to Alfred personally, but which must also have been of some importance to his bishops. The Latin text comprises four parts. The first warns that only the learned are qualified to become the teachers of others, the physicians of souls. This section also outlines the chief difficulties that the episcopate encounters and the qualities required of bishops. In the second section, Gregory prescribes how effective bishops are to organize their lives spiritually and relate to their flocks. The third explains how a bishop may identify the many classes of people and urges the effective prelate to counsel and correct his people according to their standing. The fourth section warns against the pursuit of glory and self-promotion, explaining that a bishop who would be responsible for the guidance of others must be aware of his own shortcomings. The work enjoyed immense popularity as a guide for secular clergy throughout the Middle Ages. Bede praises the work in his *Historia ecclesiastica* (II, 1), and in his 734 letter to Ecgberht, bishop of York (trans. McClure and Collins 1994), he urges him to read it.

Alfred's translation is known as the *Pastoral Care*.[4] It seems a supremely appropriate text for inclusion in Alfred's program of translation. Anglo-Saxons had a particular reverence for Gregory because he ordered the mission to England in 597 that brought Roman Christianity to the island (see H. Chadwick 1991 and Meens 1994). His influence on the Anglo-Saxon church was deeply rooted: for example, it was Gregory who first recommended the establishment of an episcopal see at York, though it was not until 735 that a bishop was permanently installed there. Because Alfred's project of national renewal was an attempt to recapture former greatness founded on Christian learning, a return to the wellhead of English Christianity, the work of its spiritual father, must have seemed particularly apposite. Gregory's association with the origins of Anglo-Saxon Christianity, in any case, is made explicit in the metrical preface (see below), where Alfred explains that this text was brought to England by Augustine. A more immediate reason for Alfred's selection of this text is that it speaks to his call for education as a crucial component of the faith (Bately 1990). Alfred's remarkable prefatory letter, announcing education as the key to restoring English civilization, is thematically of a piece with the work, given the design of Gregory's book as a teaching manual. The first chapter admonishes those who would become teachers without first having mastered their craft, explaining that a "spiritual physician," like a "worldly physician," must be able to see the wounds in order to cure them. Very likely another facet of Alfred's attraction to Gregory's book is the work's resonance as a guide for kingship. Though it is intended particularly as a primer for the episcopate, Gregory's work examines the qualities of good rulers, and his concern for the burdens of leadership no doubt spoke to Alfred personally. The fourth book warns that the greatest danger to an effective ruler is the temptation of self-satisfaction. Alfred may have recognized a lesson for secular rulers in Gregory's advice to bishops:

> Often talents and virtues become destructive to one who possesses them, when on account of arrogance he presumes too much in the talents he has, and he will not augment them. Then they become destructive for him, because talents are always at war with shortcomings. But the mind often flatters itself, and because of that flattery it abandons timidity about its own thoughts. Then the mind rests carelessly in that presumption. (Sweet 1871–2: 463)

Good governance requires subjects as well as rulers to fulfill the duties proper to them:

> Servants [ðēowas] are to be admonished in one manner and masters [hlāfordas] in another. Servants should be admonished to have humility before their masters . . . Servants should be instructed not to scorn their masters. They will scorn their masters if they disobey their wishes and commands . . . The servant should be instructed so that he knows that he is not free of his master. (Sweet 1871–2: 200)

This concern for the right behavior of all segments of a society accords with Alfred's views on social polity (see below on the three estates).

Yet even more particularly Alfred must have appreciated the value of Gregory's work for his bishops, who had the tremendous task before them of rebuilding the ecclesiastical structure from the ground up. Even before Alfred's day, "a basic standard of competence in Latin cannot be assumed for all the episcopacy" (Lapidge 1996d: 434), and his prefatory letter implies an even worse state of affairs during his reign. That the translation was indeed intended for his bishops' use is suggested by his intention, detailed in the prose preface, to send a copy to each of them – an intention we know to have been executed, since the surviving copies of the preface either are addressed to particular bishops (Wulfsige, Asser's predecessor as bishop of Sherbourne; Hehstan, bishop of London; and Wærferth, bishop of Worcester – though Wærferth himself can hardly have required a translation for his own use) or contain a blank space for the insertion of the recipient's name (in the case of BL, Cotton Tiberius B. xi , the victim of two successive fires, and known to us only from a seventeenth-century transcript made by Franciscus Junius).

In the Preface, Alfred says that after he had learned the Latin of Gregory's work he translated it "at times word for word, at times sense for sense" – and indeed, though the translation is fairly literal, Alfred very likely viewed translation "not as an unfortunate compromise, but as legitimate interpretation operating within the well-defined parameters of Christian exegesis" (K. Davis 2000: 149). Both Gregory's and Alfred's texts are practical guides with lists of virtues and qualifications illustrated by concrete Biblical examples. Yet Alfred generally simplifies the grammar, turning subordinate clauses into coordinate ones. Alfred's Preface, on the other hand, is composed of a much suppler and more complex syntax, defining a prose style that seems exceptionally well suited to the demands of pedagogic discourse (Klaeber 1923, Stanley 1988). It also displays a remarkable range of rhetorical, aural effects (Orchard 1997: 102). It is thus the most interesting portion of the work not just for what it tells us about the state of learning and Alfred's plans to improve it, but also as an illustration of what could be achieved in prose when it was freed entirely from the constraints of translation – a rare enough occurrence in the Old English corpus.

In addition to the prefatory letter on the state of learning in England, most of the non-defective manuscripts include both a second preface and an epilogue. Both of these are in verse (*ASPR* 6.110–12) and are considered by most to be Alfred's work. These poems take no metrical liberties that are not also taken by the *Beowulf* poet (*pace* Stanley 1988: 354, 355), and O'Brien O'Keeffe (1990: 96–107) has demonstrated how thoroughly conventional the formulaic diction of the preface is. In addition to relating the work's author to Augustine's mission of 597 (as remarked above), the preface indicates that Alfred had copies made for his bishops "because some of them – those who knew the least Latin – needed it" (15–16). Discenza (2001) argues that the preface is designed to assert Alfred's religious authority as Gregory's successor. The verse epilogue is more ambitious, developing an elaborate metaphor of Gregory's book as a font of wisdom whose waters emanate ultimately from the Holy Spirit. The reader is invited to visit often and bring a pitcher that will not leak. The chief source appears to be the *Regula pastoralis* itself, a point that tends to confirm Alfred's authorship of the poem (Whobrey 1991).

Alfred's *Pastoral Care* and his translation of Boethius' *De consolatione philosophiae* could hardly be more different. While one is a practical guide rendered faithfully from Gregory's Latin, the other is a philosophically complex theodicy and a translation only in the broadest sense of the word.[5] Anicius Manlius Severinus Boethius, born about AD 480 to an ancient and distinguished Roman family that had converted to Christianity in the fourth century, was son of one consul and foster child of another. He was educated at the Platonic Academy in Athens, and most of his writings reflect his classical education. When Rome came under the rule of the Ostrogothic king Theodoric (454–526), Boethius began a brilliant career, first as sole consul, then as *magister officiorum*, a position which gave him responsibility for the direction of all civil servants. In 524 or 525, however, his fortunes were reversed when he was implicated in a plot against Theodoric, who sentenced him to death. Despite Boethius' protestation of innocence, the obsequious Senate confirmed Theodoric's sentence, and Boethius was tortured and bludgeoned to death at Pavia. It was while he was imprisoned and awaiting execution that he wrote *De consolatione philosophiae* (ed. Bieler 1984; trans. R. Green 1962). The *consolatio* genre was produced in all branches of Greek and Latin philosophy, and it is the source of the "physician of souls" metaphor that can be traced from the works of classical authors to Late Antique Christian texts like Gregory's *Regula pastoralis*, as we have seen. In form, Boethius' work is a composite of Platonic dialogue and verse, divided into 5 books with 39 interspersed poems. In the prose portions, Lady Philosophy appears to Boethius in prison in order to heal him, through conversation, of his grief over the loss of his former good fortune. The whole work is then an allegorical account of Boethius' discovery of the insignificance of worldly things and of the rational workings of seemingly cruel Providence. We can be certain that Boethius was a Christian, yet the *Consolatio* is marked by a conspicuous absence of Christian doctrine and by the clear influence of Neo-Platonic philosophy.

In the later Middle Ages and the Renaissance the *Consolatio* was one of the most widely read works of literature, preserved in more than 400 manuscripts and translated into vernacular languages by, among others, Notker Labeo and Peter von Kastl (German), Jean de Meun (French), and Geoffrey Chaucer and Queen Elizabeth I (English). It entered the Latin curriculum in England in the later Anglo-Saxon period, probably because of Alfred's interest in it (hence the existence of a Latin manuscript with a continuous gloss in Old English for half of Book III, ed. Hale 1978); but before his day there is no evidence that it was read in England (Godden 1981: 419). It is thus an unusual work for Alfred to have chosen to translate, though it is not hard to see how, in the midst of the vikings' depredations and his own ill health, Alfred should have perceived the value of Boethius' Neo-Platonism and Stoicism for his countrymen and for himself.

The translation was most likely made after 893, as Asser does not mention it – or any of Alfred's own translations – though several later sources ascribe the Old English version to Alfred, including the *Chronicon* of Alfred's kinsman Æthelweard and William of Malmesbury's *De gestis regum Anglorum* (ca. 1127). There are two chief manuscripts. Oxford, Bodleian Library, Bodley 180 is a complete prose rendering, preceded by a Preface that reproduces the language of Alfred's Preface to the *Pastoral Care*:

> King Alfred was the translator of this book, and he turned it from literary Latin into English, just as it is now done. At times he translated it word for word, sometimes sense for sense, as clearly and intelligently as he could interpret it in the face of the various and manifold worldly troubles which often occupied him both in mind and in body . . . And now he (Alfred) prays and in God's name beseeches each one of those who wish to read this book that he pray for him and not reproach him if he (the reader) better understands the work than he (Alfred) could.

The Bodley manuscript, though it is from the twelfth century, must represent a copy of a draft, as in the tenth-century version in BL, Cotton Otho A. vi, all but nine of the metrical passages of the Latin have been rendered into Old English verse, referred to collectively as the *Meters of Boethius* (*ASPR* 5.153–203). The preface in both manuscripts apparently means to say that Alfred first translated the entire work into prose and then reworked portions into verse – and indeed, the Old English *Meters* are often minimally altered from the prose (see below).[6]

Alfred's *Consolation* is better considered an adaptation than a translation of Boethius' work.[7] In form it is quite different, converting Boethius' 5 books, with interspersed verses, into 42 chapters and adding a preface and a proem – though it dutifully records the point at which each of Boethius' books concludes, once in the middle of a chapter. In substance, too, the work departs continually from its source. For example, although chapters 2 and 3 adopt the first-person account of Boethius lamenting his condition, in chapter 4 Alfred renames the character of Boethius, referring to him as *Mōd* 'Mind'. Later in the work, he restores the identity of Boethius to the narrator, only to replace it further on with "I." In Alfred's adaptation, Boethius' Lady Philosophy is sometimes a dual personage he refers to as *sē Wīsdom and sēo Gescēadwīsnes* 'Wisdom and Reason', but most often he simply refers to this character as Wisdom (see K. Cook 1996). Additionally, because Boethius' complex Neo-Platonic philosophy is not always consistent with medieval Christian theology, Alfred resorts to adaptation and expansion. Thus Alfred tends to subordinate the Platonic doctrine of the preexistence of the soul, with its attendant themes, to orthodox Christian teachings on the creation of humankind, and his God seems a more forgiving one, since Alfred continually stresses the value of repentance (see Bately 1994a).

Alfred also alters Boethius' complete rejection of worldly goods. For Boethius, material possessions were but one of many distractions to mortals striving after the *summum bonum*. Alfred challenges this idea, and he recasts Boethius' dismissal of worldly goods as an endorsement of moderation:

> If you wish to have moderation and wish to know what is necessary, then that is food, drink, clothing, and the tools for whatever skill you know that is suitable for you and that is right for you to have . . . Now if you eat or drink beyond moderation, or you put on more clothing than you need, the excess will become either a pain or a plague to you, either an inconvenience or a danger. (chapter 14)

Boethius' argument is philosophical and theological, yet it avoids overt Christian reference; Alfred's translation, by contrast, is everywhere imbued with the religious idiom of his day (see Sauer 1996). Book V of Boethius' work presents his most memorable argument, that God's fore-knowledge of human events does not *cause* those events and thus does not abrogate human free will. This book is a complex cosmological ex-cursus on the roles of Providence and Fate. Boethius defines Providence as divine reason, the plan as it is conceived in God's omniscience. Fate, on the other hand, is the working of Providence on the temporal plane as humankind perceives it in the unfolding of events. As such, Fate is the manifestation of Providence. For Alfred, Fate (*wyrd*) is in no way an ex-tension of Providence (*foreþonc*): "I say then, just as all Christian people say, that divine providence rules them, not fate" (chapter 39). Boethius' concept of Fortune, whose very nature is mutability, is unrecognizable in Alfred's adaptation, in which he conflates *wyrd* and *fortuna*: "Then he (God) directs *wyrd* either through good angels or through the souls of men, either through the life of other creatures or through the stars of heaven or through the various wiles of demons – sometimes through one of them, sometimes through all of them" (chapter 39). Since the concept of Fortune is radically altered in Alfred's version, the Wheel of Fortune, invoked in Book II of Boethius' work, does not appear as the tool of a whimsical goddess (see Bately 1994b). But replacing the example used by Boethius of the working of the spheres (IV, prosa 6), Alfred invokes the image of the wheel as an illustration of humankind's relation to God: "Just as a wheel turns on the axle-tree of a wagon and the axle-tree stands still and yet bears the entire wagon and controls its entire motion . . . likewise the axle-tree is the highest good which we call God, and the best people go nearest to God just as the nave of the wheel goes nearest to the axle-tree and the average people just as the spokes" (chapter 39). All in all, the complexities of Boethius' Book V receive perhaps the most deeply curtailed treatment of all in Alfred's translation.

As in the *Pastoral Care*, Alfred is concerned with kingship and power in his adaptation of the *Consolatio* (see Discenza 1997). Chapter 37 of Alfred's work is a discussion of how kings, beneath the splendor of their royal garb, are no different from those who serve them:

> Hear now a story about proud and unjust kings, whom we see sitting on the highest thrones, who are resplendent in clothing of many kinds, and who are surrounded by a great retinue of thanes . . . But if one stripped the clothing from him and took away from him those thanes and that power, then you could see that he is very similar to any one of his thanes who serve him there, if he is not even worse.

While Alfred's preoccupation with the qualities and characteristics of good kingship is certainly present in the *Consolation*, he is also concerned with emphasizing obedience. One of the more telling modifications of Alfred's version is his alteration of Boethius' insistence that he is innocent of the charges against him. Alfred tells us in chapter 1 that Boethius plotted to wrest the kingdom from the unrighteous Theodoric, so his distress is a consequence of his treason. The *Consolation* also contains an addition in chapter 17 that amounts to a statement of Alfred's political and social philosophy. He divides his subjects into three classes, those who pray, those who fight, and those who labor, and these three estates, as they are called, are subsequently encountered often in medieval texts (see Duby 1980 and T. Powell 1994), including those of Ælfric and Wulfstan.[8] Alfred also demonstrates in the *Consolation* a concern that is pervasive in his writings: centering oneself in a life of devotion in the midst of worldly affairs (see Szarmach 1997). Alfred's Preface refers to the "worldly troubles" that beset him both in mind and in body, and the work itself promotes a view of adversity as a liberating force: "For prosperity always lies and pretends so that one should think that it is the true happiness . . . but adversity unbinds and frees each of those ruled by it, inasmuch as it reveals to them how frail these present goods are" (chapter 20). Taken in their entirety, Alfred's modifications reflect a conscious effort to highlight the overall themes and concerns that were most relevant to his time and circumstances.

This contemporizing impulse must not be ignored in evaluating the argument that Alfred's alterations to his source should be attributed to his reliance on one or another medieval commentary on Boethius.[9] Commentaries may indeed have influenced the translation, but even more important, Alfred's intent was to make Boethius accessible to those incapable of reading Latin, and it is inevitable that the philosophical complexities of the *Consolatio* should have prompted him to effect some fundamental changes even without the guidance of commentaries. His method of interpreting for the reader is nowhere clearer than in his habit of amplifying Boethius' arguments with succinct illustrations, sometimes substituting the familiar for the strange, as with his much-remarked substitution of Weland, the incomparable smith of Germanic mythology (maker of Beowulf's corselet), in Boethius' lament, "Ubi nunc fidelis ossa Fabricii manent?" ('Where now do the bones of loyal Fabricius lie?': II, metrum 7; cf. Alfred's chapter 19 and *Meters* 10.33), and his allegorizing explication of the story of Orpheus and Eurydice (chapter 25). So, too, refusing to reject material goods altogether and collapsing

Boethius' *fortuna* and *fatum* in the concept *wyrd* are perhaps best viewed as intentional accommodations to the sensibilities and understanding of a monoglot Anglo-Saxon audience.

The Meters of Boethius are widely acknowledged to be unskillful as verse compositions (see, e.g., Earl 1989), but in recent years the tendency has been to attribute their relative inelegance and difficulty to the subject matter rather than strictly to Alfred's limited ability as a poet (Bethel 1991, Clemoes 1992). Boethius' composition did not readily lend itself to Germanic versification, since its argumentative reasoning furnishes few opportunities for traditional poetic diction, rather demanding a philosophical vocabulary foreign to verse (Fulk 1992: 251). Moreover, the *Meters* are not a thorough reworking of the Old English prose but the product, in general, of such minimal changes as are required to make the prose conform to the rules of versification (see Benson 1966: 337–40 and Obst and Schleburg 1998: iv), and the result is, not surprisingly, prosaic, as a brief sample will demonstrate:

> Þonne hīo ymb hire scyppend   mid gescēad smēað,
> hīo bið up ahafen   ofer hire selfre,
> ac hīo bið eallunga   an hire selfre,
> þonne hīo ymb hi selfe   sēcende smēað. (20.218–21)

> When it (the soul) reflects upon its maker with rationality, it is elevated above itself; but it is completely within itself when, searching, it reflects upon itself. (Cf. the prose version: *Þonne hīo þonne ymbe hire scippend smēað, þonne bið hīo ofer hire selfre; ac þonne hīo ymbe hīselfe smēað, þonne bið hīo on hire selfre.*)

Alfred's purpose in versifying the *Meters* thus seems not to have been to compose memorable poetry but merely to give his translation a form comparable to that of his source, and thus to provide for those without knowledge of Latin an experience more nearly analogous to that of reading the original. From this, two conclusions follow: (1) for literary purposes it makes little sense to study the *Meters* outside of the prose context for which they were composed, and (2) it would be a mistake to judge Alfred's competence as a poet on the basis of the *Meters* alone. In regard to the latter point it is worth noting that the first of the *Meters*, corresponding to the prose proem that Alfred himself devised, is formally far superior to the rest – and generally differs more widely from the prose version – and that is no doubt because its material is narrative and in the heroic tradition, recounting the Gothic conquest of Italy and Boethius' fall from grace.

What Alfred saw as the value of literacy is suggested by the nature of the texts that he translated himself, since they are primarily reflective. He revisits some of the inward-looking philosophical considerations of his version of Boethius in his translation of Augustine's *Soliloquia*. Again, Alfred's version is a very free adaptation of his Latin source, and one may perceive in his modifications to this relatively little-read Augustinian work an effort toward a more powerful mode of personal expression (Hitch 1988). Alfred's themes are the immortality of the soul and knowledge of God, but these ideas form just two aspects of Augustine's original work. It was in 387, some ten years before he composed his *Confessiones,* that Augustine wrote his *Soliloquia* (best ed. Hörmann 1987; ed. and trans. Gilligan 1943, Watson 1990). Like Boethius' *Consolatio,* Augustine's work is imbued with Neo-Platonic philosophy and logical discourse, and it is also a very challenging text. He composed the work as a catechumen, when he was struggling to subordinate his academic predisposition to the rigorous demands of theology, and he would later point out, in his *Retractiones,* just how he had failed to accomplish this. The work is a dialogue between Augustine and Reason, who attempts to explain that knowledge of God requires that one fix the mind's eye on God alone, and this may be accomplished only by cultivating the virtues that allow one to see with perfect clarity. Book I is primarily concerned with demonstrating how the mind's eye can be made sound in resisting temptation. Book II addresses the immortality of the soul, a subject to which Augustine's later *De immortalitate animae* would be devoted exclusively.

Alfred's adaptation consists of three books and a preface.[10] An extract is contained in BL, Cotton Tiberius A. iii, but BL, Cotton Vitellius A. xv, from the twelfth century, contains the whole of the work with a colophon that attributes the translation to Alfred. The preface, which is Alfred's own composition, is an extended metaphor that compares the process of education and writing to gathering timber for the construction of a house. Alfred says, "I did not come home with a single load without wishing to bring back the whole forest, if I could have carried it all," and he advises others to return to the forest to gather what was left behind. The passage thus is consonant with Alfred's aims as a translator, since the success of his educational reforms depended upon the effectiveness of his translations in inducing others to take up the cause of learning. Alfred's method of free adaptation permitted him to draw on several sources besides the *Soliloquia,* which have been identified with varying degrees of probability. One undeniable source, however, is Augustine's *De videndo Deo* ('The Vision of God', Epistle 147, PL 33.596–622; trans. Parsons 1953: 170–224), as this is announced in the colophon to be the source of Book III – though the source is treated as freely as in the first two books, being severely abridged. Book III has been appended because the *Soliloquia* end abruptly when Augustine asks whether we will know all things in the afterlife, and Reason replies that he will find a full answer to his question in *De videndo Deo*. This third book then abandons the dialogic form of the earlier two and becomes an extended monologue on the implications of knowledge after death, arguing that although we will know all things in the afterlife, it is to our benefit to acquire knowledge in this life, for just as not all in heaven will have equal glory, so not all will be equally wise. In fact, it seems only the framework of *De videndo Deo* has been adopted, and Book III is more directly concerned with the issues treated in another, unnamed source, a homily of Gregory the Great (see Jost 1920: 263). Gatch (1986) has argued convincingly that Alfred turned to *De videndo Deo* because he wished to resolve a matter that Augustine seemed to leave dangling, and he turned to Gregory because *De videndo Deo* did not actually address the issue directly. He finds, then, that although many of Alfred's alterations are due to the inability of the king and his ninth-century readers to comprehend the Augustinian argument except in their own more limited terms, Alfred nonetheless created a translation that is more complete and unified than the chief source.

The colophon in the sole complete manuscript is the only direct medieval attribution of the work to Alfred. But the parallels between this text and Alfred's *Pastoral Care* and *Consolation of Philosophy* (in particular) make it clear that it belongs to the Alfredian canon. Portions of the *Soliloquies* that conform closely to parts of Alfred's *Consolation* that are not found in the Latin source, as well as repeated phrases in the dialogues, are the strongest evidence for Alfred's authorship (Carnicelli 1969: 28–40). And we have already noted that this work incorporates many of the ideas and themes to which Alfred had devoted his studies. It also demonstrates the theme of power and governance that is so prevalent in Alfred's works, as when Reason, probing Augustine's deference to authority, says, "I hear now that you trust the higher lord better. But I would like to know whether you think that your worldly lords had wiser and more reliable thanes than the higher lords had" (Carnicelli 1969: 88–9).

Asser (cap. 89) tells us of an *Enchiridion* (handbook) that Alfred kept with him at all times and in which he recorded favorite passages from his reading. In his *De gestis pontificum* (ca. 1125), William of Malmesbury makes mention of a handbook of King Alfred, perhaps the same book known at Worcester in the twelfth century as the *Dicta* 'Sayings' of King Alfred. A Middle English composition known as *The Proverbs of Alfred* (ed. Arngart 1979) attests to a popular tradition of wisdom literature associated with Alfred. (It is, after all, a convention of the genre to attribute the work to a famous person, such as Solomon or Cato.) The handbook that Asser and William name – if they refer to the same text – is lost. Some have conjectured that these references to Alfred's handbook are in actuality to a manuscript of his translation of the *Soliloquia*. The two do not in fact seem very similar, though Whitelock (1969: 90–1) describes a set of conditions under which William might have identified one with the other.

The prose translation of the first 50 psalms of the Paris Psalter (Paris, Bibliothèque Nationale, Lat. 8824; facsimile ed. Colgrave 1958b) is the last of the Old English prose texts attributed directly to Alfred.[11] Psalms 51–150 are in verse, but they are certainly not by Alfred (see Bethel 1991), and they seem to be later compositions. William of Malmesbury, writing in the twelfth century, tells us that Alfred was translating the psalms at the time of his death (*Gesta regum Anglorum*, ed. and trans. Mynors, Thomson, and Winterbottom 1998, cap. 123.2). To be sure, William's attributions are not always reliable (see below), and no other medieval source mentions Alfred's translation of the psalms. Still, the linguistic and stylistic affinities to Alfred's other works seem to us conclusive evidence that they should be included among his direct translations: like other of Alfred's authentic works, for example, their vocabulary betrays a preference for *mettrumnes* 'infirmity' to *untrumnes* (the usual word in prose), of *unriht* 'wrong' to *unrihtnes*, and so forth (Bately 1982). Alfred's authorship explains the peculiarity that only the first 50 psalms are in prose: the verse psalms derive from a translation that must originally have included Psalms 1–50 (see chapter 6), and so they seem to have been added to the prose translation to fill out the collection. The prose translation thus seems to have been regarded as more important – as indeed it probably would have been if it was known to have been made by Alfred.

The Paris Psalter is a manuscript that is physically unusual – its dimensions are 526 millimeters in length and 186 in width (20.5 × 5.3 in.) – because it was constructed with its eventual contents in mind (see plate 5). Pages are laid out in two long columns, the first containing the Roman Psalter, the second an Old English translation. Each Old

Plate 5   The Paris Psalter (Paris, Bibliothèque Nationale, Lat. 8824), fols. 2v–3r, made ca. 1050, with four miniatures illustrating the accompanying psalms: God's hand descending from a cloud to lift the head of a man in prayer (Ps. 3.4) and similarly gesturing toward him (Ps. 4.2), a man bringing a cup and a ram to a draped altar (Ps. 4.6), and two men bearing grain and oil or wine (Ps. 4.8). Bibliothèque Nationale, Paris.

English psalm is preceded by a brief introduction, mirroring the practice of Latin psalters that included a *titulus* before each psalm providing useful information about it. The Old English introductions for the most part explain the occasion of each psalm's composition, as well as its purpose and applications. Each is in the form of an *argumentum* that explains the theme, expressing a tripartite historical, moral, and Christological interpretation. Alfred sometimes provides a fourth expression that might be called a second historical interpretation, dealing with events of the Old Testament, and this fourfold model seems to have come from Irish commentaries on the psalms (O'Neill 1981). No single source for Alfred's translation has been identified, but it is clear that his source largely followed the Roman Psalter, which is a revised version of the Old Latin Psalter, with a number of readings from the Gallican version, which later supplanted the Roman in English usage. Again, the translation is not a slavish one, though it is of high quality (Wiesenekker 2000). Most of Alfred's deviations from his Latin text are expansions meant either for clarification or for emphasis. This observation lends support to the suggestion above that he modified Boethius' and Augustine's texts not because he understood them imperfectly or relied as much on commentaries as on the works themselves, but because accuracy of translation was less important to him than making certain that the text was readily comprehensible to those who knew nothing of Latin learning.

The psalms may well have had a special resonance for Alfred, given that they were believed to be the compositions of the greatest of Hebrew rulers, King David. And the first 50 psalms express the theme of the burdens of kingship and power that is, as we have seen, so prevalent in Alfred's work. For instance, Psalm 2 asks "Why do the people rage and why do they consider wickedness? And why do earthly kings rise up and noblemen commit to battle against God and against those whom he has chosen and anointed as Lord?" So, too, since there is no preface to this work, as there is to the three discussed above, possibly it was intended for the king's own private devotion and study. But it is hardly necessary to assume any particular personal appeal of the psalms to explain Alfred's selection of them for translation: they were a fundamental monastic text, memorized by novices even before they could comprehend Latin. The Psalter is thus a natural choice for any curriculum based on "those books that are most essential for people to know," as Alfred's Preface to the *Pastoral Care* describes his collection of translations (Sweet 1871–2: 1.6, 7). Moreover, the introductions tailor the translation to the needs of learners, and thus this work seems better attuned to the king's educational program than to his personal needs. Whatever the translation's original purpose, the eleventh-century deluxe manuscript was almost certainly made for a wealthy lay person (O'Neill 2001: 19–20).

A group of three historical texts is closely associated with Alfred's literary initiatives.[12] The first of these is the Old English rendering of Bede's *Historia ecclesiastica* (ed T. Miller 1890–8). The work survives in four more or less complete manuscripts, of which Oxford, Bodleian Library, Tanner 10 is the most important (facsimile ed. Bately 1992). The linguistic evidence of this text suggests that it was copied from a Mercian original by West Saxon scribes (see Grant 1989), placing the work outside the corpus translated by Alfred himself, though Ælfric and William of Malmesbury both attribute it to him.[13] Whether or not the translation was actually made at Alfred's instigation, that it was copied by an Early West Saxon scribe may be taken as probable evidence that the text was seen as pertinent to the program of translations undertaken by Alfred. Indeed, if Alfred intended to inspire his countrymen to rebuild its literary heritage, there could hardly have been a more useful text for this purpose, as Bede both narrates England's past glories and exemplifies them in his own scholarship. The changes wrought by the translator accord with this purpose and resemble those of Alfred's own translations: the work is reduced in scope and detail, but chiefly in regard to matters of little interest to an audience of the late ninth century (Scragg 1997a: 47). In Bede's day the issues debated at the Synod of Whitby (see section 2 of the introduction) were recent, and thus Bede provides a detailed account of the Paschal controversy and cites computistical data for calculating the date of Easter. These passages, along with the historical documents that Bede quotes verbatim, are omitted.[14] The result is a work that is more concerned with local Anglo-Saxon history than with Bede's more expansive emphasis on placing his people in a typological Christian continuum. What remains is a Bede who seems less concerned with orthodoxy in doctrine, theology, and historical method, for the deletions have the effect of lending greater prominence to the miracles and visions recounted in the work.

Also to this period belongs the Old English Orosius (ed. Bately 1980b). Paulus Orosius (ca. 380–420), a priest from Braga in Portugal, wrote his *Historia adversum paganos* (ed. Zangemeister 1889; trans. Deferrari 1964) at the prompting of St. Augustine of Hippo. It is the first Christian history of the world, describing historical events typologically. Orosius wrote in response to those who blamed the degradation of Rome at the hands of barbarian Goths on the rise of Christianity and the abandonment of the old Roman pantheon. Orosius adduces all manner of calamities prior to the establishment of Christianity in order to demonstrate that his own era was no more beset by troubles than any previous. Book I describes the geography of the known world and outlines human history from the Flood to the foundation of Rome; Books II, III, and IV trace the histories of Rome, Greece, Persia, and Alexander the Great's Macedonia; Books V, VI, and VII deal exclusively with Roman history from the destruction of Carthage to the author's time. The mode of the apologetics of the work is a demonstration of the influence of a Christian God through human history, culminating in the transformation of Rome into Christianity's capital. It is easy to imagine why this work should have been chosen for translation: as a popular Christian history of the world – over 250 manuscripts have survived – it was a fitting companion to Bede's more local *Historia ecclesiastica*.

William of Malmesbury (ed. Mynors, Thomson, and Winterbottom 1998: cap. 123.1) attributes the Old English translation of Orosius' *Historia* to Alfred, but his authorship can be ruled out conclusively on the basis of diction and syntax.[15] The method of translation is nonetheless similar to Alfred's (see Kretzschmar 1987), for comparison to Orosius' Latin reveals many omissions: e.g., Books V–VI are reduced to one, and sections that criticize Germanic barbarism and hostility are deleted. There are also some significant additions. The geographical tour of Europe in Book I has been entirely rewritten, producing some significant differences (see Gilles 1998 and S. Harris 2001), and a particularly interesting passage has been added describing two voyages. The first is that of Ohthere, a resident of Hålogaland in Norway, who "reported to his lord, King Alfred" (I, 1) on the geography of Norway and on a voyage he made around the North Cape to what was probably the Kola Peninsula or the shores of the White Sea (now in Russia), an area inhabited by Karelians. Subsequently he provides directions for the sea voyage from Hålogaland to the mouth of the Oslo Fjord, and from there to the Danish trading town of Hedeby (modern Schleswig). The second voyage is that of Wulfstan, most likely an Englishman, who sailed from Hedeby through the Baltic to the mouth of the Vistula in present-day Poland, an area inhabited by the *Este*, probably a Slavic group.[16] In a passage notable for its use of Anglian unsyncopated verb forms, he describes the Ests' funerary practices, which involve the laying-out of a corpse for as much as half a year (enabled by magically produced refrigeration) and a horse race for the deceased's possessions. The voyages of Ohthere and Wulfstan are recounted only in the Lauderdale (or Tollemache) Manuscript (BL, Add. 47967; facsimile ed. A. Campbell 1953), an important witness to the Early West Saxon dialect. Most of the other additions found in the Old English *Orosius* are explanatory developments of names, terms, or references which might not have been known to the audience, as when Dido is identified as the founder of Carthage (V, 1), *consulas* are described as *lādteowas* 'leaders' (II, 2), and the rape of Lucrece is explained (II, 2).

Asser (cap. 77) tells us that Wærferth, bishop of Worcester (872–915), was the Old English translator of Gregory the Great's *Dialogi*. This may then be the earliest of the Alfredian translations.[17] Yet the preface added to two of the surviving manuscripts, CCCC 322 and Oxford, Bodleian Library, Hatton 76, makes reference to more than one translator, stating ostensibly in Alfred's voice that the king sought out his *getrēowum frēondum* 'trusted friends' to translate Gregory's work for him personally, so that in the midst of worldly affairs he might take comfort in "heavenly things." The translation thus has generally been assumed to represent not a work of Alfred's program for public dissemination but a private text for the king's personal use: Whitelock (1966: 68), for instance, speculates that Alfred had the translation made before he had conceived of his educational program. However, Godden (1997) has argued persuasively that Wærferth himself composed this preface for Alfred. One implication of this is that if the work was not originally conceived for wider circulation, that plan was altered quite early. A different, metrical preface to the *Dialogues* (*ASPR* 6.112–13) in BL, Cotton Otho C.i says, *Mē awrītan hēt Wulfstan bisceop* 'Bishop Wulfstan had me written'. If, as it would seem, *Wulfstan* refers to the later homilist, then Alfred, who died a century earlier, cannot have given him the *bȳsen* 'exemplar' (line 23), as the preface claims. Sisam (1953b: 201–3, 225–31) identifies the last three letters of the name as standing on an erasure and reasons that the original reading was *Wulfsige*, in reference to the bishop of Sherborne who received a copy of Alfred's *Pastoral Care*. This is then further evidence that the work circulated in Alfred's lifetime.

The *Dialogues* include a series of stories of miracles which Gregory narrates to his deacon Peter, making up the first three books; the fourth book concerns the afterlife. The translation is sophisticated, but it tends to render the Latin text rigidly (Bately 1988b), and it contains numerous errors. BL, Cotton Otho C.1 contains a revision of the translation dating to ca. 950–1050. Yerkes (1979, 1982) has studied the relationship between the translation attributed to Wærferth and the anonymous reviser's text and found that the comparison reveals much about the rapidity of linguistic innovation in English in the years that separate the two versions, suggesting that many of the features that characterize modern English took shape during this period.[18] Generally, the revision represents a more carefully rendered – if not more competent – version of Gregory's work.

The complex of texts that modern scholarship calls the Anglo-Saxon Chronicle is "the first continuous national history of any western people in their own language" (Swanton 2000: xx).[19] It is our chief source of information on Anglo-Saxon history after Bede. The degree to which we should connect the Chronicle to Alfred has never been firmly established. The twelfth-century chronicle of the Anglo-Norman historian Geoffroy Gaimar (ed. T. Wright 1850) mentions that Alfred commissioned a book of English history. The Anglo-Saxon Chronicle does seem to have originated in Wessex, because the annals even before Alfred's reign demonstrate particular familiarity with the western shires. It is possible that Alfred directly commissioned the collection of national annals; we know, in any case, that some version of the Chronicle was available to Alfred and his circle because of the use that Asser made of it (see above). And we know that it was during Alfred's reign that copies were first distributed to various monastic houses, as the surviving manuscripts are in close agreement to the year 892. Subsequently the various versions were extended by the addition of supplements issued centrally or by the insertion of annals of a wholly local character. As a consequence of this method of compilation, the manuscript history of the Chronicle is complicated (see Bately 1988a, 1991a). The oldest manuscript, A, is the Parker Chronicle (CCCC 173, fols. 1–32; facsimile ed. Flower and Smith 1941), named for its previous owner, Matthew Parker (1504–75), archbishop of Canterbury. The earliest portion of A, it has usually been thought, was copied during Alfred's reign, though it may have been written out as late as ca. 920 (see Dumville 1987: 163–5); it was in any case updated continuously at Winchester until shortly after the Conquest. Versions B (BL, Cotton Tiberius A. iii, fol. 178 + A.vi, fols. 1–35) and C (in BL, Cotton Tiberius B. i) are both from Abingdon, and large portions of the former (or rather the former's exemplar) are copied faithfully into the latter, though C relies on other sources, as well. B and C both incorporate a set of 16 or 17 annals imperfectly integrated into the rest, inserted between the

entries for 915 and 934 though covering the years 902–24, a section
known as the Mercian Register (see Taylor 1983: xliv–xlvii). The D
version (in BL, Cotton Tiberius B. iv) also incorporates annals from the
Mercian Register. It is a Worcester manuscript copied from a northern
exemplar, and it evinces notably Scottish interests. The fullest version
(E), in Oxford, Bodleian Library, Laud Misc. 636 (facsimile ed.
Whitelock 1954), copied at Peterborough, also shows strong northern
influence, and it continues long after the Conquest, ending with the
death of King Stephen (1154), about whose oppressive reign the an-
nalist gives an eloquent and harrowing account.[20] This Peterborough
(or Laud) Chronicle is of particular linguistic interest because it illustrates so well the abandonment of the West Saxon written standard and
the evolution of the language into Middle English. But the Chronicle
as a whole is of unique value for grammarians, for it is one of the few
prose texts of the Old English period that contain substantial passages
uninfluenced by any Latin source, the syntax of which is thus uncon-
taminated. Versions of the Chronicle, it should be noted, exerted considerable influence on post-Conquest historians such as John of
Worcester, William of Malmesbury, and Henry of Huntingdon.

Most of the entries in the *Chronicle* are simply brief notices of the
events of a given year, and there is usually little or no elaboration: "802:
In this year Beornmod was ordained bishop of Rochester"; "829: In
this year Archbishop Wulfred died"; "976: In this year there was a great
famine among the English people." Yet, especially in the later years,
there are often extended narratives. Particularly memorable is the account of Alfred's wars against the vikings (871–97), the fullness of which,
in comparison to the preceding annals, suggests the propagandistic value
to Alfred of the Chronicle's publication (see Smyth 1995: 482–98 and
Bredehoft 2001). Also remarkable is the account, under the year 755,
of the mutually destructive feud between King Cynewulf of Wessex and
his kinsman Cyneheard (see White 1989 and Johansen 1993). The narrative detail of this annal contrasts with the spareness of the surround-
ing entries in a way that to some has suggested parallels to the Icelandic
family sagas, particularly because it portrays a situation of conflicting
loyalties typical of heroic literature.[21] Beginning in the mid-tenth century, certain poems of nationalist aims are interspersed among the annals.[22] These celebrate significant events, and the first and best of the
poems is *The Battle of Brunanburh* (discussed below, chapter 9).[23] Most
are formally not of high quality – some mix rhyme with irregular alliteration and meter – but in some of the better poems the word *hēr*

'here, in this year' that usually begins an entry is probably required by the meter, with the implication that these were composed specifically for inclusion in the Chronicle.[24] One broadly rhythmical passage on the accession of Edgar (959) in MS D is clearly based upon Ælfric's brief alliterative encomium for Edgar in the epilogue to his digest of the Book of Judges (ed. Crawford 1922: 416–17), and stylistic traits strongly suggest that it was the homilist Wulfstan who adapted this text for use in the Chronicle and composed another rhythmical passage on the death of Edgar (975) in the same manuscript (see Jost 1923).

Some other texts associated with Alfred's reign are his law code, the so-called *Bald's Leechbook,* and the *Martyrologium*. Though these may have been composed in the ninth century, they do not seem to bear any particular relation to Alfred's program of reforms, and so they will be treated later, in chapters 7 and 6, respectively.

We have seen that Alfred's own translations are particularly suited to the needs of those entrusted with the task of rebuilding the monastic structure of the Anglo-Saxon Church. By contrast, Alfredian texts not composed by the king himself, with the exception of the *Dialogi* of Gregory, are all of a historical nature. Such historical works did undoubtedly serve the political purposes of the house of Wessex. Before Alfred's reign, England was not a nation but a collection of tribal kingdoms, while his near successors could claim to be kings of all England. Either through direct portrayal of the king and his accomplishments or by promoting larger historical awareness, these works may well have served the purpose of easing that transition and helping to secure his subjects' acceptance of his sole overlordship. Yet these historical works should not be viewed solely as propaganda for Alfred's dynastic ambitions, as they almost certainly served an important function in his educational reforms. In his Preface to the *Pastoral Care*, he describes his plan as a response to his own historical awareness: contemplating the past glories of the Anglo-Saxon Church, he was moved to act. The intellectual ferment of the early Church in England seems also in part a product of historical awareness, as scholars like Aldhelm, Bede, and Alcuin reached back across the centuries to Roman and Late Antiquity and attempted to rebuild Latin civilization on frontier soil. Seen in this light, the historical works of the Alfredian period may indeed have been essential to Alfred's project of motivating his subjects to recapture what they had lost.

3

Homilies

Written homilies are set texts designed for the portion of the mass or other liturgical rite devoted to preaching.[1] It was once widely assumed that Old English homilies were uniformly composed for the use of preachers celebrating the mass before the laity on Sundays and feast days. Although some certainly were, it is now apparent that early homiliaries on the Continent and in England were also devised either for private study or, most commonly, for the internal use of religious houses, for on such days the Divine Office (series of daily prayers, hymns, psalmody, and readings at seven or eight set hours) prescribed for monks and secular clergy called for the reading of homiletic texts during the night office (Nocturns or Matins, about 2:00 a.m. in winter: see Gatch 1977: 27–39 and Clayton 1985). It is only natural that most of the surviving manuscripts containing homilies should have been designed for the use of religious houses, since monastic and cathedral libraries are the only very appreciable source of such English books of the period as are preserved into modern times: compare how, of all the liturgical books that survive from Anglo-Saxon England, not one is a priest's manual. Thus even the Vercelli Book, a manuscript designed for private study, shows signs of having been in the possession of a religious house in England (C. Sisam 1976: 44).

Technically, homilies ought to be distinguished from sermons: the former are exegetical, comprising expositions of the daily pericope (lection from Scripture, in Latin), the latter catechetical or hortatory, comprising moral instruction of a more general nature, treating of doctrine or nonscriptural narrative, exhorting the congregation to right behavior, or explaining the liturgy and its significance. The distinction was an important one in some Continental traditions, since readings from sermons and homilies were scheduled at different times in the night office (Clayton 1985: 153). In Old English manuscripts, however, the two types of texts are for the most part intermixed, and thus in current Old English studies both types are referred to as homilies. For the Anglo-Saxons the category even included saints' lives composed to be read on the feast days of saints, as such texts also form a significant component of the extant homily books. With these inclusions, the number of "homilies" preserved in Old English may be reckoned at more than 250, a large portion of the prose corpus. Fixing the precise number, however, is not an easy task, as it is a characteristic of vernacular homilies from soon after their first appearance that they tend to incorporate material from prior works, continually recombining it in idiosyncratic ways to form new compositions. Such eclectic works are referred to as "composite" homilies. The greater part of these 250 and more are by Ælfric and Wulfstan (of whom an account is given in the introduction, section 5); the remainder are anonymous.[2] Aside from the Ælfric and Wulfstan corpora, the most important collections are the *Blickling* and *Vercelli Homilies.*

Some Latin homilies were composed in England before the viking age. There survives a collection of 50 by Bede that are devoted to explaining the Gospel reading of the day.[3] Most are for occasions in the *temporale* (see below), though homilies for some saints' days are included, with a special emphasis on martyrs. Three are for anniversaries of local significance: the death of Benedict Biscop and the dedication of the Church of St. Paul at Jarrow (two on the latter). Whether they were intended for preaching or private study is debated (see Ward 1991: v, n. 10), but it is clear that Bede took care to make his exposition of the pericope immediately relevant to the lives of his audience by construing its typological significance as a direct appeal to Christians (Martin 1989). The collection that Alcuin's *vita* ascribes to him, on the other hand, has not been identified conclusively with any extant homiliary (see Gatch 1977: 187–8 n. 17). Bede's homilies do not seem to have exerted any considerable influence on the vernacular homilies that are first found in manuscripts of the later tenth century (before Ælfric), which instead draw directly on Continental sources of the pre-Carolingian, Gallican-Celtic tradition, including some proscribed heterodox or pseudepigraphic sources, and particularly on Hiberno-Latin texts like the *Liber de numeris*, the Reference Bible, and colorful sermons.[4] On Wulfstan's Latin homilies, see below.

It is uncertain when vernacular homilies were first written in England. The homilies of Ælfric and Wulfstan can be dated fairly narrowly, and certainly some of the anonymous homilies are earlier. Possibly some of the latter were composed in the ninth century (see Turville-Petre 1963: 75, but cf. Scragg 1992b: 72), yet composition before the middle of the tenth century cannot be proved for any homiletic text. Indeed, the evidence for the composition of any substantial prose in Old English in the century separating Alfred from Ælfric is sparse (see Bately 1991b: 72). Regardless of their precise age, the very existence of vernacular collections is striking, as there is nothing comparable from the Continent until the twelfth century, and written Continental vernacular homilies in any form are rare before then (see Gatch 1978). If sermons were delivered in the vernacular on the Continent, preachers may have given a running translation of Latin sermons or worked from memory or notes rather than from written texts (Gatch's view), though possibly Latin sermons could be made comprehensible to Romance speakers (see note 8).

Regardless of the exact dating of these homilies, the chronological difference of at least a generation between the Vercelli and Blickling collections, on the one hand, and Ælfric and Wulfstan on the other is a significant one, and it is reflected clearly in the content of the two corpora. Ælfric and Wulfstan represent the full flowering of the Benedictine reform, in that they show an intellectual rigor missing from the earlier, anonymous works. In the earlier homilies the concern to sift sources and eliminate contradictory teachings is not great, and thus the theology of the Blickling and Vercelli collections displays some internal contradictions, particularly in regard to the fate of the soul of the departed while it awaits Doomsday (Gatch 1965, Kabir 2001). The sources employed are often insular and heterodox, and thus, much use is made of apocryphal Christian writings like the *Visio S. Pauli*, which Ælfric holds up to ridicule as a "false composition" in one of his homilies (ed. Godden 1979: 190), as had Aldhelm earlier in the prose *De virginitate* (Ehwald 1919: 256.7–14). The themes treated are thus often of the fantastic sort encountered in the *Solomon and Saturn* poems (see chapter 8, section 1), such as "The Five Horrors of Hell" (D. Johnson 1993) and "The Devil's Account of the Next World" (Charles Wright 1993). By contrast, Ælfric and Wulfstan make a point of employing only canonical sources in the patrology and insuring that the teachings they promote are internally consistent (Gatch 1977: 120).

The *Blickling Homilies* (ed. and trans. Morris 1874–80; facsimile ed. Willard 1960) are named after Blickling Hall, Norfolk, where the manuscript resided at one time, though it is now in the Princeton University

Library. The manuscript, the work of two scribes who have not been localized, is a fragment, missing perhaps five quires at the beginning and more matter at the end, and yet it remains one of the two chief witnesses to vernacular homilies of unidentified authorship. Eight of these eighteen anonymous homilies are unique; the other ten either are found in other manuscripts, as well, or were incorporated piecemeal into later composites.[5] They are arranged, with small deviations, in the order of the liturgical year, though the first 13, celebrating the Feast of the Annunciation, Lent, Easter, Rogationtide, the Ascension, Pentecost, and the Assumption, are ordered in accordance with the *temporale* (the annual sequence of the daily offices for movable feasts, as codified in the missal or breviary) and the last five with the *sanctorale* (offices for feasts of fixed date, including Christmas and saints' days, forming a separate unit in the missal). The last five are thus saints' *vitae* and *passiones*, for Ss. John the Baptist, Peter and Paul, Michael, Martin, and Andrew (the last fragmentary, though a closely related text in CCCC 198 survives intact). The missing initial quires presumably contained homilies for the season preceding the Ascension, including, perhaps, all or part of Advent, Christmas, and Epiphany.[6]

Although the manuscript can be assigned to ca. 1000, the texts themselves cannot be dated with any precision. One obstacle is that the collection is stylistically uneven, and thus it is clearly not the work of a single homilist. One homily (XI) contains a reference to the year 971, but it cannot be determined whether this was the year of composition or whether the year was updated in the course of copying. The language of the homilies as a whole is archaic by comparison to that of Ælfric (see Vleeskruyer 1953: 56; also Schabram 1965: 75), but how archaic is impossible to say with certainty, and there is no scholarly agreement about whether the homilies represent the first fruits of the monastic reform, in the middle or second half of the tenth century, or whether some might have been composed earlier. That their composition should have been unconnected to the reform, however, is rendered plausible by the notable Anglian element in their vocabulary identified by Menner (1949) and Schabram (1965: 75).

It has been argued plausibly that the *Blickling Homilies* were intended for the use of those preaching to the laity during the mass.[7] The structure of the collection closely resembles that of an early ninth-century Latin homiliary from the Continent, that of St. Père de Chartres, one of just two from this period known to have been constructed for this same purpose.[8] The St. Père manuscript also follows the order of the

temporale up to Pentecost and the *sanctorale* thereafter (though this is
an obvious pattern: see Scragg 1985: 316), and it draws on many of the
same sources. In addition, certain of the Blickling texts do seem to be
addressed to the laity, as, for example, homily x begins with an address
to "men and women, young and old, educated and ignorant, rich and
poor," and IV concerns the obligation to render tithes.

The nature of the Blickling texts is diverse, but a few themes predominate. Charity to the poor is a persistent concern, and the congregation is repeatedly advised not to live in pride while the unfortunate
suffer. Two homilies, I and XIV, are especially gentle and loving, recounting the purity and grace of the Virgin Mary and John the Baptist.
Indeed, Dalbey (1980) has argued that mildness and compassion were
the guiding themes for the compiler. Yet the collection does not draw
Christians to good works by mildness alone, for eschatology also exerts
a strong presence, and several of the conventional themes associated
with it make an appearance, such as a graphic description of a decaying
corpse, made at one point to speak (x, pp. 101, 113) and the *ubi sunt*
topos (v, x; see chapter 8, section 2). Hand in hand with the
eschatological theme goes an apocalyptic one, treating of the last days
(VII, X, XI). Since the motivation for this naturally is to instill fear of the
wages of sin, a certain fascination with the torments of hell is mani-
fested, in v, VI, VII (the latter two in the context of the Harrowing), and
particularly in XVI on the dedication of St. Michael's Church, a much-
discussed passage of which (ed. Morris 1874–80: 209–11), drawn from
the *Visio S. Pauli*, describes hell in terms reminiscent of Grendel's *mere*
in *Beowulf* 1357b–1376a, 1408–1417a:

> Thus St. Paul was looking toward the northern region of the world,
> where all waters go down, and there he saw over the water a certain
> hoary stone; and north of the stone had grown very frosty woods, and
> there were dark mists there; and under the stone was the lair of monsters
> and outlaws. And he saw that on the cliff there hung on the icy woods
> many black souls bound by their hands; and devils in the form of mon-
> sters were attacking them like a greedy wolf; and the water was black
> below under the cliff. And between the cliff and the water there were
> about twelve miles, and when the branches broke, the souls that hung on
> the branches disappeared below, and the monsters seized them.

The significance of the parallel is a matter of debate: some have seen it
as happenstance (e.g. C. Brown 1938), others as the result of direct
influence of the homily on *Beowulf*, and thus of the latter's late date of

composition (e.g. R. Collins 1984). However, Charles Wright (1993: 113–36) has argued persuasively that if the connection is real (and he is certain that it is), then the *Beowulf* passage must draw not on the homily itself but on a version of the *Visio* that might date to the eighth century or even earlier. In any case, the homily's description of hell illustrates well the fantastic sort of material favored in this homiliary, and as argued by Godden (1978: 99–102), it must be against works like this one that Ælfric was reacting when he set out to reform the writing of homilies (see below). Indeed, nearly all the hagiographical homilies that round out the Blickling collection incorporate material from apocrypha and Latin sermons appealing to a love of colorful narrative, including an attempt on the part of collaborating devils and Jews to slaughter the apostles and steal the corpse of the Virgin (xiii) and a particularly contentious series of competing wonders wrought by Simon the sorcerer (something of a metamorphosed Simon Magus) and the apostles Peter and Paul (xv).

The *Vercelli Homilies* (ed. Scragg 1992b, trans. in Nicholson 1991) appear in the Vercelli Book, a manuscript of southeastern provenance (facsimile ed. C. Sisam 1976), where they number 23. Most are sermons, though two are homilies proper (xvi and xvii), two are largely hagiographical (xviii and xxiii), and two (i and vi) are chiefly close translations of scenes in the life of Christ from the gospels of John and Pseudo-Matthew, with no real exposition (see Scragg 1992b: xix–xx). Mixed in with them in the manuscript are the poems *Andreas* and Cynewulf's *Fates of the Apostles* (after homily v), *Soul and Body I, Homiletic Fragment I*, and *Dream of the Rood* (after xviii), and Cynewulf's *Elene* (after xxii). The poems do not seem entirely out of place in this environment, as they are homiletic or hagiographical in nature. Indeed, *Homiletic Fragment I* ends with a conventional homiletic formula of closure, and *Soul and Body I* is simply a versification of a common homiletic theme found also in homily iv. In any event it is not the case that poetry has intruded upon an otherwise coherent collection, since the Vercelli Book is in no sense a homiliary: the contents are not in the order of the *temporale,* and the book appears not to have been used for preaching but for pious reading (K. Sisam 1953b: 118). There is in that respect a Continental parallel, as the Latin homiliary of Hrabanus Maurus, compiled for the emperor Lothar ca. 855, is known to have been put to the same use (see Clayton 1985: 156). Indeed, it would be harder to explain how a vernacular book of homilies for liturgical use came to the library at Vercelli, in the Italian Piedmont, than one intended for

private study (see K. Sisam 1953b: 116–18; Boenig 1980: 327–31).
The contents are drawn from sources of heterogeneous date and linguistic composition, though certain groups of texts seem to have been
copied from the same source.[9] Indeed, three of the homilies (XIX, XX,
XXI), plus another for Ascension Day in CCCC 161, appear to be by the
same anonymous author (Scragg 1992a). In its peculiar form the Vercelli
Book has been likened to a florilegium (medieval anthology or collection of excerpts: Gatch 1977: 57; Ó Carragáin 1981: 66–7), but in any
case among manuscripts of homilies there is nothing comparable in
form from England or the Continent up to this time. The chief Latin
sources are the homilist Caesarius of Arles (d. 542) and a version of the
St. Père homiliary (see above), though in addition to the other sources
already mentioned, direct or indirect use is made of Gregory the Great,
Paulinus of Aquileia, Isidore of Seville, Sulpicius Severus, the apocryphal *Apocalypse of Thomas*, the *Gospel of Nicodemus*, the *Catechesis celtica*,
and others.

The *Vercelli Homilies*, it has been pointed out, tend to conform to a
typical structure, comprising a "formula of introduction, an appropriate number of preparatory motifs, a central narrative episode or exposition, and a closing" (Szarmach 1978: 244). What is most striking about
this collection, though, is the heavy preponderance of penitential themes,
which are the chief concern of 10 of the 23 homilies. For example,
homily III, a close translation of a popular anonymous Latin text, lists
the six steps to the forgiveness of sins: confession, repentance, vigils,
fasting, prayers, and alms. Each step is then described in turn, providing some useful insights into early medieval penitence, for example confirming that it was a confessor's practice to recite the eight capital sins
for the penitent one by one, to insure that no sin remained uncon-
fessed; and remarking that forgiveness of sins depends not upon the
number of years of penance performed but on "bitterness of spirit" –
that is, on the intensity of one's remorse. As in the Blickling collection,
penitence is encouraged by ample appeal to eschatology (most prominent in II, IV, VIII, IX, X, XV, and XXI), usually linked with chiliasm, producing conventional themes of transitoriness, which include variants of
the *ubi sunt* theme (IV, X) and the decay of the corpse (which the soul
reproaches in IV; see also XIII, XXII). The Vercelli collection has sometimes been described as more strident and militant in tone than the
Blickling (see, e.g., Greenfield and Calder 1986: 74; Jeffrey 1989: 178).
Yet all the same themes are found in the two, and the *Vercelli Homilies*
do not lack texts of a more compassionate nature, such as homily XVII,

in which the theme of peace and love in Christ is actually more explicit than in any of the Blickling texts.

There are no intact codices of anonymous homilies comparable in scope to the Blickling and Vercelli collections: the remaining 80 or so anonymous homilies, some quite fragmentary, are distributed among more than 50 manuscript sources (listed by Scragg 1979). What Scragg finds most remarkable about the anonymous homiletic tradition of the tenth century is its homogeneity. Despite the fairly large number of surviving manuscripts that contain such homilies, the variety is quite limited, as there is considerable overlap among them. Some are faithful copies of texts found elsewhere, but what is most striking is how often the same material is incorporated into different composite texts, and on how many separate occasions the same Latin source is translated independently into the vernacular. It is also remarkable that our knowledge of the vernacular homiletic tradition before Ælfric is effectively limited to what was available in Canterbury: the evidence for other major centers, such as Winchester, Worcester, and Exeter, is either much later or lacking altogether (Scragg 1979: 264–6). As the same material is used repeatedly, naturally the themes that run through the corpus differ little from those found in the Blickling and Vercelli collections. A particular preoccupation is eschatology in the service of penitence (see Gatch 1965). But the most salient feature of the corpus, by comparison to later compositions, is its relative heterodoxy: narratives involving devils are especially favored, but throughout one finds colorful themes of the enumerative style, such as "The Seven Heavens" and "The Fifteen Signs before Doomsday" (see Charles Wright 1993: 76). To date, the chief mode of research on the corpus of anonymous homilies has been source studies, and the body of such work is substantial.[10] There is also a growing corpus of studies attempting to demonstrate the common authorship of two or more of the anonymous homilies.[11]

New standards for the composition of vernacular homilies were introduced by Ælfric in the last decade of the tenth century.[12] As a student of Æthelwold in the Old Minster, Winchester, from about 970, he was educated for the priesthood at the literary center of the reform movement. The intellectual and doctrinal rigor that he attempted to bring to all his literary endeavors may thus be viewed as an expression of the spirit of Æthelwold's reforms. In the Latin and English prefaces (ed. Wilcox 1994: 107–10) to the first series of his *Catholic Homilies* he tells us his chief aim as a translator: he wished to make these homilies available in English because he "had seen and heard much error in many

English books which uneducated people in their innocence took for great wisdom." Accordingly, he says, in translating he has avoided obscure vocabulary. What he means by "error" (or "heresy" or "folly," OE *gedwyld*) is made clear by his disapproving reference to the *Visio S. Pauli* in the homily cited above. This is not to say that Ælfric does not share many of the interests of the earlier anonymous homilists. Indeed, in the same English preface he says that what lent this project urgency was the approach of the end of time, with the arrival of the Antichrist and days of tribulation, and most of the preface is devoted to these horrors. Yet there is nothing unorthodox in this. What Ælfric brings, rather, to the construction of vernacular homilies is discrimination in the use of sources. By contrast to the erroneous English works he deplores, his homilies will be based, he indicates, only on patristic authorities – that is, the Church Fathers of the first seven centuries of Christianity – as he makes clear in the Latin preface to the first series when he lists his sources as "Augustine of Hippo, Jerome, Bede, Gregory, Smaragdus, and sometimes Haymo" (the last two being Carolingian homilists who also relied heavily on the patrology), "for their authority is very willingly accepted by all the orthodox."

The *Catholic Homilies* are Ælfric's first known compositions, and already in them he has a plan of literary reform fully worked out. They were compiled in two series of 40 homilies each while Ælfric was a monk at Cernel (Cerne Abbas, Dorset, where he arrived in 987), and they were published sometime between 990 and late 995.[13] In addition to the indication of sources in the Latin preface to the first series, Ælfric frequently mentions specific sources in individual homilies, for example Bede in II, 10 and Gregory in II, 5. Even so, he is not entirely forthcoming about his sources (see Godden 2000: xxxviii–lxii). His use of Jerome was limited, and he does not even mention his chief source, the Carolingian homiliary of Paul the Deacon (720–ca. 799). The reason for this is that Paul's method was largely to anthologize patristic homilies without alteration, and apparently in the copy of this homiliary that Ælfric used, the source attributions were marked in the text or the margin, so that he felt entitled to cite the ultimate source rather than the proximate one when he appropriated the material. As his aim was to compile a body of material of impeccable authority, naturally it was to his advantage to appeal only to the authority of the Church Fathers by citing them explicitly.

The homilies conform to the order of the liturgical year, and the two series were intended to be read in alternate years, to provide variety.

Like the Blickling and Vercelli collections, they are an amalgam of homilies proper, sermons, and hagiographical narratives, but unlike those collections, they are devoted chiefly (that is, roughly two out of three of them) to exposition of the pericope. In general, Ælfric's method is to give a literal and historical explanation of the Latin lection, usually a translation with running commentary, and then he will often explain the allegorical and moral significance. For example, in II, 12 Ælfric recounts the events of Exodus and then explains their typological significance for Christians: Pharaoh betokens Satan, the Red Sea baptism, the guiding cloud in the wilderness Christ, and so forth. Rarely does he provide a full, fourfold exegesis of a point, explicating the literal, allegorical, tropological, and anagogical significance (Wilcox 1994: 24–5). His aim, after all, is not mere pedantry but useful catechesis (see E. Green 1989). He takes seriously the belief that those who are able to correct the unrighteous, and yet who do not, will be held accountable to God for the souls of the damned (as he tells us in the English preface to the first series). It is this duty to teach the unlearned that motivates his entire program, as it is from this that his concern for orthodoxy stems: the duty of the educated to instruct the ignorant is not simply a matter of translating Latin sources for a monoglot audience but of interpreting those sources; and interpretation involves not simply explanation but also scholarly discrimination. The uneducated cannot distinguish the canonical from the heretical, and so scholars must do this for them. For this reason we find in Ælfric's writings continual signs of a particular anxiety that if the simple are given free access to Scripture and the patrology in their own language, without proper guidance they will interpret it literally and thus be led into error, especially if they take what was sanctioned under the old law to be sanctioned under the new (see Gatch 1977: 13). Accordingly, he very often leaves untranslated those portions of the pericope that are most likely to give wrong notions to the uneducated.

For example, when Ælfric recounts the trials of Job (II, 30), he begins with the remark, "Now we shall relate to you only a little concerning him, because the profundity of the account exceeds our understanding, and all the more that of the unlearned. Lay persons should be spoken to in accordance with the limits of their understanding, so that they will not be disheartened by the profundity, nor wearied by the tediousness" (lines 2–6). When the offering to God of bullocks and rams is mentioned, he explains that the sacrifice of livestock was sanctioned under the old law but is not permitted to Christians (188–90). He is careful to absolve

God of any direct responsibility for Job's misfortunes, for he insists that
the fire sent to destroy Job's sheep only seemed to come from heaven
(90–7; see Godden 2000: 594). Finally, he apologizes to the clerisy for
what he has omitted from the narrative, pleading that his version is
sufficient for the uneducated (227–30). Given his fear, then, that the
uninitiated will misconstrue Scripture, it should be clear why his homilies offer so much allegorical explication – a variety of interpretation
that one might have thought too scholarly and recondite to be preached
to lay persons. If the laity are to be exposed to Scripture – and they
must be, given the obligation of the learned to teach – then allegorical
methods are precisely what they must be taught, lest they interpret too
literally.

From his prefaces and from his particular concern with catechesis of
the laity it should be clear for whom Ælfric composed the *Catholic
Homilies*.[14] Even the title *Sermones catholici* found in the manuscripts
indicates that they are intended for ecumenical rather than monastic
use. In addition, several of the homilies show signs that they were expected to be read in the course of the mass, not the Divine Office (see
Godden 2000: xxii). It was mentioned above that while hermeneutism
was the favored style of Anglo-Latin prose in the Reform period, Ælfric
declares it his aim to avoid obscurity of diction in his prose, for the sake
of his unlearned audience. Yet he was a consummate prose stylist, and
simplicity of diction should not be confused with artlessness. His early
homilies employ certain rhythmic devices, chiefly anaphora and occasional alliteration, designed to reinforce the relation of ideas and heighten
rhetorical effects.[15] He apparently did not invent this style, as similar
devices are found in other tenth-century homilies (see Funke 1962). In
the course of composing the second series of *Catholic Homilies*, however, he began to experiment with a new type of rhythmical prose that
is much more regularly alliterative. It resembles verse, but it is not metrical, and the constraints on alliterative patterns are not as strict. It also
lacks the distinctive poetic diction of verse, and, partly in consequence,
the syntax is that of prose rather than poetry, without widely separated
appositives or elaborate periods. Its resemblance to verse, however, is
unmistakable, and in the manuscripts there is extensive pointing like
that found in some poetic texts. In the second series this alliterative
prose is the chief medium for five homilies (XIV, XVII–XIX, and XXXIV),
and it plays a role in several others. Ælfric was apparently pleased with
this new style, as he adopted it for most of his *Lives of Saints* and all his
known subsequent vernacular homilies. Very likely he developed this

style as one particularly suited to the needs of the laity, whose ability to endure lengthy homilies, he frequently indicates, is limited. That the semi-poetic form made the material more appealing may be concluded from an anecdote, attributed to Alfred by William of Malmesbury, concerning Aldhelm, that he would sing vernacular songs in order to attract an audience, to whom he would then preach.[16] Ælfric's prose is also marked by the distinctive vocabulary and orthography promoted by the school of Æthelwold (see Gneuss 1972, Hofstetter 1987, 1988; also Godden 1980), and it is thus our chief witness to the Late West Saxon written standard.

The success of Ælfric's program in his own time and for the next two centuries may be gauged from the very large number of manuscripts containing homilies from the first and second series – 35 of the former, 29 of the latter.[17] Far more material from the hand of Ælfric is preserved than of any other writer of Old English, though with the passage of time we see his homilies being combined with others in new collections, and portions of them used in the composition of new texts (as detailed by Swan 1996). His mission to the laity, it should be said, remained a lifelong concern, and his relations with them intimate, as demonstrated by the variety of lay persons for whom he translated in the course of his life (see Lapidge 1996c: 88–90). One expression of his continuing concern is the amount of revision he applied to the *Catholic Homilies*. Some of the earliest changes are preserved in Ælfric's own hand in a manuscript of the first series copied at Cernel, now BL, Royal 7 C. xii (facsimile ed. Eliason and Clemoes 1966). The changes are mostly minor; the longest amounts to two sentences. Even after Ælfric became abbot of Eynsham in 1005 he continued to revise the homilies, once even doubling the length of a text, in the case of his additions to the homily on St. Alexander and his attendant priests (ed. Pope 1967–8, homily XXIII). More significant, the manuscript evidence indicates that after the publication of his *Lives of Saints* Ælfric must have returned to his earlier work and expanded the first series, augmenting some homilies and adding others (see Pope 1967–8: 1.59–62). He may also have been the one who compiled a new temporal series for Sundays into which were incorporated all the relevant *Catholic Homilies*, along with many new ones (see Clemoes 1959: 227–9 and Pope 1967–8: 1.39–52, with opposing views). Certainly, in any case, there are quite a few homilies for the *temporale*, clearly by Ælfric, whose composition postdates the issuance of the *Catholic Homilies*. Latin homilies by Ælfric are more difficult to identify. Possibly the Latin homily on which is based the first of Ælfric's *Lives of Saints*, Nativity of Christ (ed. Skeat 1881–1900: 1.11–24), is by Ælfric.[18]

The one other vernacular homilist whose name we know is Ælfric's contemporary Wulfstan (d. 1023), archbishop of York and bishop of Worcester from 1002 (see section 5 of the introduction). What the two men had in common was their reform-minded spirit toward the composition of homilies. They were also both estimable scholars: perhaps because of his disinterest in hermeneutics, Wulfstan used to be regarded as ill read, but source studies, and comparison of his Latin outlines with his finished English sermons, have shown that he was in fact widely read and careful in his scholarship (see Jost 1932). Yet the differences between the two homilists are more striking than the similarities. While Ælfric lived in monkish seclusion, Wulfstan was a public figure, a powerful force in the administration of the Church and in royal politics of the day. The difference has its correlate in the nature of their homilies, for while Ælfric's *Catholic Homilies* are for the most part true homilies – they are scholarly works of explication – Wulfstan's are sermons that show little interest in exegesis but are chiefly eschatological, catechetical, and monitory pieces designed for dramatic and effective preaching. Twenty-one English homilies (some in more than one version) are ascribed to him in the standard edition, though the canon has not been fixed conclusively, and perhaps cannot be, given the nature of the manuscript tradition.[19] As there is so much mixture of texts from different sources in Anglo-Saxon homily books, ascriptions to Wulfstan in manuscripts are frequently unreliable. Thus, much material in the edition of Napier (1883), including 15 sermons, is excluded from Bethurum's edition on the basis of stylistic and lexical criteria for authorship pioneered by Jost (1932, 1950: 110–271). In addition to the English homilies there are four in Latin, though these were apparently compiled as outlines for English versions. Two Latin sermons without English equivalents have also been ascribed to him (see Cross 1991), and a number of briefer items in Latin may be from his hand (see Cross and Tunberg 1993: 13). As just two of the English homilies are assigned to movable feasts (XIV–XV), and there are no hagiographical pieces, naturally the homilies form no coherent series like Ælfric's, and almost all might be preached on any occasion.

The identification of authentic vernacular homilies by Wulfstan is aided by the particularities of his style, which is nearly as distinctive as Ælfric's, though quite different.[20] Alliteration is used not to mark off quasi-metrical long lines but to lend some of the sonorousness of verse to pleonastic binomials, the Old English equivalent of expressions like "death and destruction" and "wrack and ruin," which particularly mark his work. These tend to alternate with pairs that rhyme rather than alliterate, such as *stalu and cwalu* 'theft and killing' and *sacu and clacu* 'strife and injury', and with various types of anaphora and parallelism. He is also fond of intensifying words and phrases like *æfre* 'ever', *ealles tō swīðe* 'all too much' and *oft and gelōme* 'again and again', which contribute to the sense of urgency that his themes convey. His style may be influenced by Latin rhetoric, perhaps combining its features with native devices (see Chapman 2002), but his figures do not in any particular instance correspond to the rhetorical effects of his often densely hermeneutic Latin sources. Rather, Orchard (1992) argues that his rhythms and his continual recycling of the same phrases and themes mark his prose as formulaic and thus closely allied to native verse traditions. His vocabulary, it should be noted, also differs from Ælfric's, for he seems to have been little influenced by Æthelwold's reform of the standard language. Overall, Wulfstan's style is crafted to maximize oratorical efficacy, with local effects of sound and sense lending emphasis to his doctrine.

Wulfstan's reputation as a stern moralist stems in no small part from the work for which he is known best, the *Sermo Lupi ad Anglos* 'Sermon of Wolf to the English'.[21] "Lupus" is the *nom de plume* by which some of his works are identified in manuscript (for a list, see Wilcox 1992: 200 n. 6). The text exists in three states, the earliest probably being the shortest.[22] On internal evidence the sermon can be dated with great probability to the year 1014, a trying time for Englishmen, as King Æthelred had been expelled in favor of Swein, and after more than two centuries of viking attacks, at last a Dane was recognized as king. The tumult of recent events – the martyrdom of Archbishop Ælfheah in 1012, the flight of Æthelred in 1013, the death of Swein in 1014 – lends force to the assertion with which Wulfstan begins, that the world is nearing the end. Like Gildas, whom he mentions, and Alcuin, along with others before him, Wulfstan sees his people's misfortunes as God's retribution for their sins, as he tells them in no uncertain terms. Most of the text is simply a catalogue of their sins, and the unremitting rhythm of crime after crime builds a portrait of English lawlessness and perversity seemingly beyond redemption. Wulfstan's special interests are revealed at the outset, for the list of crimes is headed by a scathing denunciation of lay offenses against the Church, including the plundering of church property (either for personal gain or to pay the tribute demanded by the vikings) and threats to the very safety of churchmen. The people are guilty of countless outrages, among them compelling widows to remarry; selling the innocent, even kin, into slavery abroad, or children for petty theft; betrayal of one's lord; and gang rape. Wulfstan builds to a rhetorical climax marked by two long lists of the names of crimes (murder, avarice, theft, robbery, heathen observances, etc.) and criminals (manslayers, parricides, killers of clergy or children, whores, witches, robbers, etc.), the latter imported from an earlier homily in which it describes the inhabitants of hell (VII). Significantly, it is only the last few sentences of the homily, barely a twentieth of the whole, that are devoted to the remedy: loving God and receiving the sacraments. Impassioned doomsaying like this is far from the spirit of Ælfric's reasoned persuasion. Yet it is also generally uncharacteristic of Wulfstan's work, and so it is in one sense unfortunate that this is the homily for which the archbishop is best known. In another respect, however, it is appropriate, as this is apparently the way Wulfstan himself would have wished to be remembered. Wilcox (2000b) has shown that a recurrent theme in Wulfstan's writings is that one of the chief duties of a bishop is not to be silent but to cry out and "preach God's right and forbid wrong" (in his own reiterated formulation), even when the message is unwelcome. Versions of this theme are juxtaposed with copies of the *Sermo ad Anglos* in manuscripts in such a way as to suggest that Wulfstan saw this sermon as the prime example of his own fulfillment of this fundamental episcopal duty.

Wulfstan's other homilies fall into three groups, by subject or occasion: eschatology and repentance (I–V, XIX–XXI), Christian practices (VI–XII), and the duties of an archbishop (XIII–XVIII). The first group comprises chiefly early works, apparently composed while Wulfstan was bishop of London (996–1002), yet even at that time the fundamentals of his approach to homily composition were fully formed. This group differs widely from the sensational eschatological material of the anonymous homilies, for there is almost no mention of the fires of hell, and in the homily on the Antichrist (I) the concept is so diluted that anyone who offends God may be so named. The second group is almost entirely catechetical, explaining to the laity the meaning of sacraments and prayers. Yet lay persons were not Wulfstan's only audience, for one version of the homily on baptism (VIII) is written for priests under his jurisdiction and another for both the laity and the clergy. Moreover, part of his purpose in discussing the sacraments may have been to promote the aims of the Reform by prescribing for the clergy orthodox baptismal practices in keeping with the Roman rite, which had possibly become confused with the older Gallican one (Bethurum 1957: 303). The third group represents homilies written in fulfillment of archiepiscopal duties, including a pastoral letter and sermons for the consecration of a bishop and the dedication of a church.

Wulfstan's use of sources differs from Ælfric's in that he employs Carolingian sources more frequently and does not identify either these or his sources in the patrology by name (Joyce Hill 1993: 20–1) – that is, although his sources are orthodox, he does not seem to feel obliged to prove this. Like Ælfric, Wulfstan tailors his homilies to the understanding of the uneducated. This is particularly clear in connection with several texts by Ælfric that he revised for his own purposes. The most familiar of these is *De falsis diis* 'False Gods' (xii, corresponding to Ælfric's late homily of the same name, xxi in Pope 1967–8), about heathen gods in the Bible, and those of the Romans and Danes. Wulfstan injects his characteristic binomials and intensifiers and freely alters Ælfric's alliterative patterns, though unsystematically. He also abridges his source sharply, reducing the sermon to about a sixth of its original length. More significantly, though, he frequently paraphrases in ways that suggest no clear motive but to suit the material to his own oratorical rhythms (see McIntosh 1949: 121). For example, Ælfric says of Venus that "she was Jove's daughter, so indecent in her lechery that her father had her, and also her brother, and various others, after the fashion of a whore; but the heathens worship her as a sainted godess, just as their god's daughter" (150–4). Wulfstan rephrases this: "She was so foul and so indecent in her lechery that her own brother copulated with her, as it is said, at the devil's prompting, and the heathens also worship this evil-doer as an exalted virgin" (77–80). Wulfstan often shows reticence about certain distasteful topics, and this explains the omitted reference to sexual relations between father and daughter. (A similar reference was omitted earlier, as well as a reference to Saturn's eating his sons – apparently both more repulsive ideas for Wulfstan than incest between sister and brother.) Otherwise the changes seem chiefly rhetorical, especially the heightened irony of calling Venus a *fǣmne* 'virgin'.

That the homilies of Ælfric and Wulfstan continued to be copied or (particularly in the latter case) plundered for homiletic material for as much as a century and a half after the Conquest is in part because genuinely new material was not produced: Old English homilies of such originality and learning would not be composed again after their day. That Ælfric, at least, did not inspire others to compose as he did cannot be simply because others did not see the value in his unique program of introducing the laity to hermeneutics.[23] The immense popularity of his methods is attested by the large number of manuscripts – even though homilies of the sort represented by the Blickling and Vercelli collections also continued to be copied and recomposed. Rather, that Ælfric and Wulfstan inspired no conspicuous imitators seems a sign less of the reception of their work in Anglo-Saxon times than of the unique circumstances that the historical moment presented to them. The singularity of their achievement in regard to homiletics is best thought of as intimately connected to the age, for their innovations in preaching are predicated on the reforming spirit of a monastic movement that reached full force only in their lifetimes. That movement was never to recapture the crusading spirit of the first generation of disciples educated by the reformers.

4

Saints' Legends
by Rachel S. Anderson

I The Hagiographical Background

The cult of the saints has its roots in Late Antiquity, when the graves of the holy came to be regarded as numinous places where this world and the next are in contact. At these tombs the poor and the sick gathered to seek miraculous help, and the faithful petitioned those already at God's side to intercede for them. Around the tombs there grew up shrines and churches, and around the saints there grew cults devoted to the veneration of relics and to the salutary benefits of pilgrimage to the shrines of martyrs.[1] Because of their combined human and heavenly natures, saints could be relied upon to pity humankind, and their physical remains were the site at which those two natures intersected. Indeed, the connection of the physical to the spiritual is made explicit in the construction of reliquaries, since these were often designed to allow the petitioner to touch the remains (Lapidge 1991b: 243–4).

Hagiography played no small role in these developments. Already in some of the earliest hagiographical writings – the late fourth-century poems on Felix, confessor, bishop, and patron saint of Nola, by Paulinus of Nola, and the *vita* of St. Martin by Sulpicius Severus – the saints are portrayed as friends and protectors, and in the latter work the saint's miracles are recounted in evidence of his power. Hagiography thus served to promote the cults, to attract adherents, and therefore to empower the religious institutions that grew up around the saints. One consequence of this aim is that hagiographical narrative often seems suspended in a timeless medium: historical and personal particularities of the saints tend to be smoothed away in an effort to render the appeal of a saint as ecumenical as possible. The form in fact is entirely conventional, as lives generally conform to one of two models. One is the *vita*, which typically relates the saint's noble birth, accompanied by miraculous signs; a youth marked by portents of sanctity; in adulthood, the saint's abandonment of secular life for a holy existence marked by wonders; deathbed instructions to disciples; and posthumous miracles, particularly at the remains (perhaps based on memoranda kept at the saint's shrine). The other is the *passio*, which characteristically is set in the age of persecutions, treating of a noble Christian's refusal to renounce the faith and worship pagan gods; interrogation by authorities, followed by a series of grisly tortures; and ultimately martyrdom, usually by decollation (since that was the manner of St. Paul's death, and it is not therefore to be resisted by subsequent martyrs). The distinction between *vitae* and *passiones* reflects in part chronological, in part hierarchical aspects of sanctity, as illustrated by Ælfric in a homily on the memory of the saints (ed. and trans. Skeat 1881–1900: 1.336–63): first after God he treats the patriarchs of the Old Law, then Christ's disciples, followed by the 72 who were the first traveling preachers (a number derived from Bede: see chapter 6), then the martyrs of the early Church, and finally the confessors (saints of the period after the persecutions), identified in order of eminence as bishops, priests, monks, and virgins. As for the reading context of saints' lives, such texts were composed variously for private study and for recital either in the refectory, where monks or canons dined in silence, or in connection with the liturgy, during Nocturns on the vigil of the saint's feast, the day of the saint's "birth" (actually death, when she or he was born into eternal life).

2 Legends of the Pre-Viking Age

The hagiographic tradition was still young when Roman Christianity found its first English converts in 597, and thus the Latin hagiography that first blossomed a century later in the English kingdoms retains much of the spirit and form of the earliest works of the genre.[2] But what lent vigor to this early English hagiographical movement was no doubt the extent to which Englishmen felt akin to the Church Fathers as pioneers of the faith: new saints were being made in their midst – English saints, who had shared in the same great enterprise of building an English Church, and from whom especial comfort and aid could therefore be anticipated. The writing of English saints' lives in Latin moreover might be expected to proclaim to all of Christendom the place that the English had carved out for themselves in the international Christian community. Indeed, at least one English saint whose *vita* survives, Cuthbert, was culted on the Continent (Lapidge and Love 2001: 10). Most of the earliest anonymous Anglo-Latin lives, then, are of English saints, though the narrative structures are often modeled on classics of the hagiographical tradition. (The formulaic nature of the legends in fact evolved as a method to secure membership in the ecumenical communion of saints for the person commemorated.) The *Vita S. Cuthberti* by an anonymous monk of Lindisfarne (ca. 700; ed. and trans. Colgrave 1940) even quotes extensively from Sulpicius' *Vita S. Martini* in an early chapter (I, 2), and the *Vita S. Guthlaci* (ca. 730–40; ed. and trans. Colgrave 1956) of Felix of Crowland (who is otherwise unknown) naturally takes as its model the *Vita S. Antonii* of Athanasius (translated from Greek by Evagrius), the prototype of lives of eremites, especially those tormented by devils, as Guthlac was. Cuthbert, the hermit and reluctant bishop of Lindisfarne, was the most revered of English saints; Guthlac, also a hermit, at the age of 24 abruptly gave up a military life of campaigns on the Welsh marches (compare Bede on King Æthelred of Mercia, *Historia ecclesiastica* V, 24) to live first as a monk at Repton, Derbyshire, and then from 699 alone in the fens of Crowland, Lincolnshire, until his death in 714. Both *vitae* follow the formula outlined above, though they show additional similarities, including the saint's prophecies fulfilled, struggles with devils, relations with monarchs, and rapport with nature. Bede later reworked the anonymous *Vita S. Cuthberti* into a poetic version in 979 hexameters, adding 12 miracles, probably from oral report;[3] and about 720 he wrote his own prose version (ed. Colgrave 1940), thus creating an *opus geminatum* 'twinned work', a tradition traceable to the fifth-century poet Caelius Sedulius. In a letter of dedication to his two lives of St. Willibrord, Alcuin explains the purpose of this practice: "I have arranged two books, one plodding in the language of prose, which can be read publicly to the brethren in church . . . the other running on Pierian foot, which should only be contemplated among your scholars in the privacy of the cell."[4] Bede's purpose in reworking the material on Cuthbert was to strip away all the local detail that the anonymous author of the earlier life had lovingly garnered from oral tradition at Lindisfarne, and thus to elevate Cuthbert to a higher status by rendering the *vita* appropriate to an international audience (Lapidge 1996a: 18–19). Bede also revised an earlier *passio* of St. Anastasius, perhaps because he knew of Theodore's interest in the saint – though in pronouncing the original badly trans-

lated from Greek, he seems to have assumed, perhaps mistakenly, that
Theodore was not himself the translator.[5]

   Early Anglo-Latin allegiance to classical tradition is also evident in
Bede's reworking of Paulinus' poems on St. Felix into a prose *Vita S.
Felicis*, in which his treatment of Paulinus' material reveals a particular
interest in the theme of divine justice expressed miraculously in the
everyday world through the power of the saint (MacKay 1976). Not all
early works are so classically influenced: an anonymous monk of Whitby
wished to honor with a *vita* the pope responsible for the conversion of
the English; knowing little about Gregory the Great or miracles associated with him, however, he must ask his readers' indulgence if he simply praises the saint extravagantly, randomly assembling passages from
Scripture, references to Gregory's writings, and some absurd fables (ed.
and trans. Colgrave 1968: 76). Likewise the *Vita S. Wilfridi* (ca. 710–
20, ed. and trans. Colgrave 1927) of Stephen of Ripon (sometimes
mistakenly called "Eddius" Stephanus) is a baldly political work, offering a partisan account of the tempestuous career of St. Wilfrid (d. 709),
a contentious bishop who traveled to Rome more than once to seek the
Pope's intercession after a Northumbrian king or Church council expelled him from one of the sees that he held in broken succession.
There also survives an anonymous Latin life of St. Ceolfrid, abbot of
Bede's monastery, which departs from classical models in that it provides an intimate portrait full of local color and without miracles.[6] In
addition to all these early Anglo-Latin legends, a substantial body of
hagiography by Alcuin survives; some lost works are mentioned in surviving texts; and of course many saints' legends of foreign origin were
copied into English manuscripts.[7]

3 Later Anglo-Latin Legends

Northumbria clearly dominated literary production in the eighth century: all the hagiographies mentioned above are from there, with the
sole exception of Felix's *Vita S. Guthlaci*, dedicated to Æthelbald, king
of Mercia (716–57). If Alcuin's hagiographies, produced on the Continent, and those of his students are excluded, it may be said that after ca.
740 no Anglo-Latin saints' lives were composed again for nearly two
centuries. The practical aims of this early group of works are not always
clear; nonetheless, their involvement in political issues is sometimes
evident. Stephen of Ripon, as mentioned above, clearly intended to

promote Wilfrid's positions, and perhaps thereby to secure the rights of the religious communities that Wilfrid had left behind. Felix's life of Guthlac is very likely designed to ensure continued royal patronage, for it relates how one visitor to the saint's fenland retreat, the great Æthelbald, who was then in exile but became king in 716 after a contested succession, repaid Guthlac's hospitality (and the saint's prophecy of Æthelbald's accession) by enriching the saint's shrine. Political motives have been suggested for some other works as well, though our knowledge of the political context in Northumbria is less than perfect.[8] When Anglo-Latin hagiography is reborn, starting with the reign of Athelstan (924/5–39), its aims are generally more transparent, particularly its connection with the rising relic cults. Thus Fredegaud of Brioude (anglicized to Frithegod), a Frank in the household of Oda, archbishop of Canterbury (941–58), composed his *Breviloquium vitae Wilfridi* (ed. A. Campbell 1950), a reworking of Stephen of Ripon's prose *vita* into some 1400 impenetrable hexameters, on the occasion of Oda's forced translation of Wilfrid's remains from Ripon to Canterbury in 948. The archbishop's seizure of the relics and Fredegaud's willing promotion of the cult attest to the power that attached to the possession of saints' remains. Similarly, Bishop Æthelwold the reformer was no doubt the moving force behind the hagiographical works that were composed about St. Swithun by Lantfred, a Frankish cleric at the Old Minster, Winchester, and by Wulfstan, precentor there, in the years following the translation of the saint's remains from outside to inside the Old Minster in 971.[9] Nourished by these narratives, the cult of Swithun, an obscure ninth-century bishop of Winchester, grew immense. It financed the rebuilding of the cathedral and the construction of an elaborate shrine for the saint.[10] Wulfstan, taking Sulpicius' *Vita S. Martini* as his model, also wrote a life of Æthelwold after the translation of the reforming bishop's remains in 996 – fulfilling the latter's desire to be thus commemorated.[11] On a more modest scale, the *Vita S. Dunstani*, composed about the year 1000 by an English cleric at Liège, who is identified only as .B., was plainly conceived as a plea for patronage that would enable the author's return to England.[12]

As these examples show, Anglo-Latin hagiography in the later period relied heavily on the contributions of foreign clerics. In general, Latin hagiography amounts to relatively little of the oeuvre of the best-known English scholars of the later period. Wulfstan the homilist has left nothing of this sort. Abbot Ælfric composed a simple epitome of Lantfred's work on Swithun and of Wulfstan's work on Æthelwold, rendering them suitable for an audience ill equipped to comprehend the dense hermeneutism that was the fashion throughout the later period.[13] He also abridged the *Passio S. Eadmundi* of Abbo of Fleury, though the text has not yet been identified. Byrhtferth of Ramsey wrote somewhat more, including a *passio* of the Kentish royal saints Æthelred and Æthelberht, doubtless in conjunction with the translation of their remains to Ramsey in 992. In addition, he composed a huge Aldhelmian *vita* of his master, the reformer Oswald, and a curious life of St. Ecgwine, founder of Evesham Abbey, from which it is clear that he knew so little about this early eighth-century bishop that he was obliged to improvise a series of irrelevant divagations until he reached the more familiar ground of the saint's miracles.[14] Several anonymous works of this period are also preserved, including lives of Ss. Judoc, Neot, Birinus, the Irish *peregrinus* Indract (properly Indrechtach), the infant Rumwold, the juvenile prince Kenelm, and Æthelberht of Hereford.[15] But all in all the production of Anglo-Latin hagiography in the last century of the era was small, in keeping with the limited Latinity of the age. There was a much greater volume of lives of Anglo-Saxon saints produced, mostly by foreign clerics, in the half century after the Conquest, belying the platitude that Norman churchmen were dismissive of English saints.[16] Indeed, their interest in English saints exceeded that of modern scholars, as much of this material today remains unstudied, even unprinted.

4 Vernacular Prose Legends

In contrast to the relatively meager production of Anglo-Latin saints' lives in the later period is the very considerable production of vernacular texts. In this corpus the legends of foreign saints predominate, since the purpose of vernacular composition was, chiefly, to convey the benefits of Latin literature to those who could not understand Latin, and *vitae* of English saints make up a mere fraction of the wider Latin hagiographical corpus. In any case the production of vernacular lives is not so much a culture-wide phenomenon as the work of one person, Ælfric of Eynsham, who composed very nearly two-thirds of the surviving corpus of 103 texts (in the accounting of Nicholls 1994). Some of these are preaching texts for saints' days in the *Catholic Homilies* (see chapter 3): Series I includes 12 such homilies, and Series II 13 (listed by Godden 2000: xxviii–xxix), with special emphasis on the apostles. The reason that saints' lives appear among the homilies is that the Sundays and major feasts for which the two series were composed do not all belong to the *temporale*, and thus they are generally celebrations of saints' days, for which homilies on saints' lives are appropriate. Some of these are true homilies, for example the *passio* of Ss. Peter and Paul (*Catholic Homilies* I, 26), which begins with an exposition of the pericope; the remainder at least resemble sermons, as they include parenetic (hortatory) material addressed to the congregation.[17] In the earliest hagiographic pieces of the *Catholic Homilies* (John the Evangelist, Peter and Paul, Andrew, Paul, and Gregory), the predicatory value of the life is exploited to the full, whereas, beginning with the homily on Cuthbert (the first in Ælfric's alliterative style) and continuing with those on Benedict and Martin, the mood is less "preacherly" and more contemplative (Godden 1994a).

Most of Ælfric's hagiographies, however, are to be found in his *Lives of Saints* (abbr. *LS*, ed. and trans. Skeat 1881–1900), drafted no later than 998, for the English preface is addressed to the *ealdormann* and chronicler Æthelweard (see section 5 of the introduction above), who died that year. These are not generally constructed as sermons but as self-contained narratives. The Latin and English prefaces (ed. Wilcox 1994) reveal that the work was undertaken at the request of Æthelweard and his son Æthelmær; that unlike the *Catholic Homilies* it was to include only saints honored by monks in their offices, not by the laity; and that it was Ælfric's devout wish that nothing be added to the collection. Yet no surviving manuscript conforms to these intentions, as even the best (BL, Cotton Julius E. vii) contains extraneous material: four anonymous lives (XXIII, XXIIIB, XXX, and XXXIII), five Ælfrician homilies (I, XII, XIII, XVI, and XVII), and two epitomes by Ælfric of books of the Bible (XVIII and XXV). Familiarity with martyrs, he explains in the prefaces, is valuable both for their intercessory powers and for stirring up those of flagging faith. Most of the texts thus are *passiones*, but some confessors are also represented, and five English saints. He suggests another purpose for saints' lives in the general homily on the memory of the saints (XVI) mentioned above:[18] these serve as examples to us of virtuous practices, which are especially important now that the world is drawing to an end.

The collection, however, probably originated in a more immediate consideration: Æthelweard's purpose in requesting it was very likely so that his household might imitate monastic practices in their devotions (Gatch 1977: 48–9). This supposition is supported by the ordering of the pieces in the Cotton Julius manuscript, where the collection follows the order of the *sanctorale* (see Joyce Hill 1996: 236–42), beginning with Christmas. Ordering the collection this way would seem to have a liturgical motive, though *LS* as a whole was plainly composed for the laity and is ill suited to liturgical use (Clemoes 1959: 221). Some particular items are also an ill fit with the liturgy: the life of St. Martin (XXXI), for example, is about half the length of *Beowulf*. Clearly, then, if Gatch's conjecture is correct, Æthelweard's observances cannot have closely resembled monastic offices.[19] Nevertheless, that the *Lives* are intended for public performance, perhaps in household devotions, is suggested by the observation that, like the last of the *Catholic Homilies*, nearly all the *Lives* are crafted in Ælfric's distinctive alliterative style, suiting them to effective oral delivery.[20]

That the ordering in the Cotton Julius manuscript more or less follows Ælfric's intentions is made probable by a consideration of his chief source. Though it used to be believed that Ælfric compiled these lives from a wide range of sources, it has since been shown by Zettel (1982) that nearly all but the lives of English saints and the non-hagiographical items are translated from a two-volume Latin legendary compiled probably not long after 877 in northern France or Flanders, though the surviving manuscripts are all from England. This is called the Cotton-Corpus legendary, after the manuscripts that make up the earliest surviving recension, BL, Cotton Nero E. i, parts i and ii, and CCCC 9. It is an immense collection, containing entries for more than 160 feasts and encompassing more than 1,100 pages of manuscript text. Even this earliest-attested version is later than *LS* by more than half a century, but like this version, the one known to Ælfric must have been arranged in the order of the liturgical year.[21]

As with the *Catholic Homilies*, a particular concern of Ælfric in *LS* is orthodoxy. In adapting his chief source to his own use, he makes additions – some of the few that he does make – that allude to this familiar theme, as when he opens his *passio* of St. George (XIV) with a contrast between the foolishness that heretics have written about the saint and the true narrative that he will recount.[22] He also insists, in the English preface to *LS*, that he is saying nothing new in these works, since all is derived from Latin sources, and this disclaimer of originality is reminiscent of his earlier concern that we should know that his *Catholic Homilies* are based on the best authorities (see chapter 3). Likewise, Biggs (1996) has shown how Ælfric, having found Sulpicius Severus' *Vita S. Martini* to use as his source for his life of St. Martin in *LS*, employs it to correct his earlier life of the saint in *Catholic Homilies* II,

34. In his life of Apollinaris, reduced considerably from the source, he excises the many reverses faced by the saint, which make the Latin *vita* distinctive, though he retains scenes in which retribution is visited upon God's enemies (Whatley 1997: 189–92).

Very likely Ælfric expected that *LS* would circulate widely beyond Æthelweard's circle, and thus the collection, though in the vernacular, resembles legendaries in international circulation in that it includes mostly saints of universal veneration, and no local or obscure ones. Lapidge observes, interestingly, that "Ælfric omits various French and Flemish saints who were evidently culted actively in tenth-century England (for example, Vedastus, Quintinus, Bertinus, Amandus, and others), an omission which is curious in light of the prominence which these saints are accorded in the liturgical books associated with Bishop Æthelwold, Ælfric's mentor" (1991b: 257). It may be, as Lapidge concludes, that this is again a question of orthodoxy – of commemorating only the most ecumenical saints – though possibly also it reflects a variety of nationalist sentiment, as the collection does include lives of five English saints: Alban, King Oswald, King Edmund, Æthelthryth, and Swithun.[23] There is also a life of Cuthbert in the *Catholic Homilies* (II, 10). For all of these, except perhaps Alban, there would have been no source in the Cotton-Corpus legendary, but Ælfric sought out other sources: Bede for Æthelthryth, Oswald, and Cuthbert; Lantfred (above) for Swithun; and Abbo of Fleury (above) for Edmund. In fact, a copy of the hagiographical commonplace book in which Ælfric assembled nearly all these source materials seems to survive in Paris, Bibliothèque Nationale, Lat. 5362 (see Lapidge and Winterbottom 1991: cxlviii–cxlix). Ælfric's aim in adapting the material was to simplify and create an understandable narrative devoid of rhetorical flourish (Whitelock 1970), and perhaps also to make it exhibit a pattern of divine retribution in consequence of such "apocalypse and invasion" as England was experiencing in his day (Godden 1994a).

Although the great majority of vernacular saints' legends are by Ælfric, most of the anonymous works were in fact composed before his day: these include homilies or lives for Ss. Andrew, Chad, Christopher, Euphrosyne, Eustace, Guthlac, Malchus, Martin, Mary of Egypt, Peter and Paul, the Seven Sleepers, and perhaps Margaret and Pantaleon, not to mention works composed for festivals of the Virgin Mary and John the Baptist.[24] Later legends are few: perhaps just works on the Breton saint Machutus, Augustine of Canterbury, and Mildred. Why hagiographies should have been written in English before Ælfric set out to satisfy his lay patrons is unclear; but because from Alfred's day on "the number of centres where Latin scholarship attained a respectable standard was surprisingly small" (Lapidge 1991b: 953), it is possible that they were for the use of monastics who did not understand Latin.

On the whole, scholarly interest in the anonymous saints' legends has been limited chiefly to source studies.[25] Yet the flourishing of gender studies has provoked considerable scholarly interest in female sanctity, and particularly in transvestite saints, among both the Ælfrician and the anonymous lives.[26] Scholarship has traced the predictable trajectory of a recuperative and appreciative phase followed by a more skeptical one (compare the discussion of *Beowulf* and gender studies in chapter 9). Thus G. Griffiths (1992) reads Wilfrid's contemporary Æthelthryth (*LS* xx) as an active and autonomous saint, though her mark of distinction in her brief legend is to have preserved her virginity through two marriages. Ælfric's life of Eugenia (*LS* ii) recounts how she disguised herself as a man in order to join a monastery, was made abbot, and revealed her sex only when accused of seduction by a woman whose advances she had spurned. After this the legend becomes a fairly typical *passio*. Szarmach (1990) finds that in this legend Ælfric eliminates the erotic aspects of his source, not merely to repudiate sexuality but to accord with St. Paul's prescription, "There is neither . . . male nor female, for you are all one in Jesus Christ" (Gal. 3.28). Roy (1992) contrasts the Latin source's tendency to denigrate women with Ælfric's "less prejudiced" treatment of Eugenia. By contrast, Gulley (1998), who compares the version in the *Vitas patrum* (PL 73.605–24) rather than that in the Cotton-Corpus legendary, finds that Ælfric "has shifted the emphasis so that Eugenia's sanctity rests not on her renunciation of sexuality and femaleness as represented by her virginity and transvestism but rather on her rejection of the material world" (p. 114) through her acceptance of martyrdom. In the vein of performative approaches to gender, Horner (2001: 159–60) rejects binaristic views of Eugenia's transvestism to explore a more "layered" conception of gender.

Eugenia's disguise is merely a device in her *vita* – she discards it before the tale is half told – and Ælfric's focus is instead on virginity and martyrdom. By contrast, in the anonymous life of Euphrosyne (*LS* xxxiii), another tale of a woman disguised as a monk, cross-dressing is the center of interest, and the *vita* ends when the saint's sex is revealed at the conclusion of her life (see Szarmach 1996). Scheil (1999b) argues that the foregrounding of the saint's transvestism is an appeal not simply to male erotic desire but to fascination with gender ambiguity. Frantzen

(1993b; also Lees 1999: 147) sees something less innocent at work in all these narratives, as cross-dressing, as well as mastectomy suffered in the course of torture (in the case of Agatha, *LS* VIII), evidences the way that the sexlessness demanded of virgin saints turns out to be another variety of male normativity. Yet Lees and Overing (2001) find that Ælfric's concern in *LS* "is not simply gender identification, but the overarching dynamics of chastity" (p. 129), and Donovan (1999: 121–34) argues that these saints' chastity is empowerment, representing women's control over their own sexuality. Ælfric's methods and attitudes in the treatment of female saints are illuminated by nothing so clearly as the contrast between his works and the anonymous life of the reformed harlot St. Mary of Egypt, which he, given his concern about maintaining the orthodoxy and integrity of his collection (above), would doubtless have been appalled to find is added in the Cotton Julius manuscript of *LS* (XXIIIB). Unlike Ælfric's works, the latter translates the source fairly faithfully, it celebrates eremitism over the cenobitism that was the basis for Ælfric's literary program, it is at once sexually provocative and immoderate in its asceticism, and it assigns Mary a position of authority as mentor to a monk and a priest rather than relegating her to a submissive role typical of Ælfric's women (Magennis 1996). Indeed, its transgressive nature must have constituted its chief appeal for Anglo-Saxons (Scheil 2000).

5 Vernacular Verse Legends

There survive five Old English texts that are best described as versified saints' lives: *Elene, Juliana, Andreas,* and *Guthlac A* and *B.* Why hagiographies should have been put into vernacular verse is not known for certain. Of the known or possible uses for Latin and vernacular prose lives, however, two suggest themselves in this instance: recitation at meals in the refectory and private contemplation, more likely by monastics than lay persons. That the first two of the five poems are preserved in the Vercelli Book suggests the latter explanation (see the discussion of this manuscript in chapter 3); and there is no reason to think that the Exeter Book, in which the remainder are preserved, was ever used by the laity.[27] These poems contrast with vernacular prose hagiographies in that the latter may condense and summarize their Latin sources (especially Ælfric's *LS*), but they do not add to them, while the former contain some arresting additions – for example, in *Elene,* the battle scene between Constantine and the Huns (109–52) and Elene's voyage to the "land of the Greeks" (Judaea, 225–63). Particularly in accretions like these, with obvious analogues in *Beowulf*, it is plain that versified material of all sorts is tinged by the conventions of heroic verse. The example of Grendel suggests the possibility that what may have made these legends particularly appealing, and thus attractive subjects for poetry, is that devils appear in all of them.[28]

Like *Christ II* and *Fates of the Apostles* (chapter 6), *Elene* and *Juliana* each end with a pious passage into which a name – ostensibly the author's – variously spelt CYNWULF (in the former two) and CYNEWULF (the latter) is worked in runes into a kind of puzzle. This violation of the norm of anonymous authorship is justified in *Juliana* and, less obviously, *Fates* by an appeal to the reader to pray for the poet, but in *Christ II* and *Elene* there is no such motive provided for the runic signature – though in Anglo-Latin literature there is precedent for working the author's name cryptically into verse simply as a game, as in some of the acrostic poems of Boniface and Alcuin (see Dümmler 1881: 16–17, 226–7). The nature of the puzzle varies (see Elliott 1991 for discussion), but the passages containing the runes are all on themes of mutability and eschatology. Cynewulf has not been persuasively identified with any known person, though formerly there was considerable fruitless speculation about whether he might not have been a bishop or a wandering minstrel, or something between the two.[29] He has usually been assigned to the period 750–850, though it is possible that he wrote a century or more later (see chapter 6). His dialect, as appears from his vocabulary and the rhymes required at *Christ II* 586–98 and *Elene* 1236–51, seems to be Anglian, rather of the Midlands than of Northumbria.[30] Scholars once were inclined to attribute a great many poems to Cynewulf (see A. Cook 1900: lii–lxv), but the evidence of style and vocabulary is mostly negative: among the more substantial unsigned poems, only *Guthlac B* (of which the end is missing, so that no runic signature could be preserved) could plausibly be ascribed to him on these grounds (Fulk 1996a: 4–9).

Cynewulf's *Elene* (*ASPR* 2.66–102) is a translation of some recension of the *acta* of Cyriac (or Quiriac), bishop of Jerusalem, whose feast is celebrated May 4, a version of the *Inventio sanctae crucis*.[31] It begins with a vision of the cross granted the emperor Constantine, through the power of which he overcomes an army of Huns and allied Germans. He sends his mother Helena (OE *Elene*, with initial stress) in search of the cross on which Christ was crucified. In Jerusalem she finds the Jewish elders to whom she turns for information uncooperative. In a troubling inversion of the conventions of the *passio*, Elene becomes tormentor to the wisest of the Jews, named Iudas, having him thrust into a pit. After a week he relents, and when he invokes divine aid to identify the site of Calgary, a cloud of smoke arises at the spot. Three crosses are dug up, and Christ's is identified when a young man is raised from the dead by its agency. Satan appears in order to rebuke Iudas, who answers him contemptuously. Elene covers the cross in gold and gems and has a church built on the holy spot, after which Iudas, renamed Ciriacus, receives baptism and is made bishop. Another miracle reveals where the nails are buried, and Elene has these worked into a bridle for her son's horse. After an extrametrical *Finit* (1235), a purportedly autobiographical rhyming passage speaks of the poet's advancing age, a conversion from sinful ways, and divine inspiration in song. The poem closes with an account of Doomsday. The structure of the legend is thus unusual, as it is neither a *passio* nor a *vita*, and it is debatable whether the central figure is Elene or Ciriacus – or the cross itself (see the discussion of *Dream of the Rood* in chapter 6). The title, of course, is modern.

In keeping with modern critical preoccupations, studies of *Elene* from the past dozen or so years have tended to problematize the poem's treatment of gender, ethnicity, and power. Thus Hermann (1989: 91–118, esp. 101–3, joined by Lionarons 1998) faults critics, particularly of the allegorical sort, for serving as apologists for the protagonist's oppressive politics and anti-Semitism. DiNapoli (1998b), by contrast, finds that the anti-Jewish attitudes expressed by the Latin source are deliberately muted by Cynewulf, in that the poet underscores the Jews' innocence of the charge of concealing knowledge of Christ and the cross.[32] Olsen (1990) asserts that Helena was chosen for poetic treatment precisely because she is active and heroic, while Lees (1997: 159–67), to the contrary, argues that despite Elene's prominence, all autonomy and agency in the poem belong to Constantine and Iudas, and Elene's gender matters only in figural terms, since she may be assumed to allegorize the Church. Lionarons (1998) sees gender construction in *Elene* as shifting, and predicated on a syncretism of Latin ecclesiastical and Germanic cultures. All of these approaches differ markedly from prior studies of the poem, with their largely structural, thematic, and typological concerns.[33]

Cynewulf's *Juliana* (*ASPR* 3.113–33), by contrast, is a paradigmatic *passio*. In the city of "Commedia" (Nicomedia – Cynewulf apparently mistook the first three minims in his source for "in" rather than "ni") during the reign of Maximian (d. 310), a powerful *gerēfa* (Lat. *senator*) by the name of Heliseus (Lat. *Eleusius*) sought the hand of the young noblewoman Iuliana, but she refused to marry a heathen. She was flogged successively by her exasperated father and her suitor and then imprisoned. In her confinement a demon appears to her, pretending to be an angel sent by God, to tell her to partake of the pagan worship demanded of her. She prays for guidance, and a voice from heaven advises her to seize the visitor and demand the truth. This she does, and in a series of lengthy speeches the demon is compelled to reveal all the evil he has accomplished throughout human history, and how he has gone about it. The next day, an attempt is made to burn Iuliana and to plunge her into boiling lead, but she remains unscathed, protected by an angel, until she is beheaded with a sword. Subsequently Heliseus is drowned on a voyage, with 33 companions, while Iuliana's corpse is worshipfully interred. The close of the poem, with its runic signature, is penitential and looks toward Judgment Day.

Aside from this closing passage, Cynewulf makes no substantial additions to his source, which must have resembled the legend printed in the Bollandist *Acta Sanctorum* for February 16.[34] The poem is nonetheless revealingly different in its emphases. The contest with the demon is made the dramatic center of the poem (Woolf 1993: 15), perhaps not just because of the Anglo-Saxon fascination with devils, but because it turns the saint's seemingly passive virtue of virginity into an active conquest of evil. Indeed, Horner (2001: 101–30) sees this militarization of virginity as an analogue to the empowerment of a threatened female monastic audience by the potency of discerning reading. Of course, in Cynewulf's hands the tale assumes the usual heroic trappings of Germanic verse, one aspect of which is the elimination of some of the less dignified details of the legend, such as Juliana's casting the demon into a dung heap and the devouring of Eleusius and his companions by birds and beasts – a fate with heroic rather than abject connotations in Old English, in view of the "beasts of battle" topos. Perhaps most striking is the way that Cynewulf has increased the contrast between Iuliana and her opponents by means of polarization (see section 6 of the introduction), polishing her character and besmirching theirs. Heliseus is made particularly demonic and bestial in his deranged furor at her resistance, but more interestingly some questionable aspects of Juliana's behavior are omitted, for example her temporizing insistence that she will marry no less a man than a prefect, as an initial strategy for deflecting Eleusius' advances.

The apocryphal Πράξεις 'Ανδρέου καὶ Ματθεία εἰς τὴν χώραν τῶν ἀνθρωποφάγων 'Acts of Andrew and Matthew in the Country (or πόλιν 'City') of the Cannibals' was available in England in a close Latin translation, of which one sentence is preserved, embedded in an Old English rendering, the fragmentary Blickling homily on St. Andrew.[35] In an eleventh-century palimpsest discovered at Rome there survives a longer fragment of the same Latin recension (called the Bonnet fragment, after its first editor), and in some form this version must have served as the source not only for the homily but also for the anonymous poem *Andreas* (*ASPR* 2.3–51). Some other Latin recensions of the Πράξεις survive in Continental manuscripts, but they are less faithful renderings of the Greek, which therefore serves as our best guide to the poet's source, aside from the Bonnet fragment.[36] With its bloodthirsty antagonists and heroic contests, the material of the legend seems better suited to the conventions of Old English verse than any other hagiographical work – and this, more than anything else, may explain the poem's affinities to *Beowulf* (see below). Matheus (St. Matthew), blinded and imprisoned by the man-eating Mermedonians, prays for assistance, and God calls Andreas from Achaia to his aid. Though at first reluctant, Andreas eventually sets out with his disciples and meets on the shore three mariners – in disguise, two angels and God himself (more precisely Christ in the Πραξεις) – who ultimately agree to ferry them gratis to Mermedonia. While the disciples sleep on the voyage, Andreas relates to the captain Christ's miracles, and particularly an apocryphal account of an angelic statue made to speak. Andreas sleeps, and when he and his men awake alone on the shore in Mermedonia, Andreas recognizes who the captain was. God appears, and when Andreas asks why he did not recognize him earlier, he is told that this was punishment for his initial recalcitrance. Rendered invisible to the Mermedonians, Andreas enters the city alone and finds the prison, where seven guards are struck dead and the doors open at the saint's touch. After a joyful reunion, Andreas heals Matheus and frees all the prisoners. When the Mermedonians find the prison empty, they choose one of their own to be eaten in Matheus' place, but Andreas causes their weapons to melt. A devil appears to inform them who their tormentor is, and on God's advice Andreas appears before the multitude and is taken and treated savagely. The devil comes to taunt him in prison but is put to flight by the saint's resolute reply. After the fourth day of torment, God heals Andreas' wounds, the saint commands a pillar of his prison to pour forth a deluge on the cannibals, and an angel spreads fire to prevent their flight. At the citizens' repentant pleas, Andreas opens a chasm in the earth that swallows the deluge along with 14 of the worst sinners. At his request, God raises the young people who had been drowned, and all are baptized. A church is built, a man named Platan (Lat. *Plato*, Gk. Πλατων) is made bishóp, and when Andreas sets out for Achaia, where he expects to be martyred, the lamenting people close the poem with a chorus in praise of God.

Nearly all recent studies of *Andreas* focus on issues of orality and literacy. The critical issues are of long standing, for because of certain verbal resemblances it was for many years accepted that the poet knew and drew upon *Beowulf*.[37] This consensus lapsed with the growing recognition that Old English verse is formulaic, and verbal parallels may result from a common oral tradition rather than from direct literary influence.[38] A matter of particular debate is line 1526, where *meoduscerwen* 'dispensing of mead(?)', used as a kenning for the deluge, has seemed to many scholars a clumsy imitation of *ealuscerwen* at *Beowulf* 769, referring to the terror imposed by Grendel as a dispensing of bitter drink (ale). But the *Beowulf* passage is a crux, and Rowland (1990) goes so far as to argue that the usage in *Andreas* is in fact superior. Yet the relation between *Andreas* and *Beowulf* is still debated, since the 1993 studies of Riedinger and Cavill both find that oral tradition is a poor explanation for a range of similarities between the poems. Moreover, Calder (1986) finds that the aesthetics of *Andreas* are unlike those of *Beowulf*, and comparison of the two leads to misunderstandings about the former. Aspects of the *Andreas* poet's literacy have not been neglected: both Riedinger (1989) and J. Foley (1995) highlight some of its consequences, the former arguing that traditional, secular oral elements are transmuted in this sacred, literate context, the latter that the poet's self-interruption in lines 1478–91, where he questions his own ability to complete the task before him, expresses uncertainty about his ability to adapt his written source to the oral poetic register – if it is not simply a conventional modesty topos. Fee (1994) would perceive writing and torture as analogous, and the former therefore as a central concern of the poet, much as others have argued in regard to *Beowulf*.

The cult of St. Guthlac was extensive, to judge by the wealth of textual material produced late into the Middle Ages (see Colgrave 1956: 19–46). Particularly interesting is a set of designs from sometime after 1141 for 18 stained-glass roundels depicting scenes from Felix's *Vita S. Guthlaci* (best illustrated in G. Warner 1928). Felix's difficult, Aldhelmian legend is translated, only slightly abbreviated, into unadorned Old English in BL, Cotton Vespasian D. xxi (ed. Gonser 1909: 100–73), of which an older copy of cap. XXVIII–XXXII forms Vercelli homily XXIII (ed. Scragg 1992b: 381–92). The text is probably archaic, and perhaps Mercian, though in its present form it has been modernized (Roberts 1986). Felix's legend also forms the basis for *Guthlac B* in the Exeter Book (*ASPR* 3.72–88), inasmuch as the poem loosely renders one chapter (50) describing the saint's sickness and death, and it is this dependence that lends the poem its eastern hagiographical flavor, given the similarity of Guthlac's mode of eremitism, as portrayed by Felix, to that of the Desert Fathers. The poem begins with an account of the Fall and Expulsion from Eden to explain why all humankind must die (819–878a) – vastly amplifying a brief remark in Felix's account about Adam's culpability in our mortality (see Biggs 1990) – thus establishing the central topic. Guthlac's struggles with devils, his rapport with nature, and his miracles receive brief notice (894–932a), but the bulk of the poem is devoted to the week's sickness that Guthlac suffered over Eastertide, during which he conversed with his servant and disciple (named Beccel by Felix), teaching him and revealing to him that he had for 14 years been visited daily and nightly by an angel. His last request is that his death be announced to his sister (named Pega by Felix), and thus the last part of the poem is Beccel's message to her. This is the passage that has regularly garnered the greatest critical interest, as the message (1347–79) is reminiscent of the language of *The Wanderer* and *The Seafarer* in the same manuscript. The progression of ideas in 1348–54 in fact parallels that in *The Wanderer* 11–36, moving from the value of stoicism (cf. *Wanderer* 11–20) to separation (20–1) to the burial of one's lord (22–3), followed by abject departure from the gravesite (*hēan þonan*, 23) and loss of former joy (25–36). The most recent studies, those of Phyllis Brown (1996), Ai (1997), and S. Powell (1998), employ this closing passage as a key to understanding both the poem's elegiac mode as a whole and the psychology of Anglo-Saxon consolation in general. The message, as well as the poem, unfortunately is incomplete: there is a lacuna in the manuscript, with the loss, in the view of most scholars, of an entire quire, if not more.

Though the verses of *Guthlac A* and *B* are numbered consecutively in all editions, they are clearly separate compositions. The latter, as mentioned above, is similar to the signed works of Cynewulf, notably in diction, but also in metrical style. *Guthlac A* (*ASPR* 3.49–72) is metrically more like conservative (and therefore presumably earlier) compositions such as *Genesis A*, *Exodus*, *Daniel*, and *Beowulf* (Roberts 1979: 59–62, Fulk 1992: 399–402). This is unsurprising, as the poet of *Guthlac A* tells us that all the events narrated in the poem took place within living memory (see 93–4, 154–7, 401–2, 753–4a), implying composition in the eighth century, as Guthlac died in 714.[39] If the poem could be proved to be based upon Felix's *vita*, it could be dated later than ca. 730; but there is no consensus, and the majority of scholars incline to the view that Felix is not a source (see Roberts 1988). Although the beginnings of the two poems are clearly marked in the manuscript – both begin with nearly an entire line of capitals after a blank line, a regular sign of a new composition – the poems' earliest editors, along with some later commentators, did not see the relevance of lines 1–29 and regarded them as either a separate composition or part of the preceding poem, *Christ III*.[40] Yet their pertinence is not so very obscure. Like *Guthlac B*, the poem begins with a prologue, so that the saint is not introduced until line 95. In lines 1–29 an angel greets a soul bound for heaven, praising the joys it will find there and closing with the remark that to overcome accursed spirits a person must aspire to that heavenly repose. Lines 30–92 then take up the matter of how one gets to heaven, contrasting those who put their trust in this fleeting world and those who have their eye fixed on the hereafter, narrowing the topic eventually to eremites. The bulk of the poem then is an account of how demons tormented the saint after he displaced them from their hillock in the fen where he made his hermitage. They continually tempt him to despair and to love the things of this world. On two occasions they bear him aloft, first so that he may see the self-indulgent ways of monastics (412–26).[41] Then they draw him to the gates of hell to show him the home to which they say he is destined (557–751). At this point, St. Bartholomew is sent from heaven to command the fiends to return Guthlac to his hillock unharmed. The poem closes with a vision of Guthlac carried to heaven by angels, whereupon the narrator returns to the opening theme of how the steadfast earn their place in heaven.

For taxonomic convenience this chapter has been limited to saints' legends, yet connections should be drawn to their wider literary context. A variety of compositions with hagiographical content are neither *vitae* nor *passiones*: these include Bede's martyrology and Aldhelm's tracts on virginity (chapter 6).[42] Miracles, too, which are fundamental to the saints' religious function, characterize all sorts of Anglo-Saxon narrative, playing particularly important roles in Bede's *Historia ecclesiastica* and Wærferth's translation of Gregory's *Dialogi* (chapter 2). Like miracles, visions are also proof of sanctity, and accounts of visions are numerous and varied in their contexts (see chapter 6). Saints' legends, then, should be viewed against the wider background of sanctity as a pervasive concern in the corpus of Anglo-Saxon works.

5

Biblical Literature

The Bible was not for the Anglo-Saxons quite so determinate and discrete an object as we customarily take it for. Different versions were in circulation: although Jerome's Latin Vulgate was the Bible of Western Christendom, the Vetus Latina version continued in use in England either directly (the community at Monkwearmouth-Jarrow, for example, owned an Old Latin version of the Bible, the *Codex grandior*) or through patristic and liturgical sources. Moreover, the line between authorized and apocryphal books was not drawn quite as it is now. The deuterocanonical books Wisdom, Ecclesiasticus, Judith, Tobit, and I–II Maccabees – which do not belong to the Hebrew Bible, and which generally form no part of Protestant bibles – were regarded by the Anglo-Saxons as canonical. In addition, some books that are now universally regarded as apocryphal, such as the Gospel of Nicodemus and the *Vindicta Salvatoris* (see below), were copied in among canonical texts in Anglo-Saxon manuscripts. Moreover, it is remarkable to what extent the Anglo-Saxon Bible had become inseparable from the mass of commentary that had accrued to it over the centuries. This is evident even in prose translations, but it is particularly plain in regard to vernacular verse (see below). Even the physical object itself was different: complete bibles were rare, owing to the enormous expense and to the unwieldiness of such pandects. The texts that circulated were most often smaller anthologies of biblical books suited to particular liturgical or scholastic purposes – most notably psalters and gospelbooks, but also collections of epistles, prophets, the Pentateuch, and the like.[1]

Most important, due to the nature of book production, variants inevitably arose within the Vulgate texts themselves, with the result that there was no single authoritative version. Different communities and churches adhered to different variants and readings, depending on the texts to which they had access. This state of affairs naturally has important literary consequences, for as a result, the identification of biblical sources for Old English literature is often no simple matter.[2] The textual variants of the Vulgate had in fact so proliferated by the end of the eighth century that a systematic revision was deemed necessary. At the request of Charlemagne, Alcuin undertook the laborious task of revision, and although the deluxe presentation copy of the work that he gave to the emperor in 800 is not preserved, several Bibles produced at Tours (where Alcuin became abbot in 794) append dedicatory poems naming Alcuin and attest to his revised text. Almost nothing is known about the aims and methods of Alcuin's revisions, but we can safely surmise that his work was, in the main, meant to correct the gross mistakes that had developed in the text over the course of generations of manuscript transmission (see Loewe 1969).

The texts of the Bible and their reception were strongly influenced in England by the tradition of Biblical commentary, since exegesis was regarded as the highest pursuit of the learned. Medieval biblical exegesis was usually of the allegorical variety that sprang from Origen (185–254) and the school at Alexandria. Yet English exegesis was unusual in that it combined with this the more philological variety developed in the school at Antioch, mainly through the work of St. John Chrysostom (d. 407) and Theodore of Mopsuestia (d. 428). The Antiochene exegetes practiced a historico-grammatical approach to Scripture, emphasizing literal interpretation founded on knowledge of Greek and Hebrew, the determination of literal meaning with the aid of parallel passages, and attention to historical contexts. The Antiochene trend in England was of course occasioned by a specific historical event, the appointment of Theodore of Tarsus to the see of Canterbury, as he was almost certainly educated at Antioch.[3] The biblical commentaries of the Canterbury school, in any case, clearly show the connection, as they are incomparable in the early medieval West for their eastern learning, drawing on medicine, philosophy, metrology, chronology, and rhetoric to interpret Holy Writ. They rarely resort to allegorical explanation.[4]

The influence of the Canterbury school may be discerned in Bede, even though his approach is principally Alexandrian. He was a prodigious exegete: the 24 biblical commentaries listed in the biographical note at the close of his *Historia ecclesiastica* (Colgrave and Mynors 1969: 566–8) are his most voluminous writings.[5] Indeed, his commentaries were some of the most widely circulated works of the Middle Ages, ranked in importance with those of Augustine and Jerome. Bede's usual method in his commentaries is nonetheless derivative: he provides a short meditation on a passage of scripture and synthesizes patristic sources in a clear, succinct interpretation. The allegorical mode predominates, though he avoids adventurous symbolic interpretations and incorporates philological elucidation where it is most useful. The biblical commentaries of Alcuin, which were all produced on the Continent, were not as popular, for they survive in far fewer manuscripts than those of Bede.[6] His commentary on Genesis, *Interrogationes Sigeuulfi in Genesin*, was given an abridged translation by Ælfric (ed. MacLean 1883–4).

It is in the context of these various influences – the physical forms, versions, and exegetical schools of the Bible in England – that the Anglo-Saxons produced a great deal of vernacular prose and poetry. No doubt, once again, because of the material difficulties involved, no complete Bible translation seems to have been undertaken. The Old English Hexateuch, a collection of translations of most of the first six books of the Old Testament, is preserved, mostly in fragmentary form, in seven manuscripts.[7] In a vernacular preface (of careful rhetorical structure: Griffith 2000), Ælfric identifies himself as the translator up to Genesis 22, having undertaken the task at the request of his lay patron Æthelweard – reluctantly, since he dreads putting such works into the hands of lay persons, who have no exegetical understanding, and who may imagine themselves governed by the old law rather than the new (a familiar Ælfrician complaint: see Menzer 2000, and see above, chapter 3). Accordingly, Ælfric leaves some portions untranslated, and he treats others gingerly. For example, he declines to identify the sin of the Sodomites, coyly remarking, "They wished to satisfy their lust foully, against nature, not with women, but so foully that we are ashamed to say it plainly" (Gen. 19.3). Ælfric also translated the second half of Numbers and the Book of Joshua. Clemoes (1974: 47–52) proposes that Byrhtferth of Ramsey was the translator and compiler of the non-Ælfrician portions of the Hexateuch, but Marsden (1995: 428–9; 2000) argues that patterns of variants point to a "committee" of at least three translators.[8] The Hexateuch is a direct, literal translation of Jerome's Vulgate – though given the variety of bibles available at the time, it is often difficult to determine the extent of Ælfric's and the anonymous translators' fidelity.[9] There is nonetheless evidence of Alcuinian and Old Latin influence on the text (Marsden 1994, 1995: 413–36). BL, Cotton Claudius B. iv, it should be noted, contains extensive illustrations of Late Antique or Byzantine influence (facsimile ed. Dodwell and Clemoes 1974), and the translation itself seems to have been composed and revised over a period of years.

The virtually word-for-word interlinear gloss to the Lindisfarne Gospels (BL, Cotton Nero D. iv), made ca. 970 by Aldred at Chester-le-Street, as the most substantial witness to the late Northumbrian dialect, is of inestimable importance for Old English language studies. The Rushworth (or Macregol) Gospels (Oxford, Bodleian Library, Auct. D. 2. 19), were similarly glossed by two scribes, Owun (writing a Northumbrian gloss derived from Aldred's on Mark except 1–2.15, Luke, and John except 18.1–3) and Farman (writing an unidentified variety of Mercian).[10] Somewhat later is the prose translation generally known as the *West Saxon Gospels*, preserved in six eleventh-century manuscripts, two fragments, and two twelfth-century copies.[11] It is a direct, utilitarian translation, though again the identification of its Latin source is severely constrained by the facts of Bible production and transmission. Liuzza (1994–2000: 2.26–49) finds that the Old English translation contains in excess of 650 divergences from the modern Vulgate, with about half of these unique to the Old English version. The translation shows more than a few errors, and its original purpose is unclear. In two manuscripts, Latin headings and English rubrics, probably made at Exeter in the eleventh century, delineate a system of readings for the liturgical year. These most likely served not to permit vernacular reading of the gospels at the appointed time during the mass – which would be unparalleled at such a date – but as a homiletic aid, allowing preachers to read a translation in the course of, or in place of, a homily (Lenker 1999).

Translations of two New Testament apocrypha, the Gospel of Nicodemus and the *Vindicta Salvatoris* 'Avenging of the Savior' (both ed. and trans. Cross 1996, with Latin texts), follow the *West Saxon Gospels* in the last-mentioned manuscript, and its placement in this manuscript has prompted Healey (1985: 98) to claim that "Nicodemus nearly attains the status of a fifth gospel."[12] The Gospel of Nicodemus was probably the most widely known apocryphon of the Middle Ages, containing three major episodes: the trial of Jesus and Pilate's judgment, the Resurrection, and the Harrowing of Hell. The gospel is a conflation of two originally separate works, the *Acta Pilati* (composed in Greek ca. 300–500) and the *Descensus Christi ad inferos* (a later composition), joined in the early medieval period.[13] The popular account of Jesus' redemption of souls in hell is narrated in the Old English version by Carinus and Leuticus (the sons of Simeon, who had blessed the Christ child in the temple: Luke 2.25–35), who were among those resurrected by Christ. There exist also three vernacular homiletic treatments of the Nicodemus material (ed. Hulme 1903–4). The *Vindicta Salvatoris* is related to the tradition of the *Evangelium Nichodemi* because they share episodes older than the written composition of either, and the *Vindicta* appears as a long appendix to the *Evangelium Nichodemi* in some manuscripts. The *Vindicta* comprises four legends: the healing of Tyrus (renamed Titus after his baptism), king of Aquitania under Tiberius, who suffered from cancer; Titus and Vespasian's destruction of Jerusalem (hence the title of the work); the miracle of Veronica's linen; and the exile and death of Pilate. Recently the very Latin manuscript used by the composer(s) of both translations has been identified.[14]

Biblical translations are also to be found in homilies, which are often vernacular renderings with running commentary (see chapter 3). Thus Ælfric's homilies and *Lives of Saints* include parts of Judges, Kings, Judith, Esther, Job, Joshua, and Maccabees. Furthermore, biblical texts are scattered through liturgical manuscripts, such as lectionaries, missals, and collectars. Private devotional florilegia (such as the Royal Prayerbook, BL, Royal 2. A. xx) also often contain scriptural passages among their varied texts. In addition, translations from Scripture are to be found in a variety of more incidental contexts, such as the preface to Alfred's law code, which begins with a rendering of the Ten Commandments.

Nearly all the surviving Old English verse translations of Scripture are based on the Old Testament, since the New Testament offers little narrative that is well suited to heroic treatment. Thus, although Oxford, Bodleian Library, Junius 11 contains in excess of 5,000 lines of alliterative verse, all but 729 lines render selections from the Old Testament (*Genesis, Exodus,* and *Daniel*), the remainder dealing with Christological material (*Christ and Satan*). Of the four major poetic codices of Old English, only this one is fashioned to accommodate generous illustrations. Spaces for these were left among all the poems but *Christ and Satan*, but line drawings, numbering 48, are inserted by two artists through only a little more than the first third of the book (see plate 6).[15] Indeed, if, as seems likely, the book was intended for a lay person's use, its preservation is owing to its never having been completed, as a result of which it remained in a religious house.[16] The Dutch scholar Franciscus Junius (François du Jon, 1591–1677) was given the manuscript about 1651, and he published it in Amsterdam in 1655

Plate 6 Oxford, Bodleian, Junius 11, p. 66. The most elaborate of several line-drawings of Noah's dragon-headed ark, with tiered decks supported by Romanesque arches. Bodleian Library, Oxford.

(reprint ed. Lucas 2000) – remarkably, as there was little interest in Old English poetry at that time – under a title attributing the Old Testament narratives to Cædmon. It is still sometimes referred to as the "Cædmon Manuscript," though Cædmon's authorship is no longer credited. Indeed, although the metrical features of the Old Testament poems are archaic, and although the poems' method of translation is generally free, in a few instances it is close enough to suggest a poet literate in Latin.[17] *Genesis, Exodus,* and *Daniel* are written in one hand and provided with one consecutive set of fitt numbers, implying that they were regarded as a single composition. Paleographical evidence indicates that they were copied from a single exemplar, though linguistic and metrical features show them to be the work of different poets. *Christ and Satan* is distinguished from the foregoing poems not just in subject matter but in paleography and codicology: it is written in three (or perhaps two) new hands, and after the first leaf, the format of the gathering that contains it differs from the rest of the manuscript. It is clearly an afterthought (Raw 1984: 203) – though Portnoy (1994) argues for a liturgical basis for its inclusion.

Genesis covers the events of the first book of the Bible from the Creation to the sacrifice of Isaac (Gen. 22.13). In 1875, Sievers pointed out that lines 235–851 differ markedly in versification and certain linguistic features from the rest of the poem, and he argued that this passage is translated from an unidentified Old Saxon source. Sievers' hypothesis was verified in 1894 when a Vatican manuscript (Pal. Lat. 1447) was discovered to contain several fragments of an Old Saxon *Genesis* (ed. Doane 1991: 232–52), a few lines of which (1–26a) correspond closely to the Old English *Genesis* 791–817a.[18] The translation from Old Saxon accordingly is now referred to as *Genesis B* (*ASPR* 1.9–28), and the remainder as *Genesis A* (*ASPR* 1.3–9, 28–87). Sievers thought that the parts of *Genesis A* before and after *Genesis B* are not one composition, but in this view he has not found adherents (see Doane 1978: 35–6 and Fulk 1992: 65). The simplest explanation for the makeup of *Genesis* is that *Genesis B* was translated (probably by a Continental Saxon, in view of the many un-English idioms) and inserted into *Genesis A* when the latter was discovered to lack an account of the Fall in Eden – not improbably due to a lacuna in the exemplar, just as Junius 11 suffers from the loss of leaves here and there. The translation and insertion of *Genesis B* most likely took place in the late ninth or early tenth century, since it evinces some distinctive Early West Saxon linguistic features (Doane 1991: 47–54).

Genesis A, usually dated no later than the eighth century, begins with a non-biblical account of the rebellious angels in heaven (1–111) that takes obedience as its theme – a theme that some have seen as central to the poem.[19] Though the account of the fall of Lucifer is non-biblical, it is such a commonplace in hexameral exegesis that no single source can be identified. The heavenly paradise ruined by the fall of the angels is replaced by an earthly paradise, culminating in the creation of Adam and Eve (112–234). After the interpolated lines of the translation from Old Saxon, *Genesis A* resumes seamlessly with God's interrogation of Adam and Eve and their expulsion (865–938), followed by the story of Cain and Abel and the lineage of Cain (967–1247), the Flood (1248–1554), and the remainder of Genesis through Abraham's demonstration of obedience to God by his willingness to sacrifice his son Isaac (2850–936). Scripture is by no means given a slavish translation, but the poem is far more faithful than *Genesis B*. The only really substantial additions are the Fall of Lucifer (above) and the considerable elaboration in the account of the war of the kings (1960–2101, Gen. 14.1–17). Both are passages in which the martial diction of the native verse form is given free rein. A few omissions are effected for modesty's sake – for example, circumcision, described fairly explicitly in Gen. 17.11–14, becomes a vague *sigores tācn* 'sign of victory' to be set on males (2313). Elsewhere, however, the poet does not show reticence about recounting Noah's drunken self-exposure (1562ff) or, unlike Ælfric (above), about identifying the sin of Sodom ("They said that they wanted to have sex with those heroes," 2459–60). Rather, omissions seem to be designed chiefly to promote narrative interest.[20]

Genesis B begins out of chronological order, recapitulating the fall of Lucifer after the introduction of Adam and Eve in *Genesis A* 169–234. It is unlike *Genesis A* in conception, as its treatment of the material is quite free. The poet invests the story of the fall of the angels and of humankind with unbiblical details, as when Satan's messenger appears in angelic form and approaches Adam first. Moreover, in *Genesis B* the fall of the angels is the cause of the Fall of humankind, whereas in *Genesis A* (as in the tradition of most commentaries on Genesis) the two events are not causally linked (Burchmore-Oldrieve 1985). A significant avenue in scholarship on the poem is devoted to identifying the poet's sympathies and assigning blame: is there any admiration inherent in the depiction of Satan, and how culpable is Eve in the Fall? Unlike his nameless counterpart in *Genesis A*, Satan is individualized in *Genesis B* by his heroic speeches to his fallen comrades, speeches that are Miltonic in their stoic commitment to resistance and vengeance. The sentiments and diction may be explained as heroic conventions, but it remains remarkable that the poet, like Milton, chose to narrate these events from Satan's point of view, placing God in the inscrutable distance.[21] Sources and analogues have been proposed for this portrayal of Satan, particularly the curricular versification of Genesis by Alcimus Avitus (see section 4 of the introduction), but the poet's chief debt seems rather to heroic tradition.[22] As for Eve's culpability, scholars have tended either to blame her for not seeing what Adam was capable of seeing or to exonerate her on the ground that detecting the serpent's ruse was beyond her inferior capabilities.[23] She is said to have been endowed with a *wācran hige* (590b; see also 649a), usually translated 'weaker mind' and assumed to refer to lower intelligence (e.g. by Belanoff 1989 and Renoir 1990, with references), though in actuality it probably refers to a lesser degree of courage (Robinson 1994).

Genesis illustrates the extent to which biblical exegesis was inseparable in the minds of Anglo-Saxons from the biblical books themselves. The first 111 lines, including the fall of Lucifer, are an assortment of hexameral topics which, though not included in the Bible, were thought implicit in Scripture's sense. There are also many smaller additions of an exegetical nature, such as the poet's interpretation of Seth's name to mean 'seed' (1145a) and his elaboration of God's promise to Abraham to make it prophesy the birth of Isaac (2196b–2200), since that birth was typically regarded as prefiguring Christ's. Such typological analysis, regarding events of the Old Testament as prefiguring events of the New, is a staple of medieval biblical exegesis, and so a significant portion of scholarship on the poems of Junius 11 is devoted to discerning typological elements. This is particularly true in regard to the next poem in the manuscript, *Exodus* (*ASPR* 1.91–107), depicting the flight of the Israelites from Egypt, the crossing of the Red Sea, and the destruction of Pharaoh's army. This 590-line poem corresponds to a small part of the biblical text (Ex. 13.20–14.31), but the poet composed a loose narrative paraphrase that takes the journey of the Israelites as a *typos* of Christians' passage to the promised land through Christ's sacrifice. This is made more or less explicit in a speech of Moses to his people in which, oddly, he envisages the Last Judgment (516–48).[24] Medieval exegetes (including Ælfric: see chapter 3) interpreted the crossing of the Red Sea (310–46) as prefiguring the sacrament of baptism, and Pharaoh as a type of Satan. Indeed, in the poem he is portrayed as a devil whose minions suffer the judgment of God by drowning, in a passage (447–515) that ends with the summary judgment, *Hīe wið god wunnon* 'They opposed God' (cf. *Beowulf* 113). A further sign of the poet's typological intent is the narrative's digressive course, for even this abridged version of events is punctuated by an abrupt excursus on Noah's deliverance from the flood (362–76), followed immediately by another on the sacrifice of Isaac (377–446). These divagations are not as ill-placed as some have thought. Immediately after the passage of the Israelites through the sea, a poet who regards the flight from Egypt in terms of figural history naturally enough recalls the deluge that cleansed the world of the wicked as well as the covenant God made with Abraham, granting him the land to which his descendants now turn.[25] The effects of recasting the material in the medium of heroic verse are especially pronounced in this poem. The biblical emphasis on God's stewardship of the helpless Israelites during their escape contrasts with the Old English poem's protracted preparations for a decidedly unbiblical battle with the Egyptians, attended by the beasts of battle (162–7). Contrasts are typically heightened (see Kruger 1994), and the poem is often compared to *Beowulf* for the originality and inventiveness of its heroic diction, which Frank (1988) compares to skaldic diction.

   Daniel (*ASPR* 1.111–32) follows in Junius 11. The biblical source comprises 12 chapters, the first 6 narrating the Babylonian captivity under King Nebuchadnezzar (OE *Nabochodonossor*), ending with Daniel's preservation in the lions' den, the last 6 recounting prophecies. *Daniel* renders most of the narrative portion of the source, but it ends abruptly (though at the end of a sentence), short of the end of Daniel 5, in the course of Daniel's explication of the handwriting on the wall at the feast of Belshazzar (*Baldazar*). Most likely some leaves are missing at the end (see N. Ker 1957, no. 334, and Lucas 1979), though analyses of structure and theme tend to rely on the assumption that the poem is complete. Thus Caie (1978) perceives the events to be framed by the Israelites' bibulous apostasy (*druncne geðōhtas* 18b), leading to their captivity in Babylon, and by the drunken banquet of Baldazar, in turn leading to the fall of the Babylonian empire. This parallel framework establishes the poet's theme, the consequences of breaking faith with God's law (see Bjork 1980). Harbus (1994a) argues that the poet's real interest is not the prophet Daniel but Nabochodonossor and his arrogance, and thus that the poem is misnamed. Most analyses treat the poem as an exemplum of the opposition between pride and humble obedience, though Fanger (1991) very interestingly perceives the prophet primarily as an expounder of miracles and the poem thus as bearing affinities to hagiography. Certainly in treating the Old Testament source the poet has accorded most prominence to the episode in which the three youths Annanias, Azarias, and Misael were condemned by Nabochodonossor to be burnt alive in a fiery furnace, an episode dominated by two eloquent prayers, those of Azarias and of all three youths (Dan. 3.26–45, 52–90). The position of the prayer of Azarias asking for deliverance from the furnace (283–332) has provoked some controversy, for at this point it has already been said that the youths are safe and sound among the flames, accompanied by an angel (237). Earlier scholarship accordingly tended to regard the poem as disjunct and the prayer as an interpolation. Yet it has been shown that this order of events, and other supposed peculiarities of narrative sequence, merely recapitulate the structure of the biblical source.[26]

Daniel bears a peculiar relationship to *Azarias* in the Exeter Book (*ASPR* 3.88–94), as lines 279–364 of the former correspond closely to lines 1–75 of the latter, the connection ending suddenly in mid-sentence.[27] The correspondence thus extends from the narrator's introduction of the song of Azarias through the song itself, the account of the angel's rescue of the young men, and into the beginning of their song of praise for God, ending after just six verses. The remainder of *Azarias* comprises a rather different, longer version of the remainder of the three youths' song (76–161a), followed by the Chaldeans' discovery of the miracle (161b–191). There is no consensus about how to explain the connection between the two poems – which borrows from which, and whether this might not be a case of memorial rather than literate transmission (the view, e.g., of E. Anderson 1987: 4). We find it difficult to believe that *Azarias* 1–75 is not copied from some written recension of *Daniel*, since the correspondence is in many ways so precise. Such differences as the two closely equivalent passages evince are well explained by the notion of scribal involvement in the rewriting of poetic texts (Moffat 1992: 825–6). There is also the consideration that *Azarias* incorporates the narrative framework of the longer poem, beginning *in medias res*. The poem is chiefly a rendering of the prayers of Azarias and the three young men, and a purpose for such a rendering is not hard to imagine, for the *Oratio Azariae* and the *Canticum trium puerorum* from Daniel were included in the liturgy for Holy Week (see Remley 1996: 359–78), and they seem to have been known as prayers or hymns for private recitation, to judge by their inclusion in the Royal Prayerbook (see above). The narrative framework, however, seems superfluous in *Azarias*, given what a small portion of the context it reveals.[28] *Daniel* thus seems more likely to be the source of *Azarias* than the reverse.

An Old English biblical poem based on a deuterocanonical text of the Old Testament is *Judith* (*ASPR* 4.99–109), copied into the *Beowulf* Manuscript by the second scribe.[29] It relates the story of the widow Iudith, who beguiles and kills the Assyrians' leader Holofernes during the siege of Bethulia. The 349-line Old English poem adapts its source to present, following Iudith's decapitation of the drunken Holofernes, a pitched battle between the Hebrews and Assyrians (199–323a) in high heroic style, attended by the beasts of battle (205b–212a). The poet polarizes the characters, drawing a sharp contrast between the licentious Holofernes and the virtuous Iudith, who is cast as a kind of *miles Dei*, saint-like in her faith that God will deliver her people. Whereas in the biblical account Judith plots Holofernes' downfall, lying to him and using her beauty to lure him to his destruction, in what survives of the Old English poem the designing aspects of her character are suppressed.[30] The beginning of the poem is missing, and to all appearances a mere fraction remains: the extant fragment renders less than a third of the source (12.10–16.1), and fitt numbers suggest that the first 9 of 12 sections are missing. Yet this evidence is not incontrovertible, with the consequence that there is considerable disagreement, and more than a few studies, particularly of the poem's structure and theme, rely on the assumption that no more than a few lines are missing from the beginning (e.g. Huppé 1970: 147, Lucas 1990, and Häcker 1996). The poem is not, after all, a faithful rendering of the source but a selective retelling of events. Ælfric's homily on Judith (ed. Assmann 1889: 102–16), a more literal rendering, explicitly makes of her a figural type of the Church and of chastity (Godden 1991: 219–20, Clayton 1994, Magennis 1995). Yet whereas *Exodus* fairly plainly demands some degree of typological interpretation, it is a matter of debate whether the poem *Judith*, as we have it in its fragmentary form, is to be read as a literal narrative of the victory of the righteous over the wicked or whether Iudith should be viewed as a *typos* of the Church battling iniquity.[31] *Judith* is now generally agreed to be a fairly late composition, and this seems adequate explanation of elements of its vocabulary formerly thought to be West Saxon. The poem evinces some marked Anglian features.[32]

The last poem of Junius 11 brings us to poetry based on the New Testament. Unlike the other poems of the manuscript, the 729-line *Christ and Satan* (*ASPR* 1.135–58) lacks a unified narrative trajectory, instead patching together three different strands of canonical and apocryphal passages: the lament of Satan after his banishment to hell (1–365); Christ's Harrowing of Hell, Resurrection, Ascension, and the Last Judgment (366–662); and the temptation in the wilderness (663–729). The three strands are linked by homiletic passages urging preparations in this life for judgment in the next. This structure has led some to assume that *Christ and Satan* actually represents three (or more) discrete poems.[33] There is no single source for the poem, with the Vulgate, the Gospel of Nicodemus, Blickling homily VII, and other materials figuring into the mélange of Christian sources and analogues. Sleeth (1982: 68–70) suggests that the poem evolved out of Part 2, itself developed from the homiletic tradition for Easter that narrates the events of Christ's life after his crucifixion and resurrection. The poet then expands the idea of Christ's exaltation through his meekness by counterpointing Satan's damnation through his arrogance, and he ends with the confrontation of the two in the wilderness. Wehlau (1998) instead sees the achronological order of the narrative as a device designed to remove "the veil of historical time to reveal the incarnation and the cosmic battle that underlies it all" (p. 12). Most *Christ and Satan* scholarship of the past dozen years has dealt with fairly circumscribed interpretive problems.[34] Despite its peculiar structure, the poem is not without merit. Portions of Satan's lament (esp. 163–88) bear a rhetorical resemblance to lyrics like *The Wanderer* and *The Seafarer*, as the devil rues the loss of past joys and portrays himself as a wandering exile.[35] Very likely the poem was seen as appropriate for inclusion in the manuscript because it opens with the fall of Lucifer, as do *Genesis A* and *B*. The poem, it should be noted, furnishes particularly interesting evidence of the way scribes "Saxonized" Anglian poetry, making it conform to the mainly West Saxon poetic *koine* (Fulk 1992: 394–6).

Aside from some works that are more homiletic in overall design, such as *Christ II*, the one remaining poem that takes a New Testament theme (though an apocryphal one) is *The Descent into Hell* (*ASPR* 3.219–23), a 139-line poem that draws on the tradition of Christ's Harrowing of Hell but not directly from the *Evangelium Nichodemi*.[36] The poem begins with the visit of the two Marys to Christ's tomb, but it shifts abruptly to the Harrowing – Christ's rescue of the patriarchs and the righteous from hell, where they were obliged to remain until Christ's sacrifice made it possible for humankind to enter heaven. The Harrowing is presented in the heroic terms of battle, describing how Christ, *rēðust ealra cyninga* 'harshest of all kings', destroyed the walls of hell without the aid of armed warriors (33–42a). John the Baptist, who had informed the others of Christ's arrival (26–32), then offers praise for the Lord to the end of the poem (59–137) in a speech with an iterative structure, invoking Christ, Mary, Jerusalem, and the River Jordan in the first half, and then again in the same order in the second. In structure it may draw inspiration from the Eastertide liturgy (Conner 1980), but Brantley (1999), who provides an overview of scholarship on the poem, identifies a non-textual analogue – line drawings in the Utrecht Psalter – to explain two of the poem's peculiarities, its juxtaposition of the Marys' visit to the tomb with the Harrowing, and the omission of any reference to Satan.

Clearly, were it not for Junius 11, hardly any Old English verse would survive that is primarily scriptural narrative – and Junius 11 is not a typical book, as it was probably intended for lay use (see above). The surviving continuous prose translations were also intended, at least originally, for the laity; only the continuous glosses were intended for the use of clerics. There may once have existed quite a large body of biblical literature in the hands of lay persons. Yet considering the low rate of preservation for books outside of religious houses, it is remarkable that any biblical narrative survives at all.

6
Liturgical and Devotional Texts

The ecclesiastical practices of Anglo-Saxon England demanded the compilation of a large and eclectic group of texts that can be broadly characterized as liturgical and pietistic writings. The greater part is in Latin, and while it is important in general to view Old English literature in the context of monastic Latinity, the interrelations of Latin and vernacular production are most apparent among the texts considered here.[1] The history of such texts in Anglo-Saxon England probably begins with Augustine of Canterbury's mission of 597, for naturally the administration of the sacraments and the establishment of schools for the training of a native clergy demanded the use of liturgical books. We cannot be certain that Augustine brought these from Rome, but it seems likely that he would have had with him necessary texts such as the Gospels, the Psalter, and prayerbooks. One manuscript known as the "Augustine Gospels" (CCCC 286) is a sixth-century Italian gospelbook that may have been brought to England by Augustine and his companions.[2] Quite a few liturgical books of English manufacture survive, though they are much later than this, and as a consequence, little is known of the liturgy in England in the early period.[3]

The liturgy of course was in Latin, except, in the later period, for those parts devoted to preaching (see chapter 3), and some other exceptions discussed below. In Latin we have 11 hymns composed by Bede in the style of St. Ambrose for feasts of the *sanctorale* in the performance of the Divine Office, and a body of some later anonymous hymnody in commemoration of English saints (see Milfull 1996). In Latin octosyllables there are in addition three prayers and a greeting to Bishop Hæddi that were probably composed by Archbishop Theodore (ed. Lapidge 1995b: 240–5). Yet there also exists a body of writing in Old English related, with varying degrees of directness, to the rituals of

prayer, divine worship, and the sacraments. Given the relationship between the monastic reform and manuscript production (see section 5
of the introduction), it is not surprisingly the Divine Office that provides the primary impetus.

Because of their importance to the monks' daily offices, the Psalms
might seem a natural choice for translation, were it not that novices
were expected to commit them to memory even before they could understand Latin. King Alfred's translation of the first 50 Psalms is likely
to belong to his educational program (see chapter 2) and thus to be
intended for lay use. Indeed, it seems that in a later age some lay persons, notably Ælfric's patrons Æthelweard and Æthelmær, wished to
have translated for them works that would allow them in their own
devotions to observe daily offices just as monks did (see Gatch 1977:
48–9). The poetic translation of Psalms 51–150 copied into the Paris
Psalter (Paris, Bibliothèque Nationale, Lat. 8824; facsimile ed. Colgrave
1958) to complete the psalter after Alfred's prose translation of 1–50
may thus have been designed for the laity, as the Paris manuscript itself
certainly was.[4] The very fact of their being in verse lends support to this
assumption, since it is difficult to see why a psalter to be studied by
clergy ignorant of Latin should not be more literal. The poetic translation cannot be dated, but it is usually assumed to be relatively late, as
the meter resembles that of some late poems (Sievers 1885: 474, 483–
4). It may be, though, that the unusual meter reflects less the date than
the poet's competence, since the style is generally agreed to be less than
masterful.[5] The morphology and vocabulary show it to have been made
by someone from north of the Thames, most likely a Mercian (see Fulk
1992: 410–14, *contra* Sievers), and it has been argued that the text
depends (though in a limited way) upon one or more interlinear Psalter
glosses (Keefer 1979, Toswell 1997). Another amplified poetic paraphrase, and a more successful one, appears in BL, Cotton Vespasian D.
vi, known as *Psalm 50* (*ASPR* 6.88). The first 30 lines recount the
exegetical interpretation of the psalms as David's act of contrition for
adultery, followed by the poet's expansion and paraphrase of the Latin
verses and a short conclusion in which the repentant poet asks God's
forgiveness.[6] Preceding *Psalm 50* in the same manuscript, the so-called
Kentish Hymn (*ASPR* 6.87) bears no relation to the Latin hymns of the
Divine Office. It is a poem of 43 lines in praise of the triune God,
alluding to several liturgical and biblical texts, including the Te Deum,
the Apostles' Creed, and the Agnus Dei. Both of these poems are written in the mainly West Saxon poetic *koine*, but the admixture of Kent-

ish features, along with the more obviously Kentish glosses throughout the manuscript, indicate a southeastern scribe.

A more direct illustration of how the Divine Office inspired vernacular texts is the so-called Benedictine Office in Oxford, Bodleian, Junius 121 and CCCC 201, an abbreviated version in Old English of the Divine Office employed by the Benedictines. The translation was very likely intended "to be used by literate monks for the instruction of ignorant secular clergy in the performance of the seculars' own proper divine service" (Houghton 1994: 445; cf. Caie 2000: 20–1). Six of the eight canonical hours are represented (ed. Ure 1957), though only Prime (ed. and trans. B. Griffiths 1991) is complete. The Old English was almost certainly either composed by the homilist Wulfstan (see Bethurum 1957: 47–9) or extensively revised by him (Ure 1957: 39–43), except for the versified portions, which are *The Lord's Prayer II* and *III* (in the Cambridge and Oxford manuscripts, respectively), *The Gloria I*, *The Creed*, and fragments of Psalms (*ASPR* 6.70, 77–86; the last two texts are not in the Cambridge manuscript). *The Creed* exemplifies these texts well. It offers a stanzaic amplification of the Apostles' Creed with the ordered Latin clauses as rubrics at the head of each stanza. This clause-by-clause decomposition and exposition is customary, stemming from a legend that each of the 12 Apostles composed one of the 12 articles – each clause is in fact ascribed to one apostle in additions to a gloss on the Apostles' Creed in BL, Royal 2. A. xx – though the Junius 121 poem obscures this point, having just ten stanzas. The form of *The Gloria* and the two versions of the Lord's Prayer is similar. Yet the two versions of the latter, which are unrelated translations, are quite different from each other in nature, for the former is more than a translation, rather a commentary on each lemma, remarking, for example, about *sanctificetur nomen tuum* 'hallowed be thy name' that God's name is blessed in 72 languages (the number of languages in the world, according to Bede: see section 1 of chapter 4 on Ælfric's treatment of this theme). As for the Psalm fragments, their particular interest is that they are the only Old English poetic translation of any part of the first 50 psalms. Their irregular meter shows them to be of one composition with the metrical psalms of the Paris Psalter, of which the first 50 are missing, replaced by Alfred's prose translation.

The purpose of translating these texts into verse rather than prose was presumably to lend them special dignity, and that presumption derives support from another poetic translation, *The Lord's Prayer I*, just 11 lines of verse in the Exeter Book (*ASPR* 3.223–4), since the sanctity of these, Christ's own words, is amplified in the first half by the use of hypermetrics. The first few words of the Gloria Patri are also translated into verse in BL, Cotton Titus D. xxvii (*The Gloria II, ASPR* 6.94), where they incongruously mark the close of a set of prognostics by the letters of the alphabet added in a blank space. In addition there are several prose translations of the Pater Noster and both the Apostles' and Nicene Creeds, and some original vernacular prayers, along with a variety of short texts related to liturgy, such as directions for the use of forms of service and notes on the meaning of *Alleluia*. Various Old English forms for *halsunga* 'exorcisms', translated from Latin, also survive in four manuscripts. Texts such as these are invariably brief and occur in books as varied as collections of homilies, collectars (books of prayers and brief selections from Scripture for the Divine Office), and pontificals (books of services for rites performed by bishops, such as ordinations and ordeals).[7] In addition, of course, there are many liturgical texts in Latin, sometimes with Old English glosses.[8]

Perhaps the clearest illustration of the influence of the Divine Office on vernacular literature is the poem *Christ I*. The first three poems in the Exeter Book were formerly regarded as a single composition by Cynewulf, referred to collectively as *Christ*. Yet the sectional divisions among them are of the sort used to distinguish different poems in the first part of the manuscript, and in any event the three are sufficiently distinguished by their lexical and metrical features, and by their treatment of sources, to render common authorship improbable.[9] The three works are thus distinguished as *Christ I, II*, and *III*, though the line numbering of the three is consecutive in the standard edition. It was Cook (1900: xxv–xliii) who discovered that the 12 lyrics that comprise *Christ I* (*ASPR* 3.3–15), also called *Advent* or *The Advent Lyrics*, are versified elaborations of the so-called Greater Os and Monastic Os.[10] These are the antiphons (responses) that were sung during the final days of Advent at the hour of Vespers before and after the *Magnificat*, the canticle of Mary. Each begins with a direct address, usually to Christ, such as *O Adonai* or *O Rex gentium* – hence the name "Os," each Old English equivalent beginning *Ēalā*. The Exeter Book begins imperfect, lacking at least one gathering at the start, and so it cannot be determined how many lyrics the composition originally encompassed. The Old English poet treats the antiphons freely, expanding, abridging, and rearranging the material: lyric II (18–49), for example, closely resembles its source, *O clavis David*, in just four of its lines (1920, 25–6). The Greater Os, four of which correspond to lyrics I, II, V, and VI, are all petitions to Christ to hasten his birth into the world and save humanity, repeating the imperative *veni* – as one might expect of Advent lyrics. Seven of the later Monastic Os are adapted in lyrics III, IV, VII, VIII, IX, and XII. Most strikingly original is lyric VII (*O Ioseph*, 165–213), a dramatic dialogue between Joseph and Mary connected to the "Doubt of Joseph" motif (a medieval *topos* made most familiar by the pageant of that title in the Lincoln cycle), in which a bewildered Joseph painfully deliberates whether he should expose his beloved Mary to stoning for her pregnancy or *morþor hele* 'conceal a crime' (193a). Mary explains the mystery to Joseph (197-213) and encourages him to give thanks that she was chosen to bear Christ while remaining a maiden. The final lyric (xii, 416–39) is based not on an Advent text but on an antiphon from the period after Christmas, one of rejoicing in the Incarnation, to which the poet has added a doxology to the triune God. Thus it forms an appropriate conclusion to the series.[11] The unifying themes among the 12 lyrics are plain: the need for Christ's salvation, the miracle of his birth through Mary, and the consubstantiality of the Father, the Son, and the Holy Spirit through the mystery of the Trinity.

There is a not inconsiderable body of texts pertinent to the sacrament of penance. Of particular interest are the penitentials (handbooks of penance), guides for confessors that generally take the form of catalogues of sins accompanied by their tariffs (penances to be assigned, usually fasts). In the nineteenth century, knowledge of such handbooks fed popular anticlerical sentiment, since to the casual observer they may seem to betray a prurient interest in a wide range of sexual offenses (see Payer 1984: 3 and n. 4). If the sins listed seem lurid (e.g. bestiality, incest, rape, heathen worship) or the circumstances strained (e.g. vomiting the host through drunkenness, drinking blood), this is only natural, since such handbooks were designed particularly to guide confessors in assigning penances not for common sins but for those they most likely had not encountered before. In the earliest centuries of Christianity, penance was a public ceremony performed during Lent, but the penitential practices reflected in Anglo-Saxon texts ultimately derive from the Irish monastic innovation of a monk's confessing wrongdoing and submitting to his superior's judgment.[12] This system of private confession eventually extended to the laity, and by the early eighth century the first handbook of this sort from England had been issued under the name of no less a figure than Archbishop Theodore. Many penitential texts claim to derive from the teachings of Theodore, but none was actually written by him. The earliest such work is a Latin text titled the

Iudicia Theodori but also known as the *Capitula Dacheriana* (or *d'Acheriana*) after the work's first modern editor.[13] The *Iudicia* consist of a sequence of loosely connected statements mingling penitential clauses with material largely canonical in nature (e.g., cap. 19: "Greeks do not give carrion to their swine. The hides of dead animals, however, may be used for shoes, and the wool and horns, though not for anything sacred"). Another Latin handbook, the *Poenitentiale Theodori* (ed. Finsterwalder 1929: 285–334), is more significant. The prologue describes the circumstances of its composition: a *discipulus Umbrensium* 'pupil of the Northumbrians' collected these materials based on the answers of Theodore to queries put to him concerning penance, and they were originally gathered by a priest named Eoda. So if the prologue is to be trusted, the *Poenitentiale* as we have it is at best a third-hand account of Theodore's teaching. The work consists of two books: the first is a penitential, the second a series of canons (rules promulgated by church councils). Of the 19 surviving manuscripts of the *Poenitentiale*, 18 are of Continental provenance (reflecting the exportation of insular penitential teaching to the Continent in the eighth and ninth centuries), but all of the earliest manuscripts seem to be Continental copies of penitentials from England. A third Theodoran text, the *Canones Gregorii* (ed. Finsterwalder 1929: 253–70), has the loose structure of the *Iudicia Theodori*, and it seems to have been used as a source for the *Poenitentiale* (see Fulk forthcoming a). Theodore's sources include various Irish and British penitentials, as well as the Greek fathers (especially Basil) and some Church councils (see Finsterwalder 1929: 200–5).

The Theodoran handbooks exerted a powerful influence on all subsequent penitentials, which, like it, recombine and reorganize the clauses of their sources. One such text (ed. Wasserschleben 1851: 231–47) has been traditionally (perhaps spuriously) ascribed to Bede's student Ecgberht, archbishop of York (735–66), on the basis of the manuscripts' *incipits* naming him as the author. It contains a prologue and 16 chapters, and the earliest manuscript (Vatican, Pal. Lat. 554) is from the late eighth or early ninth century. Another group of closely related suppositious penitential texts is ascribed to Bede, and most versions incorporate large portions of the Ecgberht penitential.[14] A ninth-century Frankish compilation combines the Bedan and Ecgberhtine penitentials under Bede's name (the so-called *Double Penitential*), further indicating the influence of insular penitential texts on the Continent.

It is only after the Continental ninth-century recensions of eighth-century insular texts that vernacular penitentials turn up in England. There are four of these, none found in a manuscript older than the eleventh century. One such text, traditionally attributed to Ecgberht on the basis of an *incipit* in one manuscript, contains two discrete parts, a *Confessional* and a *Penitential*, though the two co-occur in all three manuscripts that contain the complete text of the former.[15] The *Confessional* is often referred to as the *Scrift Boc*, after the *incipit* in CCCC 190. It is a disordered text that bears no close resemblance to any one penitential text that antecedes it. Its sources include parts of the penitentials ascribed to Theodore (who is named in the work), Bede, Ecgberht, and Cummean (the last represented in a seventh-century Hiberno-Latin text). Chapters I–III of the *Penitential* translate cap. III–V of the penitential of Halitgar (a Frankish text written by the bishop of Cambrai in 830); they outline situations requiring penance, along with penances for the laity and clergy. The remaining chapter, combining portions of the *Confessional* with the penitential of Cummean, is a miscellany of penances not given in the earlier books.

Following the improvements that the *Penitential* makes upon the *Confessional*, another eleventh-century text represents even greater progress in the tradition of penitential literature. The *Handbook for the Use of a Confessor* (ed. Fowler 1965) is the most succinct of the vernacular texts mentioned, and this penchant for brevity, further reflected in the reduction of the number of tariffs, seems to indicate its practical use by clergy hearing confession. Indeed, the codicology of one manuscript (N. Ker 1957, no. 10C.1; perhaps also 177B) suggests that it formed a large portion of a manual actually used in the confessional. It survives in seven manuscripts (the most complete being CCCC 201, dating to the mid-eleventh century: see Quinn and Quinn 1990: 91), in most of which the handbook, or part of it, has been copied in among other texts of a miscellaneous nature. The *Handbook* draws heavily on the *Penitential*, and it represents the zenith of penitential literature in England by virtue of its ordered and concise completeness, containing provisions that encompass all aspects of confession and penance in six books – a Latin *ordo confessionis* (in this case a penitent's preparations for confession) from the Rule of Chrodegang (see below), a formula for confession, general instructions for confessors, a penitential, directions for the assignment of penances, and acceptable commutations (e.g., a powerful man may persuade, by any means, a sufficient number of others to fast for him, so that seven years' fasting may be accomplished in three days). Somewhat briefer are *The Canons of Theodore*, often described as a partial translation of the *Poenitentiale Theodori*, but in actuality a translation of canons selected from all three of the Theodoran texts described above. The *Canons* are found in CCCC 190 and in Brussels, Bibliothèque Royale, 8558–63. A shorter text found in Oxford, Bodleian, Laud Misc. 482, is usually regarded as a fragment of this same translation. They are certainly related, but the differences are profound enough that this should be regarded as a separate work.[16] The vernacular texts mentioned here, all of them probably late compositions, represent a body of important pastoral literature which derives immediately from ninth-century continental sources like the *Double Penitential* but ultimately from eighth-century insular sources like the *Poenitentiale Theodori*.

The importance of the sacrament of penance in the Anglo-Saxon Church is attested not just by the handbooks but by a variety of less substantial texts associated with confession and penance, resembling those collected in the *Handbook*. One of these short texts directs penitents to recite Psalm 7 to obtain the mercy of God (see N. Ker 1957: 24). CCCC 190 – which contains the Old English *Penitential* and *Confessional* – includes a form of confession (and a form of absolution) that enumerates a long list of sins from gluttony to litigiousness (see Förster 1942: 14). Other forms of confession are contained in five further manuscripts. The text of the *Poenitentiale Theodori* in CCCC 320 is preceded by an exhortation to confession. An assortment of confessional prayers exist in nine manuscripts, and most of these materials follow a pattern of the penitent's invocation of God's mercy followed by a declaration of contrition and the enumeration of certain sins.[17]

The basis for the tenth-century monastic reform was the *Regula S. Benedicti* (ed. and trans. Fry et al. 1980), and naturally a text so fundamental to the monks' way of life should be expected to have left its mark on the composition of a wide range of texts. The Rule itself, composed by St. Benedict of Nursia (ca. 480–550), comprises a prologue and 73 chapters, which can be divided into three rough sections: the prologue and the first seven chapters, which pronounce the virtues of a life of asceticism, a series of chapters providing directions for the Divine Office, and a series of chapters on the administration of monastic houses. An assembly at Winchester ca. 973 issued a customary (account of rituals and usages), known as the *Regularis concordia* 'Agreement about the Rule' (ed. and trans. Symons 1953), outlining an accord for the unification of monastic observance in England under the Benedictine Rule. Authorship of the document is traditionally credited to Dunstan, archbishop of Canterbury, but it is likelier that Æthelwold, bishop of Winchester, composed the *Regularis*. It consists of 12 chapters that describe the programmatic life of monastic houses, centering on the performance of the liturgy and administrative concerns. The real significance of this document is that it made the Benedictine Rule the basis for English monasticism. This is no small consideration, given that the members of unreformed communities were not obliged to live in poverty or obey their abbot – early in his career the reformer Oswald, later archbishop of York, had in fact resigned his abbacy of a community in Winchester over his inability to exert control – and the appointment of abbots was usually the prerogative of the family of a community's founder. The *Regularis* is deeply indebted to Carolingian reforms, no doubt owing to the Continental connections of Dunstan, who had lived in exile at the monastery of St. Peter's in Ghent, and of Oswald, who exercised great influence over the reform and was ordained at Fleury, and to the fact that, as the preface states, monks from Fleury and Ghent were summoned to assist the assembly at Winchester. The document in fact is a compilation of the best practices of Ghent, Fleury, and England, and as a result it is a confusing and "imperfectly digested and harmonized collection" (Barlow 1979: 330) which must have been difficult to conform to. The *Regularis* is preserved in complete form in two eleventh-century manuscripts, BL, Cotton Tiberius A.iii, which includes a continuous interlinear Old English gloss, and BL, Cotton Faustina B.iii, both probably from Canterbury (see Joyce Hill 1991 and Kornexl 1995). Another eleventh-century manuscript, CCCC 265, preserves the unique copy of a Latin abridgment of the *Regularis* by Ælfric known as the *Letter to the Monks of Eynsham*, a traditional editorial title that obscures the fact that the work is a customary intended as a guide for Benedictine monks.[18] Ælfric follows the order of the topics addressed in the *Regularis*, but he distills the copious details to more general descriptions of monks' daily observances. Yet Ælfric's work offers some valuable departures from his source, such as his list of hymns forming the so-called New Hymnal, which was introduced to England by the reformers of the tenth century.

In addition to writing the *Regularis*, Bishop Æthelwold composed an Old English translation of Benedict's Rule. The Old English Benedictine Rule is the earliest vernacular translation of the text in Europe, and it is preserved in complete form in five manuscripts, of which four are bilingual.[19] There exists a version of Æthelwold's translation for the use of a cloister of nuns at Winteney, Hampshire, in the first quarter of the thirteenth century (ed. Schröer 1885–8), and Gretsch (1992: 151–2) has argued that versions for monks and nuns both left Æthelwold's scriptorium in the tenth century. In a document dated to the time of the reforms (though in a twelfth-century manuscript that contains only the Old English version of the Rule, BL, Cotton Faustina A. x), Æthelwold, composing what some have thought to be a prologue to his translation of the Rule, states, "I consider translation a very sensible thing. It certainly cannot matter by what language a man is acquired and drawn to the true faith . . . Therefore let the unlearned natives have the knowledge of this holy rule by the exposition of their own language" (trans. Whitelock, Brett, and Brooke 1981: 151–2). His translation is based on the version, not previously known in England, in use in reformed Continental monasteries, and it is a close rendering of his source, though it demonstrates a fine idiomatic aplomb. In connection with the Rule should be mentioned Ælfric's *Admonition to a Spritiual Son*, a translation of a text attributed to Basil.[20] It is a general exhortation to devotion to God, in which military images play a prominent role, and it is directed to both monks and nuns. The inclusion of the latter may explain the motive for translation (Wilcox 1994: 52).

Libri vitae 'books of life' preserved from such communities as Lindisfarne (facsimile ed. Thompson 1923) and the New Minster, Winchester (later Hyde Abbey; facsimile ed. Keynes 1996a), show that the practice of confraternity was in use among England's monasteries and abbeys. This consisted of an affiliation given by a monastery or an abbey to a member of another community (or to a lay person), granting liturgical commemoration in the community's prayers. Consequently, such *libri* contain long lists of names, chiefly of monks. In addition, two eleventh-century manuscripts contain Old English rules for confraternity, prescribing certain masses and prayers, along with almsgiving, in commemoration of community members and affiliates.[21]

The Old English translation of the *Regula canonicorum* 'Rule for Canons' of Bishop Chrodegang of Metz (d. 766) alternates chapter by chapter with the Latin text in CCCC 191 (ed. Napier 1916), an eleventh-century manuscript from Exeter. This work provides an authoritative rule for cathedral clergy that prescribes a regimen of communal life based on the *Regula S. Benedicti*. The quasi-monastic living arrangements it prescribes for canons were intended to combat simony and clerical incontinence. Thus it is not surprising that this rule seems to have gained importance in England only in the later period, when the behavior of the clergy came to be an important impetus for reform (see

Knowles 1963: 140 and Langefeld 1996). The language of the translation in fact shows it to have emanated from the doctrinal center of the
Reform, Æthelwold's school at Winchester (Gneuss 1972). The Old
English version is usually known as the *Enlarged Rule of Chrodegang*
because it contains additional material from the 817 Rule of Aachen, a
version of the Benedictine Rule given legal force on the Continent as
the rule for monks by the emperor Louis the Pious at the synod of that
year. Another vernacular text for secular clergy is the Old English translation of part of the *Capitula Theodulfi*. Theodulf, bishop of Orléans
(ca. 760–821), issued his first capitulary (set of ordinances) about 800
as a guide for priests, instructing them how to handle many aspects of
their pastoral duties, such as administering confession and celebrating
the mass. Again, two eleventh-century bilingual copies survive (both
ed. Sauer 1978), in CCCC 201, where the free and fluent Old English
translation follows the whole of the Latin text, and in Oxford, Bodleian,
Bodley 865 (also ed. Napier 1916: 102–18), a fragment (chapter 25 to
the end) in which the rather literal Old English follows the Latin chapter by chapter. Similar in purpose is Wulfstan's *Canons of Edgar* (ed.
Fowler 1972, so named by editors because formerly assigned to the
reign of Edgar), which he composed as a guide for parish priests, calling for annual synods to address concerns with the secular clergy. It is
infused with the familiar Wulfstanian theme of how to combat the de-
clining morals of the English.

A sizeable body of devotional literature occurs intermixed with liturgical texts in the manuscripts. The influence of the one on the other is
less obvious in the early period, when some substantial independent
Latin works of theology and moral instruction were produced. Of these,
most worthy of mention is Aldhelm's *De virginitate*, the hermeneutic
prose of which was exemplified above.[22] This immense opus comprises
a theoretical disquisition on the three degrees of virginity (virginity,
chastity, and matrimony), two catalogues of virgins (male and female,
ordered chronologically), a dilatory account of five biblical patriarchs,
and a diatribe against fine dress among ecclesiastics. *De virginitate* is
the first English *opus geminatum* or 'twinned work' (see chapter 4,
section 2), as the prose is followed by a poetic version, the *Carmen de
virginitate*, which Aldhelm, in the conclusion to the prose version, promised to compose for the sorority at Barking. The *Carmen* is chiefly a
catalogue of virgins, though it differs from the prose in that all the
matter after the catalogues is replaced by an account of an allegorical
combat between the personified chief vices and virtues, doubtless in-

spired by Prudentius' *Psychomachia*. This material is probably related to the more aggressive characterization of virginity in the first part of the poem as "trampling" upon vice (see Rosier in Lapidge and Rosier 1985: 98). This practice of turning prose into something more martial when it is versified has obvious parallels in the vernacular, in which the conventions of Old English verse demand that heroic diction and characterization be applied to even the most mundane subjects.[23] Aldhelm's *De virginitate* was widely read and studied in England and on the Continent, and as a consequence, his hermeneutic style exerted a profound influence on Latin composition in England to the time of the Conquest.

Alcuin's *De virtutibus et vitiis* (PL 101.613–38), a compilation of biblical and patristic *sententiae* (commonplaces) for the moral instruction of a Frankish count, is similar not just in its aims but in the extent of its influence: it is the chief, though indirect, source of Vercelli homily xx (see Szarmach 1986), it was used by Ælfric and other homilists (both English and Continental), and it was translated into Old English in the tenth century (see Lindström 1988). In their uses such treatises as this can hardly be differentiated from more strictly philosophical works, such as Alcuin's *De animae ratione* 'The Nature of the Soul', since this was also mined several times by Ælfric for homiletic content.[24] It takes the form of a letter to a Frankish aristocrat, recommending various books to her and arguing that it is the natural inclination of the soul to love God. Similarly, the twelfth-century Old English translation of two portions of the *Elucidarium* of Honorius Augustodunensis (d. ca. 1156) is preserved in a collection of homilies, and it was clearly used for preaching.[25] The Latin work itself, in fact, seems to have been designed to involve Benedictines in pastoral work, instructing clergy how to answer questions of doctrine posed to them. The Old English is in catechetical form, and the first portion (*De peccato*, corresponding to Book II, chapters 1–6), touching the nature of sin and free will, is devoted primarily to explaining why the good suffer and the bad prosper in this world, the second (the "Resurrection" dialogue, I, 23–5) to the doctrinal significance of events from the Resurrection to the Ascension.

Letters often seem related to homiletic literature, too, since, in the tradition established by St. Paul, in the early period they were above all devoted to moral instruction. Many survive, particularly from the circles of Aldhelm, Boniface, and Alcuin; and of Bede we have a letter composed a few months before his death, to his student Ecgberht, archbishop of York, exhorting him to his pastoral duties.[26] This apparently inspired the archbishop's authorship of the *Dialogus ecclesiasticae institutionis* (ed. Haddan and Stubbs 1869–71: 3.403–13), a discussion of the relations between civil and ecclesiastical law, also in catechetical form. In the later period we have several letters by Ælfric, mostly composed for the use of bishops, and mostly in English.[27] The earliest of these is the *Letter for Wulfsige* (ed. Fehr 1914: 1–34), composed at the request of the bishop of Sherborne to instruct the clergymen of his diocese in their duties and to exhort them to good behavior. The *Letter to Wulfgeat* (ed. Assmann 1889: 1–12) is addressed to a nobleman of the neighborhood of Eynsham who had been dispossessed of his estates, son of the same *ealdormann* Leofsige of Wessex who was banished in 1002, according to the Peterborough Chronicle, for a heinous murder. The letter supplements earlier English writings lent to Wulfgeat by offering a summary of doctrine, combining a brief account of sacred history, from the Creation to Doomsday, with commentary on Matt. 5.25 ("agree with thine adversary") derived from Augustine. Similar in design and purpose, but greater in scope, is the *Letter to Sigeweard* (ed. and trans. Crawford 1922: 15–75), composed for another local man of some prominence. It is also known by the title *On the Old and New Testament*, since it offers a conspectus of the books of the Bible as a framework for sacred history. The *Letter to Sigefyrth* (ed. Assmann 1889: 13–23), also written to a lay person, is a treatise on clerical chastity, written in response to the teaching of an anchorite living on Sigefyrth's estate that priests might marry. Finally there are two substantial letters written for the homilist Wulfstan (ed. Fehr 1914: 68–145, 146–221), originally in Latin, then translated a year later at his request. Wulfstan had requested two letters on the duties of the secular clergy. The first is chiefly, once again, an exposition of sacred history, with a brief concluding section on priests' duties. The second offers instructions for the celebration of services at different times in the liturgical year, along with comments on the Ten Commandments and the eight capital sins (a common homiletic theme). This second letter was composed for the occasion of the annual gathering of priests to distribute holy oil, and one surviving copy represents a subsequent rewriting by Wulfstan in his own style (see Fehr, pp. lxx–lxxxii).

It is only in more incidental forms that the ritual setting of devotional texts from the early period is apparent, for example in the *tituli* (metrical epigrams for the dedication of churches or altars) of Aldhelm and Bede.[28] After the eighth century, with the decline in Latin scholarship and the narrowing of resources, the literature of edification is not so learned as earlier – nor so substantial, since the texts tend to seem rather occasional. Given the centrality of liturgy in the monastic reform – the chief products of the reform have in fact been described as enhancements to the liturgy (Gatch 1977: 11) – it is not surprising that it is primarily in the later period that pietistic texts assume a character strongly influenced by the sacramental rites and communal observances of the Church. The misnamed *Menologium* (*ASPR* 6.49–55; trans. Malone 1969) is not a collection of saints' lives but a 231-line poetic catalogue of 28 feasts of saints. This vernacular poem is inspired by sanctoral calendars in Latin hexameters, which appear from the late eighth century, and which are simply versifications, for non-liturgical use, of the calendars of saints that preface missals and breviaries (see Lapidge 1984). It differs from them in its method of reckoning: while the Latin calendars give the date of each feast, the *Menologium* simply counts the days or weeks from the previous feast – though occasionally means are provided to locate feasts in relation to the beginning of months and seasons, for example "And it was two nights after that that God revealed to the blessed Helena the noblest of trees, on which the Lord of angels suffered for the love of humankind, the Measurer on the gallows, by his Father's leave. Likewise it is after the interval of a week, less one night, that summer brings to town sun-bright days for mortals, warm weather" (83–90a). This method of identifying the date is better suited to a monastic audience than the Roman calendar's reckoning by calends, ides, and nones, based on lunar cycles. The example shows that the poem also provides some information about each saint, though the Latin calendars do not, and thus its purpose may have been educational rather than mnemonic. In its manuscript context it seems to have been intended as a preface to version C of the Anglo-Saxon Chronicle. Its purpose there may be, then, to aid in identifying the dates of events narrated in the Chronicle, making it possible to relate them to dates in the Roman calendar, since the time of year in the Chronicle is often specified only in relation to saints' feasts rather than days of the month – as one might expect of a document originally compiled in a monastery. That the poet included just one English saint, Augustine of Canterbury, thus focusing on ecumenical celebrations, may also be related to this purpose.[29] A similar calendar in vernacular prose survives in two manuscripts.[30] *The Old English Martyrology* (ed. Kotzor 1981; ed. and trans. Herzfeld 1900) is similarly arranged in calendrical order, though the function of martyrologies was more clearly liturgical, since they were an element of the daily capitular office, and they are one of the texts that priests were regularly advised they should own (see de Gaiffier 1961: 52–4). Bede is responsible for the form, as he revised the fifth-century *Martyrologium Hieronymianum* (so called, though not actually by Jerome), producing 114 entries and supplementing its bare list of dates and places of martyrdom with narrative to create the first "historical" martyrology.[31] The Old English text is known only from fragments in several manuscripts, though comparatively little of the annual cycle is missing: 238 notices of saints survive, some quite lengthy. The earliest fragments (BL, Add. 23211 and 40165A, both recovered from the bindings of books) date to the ninth century, and the dialect is Mercian. Why a martyrology was put into the vernacular is not clear, especially as early as this, but it is remarkable that the *Old English Martyrology* is not a direct translation of any known Latin text, and it shows a great deal of inventiveness and independence from the entire martyrological tradition (see Kotzor 1986). It is also a learned work, incorporating material from hagiographical and liturgical writings – the *Liber pontificalis*, Gregory of Tours' *Liber miraculorum*, Bede's *Historia ecclesiastica*, and Felix of Crowland's *Vita Guthlaci*, to name a few.[32]

Given the brevity of the entries and the liturgical function of the whole, martyrologies seem unlikely material for versification. Yet most scholars have assumed that Cynewulf's *Fates of the Apostles* (*ASPR* 2.51–4) assembles and translates, from a martyrology, information about the place and means of martyrdom for each of the 12 apostles. Accordingly, the search for the source or sources of the *Fates* has dominated scholarship on the dating of Cynewulf's works. Conner (1996) briefly raised hopes with the claim that Cynewulf relied upon a version of the martyrology of Usuard, which would imply a date for Cynewulf after the middle of the ninth century, and more likely in the tenth. Recently, however, McCulloh (2000) has pointed out that Conner is mistaken about Usuard's authorship.[33] Moreover, he demonstrates that none of the extant martyrologies furnishes all the requisite information, and especially given some problems with the temporal and local distribution of martyrological manuscripts, it may be best to assume that Cynewulf relied upon an as yet unidentified passionary (collection of complete *passiones*) of the apostles rather than a martyrology. Such works are attested as early as the eighth century. As it follows *Andreas* in the Vercelli Book, the *Fates* was once assumed to be part of it, though stylistic differences militate against this (see chapter 4, section 5). Still, the poem is not an inappropriate epilogue to *Andreas*, and it is not inconceivable that it should have been composed to serve that purpose.[34]

Another Old English poem with calendrical and liturgical connections is *The Seasons for Fasting* (*ASPR* 6.98–104). It was copied from a now-destroyed Cotton manuscript into a sixteenth-century transcript discovered in 1934. This fragment in 230 lines, which has an unusual and very nearly regular eight-line stanzaic structure, exhorts the reader to strict observance of the Ember and Lenten fasts. The opening stanzas recount the Hebrews' observance of Mosaic law mandating fasts, and the poet endorses the observance of the four Ember dates set by Gregory the Great against those observed on the Continent (87–94). It is possible that this admonition alludes to the importation of Continental practices after the Benedictine Reform, confirming a date for the poem after the last quarter of the tenth century (Hilton 1986). The truncated closing stanzas (208–30) colorfully chastise priests who run to the tapster directly after mass, claiming it no sin to drink wine and eat oysters and other seafood after receiving the host. The poem has clear affinities to *The Creed*, including some identical lines (K. Sisam 1953b: 47–8), and it draws on sources, including works by Wulfstan and Ælfric, that happen to be collected in the two-part manuscript in which *The Creed* is preserved (Richards 1992). The speaker of the 11-line poem *Thureth* (*ASPR* 6.97) in BL, Cotton Claudius A. iii adopts the persona of the book itself, a benedictional/pontifical that it says was commissioned by þureð (3), for whom God's favor is asked. This is very likely the earl Þored (Old Norse *Þórðr*) who held estates in Yorkshire during the reign of Æthelred II, when he witnessed some charters (for references, see Ronalds and Clunies Ross 2001: 360, with a translation and edition of the poem).

A particularly interesting appropriation of a customary for literary purposes is *Vainglory*, in the Exeter Book (*ASPR* 3.147–9). The poem is structured on a contrast between the humility of "God's own child" (6) and the vainglory of "a demon's child" (47), a distinction that the poet claims to have learned from "a wise authority in days of old" (1), a "man knowledgeable about books" (4). The source is in fact the first chapter of the Rule of Chrodegang (a passage based on a sermon for monks by Caesarius of Arles, d. 542), which identifies humility as the first requirement of communal life, and remarks, "Whatever proud person you see, without a doubt that is the devil's child, and the humble one can be [considered] God's child" (see Trahern 1975). This prosaic material is nonetheless skillfully embroidered with the conventions of heroic verse – the poetic diction is particularly original – to produce a grand scene of drunken boasting in the meadhall.

Several poems are of a penitential nature. The brief *Alms-Giving* in the Exeter Book (*ASPR* 3.223) is simply a simile, drawn from Ecclesiasticus 3.33, comparing almsgiving's effect upon the wounds of sin to water's efficacy against fire, something of a medieval proverb (Whitbread 1945). *A Prayer* (*ASPR* 6.94–6), preserved in whole or in part in two late manuscripts, asks God's forgiveness for sins and asserts his ineffability. It is marked by a variety of rhetorical balances and oppositions (see Keefer 1998). *Resignation* (*ASPR* 3.215–18) is now usually regarded either as two separate poems, mistakenly joined by their editors in line 69, where a leaf is missing from the Exeter Book (Bliss and Frantzen 1976), or as a fragmented single poem (Klinck 1987). Both parts are monologues on the theme of sin and righteousness. *Resignation A* is a penitential prayer in which a contrite sinner asks God's forgiveness and mercy, pleading that the angels take him into God's presence, and though he committed many sins, that the devil not be allowed to lead him on a *lāðne sīð* 'hated journey' (48b–52). *Resignation B* has the speaker tell of God's punishments for him, which he cannot understand. He complains of isolation, loneliness, and persecution – hardly the sentiments of *Resignation A*. Many have seen in *Resignation B* the same themes found in so-called elegiac poetry in Old English, such as *The Seafarer* and *The Wanderer* (but cf. Deskis 1998), with this poet, too, reaching the stoic conclusion that it is best since one cannot alter one's fate to bear it patiently (118–19).

    Christ II (*ASPR* 3.15–27), also called *The Ascension*, stands apart in the corpus of Old English because it is a translation of a Latin homily – or part of one – into verse.[35] It is one of the four poems bearing Cynewulf's runic signature. Some would have us see this 427-line poem as composed to join *Christ I* and *III* (e.g. Liuzza 1990: 5–7), but the idea seems a relic of a time when the three poems were viewed as a single composition by Cynewulf: there is nothing in the layout of the manuscript to suggest that any closer connection was perceived among the three poems than between them and the following *Guthlac A*. Cynewulf based his poem on the closing chapters of Gregory the Great's homily for Ascension Day – the source of the "gifts of men" theme that recurs later in the manuscript (see chapter 8, section 1, with references) – and it is accordingly more sermonizing in character than *Christ I* or *III*.[36] The poem narrates Christ's final instructions to his apostles and his ascension to heaven (440–585) as a prelude to a consideration of humankind's capacity "to choose as well the affliction of hell as the glory of heaven" (590b–591). Though Gregory's remarks on God's gifts to humankind (an explication of Psalm 67.19) are brief, Cynewulf works them into a substantial list of human talents, such as singing, harping, writing, and sailing (654–691a), much as in *The Gifts of Men*. Gregory speaks of Christ's five "leaps," the "high points" of his sojourn on earth (Incarnation, Nativity, Crucifixion, Deposition and Burial, and Ascension) to which Cynewulf adds a sixth, the Harrowing of Hell (730–736a), inserted in the chronologically proper fifth place. The lesson he draws is that "we mortals should likewise rush in leaps in the thoughts of our hearts from strength to strength, strive after glorious deeds, so that we can ascend by holy works to the highest summit, where there is joy and bliss" (746b–750). There is a typically homiletic coda, rendering the liturgical closing formula *per saecula saeculorum* (777b–778), followed by the passage containing the runic signature, which is, like the other signatures, eschatological and penitential in theme. The final lines, however, introduce an extended simile of particular note, the image of a ship faring over perilous seas – a well-worn patristic allegory of the human condition (850–66; see Pulsiano 1983). On the whole, Cynewulf follows his chief source fairly closely, though certain discontinuities and an original pattern of descent and ascent may be ascribed to adoption of the theme of "leaps" as an organizing principle (Grosz 1970, G. Brown 1974).

Homiletic themes, and particularly penitential ones, in fact pervade the poetic corpus (see chapter 8), but in a few poems they are more than incidental elements. *Homiletic Fragment II*, in the Exeter Book (*ASPR* 3.224), is a 20-line consolation on the theme of transience, with the solace that God is the singular, eternal lord who created the world (8–11a). *Homiletic Fragment I* (*ASPR* 2.59–60), defective at the beginning, is a 47-line amplification and paraphrase of Psalm 28, focusing on the sins of slanderers, who speak fair words while filled with deceit, just as bees have honey in their mouths and poison in their stings (15b–22a). The theme of the perverseness of this world (31–42) is reminiscent of *Sermo Lupi ad Anglos* (see chapter 3), and the close (43–7) takes the anagogic form typical of so many homily conclusions (see chapter 8). The theme of the vanity of this transitory world also informs *Instructions for Christians* (not in *ASPR*; ed. Rosier 1964–6), a 264-line poem of religious maxims in the late twelfth-century manuscript Cambridge, University Library, Ii. I. 33. The tone is hortatory (e.g., "Oh, you wretched and earthly person in the world, why do you not continually recall the stroke of death, which the Lord has appointed for us?" 30–2), and familiar homiletic themes recur, especially penitential, eschatological, and enumerative ones. Passages of the poem are in fact adapted for use in two anonymous homilies, no. xxx in Napier 1883 and Vercelli xxi (showing that the poem is a late copy of an earlier work). Similarly hortatory, though milder in tone, are *An Exhortation to Christian Living* and *A Summons to Prayer* (*ASPR* 6.67–70), which are both direct addresses to the reader/listener advising prayer and piety as the keys to heaven. Caie (1994), following some earlier scholars, has in fact argued that, with other poems in the manuscript, they form the equivalent of a penitential sermon. An unusual feature of the latter poem is that it is macaronic, with on-verses in Old English and off-verses in Latin.[37] The two texts appear in sequence in the manuscript, and Robinson (1989) has argued that they are really one poem, which he names *The Rewards of Piety*. That is almost certainly the original intention, though Bredehoft (1998) shows that at least the rubricator, and perhaps the scribe himself, regarded them as separate pieces.

Another macaronic poem is *Aldhelm* (*ASPR* 6.97–8), a 17-line fragment that appears in CCCC 326 between the table of chapters and the text of Aldhelm's *De virginitate*. Latin and Greek words and verses are injected at random into a poem of praise for the scholarly talents of Aldhelm. This composition is so flawed that parts of it are impenetrable, but it is nonetheless unique in its attempt at polyglossia. Another poem attached to a longer prose text is the metrical epilogue to CCCC 41 (*ASPR* 6.113), which follows the Old English translation of Bede's *Historia Ecclesiastica*. The poet asks the reader to help the scribe who wrote the text that he may produce more copies. The ten-line poem is in alternating lines of black and red ink, and Robinson (1980) examines it in its role as a colophon to the preceding text.

Also homiletic in nature are *Soul and Body I* and *II* (*ASPR* 2.54–9 and 3.174–8; also ed. and trans. Moffat 1990) in the Vercelli and Exeter books, in which a condemned soul returns to berate its rotting corpse, described in grotesque detail, for the torments it now suffers. The longer Vercelli version adds the briefer address of a saved soul to its "dearest friend" (135), the chaste and obedient body. The soul's address to the body and the horrors of the rotting corpse are standard homiletic themes, as in Vercelli homily iv and Blickling viii. Though the Exeter version lacks the less colorful speech of the saved soul, the two versions must stem from a common written tradition, given shared errors (Moffat 1983). Attestation in two manuscripts affords a rare opportunity to examine the ways that scribes participated in recomposing native verse (see Moffat 1992). The popularity of the theme is further attested by the fragments of a similar alliterative poem in early Middle English (ed. Moffat 1987) written into a Worcester manuscript in the thirteenth century by the distinctive "Tremulous Hand" (see Conclusion, note 1). Similar also is *The Grave* (not in *ASPR*; ed. Buchholz 1890: 11), some verses copied onto a blank leaf ca. 1200 in the important homily manuscript Oxford, Bodleian, Bodley 343, and considered by some to be Middle English. It lacks poetic diction, and the meter is not according to classical standards, but it has a certain forcefulness in its imagery, inviting the reader to imagine him- or herself in the narrow confines of the grave, her or his corpse moldering. Probably it is a fragment, though the abruptness of the conclusion heightens its grim vividness: "You will not have any friend who will come to you, who will see how you like that abode, who will ever open the door and shed light on you again. For soon you will be horrible and loathsome to see. For soon your head will lose its hair – all the beauty of your hair will be ruined – no one will want to stroke it gently with fingers" (18–23).

Judgment Day I (*ASPR* 3.212–15) and *II* (6.58–67, also ed. and trans. Caie 2000) are also homiletic in nature, and the latter is connected to the *Soul and Body* tradition by the speaker's rebuke of the sinful flesh (77–81, 176–80). The homiletic nature of the works is also demonstrated by the latter's having been versified from a lost prose translation of the Latin source, a translation that was also worked into a prose homily in Oxford, Bodleian Library, Hatton 113 (ed. Napier 1883: 134–43, no. XXIX, at 136.28–140.2; also partially ed. Caie 2000: 105–7). Both poems thus rehearse such aspects of Doomsday as best contribute to the penitential theme, such as the hosts standing before Christ, the impossibility of concealing one's sins, the terror of the damned, God's wrath, and heaven and earth filled with flames. The lesson of both is the need to meditate on our sins and to deny the flesh while we can. *Judgment Day II* contains some additional elements of interest. It opens in a pleasant garden in which the atmosphere turns suddenly oppressive as the speaker is reminded of his sins, leading to thoughts of Doomsday. An anaphoric passage describing the satisfactions of heaven in mostly negative terms – "Neither sorrow nor hurt will come there, nor afflicted age, nor will any hardship ever arise there, or hunger or thirst or abject sleep . . ." (256–8, and on to 271) – has parallels in some other poems (see below). The poem is a translation of *De die iudicii* (ed. Caie 2000: 129–33), a poem ascribed to Bede in more than 30 manuscripts and now generally accepted as his.[38] It is assumed to be a late work, given its uneven metrics and prosaic vocabulary – the latter due to its being a versification of a prose translation, as noted above (see Stanley 1971: 389–90).

Christ III in the Exeter Book (*ASPR* 3.27–49) is also a vision of Judgment Day, and it is also homiletic in nature, its numerous sources including several known sermons.[39] It includes many of the same elements as the *Judgment Day* poems, such as the cataclysmic events of the apocalypse (the sun will become the color of blood, the moon will fall, the stars will scatter, and the dead will rise from their graves), the horror of the damned (who will be forced to look upon Christ's wounds as the work of their own sins for which he was crucified), the rejoicing of the saved, the poet's exhortation to all to confess and repent the secret sins which will be revealed to all on Judgment Day, and a conclusion describing how the righteous will be welcomed into heaven, where "there is neither hunger nor thirst, sleep nor illness, neither the heat of the sun nor cold nor care" (1660b–1662a). The poem's structural principle is generally agreed to be a repetitive one: Jennings (1994) traces this to the use of the service of Nocturns for the season of Advent as a model, while Earl (1999) more persuasively takes it to be a result of typological concerns, expressing a nonlinear conception of history. Metrical and linguistic features suggest that *Christ III* is a relatively early composition (Fulk 1992: 397–9).

Explicit allegory is not a common literary mode in Old English, and that is surprising, given the allegorical nature of biblical exegesis revealed in homiletic literature, as well as the role of allegories in the monastic curriculum (see section 4 of the introduction). *The Wanderer* and *The Seafarer* ask to be read allegorically, but they are more remarkable for their lyric intensity. The most explicit allegory in Old English is *The Phoenix* (*ASPR* 3.94–113), a poetic translation of the *Carmen de ave phoenice* attributed to the early fourth-century poet Lactantius (1–380), a curricular poem, followed by a versified explication (381–677) that makes use of Ambrose's *Hexameron*, among other sources.[40] Though Lactantius was a Christian, his poem contains no explicit Christian reference, recounting how the phoenix, when it grows old, gathers herbs to build a pyre on which it will be consumed in a fire kindled by the sun. From the ashes a new phoenix is born in the form of a milky worm. The Old English poet treats the material freely, expanding and condensing, omitting most names of unfamiliar figures and places, converting Phoebus, for example into "God's candle" (91). The much-anthologized opening passage, with its anaphoric, partially rhyming characterization of the bird's home – "Neither rain nor snow, nor frost's breath, nor fire's blaze, nor the downpour of hail, nor the fall of rime, nor the sun's heat, nor continual cold, nor hot weather, nor wintry showers, can do harm there, but the spot is ever flourishing and unscathed" (14b–20a) – is reminiscent of the description of heaven in *Judgment Day II* 256–71. The negative terms of the description perhaps express Anglo-Saxon antipathy to the natural world (Neville 1999: 59–62). The interpretation offered in the latter part of the poem is not a naive allegory, as the bird is said alternately to analogize Christ and humankind; but neither is the allegory worked out on the classic four levels. The poem concludes with a macaronic passage of which the general meaning is clear, though the syntax is sometimes obscure (see Cain 2001). The dialect is most likely Mercian and the date of composition no earlier than Cynewulf's day; and a small amount of evidence suggests that the same poet composed both the translation and the exegesis (Fulk 1992: 402–4). There is a brief unrelated homily in two manuscripts (BL, Cotton Vespasian D. xiv, and CCCC 198; ed. Kluge 1885: 474–9) describing St. John's vision of the phoenix.

Similar in form are the poems of the Old English Physiologus, *The Panther*, *The Whale*, and *The Partridge* (*ASPR* 169–74). The bestiary tradition is Alexandrian and pre-Christian in origin, but in its medieval form each animal's behavior is described before an allegorical interpretation is offered. The Physiologus thus shows affinities to homilies in which the pericope is explicated after the Alexandrian manner (Letson 1979). In the Old English Physiologus, the panther, enemy of the serpent, has a lustrous coat, sleeps for three days after eating, and is compared to Christ; the whale (originally an asp-turtle), in a scene familiar from the *Arabian Nights* and the *Navigatio S. Brendani* (Faraci 1991), poses as an island and drowns sailors who camp on it, emulating Satan. The whale also (like the panther) has a sweet odor that attracts others to it, though in this case for sinister purposes. *The Partridge* is too fragmentary to interpret, as the loss of at least one leaf from the Exeter Book in line 2 has produced two poetic fragments of 2 and 14 lines. A bird is mentioned at the start, and most assume this to be the partridge, as these three animals appear in this order in some recensions of the Latin *Physiologus*, representing earth, water, and air, or beast, fish, and bird.[41] Whether the two fragments may be said to belong to a single poem about the partridge depends on a variety of considerations. The Physiologus group begins with a general statement about the world's creatures (*Panther* 1–8), and it ends with an eschatological passage

(*Partridge* 5–16), followed by a *finit* (the only one in the Exeter Book) that has been taken by many to indicate the close of an abbreviated bestiary.[42] Biggs (1989) argues that the eschatological theme of *Partridge* 12–16 is characteristic of the treatment of the bird in some versions of the Latin *Physiologus*, and therefore the two fragments are likely to belong to the same poem. However, Marchand (1991) very convincingly identifies the source of lines 5–11 as the "Apocryphon of Ezechiel," not found in any Latin bestiary text, and so his view that more than a leaf has been lost, and *Partridge* 1–2 and 3–16 belong to different poems, wields considerable force.

Just as miracles are an essential element of saints' legends, proving the sanctity of the elect and forming the basis for the saint's cult by offering devotees hope of relief from afflictions, so also visions serve to prove the saint's liminal status between this world and the next. They also give evidence of divine favor, and this no doubt explains why Bede, who generally avoids sensational topics, includes in his *Historia ecclesiastica* accounts of several visions, including those of Fursa (III, 19), Adamnan (IV, 25), Dryhthelm (V, 12), and other, unnamed persons (V, 13–14). The most familiar of these visions, of course, is that of Cædmon (IV, 24), the cowherd who in a dream was inspired by an angel to sing about the Creation.[43] Twenty-one medieval copies of *Cædmon's Hymn* are known from manuscripts, in both English and Latin, of Bede's ecclesiastical history.[44] Bede translated *Cædmon's Hymn* into Latin and did not provide an English version because he was writing for an international audience of clerics (see VanderBilt 1996). In some Latin manuscripts an English version is added outside the text proper, enabling a number of scholars to speculate that the English is a translation of the Latin and that Cædmon's song is thus nowhere actually preserved – an argument founded on some notable improbabilities.[45] However that may be, the eighth-century copies remain our oldest manuscript records of both Old English verse and the Northumbrian dialect.

Precisely what Bede regarded as miraculous about Cædmon's story is disputed. Some earlier scholars sought to rationalize Cædmon's suddenly acquired talent, either as an unexpected sign of literary refinement (Wrenn 1946) or as an accomplishment previously held but concealed (Magoun 1955). Yet Bede's belief that the herdsman was the first to express a Christian theme in English poetry would seem sufficiently remarkable (Malone 1961, Lord 1993), and in any case, that his talent came to him from God in a dream would surely have been taken by Bede as proof of sanctity, given the evidentiary function of visions in the *Historia*. Indeed, regarding the song as evidence for the vision is less suspect than fetishizing it for its primacy in literary history, a consideration that probably seems of more significance to literary scholars than it would have seemed to Bede and his contemporaries. For them what made the poem worthy of committing to memory was most likely its heavenly source. More recent studies are less concerned with the significance of the miracle, tending rather to stress the political assumptions and objectives of Bede and his readers. Bede's intentions were anything but simple and naive, as his account and translation show biblical and classicizing features designed to situate the vision and text in a larger literary tradition concerning divine poetic inspiration (Orchard 1996). Special emphasis has been laid on the role of Cædmon in converting a native, oral form to literate uses (Osborn 1989, Lerer 1991: 42–8), and on modern scholars' complicity in promoting Bede's use of Cædmon in the service of triumphal Christianity and male authorship (Frantzen 1990: 130–7, Earl 1994: 85–6, Lees and Overing 2001: 15–39).

Several of the saints' legends discussed in chapter 4 contain visions: for example, Constantine is granted a vision of the cross before battle in *Elene* – enabling, rather than instigating, his conversion, according to Harbus 1994 – and Andreas' men on the boat dream that an eagle bears their souls to heaven, where they see Christ and the host of the holy (*Andreas* 859–91). In a sense, all the poetic hagiographies contain visions, since the appearance of angels and devils is a variety of *visio* – as shown, for example, by Felix's use of the *Vita S. Fursei* (also Bede's source for Fursa's visions) for Guthlac's demonic encounters. Several Anglo-Latin texts, such as some of Boniface's letters, also include visions, and Alcuin's long poem on York and Aediluulf's *De abbatibus* (chapter 1) both end with visions (studied by Kamphausen 1975: 86–114 and McEnerney 1988). Yet the *visio* also exists as a separate genre. Two prose texts are particularly noteworthy. The fragmentary Old English translation of the *Visio S. Pauli* (ed. Healey 1978), the language of which is chiefly Kentish, takes the form of a homily. The material is well suited to monitory purposes, as it has the classical features of an Anglo-Saxon vision, recounting the dreamer's experience of heaven and hell, with special emphasis on the latter. It was a popular work already in the early period, and a heterodox one, condemned by both Aldhelm and Ælfric (see chapter 3). More clearly related to the literature of sanctity is the late (ca. 1100) *Vision of Leofric* (ed. Napier 1908), actually a series of wonders experienced by one of Edward the Confessor's two most powerful thanes, earl of Mercia and husband of Lady Godiva (OE *Godgifu*). The first is a vision of heaven influenced ultimately by Book IV of Gregory's *Dialogi*, with its test of passing over a daunting bridge; the others are wonders witnessed while Leofric was at his prayers. The text is of especial interest for its insights into the quasi-monastic regimen of a pious lay person of the eleventh century, and into liturgical practices and architectural details of the day (Gatch 1992, 1993).

Next to Cædmon's dream, the best-known vision is that recounted in *Dream of the Rood* (*ASPR* 2.61–5), in which the narrator tells how Christ's cross appeared to him in a dream and recounted the events of the crucifixion and its aftermath. The cross is not simply given human qualities (an instance of *prosopopoeia*) but is made part of a *comitatus*: Christ becomes an active hero, stripping himself and ascending the cross, while the cross is something of a thane to him, wishing, but not daring, to lay low his enemies, and eventually suffering the afflictions of an exile deprived of his lord. The poem thus owes much to native verse tradition (see Clemoes 1994). Fragments of this first part of the poem are preserved in a Northumbrian version (*ASPR* 6.114–15) on a monumental stone cross preserved at Ruthwell (properly [rɪvl], though scholars tend to say [r√θwl]), Dumfriesshire. The runic inscription on the cross (see plate 7) is from the eighth or ninth century.[46] It was doubtless extracted from a longer composition resembling *Dream of the Rood*, as it contains verses without alliterating mates, and the alternation between standard and hypermetric verses can be seen as fairly regular only in the Vercelli poem. It has been suggested that the second half of the Vercelli poem (78–156) is a later addition, as it differs in form and mode, turning from narrative to exposition. Whether or not it was added later, though, the second half makes a coherent whole of the poem, lending it a structure like that of some other lyrics, particularly *The Wanderer*: at the start of the poem, the narrator introduces the speaker

Plate 7 (opposite)   The Ruthwell Cross, now inside the church at Ruthwell, Dumfries. This nineteenth-century engraving (from George Stephens, *The Old-Northern Runic Monuments of Scandinavia and England*, 4 vols., London and Copenhagen, 1866–1901, opposite p. 405 in vols. 1–2) highlights the inscriptions in the runic and Roman alphabets better than any photograph. The cross, which probably dates from the mid-eighth century (though the runic inscription may be a later addition), has suffered from both weathering and Puritan delight in overthrowing graven images. © British Library.

(the cross), which relates its experience of hardships, showing how it has acquired wisdom from the experience, which it then applies to an understanding of its own role in preparing humanity for Judgment Day. The narrator then returns, applying the cross's generalized wisdom to the life of the individual and directing our attention, in a characteristically homiletic close, to the heavenly home earned for us by Christ's passion and harrowing of hell (see Pope and Fulk 2001: 66). The different nature of the former half of the poem may then be explained not as the result of separate composition but of a matching of form and content. In this part of the poem the dreamer describes the cross as appearing alternately decked with jewels and suffused with blood, emblematizing its dual, paradoxical nature as instrument of both torture and salvation. So, too, this section alternates in form between standard and hypermetric verses, the latter often associated with moments of heightened solemnity in other poems.

Criticism of the poem has been remarkably varied, attesting to the difficulties that Anglo-Saxonists have had agreeing on an interpretive context.[47] In the past dozen years the poem has been seen as apocalyptic (Pigg 1992) or exegetical (Harbus 1996b) in outlook (both homiletic modes), or penitential (Hinton 1996); a riddle (implausibly: Laszlo 1996); or in one way or another an expression of liturgical concerns (E. Anderson 1989, Grasso 1991, Jennings 1994). Particularly interesting are studies of the gendering of the cross (Hawkins 1995, Dockray-Miller 1997), showing how an inanimate object assumes gendered qualities in its alternately powerful and powerless states. One context of the poem, however, that has received little critical attention is the hagiographic one. Its visionary content is not the only reason to examine the poem in the context of saints' lives, as two separate feasts of the Holy Cross were celebrated in the *sanctorale*, the Invention (May 3) and the Exaltation (September 14), both of which are commemorated in Ælfrician and anonymous saints' legends.[48] There is also a history of the rood-tree (ed. Napier 1894: 2–34), which in its Old English version begins with Moses and David, oddly made contemporaries, and leads up to the Invention. The cross indeed had much in common with saints, as it was widely culted, its relics especially prized, and its miracles reported. And accounts of the cross naturally involve actual saints, including Helena, Cyriac, and Longinus. When the cross is thus viewed as a quasi-saint, it seems natural enough that it is made to speak and given the human ability to suffer and ultimately triumph in *Dream of the Rood*.

Many of the texts considered in this chapter have received relatively little scholarly attention, and that is unfortunate. They reveal a great deal about the more familiar works that have preoccupied literary scholars, about which a great deal has been written without attention to the particular preoccupations and practices of those who compiled the surviving manuscripts.

7

Legal, Scientific, and Scholastic Works

I Legal Texts

Before Christianity introduced records on parchment, English law was necessarily oral. Its fundamentally oral nature was in fact never lost, as most legal proceedings continued to be conducted orally in front of witnesses, with no written record – as one might expect in a culture in which literacy belonged to the Church. The introduction of writing on parchment, however, enabled some legal innovations, one of the most important of which was the charter.[1] In earlier scholarly usage the term "charters" may refer loosely to title-deeds of property or privilege in regard to land, in the form of "writs, wills, records of disputes and miscellaneous memoranda, as well as landbooks and leases" (Sawyer 1968: vii) – though technically "charters" ought to refer only to royal documents, in Latin, of this type, and "writs" to shorter vernacular ones dealing with a wider range of administrative matters (Keynes 1999a). Based on Roman title-deeds and introduced to England in the seventh century as documentation for the estate of *bōcland* – land granted in perpetuity, originally only to the Church – they eventually included not just royal diplomas but records of private transactions. The usefulness of charters in an oral culture is plain: witnesses grow old and die, but charters continue to prove the right of individuals and religious houses to the estates in their possession. As a consequence of the large number of properties in the tenure of some religious establishments, charters, which are normally on single sheets, were often copied into cartularies (monastic or cathedral registers), the most familiar of which are the Textus Roffensis (facsimile ed. Sawyer 1957–62), an important volume of laws and legal documents made at Rochester after the Conquest (where the manuscript still resides), and Hemming's Cartulary

(BL, Cotton Tiberius A. xiii), a collection of royal charters, episcopal leases, and documents pertaining to the rights and privileges of Worcester. Given the importance of charters, it is not surprising that there was much recopying of them at a later date, and many patent forgeries (see Franzen 1996). Thus for most linguistic and many historical purposes only charters on single sheets are of value, and then only if they are originals or near-contemporary copies.[2] There are about 200 such, out of a corpus of more than 1,000 charters. The oldest original charter is of Hlothhere, king of Kent, dated 679 (no. 8); most date to the period 940–70. Charters usually are composed of fixed elements arranged in a rigid formula, including an invocation, proem, and so forth, ending with a list of witnesses (not usually signatories, as only scribes could write). One standard element is the boundary clause, in which the bounds of the property are detailed in an ambulatory circuit, proceeding from landmark to landmark. Even when the boundary clause is written in Latin, as most were before the tenth century, it will generally contain place-names and topographical features in English, and thus charters preserve many archaic forms and attest to dialect features. Charters are also useful for tracing the development of script and gauging the quality of Latinity at various times and places. Yet their evidence is limited: of the surviving boundary clauses, of which there are more than a thousand, just 35 are found in what are generally regarded as original documents dating before 900, mostly from Kent; and documents of any date from north and east of Watling Street are vanishingly rare.

Writs are much shorter, less formal documents in the form of an address by the grantor (royal or private) to the assembly of the shire court or hundred court, and they are exclusively in Old English. They developed from the late ninth century and were used for various purposes, although most of those that survive are from the eleventh century and were written as a public declaration of a change in ownership or privileges of land. Writs usually have a seal affixed as the authority of the grantor, a feature which was never part of the charter, but it is possible that both royal writs and charters, while the exclusive creation of churchmen, were at various times in various parts of England the product of royal chanceries, consisting of a group of ecclesiastical scribes attached to the royal household for the purpose of recording such legal documents.[3]

Two other sorts of records of legal transactions are manumission documents and wills. Manumissions record the legal emancipation of a person from servitude, and about 120 of them survive from the gospelbooks of churches at Bath, Bodmin, Exeter, and Durham, presumably because of the requirement, first expressed in Wihtræd's law, that a person be freed in a church.[4] The earliest surviving manumission document (ed. Harmer 1914: 32) is that of King Æthelstan upon his coronation in 925, preserved in an eighth-century Northumbrian gospelbook (BL, Royal 1. B. vii), in which he manumits one Eadhelm. The most celebrated Old English will is that of King Alfred,[5] but recorded testators span the scale from kings to commoners, in some 60 documents (many ed. Whitelock 1930) bequeathing everything from estates to a single sheep. About a quarter of these are preserved in contemporary form on single sheets of parchment, none earlier than the first half of the ninth century, and the rest are copies, often in cartularies.[6] Regardless of how they are preserved, however, nearly all survive only because they contain bequests to one or another major southern abbey. They differ from modern wills in several respects, one of which is that they rarely catalogue the bestowal of the testator's entire property, but they supplement oral arrangements.[7] Many wills of aristocrats (see plate 8) in fact seem to be merely itemizations of properties distributed during the testator's lifetime.

The relations between oral tradition and the written laws are yet to be fully explained. Almost certainly there was a body of laws transmitted orally before the Conversion, though there is no evidence for anything like such a figure as the medieval Icelandic *lǫgsǫgumaðr* 'law speaker', an elected official who recited one third of the law each year at the *Alþingi*, the annual general assembly. The first law code to be recorded (ca. 602) was that of the first Christian king, Æthelberht of Kent (d. 616). It is preserved only in a manuscript made half a millennium later, the Textus Roffensis – nearly all Old English law is in fact preserved only in post-Conquest manuscripts[8] – but the scribally updated language retains sufficient archaisms to prove that this really is the earliest English text of any length.[9] Bede tells us that Æthelberht's code was made *iuxta exempla Romanorum* 'after the examples of the Romans' (*Historia ecclesiastica* II, v), a phrase of disputed meaning, though it may refer to Frankish codes used as models. Perhaps the chief purpose of recording the code, then, was to confer upon Æthelberht a status equal to that of his in-laws, the Merovingian kings, and to signal Kent's membership in the community of civilized, law-abiding Christian nations (Wormald 1999c: 94). For Augustine and his mission, though, doubtless the urgency of having the laws recorded was that they insured the safety and security of God's servants in Kent. Being

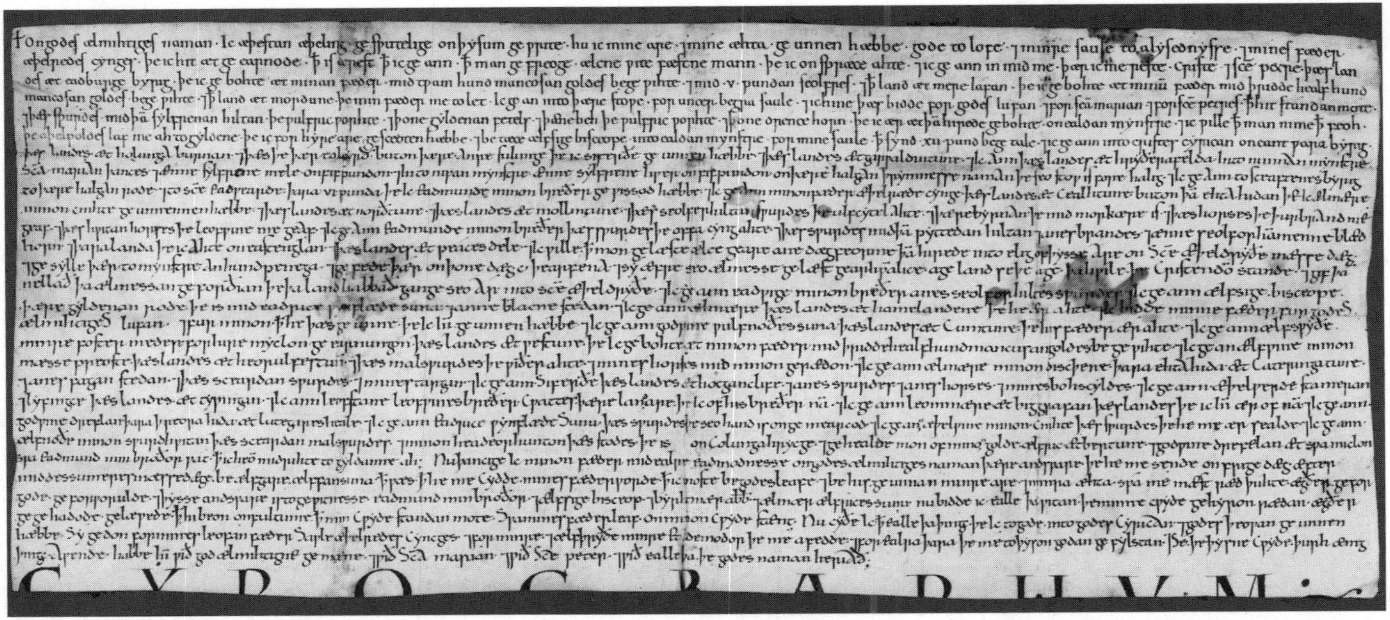

Plate 8 Chirograph will of Athelstan atheling, the eldest son of Æthelred II, made ca. 1014 (ed. Whitelock 1930: 56–62). Among the articles bequeathed are a horse, a drinking horn, several wealthy estates, money (for masses) for the repose of the testator's soul, and a variety of swords, one of them said to have belonged to King Offa (d. 796). Two copies were made on a single sheet, with the word *cyrographum* 'manuscript' written between and cut through when the copies were severed. Each copy then authenticates the other when they are rejoined: see Lowe 1998b. © British Library.

unable to engage in retributive feuding, they had no protection in law until Æthelberht placed them under his own protection by copying into his code provisions for their security inspired by Frankish laws. The most distinctive aspect of Æthelberht's code, and of Anglo-Saxon laws in general, is that they were written in the vernacular, though Continental codes till the twelfth century are all in Latin. Wormald (1999c: 101) has argued that one reason may be that laws in Latin would have been incomprehensible to the newly converted Kentish court. If he is right, though, that the laws represent not so much the king's decrees as the traditions of the people of Kent, vernacularity may also signal their consensual nature, for at such an early date, Latin laws would doubtless have seemed the product of a central state that did not reflect the actual extent of Æthelberht's authority.[10]

Æthelberht's code inspired a tradition of vernacular laws issued under the name of successive kings. But while the chief motive for Æthelberht's laws seems to have been the protection of clerics, the rationale behind subsequent codes is difficult to interpret. Above all, their nature is fundamentally conservative, and their resistance to innovation no doubt was designed to secure for each successive monarch a place among his law-giving predecessors (Wormald 1977a). The laws' system, in any case, has two bases. First is feud, which, with its attendant menu of wergilds (see section 1 of the introduction), ensured domestic order by sanctioning retribution or restitution. The greater part of the surviving codes, both in England and on the Continent, is in fact a record of compensations to be paid for various offenses, especially personal injuries, with the injured party's wergild as the highest tariff allowed – for example, from the code of Alfred, 30 shillings for striking off a man's ear, 30 for a thumb, 4 for a back tooth, 20 for a big toe, and 20 for cutting off a commoner's beard. Wergilds are separate from fines (see below), since they are not established by official ordinances, being based in traditional law. Second is ordeal, a divine rite for the proof of innocence, which placed God in the position of judge – a feature of law that probably does not date to the pagan period, but which nonetheless developed early, as it is prescribed already in the laws of the West Saxon Ine (reigned 688–726). Ordeal, at which a bishop presided, might involve the ritualized infliction of burns, with judgment predicated on whether they healed or suppurated; or it might involve observing whether the accused sank or floated in a tank of cold water.

Æthelberht's code was augmented by his successors, Hlothere and Eadric (ca. 673–85) and Wihtræd (ca. 690–725; ed. Liebermann 1903–

16: 1.9–14). The influence of this Kentish legislation may be seen in the code of Ine (above), as chapter 20 of Ine's laws is almost identical to chapter 28 of Wihtræd's. Yet Ine's laws survive only because Alfred included them as an appendix to his own laws two centuries later.[11] There is no irrefutable evidence that any royal codes were issued in the two intervening centuries, not even by the great Offa (reigned 757–96).[12] That it is only during the reign of Alfred that a new set of laws was issued confirms their political significance, in this instance contributing to the corpus of texts, including Asser's life of the king, seemingly designed to exert his authority and build his cult (see chapter 2). Alfred's laws demonstrate the same kind of historical perspective and nation-building tendencies that his other works evince. His code is preceded by an expansive translation of the Ten Commandments and other parts of Exodus, a history of the Apostles, and a history of Church law and doctrine promulgated through various councils (Liebermann 1903: 16–123). Thus Alfred positioned his laws within the continuum of Western ecclesiastical history, at once invoking and reinforcing the authority of that history.

Already in the earliest successors to Æthelberht's code we see the gradual strengthening of the hand of the monarch, with the addition of ever more fines for offenses required to be paid to the king. This trend continues throughout the period, and in the series of codes issued in a nearly unbroken sequence of kings from Alfred to Cnut we find evidence of an unprecedented centralization of power. The fundamental mechanism enabling this trend is the institution of an oath abjuring all crimes, to be sworn by all free men 12 years of age. As a consequence, crimes were no longer simply offenses against society but acts of disloyalty, and therefore the penalty even for crimes like adultery demanded the payment of fines to the king. The legal system itself acquired great force, with a more elaborate system of courts and much harsher penalties (Wormald 1999b).

This trend finds it zenith in the legislation drafted for Æthelred II and Cnut by the homilist Wulfstan. The long opening section of *I* and *II Cnut* (ed. Liebermann 1903–16: 1.278–370, at 278–307), "amounting to more than a quarter of the whole, was intended to remind the clergy and laity of their religious duties, and to secure the maintenance of . . . ecclesiastical interests" (F. Stenton 1971: 409). Under Wulfstan's direction the law thus became an instrument for God to rule the English people according to his will (Wormald 1999a, 1999c: 27). It is not the case, of course, that religious and secular institutions had been strictly segregated before this in England's political economy. But with these laws it becomes exceptionally clear to what extent royal authority had acquired a theocratic basis, as evident for example also in the crescent habit of burying kings at monastic centers, and in the growing importance of coronation ceremonies, with the inviolable authority that consecration bestowed, according to Ælfric (*Catholic Homilies* I, 14). Wulfstan's political views are laid out in detail in his *Institutes of Polity* (ed. Jost 1959), found in two versions (*I* and *II Polity*), the latter a substantial expansion. Via Ælfric's *Letter to Sigeweard* he borrows Alfred's division of the just society into three estates, comprising men of prayer, labor and warfare (a scheme that was to dominate political thought in Europe until the eighteenth century). The whole is organized to outline the responsibilities of ecclesiastical and secular posts, and it concludes with an exposition of all of society's duty to sustain the Church. Secular law is portrayed as an extension of Christian ethics, a theme evident in all of the Anglo-Saxon law codes. Of particular interest is the beginning of the work, since it opens with a section on the heavenly king, followed by one on the earthly, defining the latter's chief duties as promotion of the aims of the former and his servants.[13]

In addition to the law codes of kings, there are several anonymous ordinances concerning such matters as adultery, asylum, betrothal, the despoiling of the dead, and the administration of ordeals. Of particular interest are the *Rectitudines singularum personarum*, which set out the rights and obligations of the various orders and occupations of peasants with respect to their lords, coupled with *Gerefa*, on the responsibilities of the reeve (estate administrator).[14] There is also the treaty between Alfred and Guthrum (AD 886?), establishing the borders of the Danelaw and setting English and Danish wergilds at the same value; and the text called *Dunsæte*, an agreement for the laws of the Welsh marches.[15] Also of note is the post-Conquest interest in Anglo-Saxon law. Large portions of the Old English laws were translated into obscure Latin in the twelfth century, and at particular length in the *Quadripartitus*, an immense collection compiled during the reign of Henry I and now distributed among several manuscripts. Its purpose seems to have been to establish what laws were currently in effect (under the assumption that any Anglo-Saxon laws not abrogated by Edward the Confessor's legislation were still in force) and to prove the continuity of English law from Edward's day to Henry's, thus establishing the validity of the latter's extensive legislation.[16]

2 Scientific Literature

Even more complex than Anglo-Saxon legislation is the body of literature devoted to computus, a term that refers to both the science of computation and an individual work on that subject. The chief use of computus was to calculate the date of Easter, on which the dates of all movable feasts depended – a determination with considerable political significance in the seventh century (on the Paschal controversy, see section 2 of the introduction). But it was also a practical problem throughout the period, since the calculation depends upon the rather complex issue of how to predict the phases of the moon with precision. The more elaborate computistical texts thus may include a perpetual calendar, an Easter table, tables for determining the moon's age and the weekday, arithmetic tables, instructions for calculating, and documents relating to the history of the calendar (Baker 1999). The earliest computi are letters on competing Paschal cycles; Bede wrote the first full-length treatises on the subject, *De temporibus* (703) and the longer *De temporum ratione* (725; both ed. Charles Jones 1943). Despite its Latin title, found in two of the eight manuscripts, Ælfric's early work *De temporibus anni* is in the main a vernacular precis of the latter, though use is made of the former, and also of Bede's *De natura rerum* for its selection on celestial bodies.[17] It is a compendium of cosmological information, including the typological significance of the phases of the moon, the date of Creation, the seven divisions of the night, the signs of the zodiac, and much besides. For what audience it was intended is unclear, though Ælfric's other translations are chiefly for the laity. Byrhtferth of Ramsey's *Enchiridion* (or *Handboc* 'Manual'), on which he was at work in 1011, is composed alternately in Latin and English, the latter explaining the former in simpler terms to "the ignorant rural clergy" (I, 1.172), "those who do not understand Latin" (II, 1.421–2).[18] It is a miscellany of divagations on rhetoric, metrics, allegory, grammar, and measurement, but it is designed to serve primarily as a commentary on his Latin *Computus* (reconstructed in Baker and Lapidge 1995: 373–427), which relies heavily on Bede and on the computus of the great scholar Abbo of Fleury (martyred 1004 at La Réole), who taught Byrhtferth when he was in residence at Ramsey Abbey 985-7. Byrhtferth's overparticular discourse and hermeneutic style, modeled on Aldhelm's, often make for tortured reading, but his learning was obviously second to none during the late Anglo-Saxon period, and as a computist he is unsurpassed even by Bede. In addition there are quite a few shorter texts in Old English devoted to aspects of computus (most ed. Henel 1934), distributed in more than 15 manuscripts, thus illustrating its importance to the very end of the period. They are mostly devoted to epacts (charting the difference between the lunar and solar years) and rules for finding movable feasts.[19]

As illustrated above in regard to charms (chapter 1), the categories that we distinguish as folklore, theology, and science tend to overlap in Old English, and so the group of texts designated here as "scientific" is heterogeneous – and perhaps would have seemed so to Anglo-Saxon readers as well. An extensive subgroup comprises medical literature, again remarkable at this early date for the use of the vernacular.[20] It may be that composition in English is an accommodation not for "ignorant priests" but for lay persons, and particularly women, who were perhaps the chief practitioners of the Anglo-Saxon medico-magical tradition, given that by the time of Alfred's reign the evidence for women's literacy in Latin has evaporated.[21] The most important Old English medical text is *Bald's Leechbook* (OE *Lǽcboc*; cf. *lǽce* 'doctor'), quite probably dating to the time of King Alfred, though preserved in a tenth-century manuscript.[22] It comprises three books: the first addresses the external manifestations of diseases in the traditional head-to-foot order of Classical medical treatises; the second deals with internal ailments, borrowing extensively from Greek and Roman texts and followed by a colophon which names one Bald ('Bold', an Anglian or Early West Saxon spelling) as the owner of the book; and the third contains magical remedies and charms rooted in native folk medicine and Christian faith.[23] In addition to its folk and religious sources, the text demonstrates the compiler's familiarity with a range of Mediterranean medical works through widely known compilations of the fourth to the seventh centuries.[24] In the *Leechbook*, as elsewhere, the chief components of medicine are herbal recipes, prayers, incantations, and bloodletting.

Lacnunga ('Cures'), preserved in BL, Harley 585, while resembling the *Leechbook* in some places, is a rather chaotic assemblage of some 200 remedies, some of identifiably classical extraction.[25] In its beginning, *Lacnunga* mirrors the traditional head-to-foot arrangement found in the *Leechbook*, but this is abandoned within the first 20 entries. The folkloristic turn of the compiler of *Lacnunga* is best illustrated by the inclusion of some of the most interesting of the semi-metrical charms: *The Nine Herbs Charm, Against a Dwarf, For a*

Sudden Stitch, For Loss of Cattle, and *For Delayed Birth* (*ASPR* 6.119–24). Comparison with the more rational, classical *Leechbook* has contributed to scholars' generally low regard for *Lacnunga*: M. Cameron (1993: 47), for example, considers it valuable "as a source of superstitious medicine, and although it nowhere reflects the best in Anglo-Saxon medical practice, it gives a fascinating insight into its less rational aspects." The comparison has also led to a considerable amount of fruitless argument about suppressed paganism in these texts, and about the degree of sophistication of typical medical practice of the period (see Hollis and Wright 1992: 221–9).

Three other surviving Old English medical texts are translations of Latin works. The fourth-century *Herbarium* of Pseudo-Apuleius is translated in no fewer than four manuscripts, the oldest of which also contains *Lacnunga*.[26] An eleventh-century Canterbury manuscript, BL, Cotton Vitellius C. iii (facsimile ed. D'Aronco and Cameron 1998), is richly designed with illustrations of the plant species named in its herbal remedies (see plate 9), while another manuscript, BL, Harley 6258B, has the Latin names for the herbs arranged in alphabetical order, making it an eminently functional reference text. The work contains a treatise on betony, an herbal of 132 plants, and a supplement of 33 other plants from the *Liber medicinae ex herbis femininis* of Pseudo-Dioscorides (unidentified, before 600), all written together as a unified work with continuous chapter numbering.[27] Preserved along with the *Herbarium* in the same manuscripts is the Old English translation (ed. de Vriend 1984) of the fifth-century compilation *Medicina de quadrupedibus*, which contains a letter from a fictitious pharaoh named Idpartus to Octavian on the medical uses of badgers, a treatise on the mulberry, and a version of the *Liber medicinae ex animalibus* of Sextus Placitus (unidentified), listing medicines to be extracted, sometimes brutally, from a dozen wild and domestic animals. One surviving text from as late as 1200, an incomplete translation of *Peri didaxeon* 'About Medical Schools' (ed. Cockayne 1864–6: 3.81–145), is closely related to the sources of the *Leechbook*. The language of this work is really Middle English, and most see its connection with the pre-Conquest period as tenuous. But it demonstrates that the Anglo-Saxon tradition of vernacular medical texts was alive more than a century after the Conquest.

Like the *Herbarium* in method and arrangement is the brief Old English *Lapidary* (ed. Evans and Serjeantson 1933: 13–15, better Kitson 1978: 32–3), preserved in a Latin and English miscellany showing Kent-

Plate 9   From the herbarium in BL, Cotton Vitellius C. iii, fol. 59r, illustrating water-parsnip and a scorpion and insect or spider, against whose bite the herb mentioned on the previous folio (southernwood) is said to be efficacious. © British Library.

ish features (BL, Cotton Tiberius A. iii). The earliest vernacular lapidary from Europe, it begins with a description of the 12 apocalyptic stones based on Scripture (Exodus 28:17–20, 39:10–13, Ezra 28:13, and Revelation 21:19–20), once thought to derive from Isidore, and from Bede's *Explanatio Apocalypsis*, in which he assigns allegorical significance to the stones.[28] Now instead it has been argued that the sources of the text are closely bound up with Archbishop Theodore's circle, though the translator himself was not expert in Latin (Kitson 1978). The *Lapidary* is more designedly taxonomic than Bede's work, simply describing the appearance of the 12; yet a list of 10 stones is appended, with accounts of their uses and places of origin, and these are sometimes fanciful. Thus, "mocritum" is declared effective against sorcery, and another unnamed stone, resembling a man piping upon nine pipes and a man playing a harp, is said to counteract all venoms and powders.[29]

Taxonomy of the fantastic is the basis for the *Liber monstrorum* (ca. 650–750), a work closely associated with Aldhelm's sphere of influence.[30] The first book is a description of anthropomorphic monsters that include giants, fauns, centaurs, cynocephali, gorgons, polyglots, Ethiopians, and other staples of the genre throughout the Middle Ages. The second and third books concern mythical beasts and serpents. The *Liber* draws on identifiable Christian and classical sources, though the author repeatedly indicates his incredulity. A peculiarity is that the work begins with a joke: while all the other creatures are remote wonders, the first chapter describes a male transvestite, then admits that this "monster" is in fact frequently encountered among humans (see Fulk forthcoming a). Another remarkable feature of the *Liber* is its connection with *Beowulf*: the second chapter describes Hygelac as a monstrous giant whose bones lie on an island at the mouth of the Rhine. Two other texts of this genre also have connections with *Beowulf*, as versions are found in the *Beowulf* Manuscript.[31] The *Wonders* (or *Marvels*) *of the East*, in two manuscripts, contains brief descriptions of alleged Eastern exotica (see plate 10), some of the same ones itemized in the *Liber monstrorum*.[32] The translation derives from a group of Continental Latin texts in epistolary form in which a traveler writes to his emperor of Eastern marvels, a narrative structure lacking in the Old English version. This structure is reflected, however, in the text that immediately follows in the *Beowulf* manuscript, *The Letter of Alexander to Aristotle* (in the same hand as the first scribe of *Beowulf*), the earliest vernacular translation of the *Epistola Alexandri ad Aristotelem*. This purports to

Plate 10   Two-faced giant from *The Wonders of the East* in BL, Cotton Tiberius B. v, fol. 81r, from the second quarter of the eleventh century. His race are said to be 15 feet tall, with white bodies, red feet and knees, long noses, and black hair. They sail to India to give birth. © British Library.

be Alexander's report of wonders and monstrosities encountered in India, like two-headed serpents. It shows clear signs of being derived from an Anglian original. K. Sisam (1953b: 65–96) was the first to suggest that these texts provide a solution to the riddle why *Beowulf* is preserved at all: BL, Cotton Vitellius A. xv would appear to be a collection devoted to monsters.

3 Texts for the Schoolroom

While the Latin curriculum seems to have exerted some influence on the kinds of vernacular texts that were produced (see chapter 6), more particularly some kinds of texts were devised in the service of the more fundamental aspects of the curriculum. There existed from Late Antiquity the Latin grammars of Donatus and Priscian, but while these served the purposes of students on the Continent, where the Romance vernaculars were still inchoate, they were not suited as well to the teaching of Latin as a foreign language in England. Thus new grammars had to be devised (see Law 1982 and Bayless 1993). In the early eighth century, Tatwine, archbishop of Canterbury and enigmatist (chapter 1), wrote such an elementary grammar (*Ars de partibus orationis*), as did Boniface (*Ars grammatica*), both of them taking Donatus' *Ars maior* as their basis but adapting material from other authors and various *declinationes nominum* texts for their specific purposes.[33] Indeed, Boniface's grammar is the first fully to conjugate all classes of verbs, as required by non-Romance speakers. Among Alcuin's grammatical writings is the *Ars grammatica*, containing the *Dialogus Franconis et Saxonis de octo partibus orationis*, a question-and-answer dialogue between two teenagers.[34] As Alcuin was chief architect of the scholastic reforms introduced by the Carolingian Renaissance, the main conduit for transmission of many classical texts to later times, his *Dialogus* was responsible for popularizing the *Institutiones grammaticae* and the *Partitiones* of Priscian in the Middle Ages.

One sign of the decline in Latinity after Alcuin's day is that no new grammars were devised for two centuries; and when new work does appear, it is, predictably, in the vernacular. It was Ælfric who produced the first vernacular grammar of Latin, the *Excerptiones de arte grammaticae anglice*.[35] It was supplemented by his *Glossary* and *Colloquy* for the purpose of teaching oblates in the monastery at Eynsham.

Based on the *Excerptiones de Prisciano*, it contains sections dealing with syllables, vowels, consonants, diphthongs, the eight parts of speech, and various other subjects, focusing particularly on declension, conjugation, and lexicon. Some 16 manuscripts of the *Grammar* survived the Middle Ages in whole or fragmentary form, attesting to its popularity as a pedagogical text. The *Colloquy*, intended as an aid to Latin conversation (since only Latin was to be spoken in the cloister), adapts the traditional boy-and-slave dialogue to a conversation between a schoolmaster and his pupils, who assume the role of various fictitious tradesmen and craftsmen, and it is clear that the class-glossary that Ælfric compiled (see chapter 1) is meant to be used with it.[36] One of its four extant manuscripts contains a continuous Old English gloss that is one of the more entertaining pieces of vernacular prose, combining its pedagogical purpose with glimpses of everyday life at the dawn of the eleventh century:

Master: Shepherd, do you have any work?
Shepherd: Yes, sir, I do. In the early morning I drive my sheep to their pasture, and I stand over them in heat and in cold with dogs, lest wolves devour them. And I lead them back to their fold, and I milk them twice a day, and I move their sheepfold, in addition to which I make cheese and butter, and I am faithful to my lord.
                                            (Garmonsway 1991: 21–2)

Ælfric's student, Ælfric Bata, composed two Latin colloquies, the *Colloquia*, a scholastic colloquy that illustrates monastic school life, and the *Colloquia difficiliora*, a challenging text drawing much thorny vocabulary from Aldhelm. He also composed an expanded redaction of Ælfric's *Colloquy*.[37]

Anglo-Saxons composed treatises on other of the fundamentals of the Latin curriculum, including meter, orthography, and rhetoric, all in Latin, and all from before the Viking Age. Bede and Alcuin both produced works on correct Latin spelling, both called *De orthographia*. Like Boniface, Bede also composed a treatise on metrics, *De arte metrica*, which became (along with his *De schematibus et tropis*) the primary text on Latin meter in the Middle Ages.[38] Aldhelm wrote on meter as well: much of his immense *Epistola ad Acircium*, written to the Irish-educated Aldfrith, king of Northumbria (d. 705), is devoted to scholastic matters, as it includes a treatise on Latin meter, *De metris*, an illustration of scansion, *De pedum regulis*, and his hundred *enigmata* (chapter 1), offered in demonstration of the hexametrical line.[39] Furthermore, Alcuin composed a treatise on rhetoric, *De rhetorica*, as well as a work on dialectic, a specific mode of logical argument, *De dialectica*.[40] Finally, reference may be made again to the great Abbo of Fleury, since he composed his *Quaestiones grammaticales* for his students at Ramsey when he taught there 985–7. It contains primarily instruction on the scansion of Latin verse.[41]

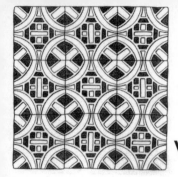

8

Wisdom Literature and Lyric Poetry

I Sententious Lore in Prose and Verse

Two Anglo-Saxon literary habits seem incomprehensible from the point of view of post-Romantic aesthetics. One is the compilation of lists. Catalogues of the feasts of the Christian year (*The Menologium*), of Germanic tribes and their rulers (*Widsith*), and of the causes of death and resting places of Christ's 12 disciples (*Fates of the Apostles*) hardly seem appropriate material for verse to those accustomed to thinking of poetry as primarily affective in purpose. The other peculiar Anglo-Saxon habit is a persistent predilection for sententious expression that, because it is universalizing, offends against the modern aversion to didacticism in a genre perceived to be devoted to personal expression. The result when these two habits combine is a body of material that has received limited critical attention because of its exceptionally high degree of alterity.

The problem, of course, is not that such works are unliterary but that we can hardly escape viewing them through a lens of internalized literary and cultural ideology. The circumstances of their composition were naturally different, and it is only in historical and cultural perspective that it is possible for moderns to gain any appreciation of them. Though apothegms (e.g. "all that glisters is not gold") were once a staple of English conversation and are still favored in many cultures (e.g. Icelandic and Chinese), our legacy from the Romantics of valuing only what is spontaneous and original has tended to devalue the use of adages, which are all reduced to the status of clichés. But it may not be too difficult to imagine a society in which the polarities were reversed and universal utterances were valued over personal expression. Especially in a setting in which books were rare and costly objects and their production was a painfully slow process, naturally the preference would have been to give their contents the broadest application and fill them with material that spoke to the greater human condition rather than to the peculiarities of individual feeling. Aphoristic literature is the natural product of such an aim, since it distills universals in their most pithy and economical form. (It is no coincidence, of course, that Alexander Pope, who, like many of his contemporaries, professed to value the universal over the particular in human experience, is perhaps best known for the aphoristic quality of his heroic couplets.) Of course book production was not the only determinant of the Anglo-Saxons' predilection for maxims and proverbs, which was apparently an inheritance from ancient times, but it is one example of the sorts of material conditions peculiar to the Middle Ages that were capable of shaping literary production.

A more direct connection can be traced between book production and literary lists. In a culture in which all literature was originally oral and the making of books was labor-intensive, writing assumed very specific functions. Primarily it was the means of transmitting literature which was in Latin and which therefore was not well suited to memorial transmission. All but a few examples of the vernacular recorded before Alfred's reign (nearly all collected in Sweet 1885) are thus somehow attached to Latin texts, as glosses or in the bounds of Latin charters. The exceptions are almost entirely lists of one kind or another, such as genealogies, regnal tables, monastic registers, and perhaps a catalogue of martyrs – just the sorts of texts better preserved on parchment than in memory. The cataloguing function of writing in the early period is perhaps nowhere better exemplified than in the glossaries compiled from the glosses employed in the school of Theodore and Hadrian at Canterbury (see chapter 1). Thus the frequency with which catalogues are found in manuscripts was enhanced not only by the material conditions of book production, dictating that books should be reserved for tasks not suited to memorial transmission, but also by traditions of manuscript compilation dating to the earliest part of the Christian era in England. In such a literary milieu it is not surprising that catalogues should have been versified, rendering them worthier of the precious space they occupied in manuscripts. The scholastic setting in which such lists were developed is in fact what leads Lerer (1991: 99–103) to identify the Exeter Book as pedagogically oriented, since he sees the manuscript as a collection of lists. That the catalogue is an unfeeling construct is wholly a modern prejudice: *Deor* illustrates perhaps better than any specimen how the aggregation of seemingly random examples can be made to produce a lyrically effective work, expressing a profound sense of loss against a sweeping background of legendary history. The paratactic nature of the catalogue form in fact suits it admirably to the aesthetic of ironic juxtaposition illustrated above under the term "contrast" (section 6 of the introduction).

The aphoristic mode pervades Old English literature, and so there is hardly a work that does not in some degree belong to the category "wisdom literature." But there is a fairly discrete body of works devoted particularly to gnomic expression, most of it in verse.[1] In its most elemental form, Old English wisdom literature amounts simply to collections of maxims or proverbs (the distinction is difficult to define),[2] and the most salient example of this type in prose is the *Distichs* (or *Dicts*) *of Cato*.[3] As a translation this work is of considerable interest, since, contrary to expectations, it is anything but literal. The translator (like the poet of the Old Icelandic *Hugvinnsmál* (ed. Finnur Jónsson 1912–15: B 2.185–210), a translation of the same text) tends to substitute native cultural values for what he finds in the Latin (see Shippey 1994a). Thus, for example, where the Latin source advises the elderly to remember what it was like to be young, the Old English translator instead urges the old to share their wisdom freely (no. 9). The *Disticha Catonis* were a fundamental text in the Latin curriculum, and it is not implausible that they should have inspired the collecting of vernacular maxims in verse (see Lapidge 1996a: 4). But surely the gnomic mode is an ancient one (as argued by Heusler 1915: 309) and was characteristic of all kinds of native verse from very early times. This is suggested by a variety of considerations: by this translator's ready substitution of native wisdom for Latin maxims; by the pervasiveness of the gnomic mode, which inspires greater or lesser passages in the entire gamut of Old English writings, from homilies to *Beowulf*, and by the similar pervasiveness of the mode in cognate traditions, particularly Old Icelandic, where we find both ancient poems that are entirely gnomic in nature (e.g. *Hávamál* (ed. Neckel and Kuhn 1983) in the poetic edda, and the late skaldic *Sólarljóð* (ed. Finnur Jónsson 1912–15: B 1.635–48), among others) and a persistent tendency to aphorism even in prose.

Another consideration that suggests the native nature of the aphoristic tradition is that in the other chief Latin-English collection, the eleventh-century *Durham Proverbs* (ed. Arngart 1981; bibliography Hollis and Wright 1992: 34–48), it is very likely the Latin text rather than the Old English that is the translation. Some of these 46 short proverbs, copied onto some blank leaves in a liturgical manuscript, are in the form of classical alliterative verse, though sometimes there is rhyme or assonance intermixed, and more often the form is simple prose. Their tone is more varied than in the poetic collections of maxims (see below), and occasionally they even reveal some humor, as with no. 11: "'Nonetheless I would not trust you though you walked well', said he who saw a witch passing along on her head" (trans. Arngart, p. 296). But the most significant aspect of the collection is no doubt its frequent echoes of lyric verse. The closest parallel is found in no. 23, which recalls *The Wanderer* 68: *Nē sceal man tō ær forht nē tō ær fægen* 'One should be neither too soon fearful nor too soon glad'.

Stray proverbs are also found scattered in Old English manuscripts (listed by Hollis and Wright 1992: 34), but the chief variety of wisdom literature in prose takes the form of unorthodox catechism. The *Prose Solomon and Saturn* (ed. and trans. Cross and Hill 1982) begins, "Here it is revealed how Saturn and Solomon contended over their wisdom," and then there follows an unadorned and random list of 59 questions and responses of the form "Tell me where God sat when he created heaven and earth. I tell you, he sat on the wings of the winds." The questions probe for knowledge of obscurities, and several take the form of riddles designed to mislead the respondent. Roughly half of them, including the example above, are either translated from or based upon questions and responses in Latin dialogues of a similar nature, including the *Ioca monachorum* 'Monks' Sports', the *Altercatio Hadriani et Epicteti*, and the *Collectanea Bedae*. A related text is the Old English *Adrian and Ritheus* (ed. and trans. Cross and Hill 1982), which contains some of the same questions, asking how long Adam was in paradise, on what day of the week he sinned, how large the sun is, why the raven is black and the sea salt, and other expressions of a preoccupation with heterodoxy and trivia. We are told nothing about the disputants: Adrian is clearly the emperor Hadrian, derived from the *Altercatio Hadriani et Epicteti*; Ritheus is unidentified.[4]

A brief text that possibly belongs to this group is *The Penitence of Jamnes and Mambres* (ed. Förster 1902), about the two Egyptian sorcerers said to have opposed Moses and Aaron (II Tim. 3.8). In two brief Latin passages with accompanying Old English translations we are told that Mambres opened the magic books of his brother and conjured him from the dead. Speaking in the first person, Jamnes then tells of the horrors of hell and how to avoid them, in a speech reminiscent of nothing so much as the close of *Solomon and Saturn I* (see below). This may be an extract from the lost apocryphon about Jannes and Jambres cited by Origen and the Roman synod of 496. The two figures were in any case well known in Anglo-Saxon England, as they are mentioned in the additions to the Old English Orosius and in Ælfric's *De auguriis*. The text, which is unnoticed by both N. Ker 1957 and the *Dictionary of Old English*, is found, along with two illustrations, immediately after *The Wonders of the East* in BL, Cotton Tiberius B. v, fol. 87r.

There are two poetic dialogues of Solomon and Saturn in a Cambridge manuscript (CCCC 422), texts that are fragmentary, metrically irregular, and textually corrupt, and thus difficult to interpret. They are almost certainly by the same author and should be dated no later than the reign of Alfred.[5] In the first, called *Solomon and Saturn I* (*ASPR* 6.31–8, of which there is another copy, a shorter fragment, written in the margin of CCCC 41: see O'Brien O'Keeffe 1990, plate v), Saturn, who counts himself master of the knowledge of the entire ancient world (references to Greece, Libya, and India standing for the three known continents: see O'Neill 1997: 143), offers 30 pounds of gold and his 12 sons if Solomon can instruct him in the mysteries of the "palm-branched" (i.e. palmary) Pater Noster – or so it seems, though the exact nature of the request is uncertain, given the state of the text. Solomon explains the powers of the prayer: it opens heaven, gladdens the saints, makes God merciful, strikes down crimes, douses the devil's flame, and kindles God's (39–42). It is doctor to the lame, light to the blind, door to the deaf, tongue to the dumb, shield of the guilty, and so forth (77–9). Near the end of the poem Solomon anatomizes each letter of the prayer, describing its virtues as a weapon against the Devil: *P* has a long rod, a golden goad, and continually scourges him; *A* follows in his track and strikes him down with overpowering might; *T* injures him and pierces his tongue, throttles him and punches his cheeks, and so forth (89–95). The prayer thus resembles a charm (M. Nelson 1990), though Hermann (1989: 32–7) perceives a closer parallel in Prudentius' *Psychomachia*, and Jonassen (1988) various other parallels, including historiated initials in human form in the Book of Kells. In the fuller manuscript each letter is supplied with a runic equivalent, although it is the letter's Latin name (e.g. *ess* rather than *sigel*) that is required by the alliteration. If each letter of the prayer were described once, the sequence would be *P A T E R N O S Q U I C L F M D G B H*, and this is not far from what we find. The poem ends with some reflections on the prayer's power against devils of whatever form, including serpents that bite cattle, fiends that pull down and gore horses in the water, and those that make a man's hand heavy in battle by carving baleful letters on his weapon. Thus one should never draw one's sword without singing the prayer.[6] There follows a prose dialogue resembling the ones described above, except that the questions and answers are exceptionally extravagant. Saturn first asks how many forms the Devil and the Pater Noster take when they engage each other in battle, and Solomon answers 30: first, the Devil takes the form of a child; second, the prayer takes the form of the Holy Spirit; third, the Devil is a dragon; fourth, the prayer is an arrow called *brahhia Dei* 'arms of God', and so forth.[7] Solomon asks about the nature of the head, heart, and banner (or apparel in general?) of the prayer, and he receives similarly fantastically detailed replies, for example that the head is gold, the hair (under one lock of which one might remain dry though all the waters of heaven drowned the earth) silver, the eyes 12,000 times brighter than all the lilies of the earth, though each petal had 12 suns and each bloom 12 moons 12,000 times brighter than the moon was before the killing of Abel. The floridity of such material is unmatched in Old English, and affinities have been drawn to haggadic forms of description (Menner 1941: 8) – though some of the exotic material of the dialogue in verse and prose is paralleled in more familiar sources, including the *Cosmographia* of Aethicus Ister (O'Brien O'Keeffe 1991a) and particularly Vercelli Homily IX and related Irish texts (Charles Wright 1993: 233–56). R. Johnson (1998) has in fact shown that the shorter version in CCCC 41 occurs among marginalia that can best be characterized as an Irish context of apotropaic preoccupations. This prose dialogue ends imperfectly where a leaf is missing from the manuscript, and after the gap we return to the poem in mid-sentence, the few remaining verses forming the conclusion of a speech by Solomon about the horrors of hell, followed by four lines to the effect that although Solomon had bested Saturn in the contest, never had the latter been happier.

Solomon and Saturn II (*ASPR* 6.38–48, trans. Shippey 1976) follows immediately in the manuscript, and it is framed from the start as a genuine debate, with the rule laid down that whoever lies or denies the truth is to lose the contest (181–2). Saturn is again portrayed as the sage of the ancient world, the Eastern lands through which he has traveled being catalogued at length (185–201, in a list reminiscent of *Widsith* 75–87). He thus speaks from the perspective of a pagan curious about Christ, and Solomon obliges him, showing how Christianity answers troubling questions about life (Menner 1941: 50). The questions, most of which are posed by Saturn, are various, dealing chiefly with natural phenomena (why snow falls, why water is restless, etc.), the workings of fate (why wealth is distributed unevenly, why twins may lead different lives, etc.), and Judgment Day (why we cannot all go to heaven, whether we can die before our appointed time, etc.), in no particular order. Some of the more arcane questions are about unfamiliar legends. Solomon asks about a land where no one may set foot, and Saturn responds that it is the source of all poisonous creatures, since there *weallende Wulf* 'wandering Wolf', friend of Nimrod, familiar to the Philistines, killed 25 dragons at dawn and was himself slain (212–24). In response to a vague question, Solomon tells of a four-headed demon of the Philistines called *vasa mortis* 'vessels of death', a legend that is clearly derived from the talmudic account of Solomon's binding of the demon Ashmedai. Such material demonstrates the poet's access to sources that are otherwise unknown in Anglo-Saxon England.[8] The poem unfortunately contains substantial lacunae, and it ends incomplete during a discussion of the good and evil spirits that attend each person. Forensic contests over arcana are also a feature of Old Icelandic poetry, most famously in the eddic *Vafþrúðnismál* (ed. Neckel and Kuhn 1983: 45–55), in which the field of combat is pagan cosmology and lore. This is a poem that is dated early by most – usually to the tenth century at the latest (see Einar Ól. Sveinsson 1962: 269–70) – and clearly the material of the poem, at least, is ancient, though whether the form is of any real antiquity cannot be determined. It does seem likelier, though, that the form in Old English and Old Icelandic should be derived from Latin models.

Of a similar kind is the brief poetic dialogue in the Exeter Book called *Pharaoh* (*ASPR* 3.223). One speaker asks how great Pharaoh's army was in pursuit of the Israelites, and the other replies that although he is not certain, he supposes there were 600 chariots. Trahern (1970) has pointed out that the poem bears a certain affinity to one version of the *Ioca monachorum*, in which the question is posed how many the Egyptians were who pursued the Israelites, and the answer (1,800) depends upon one's knowing that there were 600 chariots (Ex. 14.7) and three men in each (according to the canticles in the Roman Psalter). One of the two damaged places in the text, Trahern suggests, may actually have provided the reader with the ability to divine the correct answer by referring to three-man chariots. Though the form is reminiscent of the dialogues discussed above, there is no particular reason to think that *Pharaoh* is extracted from a longer vernacular work (see Whitbread 1946).

Another poetic variety of wisdom literature – one more directly comparable to lyrics like *The Seafarer* – is the proverbial or gnomic type: the reader is offered a series of didactic generalizations that may be understood either literally (e.g. "a blind person must do without his eyes") or metaphorically (e.g. "a fallen tree grows least"). Typically subject and predicate of a gnome are balanced across the verb *sceal* 'shall, ought to, is accustomed to' or *biþ* 'will be, habitually is'.[9] In the Exeter Book there is such a collection, referred to as *Maxims I* (*ASPR* 3.156–63), though whether it is one poem or three is unclear: the small capitals marking divisions in the manuscript are such as are used equally to delimit poems and to mark sectional divisions within poetic works (see Jackson 2000:183–4). Part A (1–136) bears a certain affinity to the dialogues described above, as at the start the speaker invites questions and urges his opposite not to conceal his own thoughts, since "wise people ought to exchange sayings" (4). The content of the gnomes ranges widely, from theology ('God is eternal for us' (8)) to natural and moral philosophy (without disease the human race would multiply endlessly (33–4)) to political economy (a king hates those who claim land and is well disposed to those who give him more 5(9–60)). There is also a salient admixture of simple natural observation (a storm often brings the ocean to a furious state, 51–2). Although it is often difficult to perceive the connection of one idea to the next, usually there is some measure of conceptual relatedness; yet the relations among ideas are loose, and there is nothing like a perceivable organizing plan.[10] Still, the three sections differ in tone and attitude: Parts B and C, for example, evince a "hard materialism" in their attitude toward wealth, food, and friends (Shippey 1976: 16–17). Part B (71–137) is more human in scope than A, speaking less of timeless universals than of people going about their daily activities, for good or ill. Particularly vivid is what the poet has to say about what befits women: the noblewoman's duties (81–92) were described above (section 2 of the introduction); a Frisian woman is said to be pleased at her husband's return from the sea, washing his clothes and granting him what his love demands (94–9); women are often defamed, and though some are true, some are "curious" when their man is away (100–2); and a noblewoman ought to wear jewels (126).[11] In this section, too, the remark that sin is the way of heathens prompts the observation that "Woden made idols; the Almighty [made] glory" (132), one of the few direct references to Woden in Old English. Part C (138–204) is the most military and masculine in spirit, speaking of acquiring fame, running with wolves, binding wounds, singing and playing the harp, hunting boars, sleeping in an armed troop, rowing against the wind, and having one's weapons ever ready. The meter of *Maxims I*, it should be said, is remarkable in that more than a third of the verses are hypermetric – a device that, in some other works, seems to have been used to lend particular gravity and dignity to a passage – though quite a few are of varieties that are rare or not encountered elsewhere in verse (Russom 1987: 100). The much shorter *Maxims II* (*ASPR* 6.55–7), in another manuscript (BL Cotton Tiberius B. i), is similar in meter and content. Its syntax is less varied, but the effect of so many short aphorisms making use of *sceal* is to produce a sense of the inevitability and rightness of all of God's creation, especially as the poem ranges over its whole extent, treating of the elements, the beasts of air, earth, and sea, and human society. The society portrayed is a heroic one, in which a king should share out rings, a warrior must have both courage and good weapons, and a dragon hoards treasure in its lair. Again the poet takes an interest in women's sexual mores, remarking, "A woman or a girl secretly seeks out her lover if she does not wish that a bride-price be paid for her in public with rings" (44–6) – a remark that Deskis (1994) argues is ironic in intent. Like *The Seafarer* and *The Wanderer*, and like Part B of *Maxims I*, the poem ends with a reminder of Judgment Day and of God in his heavenly realm – a method of closure that is common enough to merit a name, *anagogic*, as it will be called here.[12] Thus the poem assumes a recognizable structure, surveying what is natural or right in this world before leading to the next. It may be the way the poem ranges over all of creation and from the present day to Judgment Day that was thought to make it suitable for inclusion in a manuscript of the Chronicle, a work of similarly broad historical scope.

In addition there are aphorisms scattered amongst the contents of Old English manuscripts (itemized by N. Ker 1957: 545). Those in verse are the following. In blank spaces at the beginning and end of texts in two manuscripts are two rhyming maxims in Latin about mutability, with verse translations, one of which also rhymes (*ASPR* 6.109). Trahern (1982) identifies a proverb, translated from the metrical fables of Phaedrus, in two nearly perfect alliterative lines in the homily *De descensu Christi ad inferos* 'The Descent of Christ to Hell': "He who unjustly violates another's goods often thereby loses his own." The so-called *Proverb from Winfrid's Time* (*ASPR* 6.57, better considered a maxim, as its significance is literal rather than metaphorical) is found in a Latin letter (ed. Tangl 1916: 283–4) by an anonymous monk. Dated to the period 757–86, the letter is found among those of Boniface (Wynfrith: see section 4 of the introduction), and in it the writer advises his correspondent to persevere in his course of action and remember the Saxon saying, "The sluggard often delays in regard to glory, to every successful venture, and thus dies alone." The poem is written in Continental orthography, but the dialect is probably eighth-century West Saxon, given the form *daedlata* (on *foreldit*, see A. Campbell 1959: 79 n. 4). Aphoristic also is *Bede's Death Song* (*ASPR* 6.107–8), which was probably composed by Bede shortly before his death on May 26, 735, though possibly he merely recited it from memory (as argued by Bulst 1938). Medieval copies (15 of them in the early Northumbrian dialect) are known to be preserved in 35 manuscripts of the *Epistola Cuthberti de obitu Bedae* 'Letter of Cuthbert on the Death of Bede', by a disciple of Bede who was later abbot of Monkwearmouth and Jarrow.[13] Given the wealth of manuscripts from both England and the Continent, the letter clearly was an enormously popular work. For all its brevity, the song is a poignant expression of humility by the greatest scholar of the age, remarking simply that all the intellect one requires in preparation for the afterlife is the ability to consider how one's soul will be judged.

The poem *Precepts* (*ASPR* 3.140–3, trans. Shippey 1976: 49–53), or *A Father's Instructions to His Son*, which immediately precedes *The Seafarer* in the Exeter Book, belongs to a slightly different variety of wisdom literature, as it does not aim to capture universal truths about the natural and the human worlds. Rather it is expressly prescriptive, taking the form of an elderly father's ten brief lectures to his child on how to behave decently. Howe (1985: 145-51) has subjected the poem's structure to a penetrating analysis and concluded that the precepts are arranged to apply progressively to three stages of life: youth, maturity, and old age. The decalogic form is perhaps inspired by the Ten Commandments, though just one injunction (love your father and mother (9)) bears any specific resemblance to them. In tone the poem seems more akin to the Book of Proverbs. Much of the advice is quite general (do right, do not do wrong, distinguish good and evil, be wise), and even the more specific precepts are fairly timeless (mind your elders, do not cheat your friends, keep your temper). The most remarkable prescription is to escape romantic entanglements, a directive that elicits some unexampled warmth: like drunkenness and lies, the love of a woman is to be avoided, for one who enters a woman's affections may expect to depart them disgraced. In such is to be anticipated only sin, despicable shame, God's enduring displeasure, and a drowning flood of arrogance (34–41). This smacks of the misogyny, some of it quite virulent, of the monastic Latin literature of the day, and thus there is some justification for McEntire's reconstruction of a monastic context for the poem (1990).

The Order of the World (*ASPR* 3.163–6, trans. with some liberties by Huppé 1970: 29–33), sometimes called *The Wonders of Creation*, begins in the by now familiar dialogic mode, inviting a "ready hero" (the reader?) to question a "wise seer" about God's creation (1–22). The central portion of the seer's lesson (38–81) – called by the speaker a *herespel* 'eulogy' and concerned chiefly with the sun's glorious passage across the sky and under the earth – in its wide-eyed admiration of God's handiwork seems to have been inspired by Psalm 18.2–7. Yet it is not so much a rendering as an original meditation with the psalm as its point of departure (Wehlau 1997: 35–41). The psalm in any case is an unsurprising source if wisdom poetry is to be seen as the product of a monastic way of life, in which recitation of the Psalms played a fundamental role (see section 4 of the introduction). That the psalm inspired the poem explains why the speaker places the wisdom of men of old in a musical context (8–16) – an explanation that, given the poem's focus on the Creator's majesty, seems a likelier one than that the poem is a celebration of the visionary power of traditional native verse (as argued by DiNapoli 1998a; see also Jager 1990). Despite the probable source, the poem seems squarely at home in the genre of wisdom literature rather than biblical poetry (or allegory, according to Conner 1993a: 152, 158): it has many of the familiar conventions, including the invitation to dialogue, reverence for the wisdom of old, and a controlling theme of the wonder of God's handwork – the very essence of wisdom literature, in the view of Hansen (1988: 81). Yet it also bears affinities in structure to lyrics like *The Wanderer* and *The Seafarer* in that its anagogic close is particularly well developed: the glory of God's creation naturally enough leads to the vision of heaven (90–7), which in turn introduces the closing exhortation (but with gnomic *scyle* rather than homiletic *uton*) to leave the idle pleasures and fleeting joys of this life in order to merit "that better realm."

The Gifts of Men (*ASPR* 3.137–40), which follows *The Wanderer* in the Exeter Book, is also an elaboration of a biblical theme, recurrent in the Pauline epistles (chiefly at I Cor. 7.7 and 12.4–10), that God's gifts to humankind are various. The greater part of the poem is a catalogue of human abilities and qualities, structured by the repetition of *sum* 'one': one person is strong, one attractive, one loquacious, one a hunter, one a warrior, and so forth, all with a decidedly male slant. The larger point is that God's gifts are distributed widely rather than concentrated in a few individuals, and thus although one may lack wealth, strength, or some particular talent, there is always compensation of some sort. In general the catalogue is unordered, though Howe (1985: 114) has pointed out that it culminates in a series of traits – piety, valor in the struggle against the devil, skill in liturgy, and devotion to books – that might best be characterized as monastic. In the ensuing final verses, humankind is then portrayed as God's *comitatus*. Thus in the contemplation of the matter of the poem we are led to something of an anagogic conclusion, much as in *Maxims II, The Wanderer, The Seafarer,* and other lyrics. The theme of the variety of God's gifts is a commonplace of Old English verse, occurring also in *Christ II* 659–91 and *The Panther* 70–4. The theme was possibly popularized in England by familiarity with Gregory's *Homiliae in evangelia* IX and XXIX,[14] the former homily, on the parable of the talents, having been used by Ælfric for his sermon *In natale unius confessoris* (see Cross 1962). The latter Gregorian homily contains a brief passage generally thought to be the primary inspiration: "He gave gifts to men, because after sending the Spirit from above he gave to one the utterance of wisdom, to another utterance of knowledge, to another the gift of virtue, to another the gift of healing, to another various tongues, to another the interpretation of utterances. He gave gifts to men" (trans. Hurst 1990: 233). Short (1976), however, perceives a different source in the Alfredian *Pastoral Care. The Gifts of Men* is obviously far in tone and intent from the Solomon and Saturn dialogues, yet it has much in common with *Maxims I* and *II* in its focus on the diversity and justness of God's works, and particularly in its sententious itemizing of familiar knowledge.

This anaphoric *sum* is a rhetorical construct encountered at several places in Old English verse, including a brief passage in *The Wanderer* (80–4), and there is another entire poem predicated on the device in the Exeter Book, *The Fortunes of Men* (*ASPR* 3.154–6), for which no very specific Latin source has yet been identified. A significant portion of the poem is in fact a reiteration of the theme of *The Gifts of Men,* detailing the multiplicity of human talents (64–92). But the greater part (10–63) is a catalogue of misfortunes, illustrating the variety of ways that men may meet their end: through famine, warfare, or falling from a tree, on the gallows or the pyre, or in a beer brawl – though the list includes some non-lethal misfortunes: blindness, lameness, and friendless exile. It is the beginning of the poem that is of greatest lyric interest. A man and a woman are imagined raising their child (or children – it is ambiguous), clothing and educating him, lovingly, until he reaches maturity. But God alone knows what the years will bring to him as he grows. To one it happens that his end will befall him in his youth: a wolf will devour him and his mother will mourn. It is not within human power to prevent such events (1–14). One cannot help feeling that the pathos of the parents' sad misfortune was the inspiration for the poem, since the morbid collection of untimely ends seems insufficient motive. Yet some more purposeful control over the design is evidenced by the final fortune mentioned: one shall expend all his misfortunes in his youth and live to enjoy wealth and the mead cup in his family's embrace (58–63). Thus Howe (1985: 115–32) may be right that the poem reenacts the process of finding one's way to God – again evincing a final anagogic impulse.

Finally, *The Rune Poem* (*ASPR* 6.28–30, trans. Shippey 1976: 81–5) is perhaps both the least typical example of wisdom literature and at the same time the specimen with the strongest claim to membership in the group, since it concurrently transmits two types of lore: the meaning of the runes that make up the *futhorc* and the apothegms that form each stanza and illustrate that meaning.[15] The third strophe is typical: "*Þorn* 'thorn' is quite sharp, harmful for any thane to grasp, immensely cruel to anyone who lies among them." The sequence is of course governed by the order of the runic alphabet, yet the order of the final two runes has been reversed (Elliott 1989: 69). The likeliest explanation is that *ēar*, here with the meaning 'gravel, mud, earth' (Smith 1956: 1.143–4), furnished a better sense of closure, enabling an eschatological ending with a strophe on the horrors of the grave (see Page 1999). The manuscript (BL, Cotton Otho B. x) was almost entirely destroyed in the Cottonian fire of 1731, and so the poem is preserved only in the 1705 edition of George Hickes (reproduced by Halsall 1981: 84) – an edition that leaves some questions as to the poem's original form, because Hickes, an enthusiast of runes, probably added the rune names and the roman values of the staves, if he did not tamper with the text in more thoroughgoing ways.

The poem is also of some importance to determining the antiquity of the sententious mode, since it has three close parallels in Scandinavian and Continental literature (all ed. Halsall 1981). That the rune poem type (though not the poem in its present form: see Niles 1991a: 135–6) is ancient is argued by the nature of some of the lore: the second rune, *ūr* 'aurochs', refers to a beast that survived only in woodland areas of the Continent in Anglo-Saxon times; and the fourth rune, *ōs,* though it has been given the meaning of Latin *ōs* 'mouth', corresponds to *áss* 'pagan god' in the Old Icelandic *Rune Poem* – even if, as Clunies Ross (1990) argues, this is an antiquarianism in the Icelandic poem – and this is the meaning that the rune's name must originally have had, given its etymology. So also the seventeenth rune should be *tīr* 'victory', the usual name assigned to it in Old English; yet the accompanying strophe seems to assume the name *Tīw*, that of the Germanic god of war, to whom this rune refers in all three cognate poems – meaning that the Old English poem seems to preserve lore older than the late Old English form of the *futhorc* itself. It is thus easier to believe that the poetic type – though little of the specific lore except for the rune names themselves – reflects a form inherited from Germanic antiquity than to believe the most recent editor's conclusion that the four Germanic rune poems are entirely independent developments (Halsall 1981: 33–45). A considerable tradition is also suggested by the formulaic nature of the composition (see Acker 1998: 35–60).

2 Lyric Poetry

The history of critical approaches to *The Wanderer* and *The Seafarer* (*ASPR* 3.134–7, 143–7) is a microcosm of the development of critical trends in Europe and America. The philological methods that informed late nineteenth-century textual analysis were strongly influenced by the dominant model of linguistic study, a historical one designed to trace language origins. Especially but by no means exclusively in German scholarship, literary practitioners sought in the records of Old English a cultural state to correspond to the Germanic protolanguage reconstructed by philologists. To find this lost state it was felt necessary to strip away the accretions of Mediterranean learning to discover the remains of the literature of the early Germanic peoples before it was altered by foreign influences (see Frantzen 1990). Clearly, then, much more is at stake in the use of the terms "Christian" and "pagan" than the religious beliefs of the *scopas*, since the latter term signifies a complex of imagined cultural features independent of pagan theology.

To this way of thinking, *The Seafarer* seemed a prime example of the result of Christianization. The world of the poem corresponds in significant ways to the culture imputed to the pagans of Tacitus' *Germania* (section 1 of the introduction, above), since the speaker leads a hard life of seafaring, speaks of burying gold with the dead, and seems to manifest such a resignation to fate as is encountered in a genuinely heroic composition like *Beowulf*.[16] In length, too, it is comparable to the poems of the poetic edda, and so it seemed to confirm the assumption that Germanic literature before the advent of Christianity took the form of lays. The fact that the poem's most explicitly devotional content is concentrated in the concluding section (103–24) appeared to accord with the assumption that the poem's Christian elements are later accretions to an earlier, more primitive composition, and in fact in editions even of the second half of the twentieth century these lines were sometimes omitted or segregated from the rest.

Such a view of the poem could hardly persist long after the rise of the New Criticism (or Practical Criticism, as it is called in Britain). The literary formalism that arose in the course of the last century valued integrative qualities like balance, symmetry, unity of design, and structural elegance – qualities incompatible with an analysis that segregates Christian and pre-Christian elements. Moreover, whatever its conceptual limitations, the chief practical obstacle to such an anatomizing approach is that mention of burying gold with the dead is the only feature of the poem that is specifically pre-Christian in nature – and the speaker, rather than endorsing the practice, speaks of its futility. The speaker's sentiments throughout the poem, moreover, not just in the concluding lines, are wholly consonant with Christian belief. Ultimately recognizing the tenuousness of the poem's connection to the world of Tacitus' *Germania*, as the critical climate changed, scholarship grew receptive to the attempt of Whitelock (1950) to construct a different historical context, viewing the speaker as a *peregrinus pro amore Dei*, a religious person in pursuit of self-imposed exile for the purpose of mortifying the flesh to merit reward in the next life. For this she offered the evidence of recorded cases of Anglo-Saxon pilgrimage; and literary models in the writings of Celtic ascetics have been adduced in support (Ireland 1991). Her purpose was thus to promote a literal reading of the poem, and she expressly discouraged allegorical interpretation.

Allegory, however, is difficult not to perceive. The word *lǣne* in the speaker's reference to *þis dēade līf, lǣne on lande* 'this dead life, fleeting on land' (65–6) makes little sense if, in the spirit of the closing section, the speaker is not presenting seafaring as a symbolic representation of the rigors and the rewards of a life devoted to the spirit. So, too, the poem seems a much flatter and less interesting thing if the "lord" who lays plans for him (43), and whose joys are "hotter" than "this dead life" (64–5), is understood to refer to one thing only. Accordingly, the school of allegorical and exegetical criticism that flourished after the middle of the century strove to illuminate the poem by identifying its sources in patristic thought.[17] Such so-called historical criticism is no doubt a more plausible approach to *The Seafarer*. Yet studies of this sort tend to evince a common set of shortcomings. Sources tend to be overdetermined, so that even the most commonplace sentiments must be assigned a specific source in the patrology. As a result, works like *The Seafarer* assume a fragmented quality, drawing on so many different Latin texts and taking so many of the Church Fathers' ideas out of context that the poems begin to lose any recognizable shape, and the poets seem at once deeply learned and woefully distracted.[18]

The chief obstacle to effective "historical" criticism, though, is that even when we know for certain that a poetic text renders a particular Latin source, the result is invariably more paraphrase than translation. As a consequence, in most cases it is extremely difficult to prove the derivation of a lone idea from the patrology. Thus when Smithers (1957–9: 2.1–4) culls passages from Cyprian, the *Glossa ordinaria*, Origen, and others associating exile with seafaring, most readers will probably feel that as an explanation for the association of the two ideas in *The Seafarer* this is rather straining at gnats. The point is not that the influence of patristic writings is not strong in some of these lyrics, but that it is diffuse, and filtered through homiletic and other traditions in the vernacular.

The Seafarer is one of a group of poems commonly referred to as "elegies" – not in the sense of the word as it is applied to Classical or later English verse, but to lyric compositions of a type peculiar to Old English. Greenfield's definition of elegy is the most widely appealed to: it is "a relatively short reflective or dramatic poem embodying a contrasting pattern of loss and consolation, ostensibly based upon a specific personal experience or observation, and expressing an attitude towards that experience" (1966: 143). Yet several other definitions have been offered, and this fact, along with the concurrent complexity and vagueness of Greenfield's, which combines considerations of length, structure, content, narrative perspective, and affect in an attempt to accommodate all the short poems that interest modern scholars most, invites skepticism about the validity of the concept. Moreover, the number of elegies in Old English ranges widely in different estimates, from 2 (Timmer 1942: 40) to 14 or more in the view of those who would make elegy a mode rather than a genre by including elegiac passages in longer works, such as the lament of the last survivor (2247–66) and the father's lament for his hanged son (2444–62) in *Beowulf,* and the messenger's (Beccel's) announcement at the close of *Guthlac B.* Naturally the definition and membership of the class are not independent issues. But most would regard *The Wanderer, The Seafarer, The Ruin, The Wife's Lament, Deor, Wulf and Eadwacer, The Husband's Message,* and *Resignation B* as elegies. Greenfield himself regarded elegy as a genre only "by force of our present, rather than determinate historical, perspective" (1972: 135). Indeed, there is no close parallel to such anonymous laments on usually unidentifiable events in the earliest records of other Germanic languages;[19] and given the difficulties that attend delimiting and defining the genre, it is hardly plausible that Anglo-Saxon poets should have had any such concept.[20] Accordingly, most seem to agree with Greenfield, and retain the concept only on the ground that "elegy" remains a useful term in discussing this body of works. Klinck, for example, feels the concept sufficiently justified because it "provides us with a convenient locus for particular themes: exile, loss of loved ones, scenes of desolation, the transience of worldly joys" (1992: 11).

Yet these themes pervade Old English verse – they are all present in *Beowulf,* for example – and so what needs to be recognized is that the term is convenient only because it reinforces generic preconceptions. Elegy as a compositional class is a projection of the sensibilities of the Romantic Age back onto the early Middle Ages, and indeed it is as early as 1826 that we find reference to Old English "compositions of an elegiac character" (W. D. Conybeare in Conybeare 1826: 244). Victorians of a Romantic disposition saw mirrored in these works their own tendency to melancholic introversion and awe of nature mixed with a Keatsian awareness of mutability. Regarding these poems as a recognizable group only serves the purpose of seeming to justify the lavish critical attention bestowed upon them, to the neglect of many other poems mixed together with them in the Exeter Book. Yet the critical preoccupation with them is predicated on the modern preference, inherited from the Romantics, for poetry that takes the form of lyric self-expression. To privilege and highlight the self-expressive elements of these poems is probably to misconstrue them, since the lyric speakers in them are generally anonymous, and little attempt is made to individualize them.

Moreover, the features that bind the group together are often less striking than the features that bind each of them to poems outside the group. *The Wanderer*, for example, has relatively little in common with *The Husband's Message*, while it has a great deal in common with *Dream of the Rood* in both form and content: in each, a narrator identifies and introduces the main speaker, who relates his personal experience of hardship, from which he has derived wisdom evidenced by aphoristic pronouncements; and finally the narrator returns to relate this wisdom to the injunction to fix one's gaze on the life to come. What excludes *Dream of the Rood* from the elegiac group, of course, is that it is a story of the Crucifixion. The category "elegy" thus tacitly seems to require secularity – a category that surely would have made little sense in the monastic contexts in which the poetic manuscripts were compiled, but which accords with the Romantic distinction between Christian and pre-Christian compositions. Likewise *The Riming Poem* is not often included among the elegies, yet as a narrative of personal experience – of prosperity turned to loss, leading in Boethian manner to awareness – it would seem to be closely related to *The Wanderer* and *The Seafarer*. The chief difference is that it strikes most as a clumsy composition, suggesting that aesthetics play a covert role in defining the elegies. Accordingly, we believe the term "elegy" contributes to ahistorical and ethnocentric misconceptions about these poems, and we prefer to avoid it. In referring to the poems examined in this section as "lyrics" we do not intend to imply any commonality among them other than the subjectivity imposed by their lyric speakers – a feature that certainly is not exclusive to this group. This is rather a negative grouping: it is what remains when all the other poetic categories (biblical, liturgical, heroic, catalogic, etc.) are abstracted from the corpus. Indeed, poetic types are so intermixed in these compositions that to attempt to define the category on a principled basis would be fruitless and misleading.

The closest affinities of *The Seafarer* may be to wisdom literature, as argued by Shippey (1972: 67–8, 1994b). A good deal of the poem is sapiential in tone, though maxims are particularly concentrated in a catalogue near the end (103–16), where the clauses are all of the gnomic *biþ* and *sceal* type, and some have close analogues in other wisdom poetry (to 106 and 109 cf. *Maxims I* 35 and 50, respectively). More important, these gnomes are in no way incidental but are essential to the poem's meaning, since they are offered as palpable evidence of the wisdom that the Seafarer has acquired from his experience of hardships. They thus serve to justify his trials, and so they address an issue that seems to have been a particular preoccupation of the Viking Age – witness Alfred's translation of Boethius – why the good should be made to suffer.

Yet the parallels that seem most striking are to homiletic prose. The Seafarer remarks the passing of kings and emperors and their glory, and he says that earthly glory grows old just as every mortal does (81–90). This theme of the decay of the world (on which see Cross 1963 and Trahern 1991: 165–8) resembles a familiar homiletic one reworked in several related texts (see particularly Cross 1956), of which one, *Be rihtan cristendome* 'True Christianity' may be cited:

> Though emperors and powerful kings or any other exalted persons have monuments of marble made for them and decorated with lustrous gold, still death scatters it all. Then the ornaments will be melted down, the splendor shattered, the gold stripped away, the gems vanished, and the bodies corrupted and turned to dust. Thus the beauty and riches of this world are as nothing: they are transitory and fleeting, just as powerful persons are in this world. (ed. Napier 1883: 148)

The rhetoric of the poem, too, is homiletic, for the gnomic catalogue and the poem itself are closed by a passage typical of homiletic endings, starting with an exhortation and leading to an anagogic conclusion: "Let us consider where we have our home, and then think how we may get there, and then also endeavor to come into that eternal felicity where life – joy in heaven – is comprehended in the love of the Lord. Thanks be to Holy God, Prince of Glory, Eternal Lord, for exalting us for all time" (117–24). The word "Amen" has even been added to this in the Exeter Book, though it is not part of the poem, as shown by the meter. Compare the fairly typical close of the homily cited above:

> Let us do what we have great need to do, love God Almighty and faithfully observe his behests. Then we shall merit eternal joy in the kingdom of heaven with the Lord himself, who lives and reigns for ever and ever. Amen. (p. 152)

It is probably vain, however, to search for a specific source for the ideas of the poem, as so many of them are commonplaces. Rather, their resemblance to ideas in general circulation serves to demonstrate how deeply imbued the poem is with the intellectual temper of late Anglo-Saxon monastic life.

The text of *The Seafarer* is notably corrupt, and in a few places (especially 68–9, 97–9, and 111–15) the meaning must be conjectured.

The instability of the text is heightened by the observation that one or more quires may be missing from the manuscript between lines 102 and 103 – which would mean that the catalogue of maxims and the homiletic conclusion belong to a different poem (see Dunning and Bliss 1969: 2–3 and Pope 1978: 32–4, among others). This would explain the sudden shift to the gnomic mode and hypermetric form; but the assumption is by no means necessary, since the transition is smooth enough in syntax and sense, and the theme of the fear of God that is taken up in 103 is anticipated in 100–2: "Gold cannot preserve the soul that is full of sin from the fear of God, when he has stashed it away while he lives here."

Another sudden transition, at line 33, has been the basis for conflicting interpretations of the poem's structure. The Seafarer has been narrating the hardships of life at sea, when unexpectedly he reveals a different view of his situation: "Truly (*forþon*), the thoughts of my heart compel that I myself (*sylf*) make trial of the deep sea currents, the tossing of salt waves. At every moment my mind's desire urges my spirit to depart, to seek out the home of foreigners far from here." The unanticipated yearning for seafaring, so at odds with the speaker's complaint of loneliness and exposure to the elements at sea, along with the emphasis on *sylf* and the uncertain import of *forþon* (usually meaning 'therefore' or 'because'), led Pope (1965) to revive the view of Rieger (1869) and others that the poem is a dramatic exchange between an old seafarer and a young, the change of speakers occurring at this point. Though Pope's view gained adherents and is still advocated now and then in the current literature, he subsequently repudiated it (1974), in large part as a result of reconsidering and adopting the view of Whitelock that the speaker is a religious exile (noted above). The unusual meaning of *forþon* and the peculiar use of *sylf* remain troubling problems (see Jacobs 1989), but most now regard the poem's structure as sufficiently coherent without recourse to a dialogic reading.[21]

The construction of "elegy" as an Old English poetic type no doubt owes much to the close similarity of *The Seafarer* to *The Wanderer*, suggesting a genre of sorts – though this may be a simple case of direct influence. Their structures and themes are analogous, presenting a personal narrative of harsh experience away from home and family, from which is derived wisdom in gnomic form that amounts primarily to recognition of the evanescence of earthly things and the need to fix one's view on the hereafter. *The Wanderer* even shares some of the other poem's interpretive problems, with its frequent use of *forþon* in an ambiguous sense and uncertainties about speech boundaries: certainly lines 6–7 are spoken by a narrator who introduces the Wanderer and who returns in line 111; but who speaks lines 1–5 and 112–15, and whether lines 92–110 are delivered by the Wanderer himself or by a hypothetical speaker imagined by him, is by no means certain (see Leslie 1985: 2, 21 and Richman 1982). Such ambiguities suggested to Pope and others that *The Wanderer*, like *The Seafarer*, was a dialogue,[22] though its structure is now generally seen instead as an "envelope pattern" (Bjork 1989) representing a process of *Bildung* in which the speaker evolves from an *eardstapa* 'wanderer' (6), a shiftless plaything of fortune, to one who is *snottor* 'wise' (111). (Because the complete clause is *Swā cwæð snottor on mōde*, lit. 'Thus spoke the one wise in mind', some studies refer to him as 'wise in spirit', though now it has been shown that 'in mind' almost certainly goes instead with the verb, indicating that he has been speaking to himself – as suggested also by *sundor æt rūne*, probably 'apart in private' (111): see Richman 1982 (but cf. Clemoes 1995: 406 n. 122). Thus the Wanderer does not violate his own dictum that a man ought to keep complaints to himself (11–18).)

Yet the poem presents its own problems of interpretation, as well, which are chiefly syntactic. It is frequently impossible to tell whether clauses are dependent or independent, especially those beginning with *þonne*, which may mean either 'when' or 'then'.[23] Syntactic ambiguity combines with obscurity of reference in a particularly poignant passage (49–57) in which, although the details are uncertain, memories of family seem to assume the vividness of present companions, appearing so real that the speaker attempts to greet them, only to see them swim away – perhaps with the suggestion that in his dreamlike state the speaker has superimposed these memories on the indifferent sea birds that he has seen just previously upon waking from a reverie about reunion with his lord (45–8).[24] Much of the appeal of this passage stems no doubt from its very ambiguity of reference, demonstrating that while indeterminacy of meaning is a quality that recent critical theory has striven hard to uncover in modern texts, it is a quality everywhere obvious in Old English literature, which has long discouraged critical closure and instead promoted multivalence in interpretation.

The Wanderer also differs from *The Seafarer* in that it offers no hint that the speaker's trials are to be understood typologically or as colored by a theme of repentance. Thus allegorical and penitential readings have met with little approval.[25] But perhaps the chief difference between the two poems is the more patterned rhetoric of *The Wanderer*, with its many examples of anaphora. Aphoristic clauses are condensed to single verses, with gnomic *sceal* understood in each, in a series of negative parallels: "A wise man must be patient and must never be too hot-hearted, nor too word-hasty, nor too hesitant in war, nor too reckless, nor too frightened, nor too glad, nor too money-hungry, nor ever too forward in committing himself before he knows for sure" (65–9; cf. *The Phoenix* 14–18, 51–61, 134–8, 611–14; *Juliana* 590–2; Riddle 22.13–17, etc.). The rhetorical *sum* pattern of *The Gifts of Men* and *The Fortunes of Men* (as above) shapes a passage that recalls the "beasts of battle" device of heroic poetry (see section 6 of the introduction): "The proud war troop all fell by the parapet. War bore away some, put them on their way forth; one a bird carried off over the deep sea; one the grey wolf handed over to death; one a sad-faced man buried in earth" (79–84). Most strikingly the poem exemplifies the *Ubi sunt* ('Where are?') topos derived from late Latin antiquity:[26] "What has become of the horse? What has become of the young man? What has become of the treasure-giver? What has become of the places at the feast? What has become of good times in the mead hall? Oh, for the shining beaker! Oh, for the chain-mailed warrior! Oh, for the prince's majesty! How that time has departed, faded into night, as if it had never been" (92–6). This passage obviously has much in common with the homiletic one cited above, which in fact is immediately followed in its several versions by an analogous *Ubi sunt* topos:

> Where are the powerful emperors and kings who were long ago? Where are their lieutenants and their proud and mighty stewards, who fixed their laws and decrees? Where are the judges' courts? Where is their arrogance and their pomp and pride, but covered in earth and reduced to misery? What has become of this world's wealth? What has become of this earth's beauty? What has become of those who worked hardest to acquire goods and left them all in turn to others? (ed. Napier 1883: 148–9)

The final anaphora in the poem closes the speech in 92–110: "Here livestock [i.e. wealth] is fleeting, here a friend is fleeting, here a person is fleeting, here a kinsman is fleeting, and this entire frame of earth will grow empty." The closest parallel is not Latin but Norse, occurring at *Hávamál* 76.1–3 (ed. Neckel and Kuhn 1983): "Livestock die, kinsmen die, likewise you die yourself." The threesome of goods, friends, and kin, it may be noted, is still deserting Everyman in the late fifteenth century.

There is little critical agreement about the generic sources of lyrics like *The Seafarer* and *The Wanderer*. Because of the reaction against Germanist criticism since the Second World War, there is currently little discussion of possible genetic relations to *Lieder* in other early Germanic languages (see note 19). In any case, the differences are considerable, as the speakers in these lyrics are anonymous and divorced from heroic legend, and the influence of homiletic literature and Latin rhetoric is strong. There are notable parallels between some Old English lyrics and early Welsh poems that combine personal lament with nature description and aphorisms; and the use of the cuckoo as a harbinger of sorrow in *The Seafarer* and *The Husband's Message* in particular (the bird is usually a welcome one, since it presages summer) is paralleled only in Welsh (I. Gordon 1960: 15–18, Henry 1966, Jacobs 1990, Higley 1993). Yet the differences are also considerable, and the conduit for Welsh influence on such compositions remains to be identified convincingly. This is not an obstacle, however, in regard to Latin works by provincial poets of the fourth through sixth centuries, which were known in England, and some of which bear remarkable affinities to *The Seafarer*, treating "(i) the passing and failing of this world, as of every man's life, day by day; (ii) the brevity of earthly prosperity and well-being; (iii) the unknown day of death; (iv) the transitoriness of the power of kings and leaders; (v) the miseries of old age, with a description of the failings of the flesh; (vi) the uselessness of gold beyond the grave" (I. Gordon 1960: 23). Poetic works of the Carolingian Renaissance have also been suggested as analogues or models (Lapidge 1986a: 23, Conner 1993a: 158), and certainly the monastic curriculum in Latin in the later period included Carolingian Latin poets (Lendinara 1991: 276). Alcuin's lament on the sack of Lindisfarne (ed. and trans. Godman 1985; also ed. Dümmler 1881: 229–35 and trans. Calder and Allen 1976: 141–6), for example, includes most of the themes just listed. Boethius has been perceived repeatedly as inspiration or even a direct source for some of the motifs of *The Wanderer*, especially in its attempt to assure those who suffer hardship that the things of this world are illusory.[27] It seems significant, though, that all the parallels cited above are to the sapiential and homiletic portions of *The Seafarer* and *The Wanderer* – the portions that are least personal in nature, and most universal in thought and application – and that no convincing close antecedent analogue to their accounts of personal hardship has been identified.

A lengthy contemplation of ruined buildings (73–91), the "ancient work of giants" (87), is what occasions the *Ubi sunt* lament for the mortal condition in *The Wanderer*. So, too, the city in desuetude described in *The Ruin* (*ASPR* 3.227–9) is the "work of giants" (2) – the poet is undoubtedly describing Roman ruins, as relatively few Anglo-Saxon buildings were of stone – though it leads to no explicit eschatology. Still, the point of the rather detailed description of the devastation is clear enough, since the speaker more than once draws a pointed contrast to imagined scenes of wealthy grandeur and communal contentment in the mead hall (21–3, 31–7) swept away by malign fate (26). In fact, there is a general movement in the poem away from "present desolation" to "past splendour" (Greenfield 1966: 145): by the end the speaker is wholly devoted to recalling the place as it must once have been (Klinck 1992: 63). The text is itself something of a ruin, with substantial lacunae wrought by the burns that penetrate the last 14 folios of the Exeter Book. Yet even though the end of the poem is severely defective, it is clear from what remains that the poet never deviates from his descriptive aim into obvious philosophy. As the speaker describes a hot spring and baths, and the detailed nature of the description suggests a particular site, the ruined town is generally assumed to be Bath, since nowhere else in England are such features found alongside Roman ruins, and the details of the description are not entirely incompatible with what can be divined about the state of the ruined baths there before the tenth century (Leslie 1988: 22–8). The poem may well have been inspired by a tradition of primarily Latin laments over ruins – the so-called *de excidio* tradition (Dunleavy 1959 and Doubleday 1972) – the closest parallel, as argued by Brandl (1919), being the *De excidio Thoringiae* ('Destruction of Thuringia', ed. Leo 1881: 271–5; trans. Calder and Allen 1976: 137–41) of Venantius Fortunatus (AD 570).[28] Yet if this is the inspiration for the poem, it is so only in a general way, as specific similarities are few (Hume 1976). The ruined city has been viewed as an allegory of the Temple of Jerusalem, or of Babylon, or of the temple of the flesh; most of the remaining studies deal with identifying the site.[29] The vocabulary of the poem, it should be said, is unusual, as the poet uses unexampled compounds in an attempt to describe in poetic manner unfamiliar architectural features: thus the precise meanings of words like *scūrbeorge* (5), *tēaforgēapa* (30), and *hrōstbēah* (31) are obscure.

A different type of urban poem is represented by *Durham* (*ASPR* 6.27; trans. Kendall 1988: 509), most likely composed shortly after the translation of St. Cuthbert's remains to Durham Cathedral on August

29, 1104, and certainly no later than 1109 (see Kendall 1988: 507 n. 2). The poem praises the city of Durham, mentioning the fish-filled River Wear and the nearby woods full of wildlife before listing briefly the kings and saints at rest in the city. This is the only vernacular specimen of a type called *encomium urbis* 'praise for a city', of which there are numerous Latin examples from late antiquity and the early Middle Ages (see Schlauch 1941: 14–28), the best known of which is Alcuin's poem in praise of the city and church of York (see chapter 1) – a work that similarly mentions the River Ouse, teeming with fish, and the wooded countryside nearby (6.30–4) before recounting the city's history and identifying its famous inhabitants. The *ASPR* text is derived from two medieval copies (one destroyed in the Cottonian fire of 1731 but recorded in an early edition), though subsequently it has been shown that an extant seventeenth-century transcript by Franciscus Junius is of an otherwise unknown manuscript, adding a third witness (Fry 1992). As perhaps the last poem recorded in Old English – depending on whether *The Grave* (chapter 6), from ca. 1150, is regarded as Middle English – *Durham* is of considerable formal interest, since it shows significant metrical departures from the norms of classical verse (Cable 1991: 52–7 and Fulk 1992: 260–1), in addition to its peculiarities of spelling (e.g. *gecheðe/gicheðe* for OE *geoguðe,* 16) and a brief gesture toward macaronism (*reliquia* 'relics' 19).

The Wife's Lament (*ASPR* 3.210–11) has more in common with *Wulf and Eadwacer* (below) than perhaps with any other Old English poem, even discounting the fact of its female speaker (proved by the feminine grammatical endings in 1–2). Like *The Seafarer* and *The Wanderer* it is a complaint (or *planctus*: Woolf 1975), but unlike them it offers no religious consolation. Unlike them, too, it portrays the speaker's plight of loneliness and yearning for her husband in fairly concrete terms as an unfolding story rather than as a backgroundless condition of hardship. This narrative element inevitably has invited attempts to identify the speaker with a particular figure from oral legend or folktale, as with *Wulf and Eadwacer* (Grein 1857–8: 1.363, Rickert 1904–5: 365–76, Stefanovíc 1909: 428–310, Fitzgerald 1963), but none of the parallels is particularly close. Reading the poem in conjunction with eddic laments by female speakers (Guðrún, Brynhildr, Oddrún) and other early Germanic examples of *planctus* constructs a useful and informative reading context for the poem (see Renoir 1975), but it reveals nothing very satisfying about the speaker's identity or exact situation. This frustration has fostered in some a sense that the speaker must be the poet's own construct, and yet her condition is described in such detail as to suggest a purposeful riddle in regard to her identity. Accordingly, she has been identified variously as a thane lamenting the loss of his lord (Bambas 1963), a consort in exile for her failure of an Irish monastic ordeal of chastity (Dunleavy 1956), a minor pagan deity bewailing the alienation of a devotee or lover (Doane 1966, Orton 1989, Luyster 1998), an analogue of nuns who wrote to the missionary Boniface in search of friendship, or even an actual nun (Schaefer 1986 and Horner 2001: 48–55), the allegorized Church yearning for her bridegroom Christ (Swanton 1964), a speaking sword (taking the poem as a riddle: Walker-Pelkey 1992), and, in a surprisingly tenacious vein of criticism, a revenant who speaks from the grave (Lench 1970, Tripp 1972, W. Johnson 1983).[30] The poem's most recent editors (Klinck 1992, Muir 2000, Pope and Fulk 2001) regard it simply as a particularly anguished love song of separation, and they treat the details of the speaker's situation, such as the cave or underground chamber that she inhabits and her enforced remove from her husband, not as clues to her identity but correlates and causes of her feelings. Accordingly, they do not treat the poem as a riddle, and they tend to lend its exceptionally ambiguous syntax and narrative line the simplest interpretation possible.[31] Thus they assume that references to a *gemæcne monnan* 'suitable man' (18) and *geong man* 'young person' (42) do not introduce a third character and a previously unmentioned feud (as first proposed by Grein 1865: 422), and the notorious crux *her heard* (15) is not a reference to a pagan shrine (i.e. *herh-eard*: see T. Davis 1965: 303–4, and Wentersdorf 1981: 509, though this view, too, owes much to Grein 1857–9: 1.256 n.).

Sometimes paired with *The Wife's Lament* is *The Husband's Message* (*ASPR* 3.225–7), regarded by some (e.g. Howlett 1978) as the happy sequel – another interpretation originated by Grein. Appearing immediately before *The Ruin* in the Exeter Book, it shares with that poem the textual effects of the burns to the closing leaves of the manuscript. There is a brilliant and rather plausible reconstruction of the lost text, from the small remains of letters around the burnt portions, by Pope (1978), which supports the common view that the speaker is a rune stick (of yew, Pope finds) sent by its maker to invite his love to join him overseas, where he was driven by a feud, and where he is now well off. This interpretation explains the presence of runes in lines 49–50, and it is particularly attractive to the many who believe that Riddle 60, which immediately precedes it in the Exeter Book, is actually the first part of this poem, describing, as it appears to, the making of an object suitable for conveying a written message (see, e.g., Kaske 1967 and J. Anderson 1986: 236–7). This would lessen the strangeness of one feature of the poem, since inanimate speakers other than books are rare in Old English poetry. (*Dream of the Rood* and the riddles are the closest analogues.) Like *The Wife's Lament,* the poem has inspired attempts to identify the characters with figures from heroic legend (e.g. Sigurðr and Guðrún, as argued by Bouman 1962: 41–91), and when these have failed to convince, allegorical and exegetical interpretations have been advanced (see Swanton 1964, Kaske 1967, Bolton 1969, and Goldsmith 1975). The couple's projected happiness is nonetheless an archaized, heroic version of contentment in which, the feud past, as aristocrats they will distribute rings of gold to a loyal band (see Leslie 1988: 20). Though the undamaged portions contain none of the obscurities of syntax and reference of *The Wife's Lament,* the poem equally invites consideration as a puzzle to be solved, not simply because of the possible unity with Riddle 60, but because the runes (49–50) have never been interpreted satisfactorily.[32]

Closely allied to *The Wife's Lament* in its cryptic narrative, its grim spirit, and its rueful female speaker (cf. fem. *reotugu* 'sorrowful' 10) is *Wulf and Eadwacer* (*ASPR* 3.179–80), a poem that has provoked controversy out of proportion to its mere 19 lines.[33] The speaker tells us that Wulf and she are on separate islands, and on his, surrounded by fen, there are cruel men. In rainy weather she sat in mournful expectation of him, and when *se beaducāfa* 'the one bold in battle' (presumably Eadwacer) embraced her she felt both pleasure and loathing. It was sorrow over his absence, rather than starvation, that made her sick. "Do you hear, Eadwacer?" she asks. "Wulf will bear our cowardly (?) whelp to the woods. That is easily sundered that was never joined, our performance together" (16–19). The significance of some entire lines is uncertain ("For my people it is as if they were given a gift" (1); "Things are different for us" (3, 8)), and one line, *Willað hȳ hine aþecgan gif hē on þrēat cymeð* (2, repeated in 7), remains untranslatable, the syntax being ambiguous and the precise shade of meaning of *aþecgan* 'receive? consume?' and *þrēat* 'host? peril?' being indeterminate.[34] Even the most fundamental aspects of the situation are susceptible of alternate interpretations, including whether *Wulf* and *Eadwacer* are names at all (see Adams 1958, Orton 1985, and Greenfield 1986: 12). If, as seems likely, these really are two personal names, it is difficult to see why these persons should be named unless the audience was expected to recognize their story. No convincing identification with figures from heroic legend has been made, though it is not implausible that the poem should allude to some legend that grew up around Odoacer (= OE *Ēadwacer*), the Herulian foe of Theodoric the Ostrogoth and deposer of the last Western emperor in 476 – especially given the great variety of lost legends about the Goths that *Widsith* implies an English audience could be expected to know.[35] And the speaker's situation bears certain affinities to that of Signý in *Volsunga saga* (with notable differences, as well), especially if *earne* (16) is understood to stand for *earhne* 'cowardly'.[36] Some connection with heroic legend probably best explains the very existence of such a peculiar composition, since it is the tragic situation of a person compelled by opposing duties to choose a terrible course of action that forms the center of interest in early Germanic heroic poetry. Thus, as mentioned above (section 2 of the introduction), it is a married woman who is so often at the center of heroic narratives, because when her father's family and her husband's are in conflict, she must choose between them (see esp. Phillpotts 1928). The medieval tradition of *Frauenlieder*, popular songs uttered by and about women (see Malone 1962a, Davidson 1975), grows out of this heroic convention. Even if *Wulf and Eadwacer* does allude to a heroic legend, however, obviously it more closely resembles the complaints of Old English lyric speakers than the heroic poems that recount feats of arms.

Yet because no definite identification of Wulf or Eadwacer is possible, alternative interpretations of the poem have proliferated. It has been identified as a charm, a complaint that a passage of verse has been misplaced, an account of romance among dogs (facetiously), and of an anthropomorphic pack of wolves.[37] More recently it has often been viewed as a mother's lament, or an expression of her concern over an illegitimate child.[38] So cryptic is the poem that it was at first universally regarded as a riddle or a charade, and it was not until H. Bradley discussed the poem in 1888 that it was first recognized to be a dramatic monologue – though even now it is occasionally claimed to be a riddle (J. Anderson 1983 and North 1994). Not surprisingly, then, analyses continue to focus on identifying the narrative situation. No more than one recent study broaches larger issues in a significant way: Olsen (1994) rejects readings of the poem that render the speaker a passive victim, and she reanalyzes the language to show that such readings are not inevitable.

Finally, *The Riming Poem* (*ASPR* 3.166–9, trans. Macrae-Gibson 1983 and Earl 1987, both rather freely) has a remarkably straightforward structure, recounting in the past tense the speaker's life of ease and plenty, apparently as a noble (1–42), then, in the present tense, his ill-defined but pervasive discontent (43–79), leading to an anagogic close. Only in detail is the poem obscure, since the exercise in rhyming every pair of verses, or often four verses in sequence, while retaining the alliterative form, leads to almost impenetrable obscurity of diction. Nonetheless, some of the sources of the speaker's present misery are identifiable and familiar: sickness, the mutability of worldly existence, and the aging of the earth. The contrast between former contentment and present misery is abrupt and pointed, serving the pervasive oppositional aesthetic of Old English verse. The transition from the speaker's complaint to his profession of faith, on the other hand, is subtly executed, for as the culmination of so many afflictions he imagines the body moldering in the grave (75–7), and this leads seamlessly to the observation that a good person takes thought beforehand, avoids sin, and considers the joys of heaven (80–3). The immediately following close is of the familiar homiletic type, beginning with an exhortation ("Let us hasten . . .") and ending with God's truth and eternity. Despite its obscurity the poem bears obvious affinities to *The Seafarer* and *The Wanderer*. Yet because the speaker's experience of joy and woe is expressed in such abstract and formal terms, the poem's closest analogues are Cynewulf's runic signatures and, of course, the far less obscure rhyming passage in *Elene* (see chapter 4, section 5). Rhyme is a feature of Latin verse that was developed particularly early in Ireland, and it is very likely in imitation of Hiberno-Latin verse that *The Riming Poem* was composed (Macrae-Gibson 1983: 24). As in the case of Cynewulf, some of the rhymes would be made regular by the substitution of Anglian forms, and the proposal that others are best explained as Late West Saxonisms is ill founded (see Fulk 1992: 365 n. 42). A peculiar metrical feature of the poem is that it contains no light verses, as a consequence of the poet's attempt to employ double alliteration in every on-verse, just as in the rhyming passages in Cynewulf and *The Phoenix*. Literary studies of the poem are few – see Wentersdorf 1985 for a synopsis – though the editions of Macrae-Gibson (1983) and Klinck (1992) have made it far more accessible.

9

Germanic Legend and Heroic Lay

The body of material in Old English verse devoted to native heroic legend is small – a mere speck in the corpus, actually, if *Beowulf* is removed from consideration. It could hardly be otherwise, since books were precious objects, the products of intensive labor, and it is hardly to be expected that they should have been filled with matter unrelated to the sacred duties of the religious houses in which they were exclusively made. Germanic oral legend was in fact regarded by some as inimical to religious devotion, as witnessed by the much-cited remark of Alcuin in regard to the practice of listening to heroic songs at the dinner table, *Quid Hinieldus cum Christo?* 'What has Ingeld to do with Christ?' This is in apparent reference to the Heathobard hero named at *Beowulf* 2064 and *Widsith* 48 The remark also reveals that some apparently saw no harm in such entertainments, and this doubtless explains why the few surviving scraps of Germanic legend found their way into manuscripts at all.[1] This small collection of mostly fragmentary works is the attenuated remnant of what must have been a vast body of oral tradition, the outlines of which we can only guess at, with hints from related traditions in Scandinavia and on the Continent. The material is bound together, however, by more than simply its matter drawn from nonliterate traditions. Certain conventions that help to define the heroic ethos may be defined from a comparison of this material with other literary types, particularly lyric and wisdom poetry, as well as poems about the champions of Christ, which are cast in the same heroic mode.[2]

Chief of these conventions is the bond between a lord and his retainers. The men owe to their lord their winnings in battle and their military support, and when they fail this latter obligation they bring disgrace upon their families and are to be dispossessed of their property, as we see in regard to Godric and his brothers, who flee the battle of Maldon, and in regard to Beowulf's retainers who hang back from fighting the dragon. In return the lord is obliged to reward his loyal thanes' service with splendid gifts, a duty that evokes high praise in *Beowulf* when it is properly performed (e.g. at lines 1046–9 and 2989–98) and heavy censure when it is not (1719–22). The chief lasting good in such an economy, the true measure of a life well lived, is the enduring fame of heroic deeds and lordly munificence. The heroic bond between lord and retainer is confirmed and celebrated in the mead hall, which is the site where fame is enacted in the oral traditions recounted of ancestors and legendary heroes. The occasion for acquiring fame may be the pitched battles of opposing armies, but very often it is a more personal contest stemming from the duty to vengeance required by feuds. Thus heroic traditions do not shun material we should regard as historical in focus, as in the case of the Geatish wars recounted in the second half of *Beowulf*; but opportunities for personal glory are greater in the pursuit of individual feats of arms, and so it is legendary material that produces figures, good and bad, of the most memorable stature, such as Sigemund and Eormenric.

Beowulf is the work of Old English literature that has prompted, by far, the most intensive study.[3] There are several reasons for this. It is the most substantial piece of writing in the language that does not derive from a Latin source, and thus it is a rare window on an unfamiliar world. Its allusive and digressive qualities present to view a mass of half-concealed meanings and allusions that beg explication. The poem held a place of particular importance in nineteenth-century scholarship, with its nationalist preoccupation with Germanic origins, because it is the most substantial and informative work within the Germanic heroic tradition outside of Scandinavian sources, and it antedates the earliest Icelandic manuscripts by several centuries. But even after the decline of scholarly interest in Germanic antiquities (see below) it has retained its appeal, and it has even, in recent years, provoked considerable popular interest, most notably in the translation by the Nobel laureate Seamus Heaney (1999). No doubt this is in part because its many indeterminacies have invited successive critical movements to see mirrored in the poem their own hermeneutic concerns, as detailed below. And yet the general consensus that this is the finest work of Old English literature surely is not unfounded. Despite early critics' dissatisfaction, the structure of the poem is most appealing, presenting to view complexities of design at both the micro- and the macrostructural levels; and the hero's character is quite original, resembling less the fierce heroes of the Icelandic family sagas than God's pious champions in the Old English verse saints' lives, given his tactful dealings with the watchman on the Danish coast (lines 260–85), his good will toward Unferth, who earlier insulted him (1488–90, 1807–12), and his refusal to take the Geatish throne from the minor Heardred (2369–79; see Wieland 1988).

There is no consensus whether *Beowulf* represents a very ancient poetic form or an innovation. Anglo-Saxonists not infrequently incline to the view that the poem is the sole remaining example of an early Germanic genre of oral epic. Yet the more conventional one assumes the form of *Beowulf* to be, the more difficult it is to explain why the poem should have been written down at all: much precious vellum is devoted to it, and yet Old English manuscripts tend not to contain matter that did not either pertain to literate tradition or serve some religious purpose.[4] Comparatists, by contrast, tend to conclude that, unlike *Beowulf*, narrative heroic verse on native subjects took the form of shorter "lays" (German *Lieder*) – perhaps originally embedded in saga-like prose narratives – since this is what we find surviving in the other early Germanic languages (see Heusler 1941: sections 148–50, A. Campbell 1962b, Niles 1983: 96–117, Andersson 1988, and Reichl 2000: 145–53). The heroic poems of the elder edda (ed. Neckel and Kuhn 1983; trans. Terry 1990) and the fragmentary Old High German *Hildebrandslied* (ed. Braune and Ebbinghaus 1994: 84–5; trans. Bostock, King, and McLintock 1976: 44–7) are the chief evidence. The Old English *Finnsburg* fragment is also generally believed to be the remnant of a lay rather than a longer composition like *Beowulf* (but cf. Frank 1991a: 95–6); the status of the *Waldere* fragments (see below) is less certain. There exist other narratives on the ancient heroes, such as the Old Icelandic *Vǫlsunga saga* (ed. and trans. Finch 1965) and the Latin *Waltharius* (see below). But these obviously bear little resemblance to *Beowulf* in form. It is thus still widely believed that the lay was the normal form assumed by heroic compositions in ancient times, and it follows from this that *Beowulf* is innovatory in respect to form. In the nineteenth century it was widely believed that the Homeric epics were compiled from shorter compositions (an argument associated particularly with Karl Lachmann, d. 1851), and thus it must have seemed natural enough to regard *Beowulf* as a cento of earlier lays, especially given its episodic structure and digressive style. This so-called *Liedertheorie* is particularly associated with Lachmann's student Karl Müllenhoff (1869, 1889), who first formulated it in detail, though the poem was regarded as a composite as early as 1836 in the pioneering work of John M.

Kemble, and this view was once shared widely, being argued with particular conviction by ten Brink (1888) and Schücking (1905).

Though the *Liedertheorie* was outmoded by the early years of the twentieth century,[5] there remained as its vestige a fairly broad consensus that the poem is not well unified in design – the influential view, for example, of W. P. Ker (1908: 158–75), who perhaps did not recognize the extent to which his identification of the poem as an epic and his extended comparison of it to the *Iliad* and the *Odyssey* influenced his views on the poem's structure. It was Tolkien, in his British Academy lecture of 1936, who first opposed the consensus with a full-fledged defense of the poem's design, arguing that it is not an epic but a heroic-elegiac poem and that the monsters, far from trivializing the narrative, lend it greater significance by their embodiment of cosmic themes.[6] The poet's refusal to follow a single line of narrative is not a defect but one more expression of his strategy of juxtaposition and contrast, a strategy that also informs the poem's purposely static structure, contrasting the hero's youth and age to produce an effect more akin to elegy than to epic or romance. Tolkien's analysis has not gone unchallenged (see, e.g., Gang 1952, van Meurs 1955, and K. Sisam 1965), but it has been extremely influential, and even those who reject it in the end tend to accept the formalist principles on which it is based, especially the assumptions that the poem's structure, whatever it is thought to be, is carefully crafted, and that the design is *sui generis* and should not be evaluated by comparison to epic or any other unrelated genre.

Yet the temptation to attribute compositional significance to the poem's division into two or three larger episodes of battles with monsters is great, and although the advent of New or Practical Criticism swung the debate in Tolkien's favor and largely put an end to claims of disorder in the poem's structure, not all have been convinced that the poem's parts were never separate compositions.[7] One warmly debated view has been that of Kiernan (1981a, b), who perceives evidence in the manuscript that the passage linking Beowulf's youthful exploits to his old age and death was composed by the scribes of the extant copy themselves to join two originally discrete works, and the poem as we have it is an eleventh-century composition. This hypothesis harks back to the argument of Schücking (1905) that the narrative of Beowulf's return to his homeland (lines 1888–2199, "Beowulf's Homecoming") was composed to join two earlier compositions (see also Sisam 1965: 4–5). Schücking's evidence is chiefly linguistic and stylistic, and all of it is subject to alternative interpretations (see Chambers and Wrenn 1959:

117–20). To this and to Kiernan's argument there is some linguistic and metrical counterevidence: Bately (1985) points out that the grammar of the poem's *siþþan* clauses is distinctive, unlike that in other poetic works, and that the characteristic pattern is distributed throughout the poem. The findings of Shippey (1993a) on *þā . . . þā* constructions suggest a similar conclusion, and Sundquist (forthcoming) presents statistical evidence for unity in the poem's distribution of relative clause types.[8] Likewise Fulk (1992: 166–7) observes that verses of the archaic type *frēowine folca* (430a), which are rare outside of *Beowulf* but common in the poem itself, are distributed throughout the work. They are found both before and after "Beowulf's Homecoming," and they are common as well in the transitional section.[9] Other conservative metrical features that vary in frequency from poem to poem, such as noncontraction and nonparasiting, are distributed rather evenly across the two major divisions of the poem (Fulk 1992, *passim*). None of these observations by itself is conclusive proof against the claim of composite origins, but their combined force is far from negligible. More studies of the poem's grammatical, stylistic, and metrical idiosyncrasies should contribute fruitfully to the discussion of the poem's compositional unity, and this seems an area of research in which philological study may still yield significant results.

Kiernan's argument about the date of the poem has received more attention than his hypothesis about its composite nature, since even at the historical juncture in *Beowulf* studies during which it appeared, when the date of the poem was undergoing widespread reevaluation, the eleventh-century date that he proposed seemed sensational. Long before the end of the nineteenth century, and before the development of so-called metrical and linguistic tests for dating, there arose a fairly broad consensus about the general chronology of Old English verse, placing *Widsith, Beowulf,* and the scriptural narratives of the Junius Manuscript among the earliest compositions, dated most commonly to the age of Bede. The reasons for this consensus were rather slender, including considerations of style and supposed influence (before the formulaic nature of Old English verse was widely recognized), and especially the assumption that verse on themes from Germanic legend must antedate hagiographic and devotional poetry. Metrical and linguistic criteria in fact seem never to have played a very significant role in dating *Beowulf* (see Fulk 1992: 3–4 n. 5), though it was widely regarded as a major critical development when A. Amos (1980) reexamined such criteria and concluded that they were by and large unreliable. At the same time a 1980 Toronto conference on the date of the poem (proceedings ed. Chase 1981) produced such a variety of opinions, on so many different (mostly non-linguistic) grounds, that no consensus has formed since among literary scholars.

In recent years the most detailed arguments in regard to dating have tended to favor a fairly early date, on a variety of grounds, including metrical (Fulk 1992), cultural (Clemoes 1995: 3–67), and paleographic (Lapidge 2000). Hills (1997) surveys the archaeological evidence and finds that while the material culture of the sixth through eighth centuries in Britain agrees well with the references to material objects in *Beowulf*, in regard to the ninth and tenth centuries, "ring swords, pattern-welded swords, boar-crested helmets, lavish burials in ships or as cremations, and royal halls of timber would by then be memories from the past" (p. 309). Viking culture in England, however, in the ninth and tenth centuries would have provided models for many of these archaic features, and thus the archaeological evidence is not incompatible with a later date of composition. "The cultural processes that allowed Odin to appear on Christian crosses," she concludes, "could also underlie the creation of an Old English epic from Danish traditions" (p. 309). That specific comparison, however, we believe suggests the improbability that so much of the material of the poem should have been brought to England with the vikings, as the names in the poem are fully nativized, unlike Scandinavian names brought to England in the ninth and tenth centuries (see below), attesting to circulation of the elements of the tale in England from much earlier times than the Viking Age. Thus although it is certainly possible that the poem should be a later composition, an earlier date is easier to reconcile with the archaeological evidence. This is by no means, however, the view of all Anglo-Saxonists. Though few new arguments for a later date have been adduced recently,[10] most now tend to regard the problem of dating the poem as insoluble and the insolubility of the problem as a congenial state of affairs.[11] After all, to date *Beowulf* would be to constrain interpretation, discouraging certain views of the poem. Yet uncertainty about the date has no doubt had a deleterious effect upon *Beowulf* studies. Because dating is closely tied to many other issues in *Beowulf* criticism, wide disagreements about, for example, its place of composition, its religious outlook, its relative orality, and its very unity as a composition cannot be settled conclusively. Thus, unable to contextualize the poem's composition, *Beowulf* criticism tends still to be dominated by ahistoricizing, formalist approaches that contribute to the widespread impression of scholars in later periods that it is antiquated and out of touch with the wider concerns of the profession, and even of medieval scholarship.

What, more particularly, is at stake in this controversy? Those who date the poem early assume that although the manuscript was made about the year 1000, the poem has been copied from an earlier text, which in turn may have been copied several times in a series extending back to the date of composition. The greater the period of time assumed between the extant manuscript and the date of composition, the more speculative the date of the poem seems; yet the later one dates the poem, the less plausible is the conservation of so much impressive detail in its ancient material in oral form over the course of several centuries prior to the recording of the extant poem. In this latter case it would be particularly striking that the two historically datable references in the poem are to rather early figures, rather than to such later ones as might have been expected to enter into an oral tradition lasting several centuries: these references are to Hygelac's raid on Frisia (datable to ca. 520 on the basis of Gregory of Tours' account of it) and to "the Merovingian" (2921) – that is, a member of the Frankish dynasty that lasted from 481 to 751 (though the identification is not undisputed). In regard to this difficulty of lengthy oral transmission, Frank (1991a: 93–4) argues that the scattered remains of Continental heroic literature do not represent a continuous, common tradition among the Germanic nations but are the result of a Carolingian revival of interest in such matters. Whether or not one accepts this hypothesis, it highlights one of the chief obstacles to establishing a date for *Beowulf*: the nostalgic, antiquarian nature of the poet's representation of heroic society, as pointed out by Tolkien and many subsequent observers. Thus the very outlook one perceives in the poem is connected to its presumed date: the earlier it was composed, the less ironic distance is plausibly to be assumed between the poet and the world he portrays. It is certainly no accident that so many now regard the poem as a relatively late composition, given the tendency of contemporary literary analysis to "read against the grain" and value particularly the ways in which texts resist interpretive closure and bare their own contradictions.

Another issue to which the dating of the poem is important is the status of the sole surviving manuscript as textual authority. Every time a medieval text was copied, it underwent change. Some of this was intentional: texts composed in the Anglian dialects were clearly Saxonized by scribes during the period when West Saxon was the literary standard for all of England, as shown most clearly by the West Saxon copies of early Northumbrian poems like *Cædmon's Hymn* and *Bede's Death Song*, but also by the incompleteness of the transformation in some prose texts, as with the gradual Saxonization of the vocabulary of Old English copies of Bede's history (see J. J. Campbell 1951). So also some scribes participated in the recomposition of verse they copied (see section 6 of the introduction). More important, copying always resulted in simple errors of transcription: omitted words, misinterpretation of unfamiliar words or spellings, eye skips, and other various misreadings. Kiernan's argument that the poem is the scribes' own composition should lead us to expect few, if any, scribal errors – a supposition that is difficult to maintain in the face of the many forms in the manuscript that are explicable only as mistranscriptions of a written source (see Lapidge 2000). Yet even those who regard the text as a copy are often reluctant to emend it. It is by no means a fixed rule, but those who think of the poem as a relatively early composition tend to be less reverent of the text in the unique manuscript, doubtless because of the assumption that the text must have undergone considerable scribal change in the course of transmission.

Assumptions about the date of the poem have also influenced scholarly views on the composition of the poem's original audience, and thus the poem's purpose. Earlier scholarship tended to view *Beowulf* as an example of an aristocratic genre, of interest chiefly to a secular audience. Whitelock's influential study (1951) is founded upon that assumption, and it is on the basis of her findings about the nature of lordship and secular society in the eighth century that she concludes that the poem might have been composed as late as the second half of that century. Scholars now tend instead to view the poem against the background of the monastic or other ecclesiastical setting in which it must have been recorded, given that writing was not a lay activity.[12] Thus, for example, while Whitelock (1951: 77–8, with Tolkien 1936) is obliged to explain the poet's expression of regret over the Danes' heathenism (lines 175–88) as an interpolation, few scholars now see any need to account for an attitude that is wholly consonant with the assumption of composition in a religious house. The fairly uniform assumption of an early date of composition was no doubt in part responsible for this habit of situating the poem in a reception context not unlike the society portrayed in the poem itself. Still, an early date of composition need not compel such a view, as there is evidence of such secular entertainments in the monasteries (and efforts to banish them) during the early period: even if Alcuin's remark about Ingeld and Christ is not directed to a monastic audience (see note 1), we have the canons of the council held at *Clofeshoh* (an unidentified spot) in 747, banishing the vain entertainments "of poets, harpers, musicians, and buffoons" from the monastic premises.[13] Indeed, there is massive evidence for the secular qualities of the early Anglo-Saxon Church, in a period when aristocratic families possessed and governed the churches and monastic houses they endowed (see Wormald 1978, 1991a on *Eigenkirchen*).

Regardless of when the poem was first committed to parchment, the legends of which it is composed are clearly quite ancient, for while the legendary figures named are nearly all Scandinavian, their names do not have the character of names brought to England by the vikings, but they are fully native forms showing inheritance from a much earlier period of the English language (see Björkmann 1910: 198–202). It is in fact striking how many of the named persons correspond to figures mentioned in Scandinavian records from the twelfth century onward, and yet the facts reported about them may either show strong resemblances in the two traditions or differ widely.[14] For example, the story pieced together from *Beowulf* and *Widsith* is that Hrothgar and his nephew Hrothulf defeated the Heathobard prince Ingeld, son of Froda, in battle when Ingeld renewed an old feud. Most Norse sources (e.g. *Skjǫldunga saga*, ca. 1200) instead award the victory over Ingjaldr, son of Fróði, to Hróarr (Hrōðgar) and his brother Helgi (Hālga), father of Hrólfr kraki (Hrōðulf); yet in the eddic *Helgakviða Hundingsbana I–II*, the hero Helgi (a Vǫlsung rather than a Dane in these texts, though Saxo Grammaticus ca. 1200 ascribes the feat to Helgi the Dane) is made sole victor over one Hǫðbroddr (cf. OE *Heaðobeardan*: see Sarrazin 1888: 42). In Norse sources, Hróarr (Hrōðgar) is far less important a figure than his brother or nephew; Hermóðr (Heremōd) is accorded great respect; Hugleikr (Hygelac) is made a Swedish king (or, as Hugletus, a Danish one who defeats the Swede Hømothus, i.e. Eymóðr = Ēanmund in Saxo's account), though Gregory of Tours (d. 594) agrees with *Beowulf* in describing him as having mounted a disastrous raid on Frankish territory during the reign of Theodoric, king of the Franks (d. 534); Áli (Onela), is made a Norwegian king (due to confusion of Uppland in Sweden with the Norwegian "uplands"), and thus he is no relation to Óttar (Ōhthere), whose son Aðils (Ēadgils) defeats and kills him; and Sigmundr (Sigemund) is both father and uncle to Sinfjǫtli (-fjǫtli = Fitela). The form of the names demonstrates the transmission of some stories to Scandinavia from other parts of the

Germanic world (e.g. Erminrekr in *Þiðriks saga af Bern* = OE Eormenrīc), but even in these cases there may be older native forms attested to the same names (cf. Jǫrmunrekkr in the eddic *Hamðismál* and elsewhere).

Analogues in Scandinavian myth also show varying degrees of parallelism, but Scandinavian sources are sometimes required to explain the *Beowulf* poet's terse allusions. Thus Weland, the maker of Beowulf's sword (455), is referred to in *Deor* and in Alfred's translation of Boethius (see chapter 2), and he is depicted in his smithy on the Franks Casket (see plate 4); yet we know his story in full only because it is recorded in Old Icelandic, and particularly in the eddic *Vǫlundarkviða*. The necklace of the Brísingar (Brōsingas, 1199) is alluded to in both the eddas, and it plays a significant role in *Sǫrla þáttr* (ca. 1300–50; ed. Guðni Jónsson 1954; the relevant portion trans. Garmonsway and Simpson 1968: 298–300), where as Freyja's greatest treasure it constitutes evidence of her infidelity to Óðinn. The story of Hæthcynn's accidental slaying of Herebeald (2432–43) is paralleled by the myth of the death of Baldr (= -beald), the Norse Apollo, when his blind brother Hǫðr (= Hæð-) is made to cast a sprig of mistletoe at him for the gods' amusement, as related in *Snorra edda* (ed. Faulkes 1982: 45–6; trans. Faulkes 1987: 48–9). The story of Scyld Scefing ('shield of the sheaf') that begins the poem is tied up in a less direct way with the myth of the flood survivor Bergelmir, whose name means 'bundle of barley', in both of the eddas (see Fulk 1989).

Outside of the poem itself, to the hero there is no reference anywhere. Certain analogues, however, parallel the poem in intriguing ways. The closest of these is a passage in *Grettis saga* (ca. 1315), in which the hero Grettir grapples in a hall with a troll, slicing her arm off at the shoulder. The following day he dives into the river into which she disappeared, where he finds another troll behind a waterfall and kills him when the monster attacks with a *heptisax*, a short-sword with a wooden haft (like the *hæft-mēce* that fails Beowulf in his struggle with Grendel's mother) which Grettir manages to slice through. A priest waiting on the bank above for Grettir's return sees the blood of the troll in the river and leaves, assuming that the hero has been killed. For many it is difficult to believe that so many elements common to the two tales should have descended independently and intact from ancient tradition. Instead it is not impossible that some folktale resembling Beowulf's fight with Grendel and his mother should have been transmitted to Scandinavia from England at a fairly late date.[15] That the hero's fight with Grendel was a popular story in England is suggested by the preservation of the name *Grendel* in connection mostly with pits and ponds in the boundary clauses of no fewer than seven charters, some purporting to date from the eighth century (though the extant copies are actually later) and ranging widely over the South and West of the country (see Garmonsway and Simpson 1968: 301–2 for translations; and Lapidge 1982: 179–84 for discussion). The story has folktale qualities, and the fight with Grendel has in fact been identified as conforming to an international folktale type (B635.1 in S. Thompson 1966) called "The Bear's Son" (see esp. Panzer 1910, Shippey 1969, Barnes 1970, and Stitt 1992). Indeed, Beowulf has the bear-like quality of crushing his opponents with his great strength rather than using weapons against them. His name, too, has very commonly been interpreted as "Bee-Wolf," i.e. bear, stealer of bees' honey.[16] This connection lends force to another Icelandic analogue to the hero, the chief champion of the great king Hrólfr kraki (= Hrōðulf), Bǫðvarr bjarki, whose by-name means 'little bear', and who is the son of Bjǫrn (i.e. 'he-bear') and Bera ('she-bear'). Like Beowulf, he comes from the land of the Gautar (= Gēatas) to Leire on the island of Zealand, the ancient seat of Danish kings and thus the presumed site of Heorot. There by night he kills a huge troll-like beast (so *Hrólfs saga kraka*; a she-wolf in *Bjarkarímur*, both ca. 1400) that is immune to the bite of weapons and has been slaughtering the king's cattle and champions for two years. If there is a connection to *Beowulf* in this material – it is doubted by many, including Benson (1970: 15–19) and Andersson (1997: 131–3, with references), both skeptical in general about analogues – it is more plausibly ancient than in the case of *Grettis saga*.

Such analogues to *Beowulf* had mostly been identified by the end of the nineteenth century, reflecting the preoccupation of that age with discovering perceived cultural roots, excavating the dim past of the Germanic ethos. Because the *Liedertheorie* promoted the dissection of the poem into so many disparate accretions on the central narrative of the monster fights, it also suggested that there was nothing untoward in the practice of identifying the poem's religious sentiments as later intrusions on an original "pagan" composition.[17] "Paganism" in such a context almost never refers to a body of religious belief, and so in denoting all that is not Christian it becomes a thinly veiled reference to a notion of cultural purity, exposing a program to recover an imagined era in which the Germanic peoples lived in noble simplicity, uncorrupted by foreign influences. Naturally, the xenophobic implications of such a critical practice were in tune with the social conditions that gave rise to Nazism (a movement supported by a great many philologists, not all of them German: see Mees 2000),[18] and the turn away from philology and from the study of *Beowulf* in comparative Germanic contexts in the twentieth century was certainly in part a consequence of the ongoing critical reaction to German nationalism (see Shippey 1993b: 122–3). In at least equal part, though, it was the product of English nationalism, which prompted a "reclaiming" of early texts from German textual methods and even a renaming of the language, from "Anglo-Saxon" (Germ. *Angelsächsisch*) to "Old English" (see the conclusion below).

Tolkien's influential critique of *Beowulf* scholarship (1936) is an integral part of this reaction, since it is an explicit rejection of the prevailing critical interest in the poem primarily as a source for the comparative study of Germanic antiquities. The poem may be like a tower built of old stones, but to call the tower a muddle, to knock it down and sift through the pieces for traces of earlier structures, is to misconstrue its purpose, since "from the top of that tower" its builder "had been able to look out upon the sea" (pp. 248–9). It is certainly not the case that no one had thought to examine *Beowulf* on such an aesthetic basis before this, but Tolkien managed to distill the critical mood of the day and mark in *Beowulf* studies a transition that was taking place on a much wider stage: the rise of "literary criticism" in the modern sense as a respectable academic activity. The tenets of the New Criticism were formalist, and it is striking how many of those tenets are already implicit in Tolkien's essay: the rejection of historicism and other extraliterary considerations; the value placed on "universal" literary virtues like balance (in the poem's structure), system (in the monsters' relation to that structure, paralleling the development of the hero), and organicism (in the iteration of balance at various levels of analysis, including the line, the episode, and the poem as a whole); the fetishization of the work as an autonomous and transcendent object, a work of assumed genius; and a fondness for irony. The thoroughness with which *Beowulf* scholarship was transformed by this change in critical fashion is reflected in anthologies of *Beowulf* criticism (Nicholson 1963, Fry 1968, Fulk 1991, Baker 1995), which uniformly include little or nothing written before 1936.

Nothing illustrates the critical transition better than the change in scholars' attitudes toward the poet's digressive manner. While this manner produces most of the legendary material that was of chief interest to nineteenth-century scholarship, it also was responsible for a good deal of the dissatisfaction with the poem's structure, since it produces, in the much-cited phrase of a section heading in the introduction to Klaeber's edition, a "lack of steady advance." With the ascendancy of formalist approaches, the poem's digressions and minor episodes proved fodder for demonstrations of intricate structural design.[19] Studying all of them in detail, Bonjour finds that they render the background of the poem "alive," making it a realistic foil to the more symbolic main action (1950: 71). For example, the story of Scyld Scefing that begins the poem is intended to provide parallels to the life of the hero; the Finn and Heathobard episodes (1066–1159 and 2024–69) furnish the sort of historical background for the Danes that the allusions to the Swedish wars in the second half of the poem do for the Geats; and those same historical digressions on the wars with the Swedes and Franks are the chief means of building the sense of impending national disaster that underscores the tragedy of the hero's death. The Finn episode (1068–1159, discussed below) has been shown to play a particularly significant structural role (see, e.g., Camargo 1981). The tragedy of internecine killings sets the scene for the entrance of Wealhtheow – an entrance pointedly interrupted by the introduction of the ominous tableau of Hrothgar sitting with Hrothulf, Unferth at his feet. Her irony-laden declaration of trust in Hrothulf's kindness to her children, should Hrothgar die, reinforces the impression given by lines 1014–19, by *Widsith*, and by Scandinavian sources that Hrothulf will not keep faith.[20] The atmosphere of treachery and bloodshed that begins with the Finn episode is thus woven into the political context of the Danish court, all of this dreary foreboding being designed to set the stage for the more immediate tragedy that is about to descend: the attack of Grendel's mother.

The particular critical preoccupations of the mid-twentieth century naturally were the poem's formal features: diction, rhetoric, style, structure, symbolism, and theme. Yet the study of at least the more local of these considerations developed in dialogue with the theory of oral-formulaic composition proposed by Magoun (1953; see section 6 of the introduction). That the poem should have been composed of wholly traditional elements was widely perceived as a threat to the very foundations of the formalist program, since it seemed to deprive the poem of "originality," the quality considered vital for literary works to be regarded as autonomous objects transcending any historical context. Thus challenges to Magoun's analysis (e.g. Brodeur 1959: 6 and Benson 1966) tended to have as their aim to uncover evidence of the poem's originality. Magoun's claim that formulism entails oral composition was easily disproved by such means, but his detailed evidence for the formulaic nature of the poem's diction was not to be ignored. As a result, it now seems wholly impossible to discuss the diction of the poem – its compounds, kennings, and poetic vocabulary – outside of a formulaic context, except as dialect features. Thus the most important literary studies of diction after Brodeur's (1959: 1–38) seek to demonstrate not the originality of the diction but the poet's strategic use of it (preeminently Greenfield 1972: 30-5-9 and Niles 1983: 138–51).

Oral theory has been less engaged with the rhetoric and style of *Beowulf*, though some significant contributions have been made from an oral perspective (e.g. Niles 1983: 163–76 and Irving 1989: 80–132).[21] Yet some of the same issues arise in regard to style as to diction. Chief of these is the conventional nature of the oral tradition, which dictates that individuality in style should be no greater a desideratum for oral poets than innovative diction. Almost certainly we should assume that a good poem (i.e. a good performance) was valued not for its individuality of style but, quite the opposite, for its ability to recreate a centuries-old tradition. Style in Old English verse thus is not a matter of personal expression but something unintended, a variety, one might almost say, of failure, to the extent that it individuates a work rather than recreates the tradition.[22] As a consequence, approaches within a formalist framework again tend to stress the poet's tactical deployment of the stylistic effects at his disposal rather than to search for stylistic innovations. The primary stylistic result of the impulse to maximize variety in poetic diction is the principle of variation (see section 6 of the introduction), which naturally has received detailed critical attention, beginning with the comparatist taxonomy of Paetzel (1913; see also Standop 1969). Perhaps the two chief critical insights have been these: (1) The poet's variational patterns are structured for effect (Brodeur 1959: 39–70). For example, one common pattern is to build a rhetorical climax, as in the series *fēo . . . ealdgestrēonum . . . wundnum golde* (1380–82a: 'wealth . . . old treasures . . . twisted gold'), where the first term is the most abstract and the last the most concrete and vivid. (2) Variation is not simply a local effect (Robinson 1985). If it is defined in appositional terms, then apposition may be seen as structuring the poem at a variety of levels, including the apposed, alternate meanings of individual words, the generation of compounds by the juxtaposition of their elements, the paratactic nature of the poem's syntax, and larger, contrastive structural patterns such as the contrast between the hero's youth and his old age perceived by Tolkien. In other words, variation and contrast may be seen as expressions of the same underlying compositional principle of apposition. It was pointed out above (section 6 of the introduction) how irony and understatement may also be viewed as expressions of the principle of contrast. If the *Beowulf* poet can be said to have an ironic style, it is not a style different from that of other heroic poets, except insofar as he happens to be very good at deploying the features of this style.[23]

A significant body of criticism has been devoted to the detection of figures of classical rhetoric in *Beowulf*. Nineteenth-century criticism, given its aim of rescuing the Germanic past from corrupting influences, was uncongenial to such a project, and the followers of Magoun naturally have tended to focus on the oral rather than the literate features of texts (see Schaefer 1997: 118–19). Yet greater recognition of the probable monastic setting in which the poem was recorded has tended to legitimate claims for the influence of classical rhetoric, given the prominent and early role of the study of figures in the Latin curriculum.[24] Schemes have garnered more attention than tropes. Thus Bartlett (1935; see also Hieatt 1975) perceives in *Beowulf* a series of "envelope patterns" in which a passage is framed by repetition, at its close, of an element presented at its opening. For example, *Gyrede hine Beowulf* 'Beowulf prepared himself' (1441b) is echoed by *syðþan he hine tō gūðe gegyred hæfde* 'after he had readied himself for battle' (1472), and the repetition serves the purpose of "rounding off the verse paragraph" (p. 15) in which Beowulf's courage is implicitly compared to Unferth's cowardice. A related but more elaborate pattern is "ring composition" (Tonsfeldt 1977, Niles 1983: 152–62, Parks 1988, Irving 1989: 94, 150), a type of compositional strategy controversially posited for the Homeric epics and some other classical texts. Not only does an initial element balance a final one, but a second element balances a corresponding one placed second to last, and so forth, working inward to a kernel at the center. Niles offers the example of lines 12–19 (his translation, p. 153):

> To him in time   a son was born,
> young in the land,   whom the Lord sent
> to comfort the folk;   He knew the dire need
> they had suffered earlier,   lacking a king
> for a long time.   The Lord of life,
> Ruler of glory,   granted them grace for this.
> Beow[ulf] was famous,   his name rang widely,
> Scyld's son,   in the lands of the North.

Here the word *eafera*, translated 'son' (12b and 19a), frames references to Beow (13a and 18a), which in turn frame phrases to the effect that God sent a gift (13b–14a and 16b–17). Such analyses are reminiscent of Jakobsonian literary structuralism at its most refined, and thus plainly they lend themselves better to a view of the poem as a Fabergé egg of literate art than as the record of an *ex tempore* performance.

Such schematic aspects of the study of rhetoric are differentiated only in scope from larger considerations of the poem's structure, a feature of particular formalist interest. Especially influential has been Leyerle's analysis of the poem's "interlace structure" (1967; see also Irving 1989: 80–102). Drawing on parallels in the Anglo-Saxon decorative arts, particularly zoomorphic designs in which animals' elongated limbs are intertwined in complex patterns, as for example in the carpet pages and historiated initials of early illuminated gospel books, Leyerle argues that there is an effect of continual narrative interweaving both locally and globally in *Beowulf*. This is most obviously so when the history of the Geats' prolonged conflicts with neighboring nations is woven at intervals through the account of Beowulf's dealings with the dragon, presumably for the purpose of emphasizing what a disaster the hero's death will be for his people, when he can no longer defend them against the Swedes and Franks. Andersson (1980) offers a different structural perspective, as he perceives in the poem a continuous pattern of dramatic reversals – of successes and counterpoised failures, of raised and dashed hopes – that, when diagrammed, resembles a series of waves. For instance, the joyous construction of Heorot is balanced by Grendel's ravages, which are countered by the high hopes attending Beowulf's arrival in Denmark, which are opposed by Grendel's attack and killing of Hondscioh, in turn reversed by Beowulf's victory over Grendel, and so forth.

There is hardly any agreement about the nature of the poem's structure, but whether it is bipartite or tripartite (the latter being the view of many folklorists and feminists), and whether the episodes and digressions are all equally relevant to the poem's overarching design, the question of its structure is closely tied up with views on its theme. The connection is nowhere clearer than in Tolkien's influential lecture, which derives the theme of "man alien in a hostile world, engaged in a struggle which he cannot win while the world lasts" (1936: 269) from the poem's structure of contrasting youth and age, which expresses the inevitability of failure. Goldsmith (1962), followed by many, regards Hrothgar's "sermon" (1700–84) as the pivot on which the poem turns,

dividing it into halves and furnishing its moral center, and from its structural function she derives a theme of the danger of pride and covetous-
ness, as exemplified in the poem's deeply flawed hero. Chance (1986:
95–108) also sees in this passage an index to the poet's thematic intent.
She identifies Hrothgar's three concerns as envy, pride, and avarice,
qualities exemplified respectively in the three monsters, and thus she
concludes that the fight with Grendel's mother has central structural
importance in the development of the poem's moral theme. Tolkien
(1936: 281) observes that the poem begins (24) and ends (3182) with
remarks on the lasting value of *lof* 'praise', and Clark (1990: 136–42;
see also Greenfield 1976: 51–2) accordingly identifies the preservation
in memory of heroic accomplishments as the poet's chief concern. To
any of these analyses it might be objected that it is a peculiarly modern
and academic view to assume that a composition must have a central
theme; yet undeniably the poet's nostalgic, mournful treatment of the
material hints at a larger intent that begs to be interpreted. Still, if it is
primarily on the basis of the poet's elegiac tone that his theme is to be
identified – as Tolkien would have it, and many following in his foot-
steps – then the poem's theme must be applicable to the greater part of
early Germanic heroic verse, since most of it shares *Beowulf*'s sense of
doom and tragic necessity. That is, the theme must be seen as inherent
in the genre and its traditions rather than in the inspiration of the autonomous poet assumed by New Criticism.

Clark (1997) argues persuasively that notions of theme are also inseparable from consideration of the hero's character – as illustrated, for
example, by Goldsmith's assertion of the hero's moral shortcomings. It
is the dominant view in studies of the poem that Beowulf is indeed a
failed hero, and Clark traces the "moralizing and antiheroic movements
of postwar *Beowulf* criticism" (p. 280) to Tolkien. To be sure, if the
theme is to accord with the poem's prevailing mood, then Tolkien's
influential view of the poet as rueful and antiquarian leads almost inevitably to the currently prevailing view of him as distancing himself from,
and critiquing, the values of the world he portrays.[25] Yet the contribution of so-called historical criticism (see section 2 of chapter 8) to the
formation of this view must be recognized in equal measure.[26] Repu-
diation of the *Liedertheorie* and related attempts to identify "Christian
interpolations" demanded the conclusion that the poet was himself a
pious sort, and this posed the problem of identifying what kind of religious outlook the poem expresses. Even before Tolkien's lecture it was
recognized (by Phillpotts 1928) that bloody-minded tales of divided

loyalties leading to terrible vengeance, so characteristic of early Germanic literature, haunt only the periphery of *Beowulf*, and they are excluded from the exemplary life of the hero himself – who exhibits, as pointed out above, certain charitable traits that differentiate him from the saga heroes. Klaeber (1911–12) and others early in the century grappled with the problem of identifying the poem's Christian nature, but it was primarily after the Second World War, with the reaction to *Germanistik* that it nourished, that the poem came to be viewed as expressing profound learning in the patrology. Augustinian analyses of the theme have been particularly favored, e.g. by Schücking (1929: St. Augustine's understanding of the *rex justus* 'just king'), M. Hamilton (1946: influence of *De civitate Dei* on the poet), Donahue (1949–51: the two cities, of good and evil), D. Robertson (1951: *caritas* and *cupiditas*, from *De doctrina Christiana*), Kaske (1958: *sapientia et fortitudo*), Huppé (1984: how the hero's vengeful heroic ethos dooms him), Robinson (1985: compassion for unconverted, and thus, according to Augustine, damned, ancestors), and Dahlberg (1988: monsters as representatives of the earthly rather than the heavenly city), among many others. Because of the emphasis of such exegetical analyses on the hero's failings, this approach is usually (though not always) at odds with the other chief branch of historical criticism, the allegorical, which tends to see the hero as a type of the divinity (especially Klaeber 1911–12, Cabaniss 1955, McNamee 1960, Donahue 1965, Helder 1977, Wieland 1988, and others cited by Lee 1997). The two approaches, however, may be reconciled in the study of characters other than Beowulf himself. Unferth is of particular interest in this regard, as he has been taken, within a framework of patristic exegesis (beginning with Bloomfield 1949–51), as a figure of discord, under the assumption that his name means 'mar-peace'.[27]

It is the perception of the hero as a failure that forms the surest link between "historical" and poststructuralist approaches to the poem, since deconstructive criticism's project of subversive reading has left a critical legacy of perceiving texts as self-conflicted constructs. Even before the appearance of studies self-consciously identifying themselves as poststructuralist in orientation, it was possible to discern a growing habit of perceiving the poem as preoccupied with the same conflicts that pervade its critical heritage. For example, in cognizance of (especially) exegetical criticism's judgment that Beowulf is wrong to fight the dragon himself, de Looze (1984) analyzes Beowulf's monologue before he faces the dragon (2426–509, including the story of Hæthcynn and

Herebeald, the father's lament for his hanged son, and memories of earlier battles) as the hero's attempt to decide whether his greater duty is to his role as king or as hero, and thus whether he should undertake this battle. More self-consciously, Georgianna (1987) finds that the poet evinces a "modern or postmodern taste for subversive elements in narratives" (p. 834), since the futility and self-contradiction of the heroic ethos (another exegetical commonplace) are highlighted through the endless delays in the action and the self-doubts of the hero in the second half of the poem. And Lerer (1991: 188) contends that the purpose of having Beowulf recount his exploits in Denmark when he returns to Hygelac's court is to confer upon him the role of literary critic. A particularly robust vein of such criticism has been the analytic focus on the ways in which the poem reenacts the tension between orality and literacy that informs current critical discourse: Frantzen (1990: 184–7), Lerer (1991: 158–94), Near (1993), and Pasternack (1997: 182–9) all focus on the one specific reference in the poem to an act of reading – Hrothgar's study of the hilt of the melted sword that Beowulf brings from his encounter with Grendel's mother (1687–99) – to discern a self-reflective strain in the poem centered on an awareness of its textuality. Similarly, Overing (1990: 57–67) makes of the hilt an icon of the text of Hrothgar's "sermon."

The number of poststructuralist studies of *Beowulf* is small.[28] There are several reasons for this. One of the most significant is that critical discourse of the past quarter century has taken as its central concern the project of "call[ing] into question the very stability of language" (Lerer 1997: 328). This project has been fruitful when applied to modern and contemporary literature because it has had the effect of unsettling texts whose language might seem stable to interpreters who use the same language daily. It is less plainly relevant to texts whose meaning is not in danger of being taken for settled, simply because the language itself is radically uncertain. But probably the most important reason for the limited number of studies of this sort is that the techniques derived from deconstructive criticism that dominated literary theory for much of the last part of the twentieth century were formulated in reaction to New Criticism and structuralism, and to focus upon particular texts is to iterate the habit of close reading that undergirds formalist approaches. Hence the aim of exposing and unsettling critical preassumptions that have passed for transcendent verities lends itself better to the study of institutions and cultural practices than of literary texts. The most direct critique of this sort is that of Frantzen (1990), who argues that institutional practices are best understood on the Foucauldian, "archaeological" basis of an examination of their origins. From such an examination he concludes that Anglo-Saxon studies are hopelessly mired in the illusions fostered by the Romanticism under which the discipline developed, as expressed in the way *Beowulf* in particular is both taught and edited. Anglo-Saxon studies are in need of rescue and revival, since they are dominated by antiquated philological methods and subjective textual practices. This is an important and an influential argument – and a surprising one, we believe, given the precipitous decline of interest in philology among Anglo-Saxonists since Tolkien's day and the antiphilological conservatism that has reigned over Old English textual editing since the start of the twentieth century (see Lapidge 1994c and Fulk 1996b, 1997). Lerer (1997) offers a rather different critique of the history of *Beowulf* criticism, pointing out how literary scholars from Tolkien to Frantzen and Overing continually frame their critical maneuvers as acts of salvation, rescuing the poem, or the field of Old English studies itself, from the critical morass into which it is said to have fallen. Lerer's earlier study (1991) is perhaps the most ambitious and inspired of the cultural critiques, as he attempts a less polemical archaeology of Anglo-Saxon literacy, unearthing the roles of reading and writing as concomitants of power in Anglo-Saxon society, at the same time that he considers questions of canon-formation.

Gender studies in relation to *Beowulf* were not at first inflected by poststructuralist thinking, but they followed the pattern in other literary periods (see, e.g., Lees 1994: 130) of beginning with a feminist recuperative phase, which had the aim of identifying a neglected feminine presence in the poem and affirming its importance. Damico (1984) has reconstructed a fragmentary valkyrie tradition of numinous women within which she situates Wealhtheow as a commanding figure in the poem; the argument of Chance (1986) that the fight with Grendel's mother is of central structural importance was mentioned above; and Olsen (1997) draws together much earlier scholarship to set forth an evaluative epitome of women's traditional roles as hostesses, peaceweavers, ritual mourners, goaders, and counselors – to which Dockray-Miller (2000: 77–115) adds mothers. Something of the impulse of this first phase for same-sex relations is represented by Frantzen's examination (1998: 92–8) of the erotic undercurrents in Hrothgar's sorrow at Beowulf's departure (1870–82) and Hrethel's devastation at the death of Herebeald (2462–71). The second phase involves the application of recent gender theory, particularly the Lacanian psychoanalysis that has inflected the work of such scholars as Hélène Cixous and Luce Irigaray, along with queer theories of gender performance, in particular reference to the work of Judith Butler.[29] More especially, though, one should expect studies inflected by recent feminist theory to be concerned more generally with power relations in the poem, the culture, and the history of scholarship, focusing on the role of gender in the construction of those relations and resistance to the gendered status quo. These latter concerns entail a critique of the masculinist critical enterprise, perceiving work of the first phase as validating that enterprise by iterating its methods, without questioning its underlying assumptions. As a consequence, the opposition of the two phases has generated a degree of critical rancor: practitioners of the latter have characterized the work of the first phase as passé and out of touch with feminist goals (see, e.g., Frantzen 1993b and Lees 1997), practitioners of the former criticizing the work of the second phase for accepting patriarchal assumptions about women's passivity and victimization (see Olsen 1994). Yet in fact women's empowerment is a central concern of much work in the second phase (e.g. Bennett 1992 and Overing 1995).

Finally on the topic of *Beowulf* it should be said that the poem has played a central role in the development of Old English prosody as a subdiscipline. Modern theories of Old English meter begin with Sievers 1885, the greater part of which is devoted to the meter of *Beowulf*.[30] This study is of importance not only because it is the first presentation of Sievers' metrical theories, on which all subsequent work on Old English prosody depends – and usually quite heavily – but also because Sievers' observations about the diachronic and diatopic significance of variant metrical features continue to be of use. The influential work of Bliss (1967), devoted exclusively to *Beowulf*, is self-characterized as a "vindication" of Sievers. Probably the greater part of Old English metrical study has taken *Beowulf* as its basis for analysis: some of the more significant contributions of this sort are those of Pope (1942), Cable (1974), Obst (1987), Creed (1990), Kendall (1991), Suzuki (1996), Stockwell and Minkova (1997), and Russom (1998).[31]

Aside from *Beowulf*, the remains of Germanic legend in Old English are sparse. The text of *The Battle of Finnsburg* (the "Fragment," *ASPR* 6.3–4) was published by George Hickes in his *Thesaurus* of 1703–5 (1.192–3) from a single leaf found in a homiliary in Lambeth Palace Library, a leaf that seems to have been misplaced even before the *Thesaurus* was in proof, and which has not turned up since.[32] It would seem an extraordinary stroke of luck that we have this shard of a poem on the same conflict described in lines 1068–159 of *Beowulf* (the "Episode"), except that it does nothing to clarify the murky sequence of events narrated there, and it presents several problems of its own, including indications of an exceptionally corrupt text. The most widely accepted interpretation of the Episode is this: While Hnæf and a party of Danes were visiting his sister Hildeburh and her husband Finn in Frisia, a battle erupted (probably due to an old feud) between the Danes and Finn's men, the latter referred to alternately as Frisians and Jutes.[33] The casualties, including Hnæf on one side and his nephew on the other, were so great that neither party could claim a decisive victory. The Danes, left leaderless, without the means to provide for themselves, and unable to sail back to Denmark till the return of fair weather, were compelled to the shameful expedient of concluding a truce and pledging loyalty to Finn. Hengest, who apparently assumed leadership of the Danes, abided by the truce all winter, but with the arrival of spring, goaded by his men, he exacted vengeance, killing Finn and returning with Hildeburh to Denmark (see Krapp and Dobbie 1931–53: 6.xlvii–xlviii). The view of the conflict in the Episode is thus expansive, tracing its entire history and focusing in particular on the terms of the truce agreed to by the opposing parties, the funeral rites for the slain, and Hengest's state of mind. The Fragment, by contrast, focuses on heroic combat, narrating the specifics of the attack in which Hildeburh's brother and son were killed. It begins in the middle of an exchange, inside the hall, in which the first speaker apparently has seen the glint of moonlight (or torchlight?) on weapons outside and misinterpreted its source. His respondent (probably Hnæf) corrects him: this is not light from the approaching dawn or a flying dragon or flames in the gables, but battle is at hand. Such an exchange is strongly reminiscent of a motif common in Celtic literature (see Henry 1966: 216–21 and Sims-Williams 1976–8), as is the later reference to *hwītne medo* 'white mead' (39) as reward for valor (Henry 1961: 154–6). Encouraged by Hnæf, defenders move to the doors of the hall. Outside, Guthere exhorts Garulf to spare himself and not be the first to rush the doors – advice he disregards, losing his life as a consequence.[34] After five days of fighting, none of the defenders has been killed, and Finn (or possibly Hnæf: see Greenfield 1972: 45–51) questions one of his injured men how the troops bear their wounds. At this point the Fragment breaks off. There is thus no real overlap between the accounts of the Fragment and the Episode, since the latter tells us only about the consequences of the battle, and nothing about the events of the fight itself, on which the former is narrowly focused. This narrower focus is what one might expect of an actual lay (as opposed to a recounted one, as in the Episode: see Reichl 2000: 93–9), and indeed, the chief importance that scholars have attached to the Fragment, aside from its difficult connection with *Beowulf*, is its pertinence to the question of what form was taken by early Germanic heroic literature. If it is a lay, it would appear to evidence the innovative form of *Beowulf* (see above). Recent studies of the Fragment are few. The chief issues of critical concern have been to determine the sequence of events narrated (on the great variety of opinion, see the editions and North 1990) and to explain some of the puzzling readings in Hickes' edition (e.g. Breeze 1992). Waugh (1997) attempts to place the poem in an oral context, identifying Hnæf's initial speech as an analogue to the oral poet's desire to sweep away the past and assert his own moment of eminence.

Also fragmentary is *Waldere* (*ASPR* 6.4–6), preserved on two leaves discovered in 1860 in a bundle of papers and parchments in the Royal Library in Copenhagen (Ny Kgl. S. MS 167b).[35] How they came to Denmark is unknown, but the leaves show signs of having been used in a book binding – not an uncommon fate for Old English manuscripts after Henry VIII's dissolution of the monasteries, when the contents of the monastic libraries were set adrift on a sea of materials to be scavenged by Tudor printers. The two leaves do not form a continuous text, and their order is not known for certain, but most scholars agree with the *ASPR* ordering, assuming the loss of no more than about 150 lines between the fragments. The tale of Walter of Aquitaine is a familiar one, being preserved in medieval Latin, Norse, and Polish versions, as well as in several fragments and brief accounts in Middle High German. The earliest of the complete versions is *Waltharius* (ed. and trans. Kratz 1984), a poem in 1456 Latin hexameters produced in a Continental monastic setting (possibly St. Gall in Switzerland) in the ninth or tenth century. It relates how Waltharius and Hiltgunt, lovers from Aquitaine and Burgundy, respectively, fled the court of Attila, where they had been hostages, with two chests of stolen treasure. On the way home they were intercepted by Guntharius, king of the Franks, and his compatriot Hagano, another of Attila's escaped hostages, desirous of the treasure. In a narrow defile Waltharius killed 11 attackers. The next day the Franks set upon him in the open, and in the battle Waltharius lost an arm, Guntharius a leg, and Hagano an eye and six teeth. Thereupon hostilities ceased, the combatants were reconciled, and Waltharius and Hiltgunt returned to Aquitaine, where they were joined in marriage, and where Waltharius ruled for 30 years. The tone of *Waltharius* is generally agreed to be ironic (but cf. Olsen 1993) and its unheroic ending a bookish alteration of the legend (see Phillpotts 1928: 17), while *Waldere* is straightforwardly heroic. The first Old English fragment introduces a speech by (presumably) Hildegyth, a stronger-willed and livelier figure than her counterpart in *Waltharius*, exhorting (presumably) Waldere to attack Guthhere and advising him that his sword Mimming, the work of Weland, is equal to the task. This speech is never completed. The second fragment opens in the middle of a declaration made by one of the male contestants, more likely Hagena than Guthhere or Waldere, praising the superior qualities of his own sword, identifying it as Theodric's gift to Widia (son of Weland and Beadohild: see below) in thanks for the latter's rescuing him from the power of monsters.[36] Waldere then addresses Guthhere, daring him to attack without the assistance of Hagena, and thus the fragment ends. The poem is thought to have been, when it was complete, a work of greater scope than a lay. Indeed, it must have been longer than any of the heroic works in the poetic edda, since the speeches have the same leisurely quality as those in *Beowulf*. Still, it need not have related anything more than the course of the combat, and thus it is inconclusive as evidence for epic as a native form. Andersson, who is in general skeptical about Virgilian influence on *Beowulf* (1997), nonetheless perceives the *Aeneid* as a model for the rhetoric of the speeches in *Waldere* (1992), perhaps because he is also skeptical about the existence of early Germanic folk-epic (1988).

Deor (*ASPR* 3.178–9), a poem of just 42 lines in the Exeter Book, is *sui generis*, being divided into strophes of unequal length, each bearing a cryptic refrain.[37] In form it is simply a sequence of allusions to heroic legends exemplifying hardships, with one passage of gnomic reflection inserted (28–34); and yet although it thus shares with *Beowulf* the quality of allusiveness (since the poet clearly did not expect his audience to need more than the barest hints to recognize all these tales), it is even more laconic. Another parallel that has been remarked (by J. Harris 1987: 53) is the Franks Casket (see plate 4), in that both arrange scenes from history and legend in "panel structures." Some of the allusions in *Deor* are unambiguous to us – the stories of Weland and Beadohild are familiar enough – while others are mysterious, because we do not know either who the persons cited are or what aspects of their legends are relevant to the poem's theme. The figures Mæthhild and Geat are simply unknown;[38] Theodric's legend is obscure;[39] and the strophe on

Eormenric must be taken to reverse the significance of the allusions, exemplifying not a victim of misfortune but the cause of others' misfortune. Deor, the *scop* who names himself in the final stanza, is mentioned in no other source, but his people the Hedenings and his rival Heorrenda figure in medieval Icelandic and German legends. The theme of the poem is a matter of some dispute. The verses that close each stanza seem to mean "That passed away; so can this" – though the peculiar syntax of the expression, with both demonstratives in the genitive case, has spawned several alternative analyses (for discussion see Erickson 1975 and Klinck 1992: 160–1). Most recent commentators regard this refrain as optimistic in nature, indicating that the legendary figures who suffered these hardships lived through them to better days. The poem is thus to be regarded as an example of *consolatio*, a Boethian composition, since it offers hope of improvement. This interpretation renders the purpose of the refrain at the close of the final strophe somewhat obscure: it may refer generally to all the previously mentioned adversities, or to Heorrenda's displacement of Deor, or (the commonest analysis) to Deor's good fortune before his fall from grace. It is perhaps likelier, however, that the poem is not Boethian at all. When it is viewed in the context of the heroic literature to which it shows the clearest affinities – the eddic *Guðrúnarhvǫt* makes a particularly apt comparison (see Pope and Fulk 2001: 112) – it seems more naturally to express the grim admiration of sublime suffering so characteristic of heroic poetry. The poet's purpose would then appear to be to celebrate the trials of a great fellow *scop*, and in that event perhaps the refrain compares Deor's hardships to unspecified ones faced by the poet himself.

Widsith (*ASPR* 3.149–53) is also to be found in the Exeter Book, and like *Deor* it is mostly a catalogue in form.[40] An impersonal narrator introduces Widsith as the most traveled of men, a man of the Myrgings (neighbors of the Angles in what is now northern Germany) who first accompanied the Angle Ealhhild to the court of the great Gothic king Eormenric, to whom she was to be married (*pace* Malone 1931). Widsith then recites a list (or *thula*, a term adapted from Icelandic; pl. *thulur*) of legendary or historical figures and the nations they ruled, chiefly taking the form "Attila ruled the Huns, Eormenric the Goths, Becca the Banings, Gifica the Burgundians" (18–19), and so forth. At the close of this list, he again remarks the breadth of his travels and the excellence of the rewards he has received. A second *thula* follows, of the form "I was with the Huns and with the Glory-Goths, with Swedes and with Geats and with South-Danes" (57–8), and so forth. But the court of Eormenric was his usual abode, where the king gave him a most valuable torque, which he conveyed to his lord Eadgils, king of the Myrgings, in exchange for the inheritance of his father's estate. Ealhhild gave him another, and he repaid her with songs that spread her fame far and wide. When he and Scilling (another *scop*? or his harp? attested as an actual man's name) made music together, people said they had never heard a better song. The third *thula* is a catalogue of Goths he has known (112–30). Finally, Widsith observes that he to whom God gives the right of rule is best loved by men. The poem then closes with praise for the wandering *glēoman* 'minstrel' who is knowledgeable about songs and generous with his talent, bestowing and earning praise while he lives. It is not clear whether this praise for the *glēoman* is spoken by Widsith or whether the narrator has returned.

All in all, the lists seem an incomparable window on the rather large repertoire of legends that an Anglo-Saxon *scop* (admittedly, of uncertain date) might be expected to know – though even this critical commonplace about the poem has been disputed.[41] As with *Deor*, some of the names in *Widsith* are identifiable from other sources, while some are entirely mysterious. Several in the first *thula* correspond to figures in *Beowulf*: Eormenric, Breoca, Fin Folcwalding, Hnæf Hocing, Ongendtheow, Offa, Hrothwulf, Hrothgar, and Ingeld. Hrothwulf and Hrothgar are singled out for particular comment: they "observed the duties of kinship together for the longest time, nephew and uncle, after they drove off the tribe of Vikings and turned aside Ingeld's vanguard, cut the force of the Heathobards down to size at Heorot" (45–9). This perhaps hints ironically at later strife between the two, much as in *Beowulf* (esp. 1014–19); it in any case better clarifies the allusions to Ingeld and the Heathobards in *Beowulf* than any other source in antiquity. Particularly remarkable is the list of Goths and presumed Goths (112–30), since this implies an audience familiar with a wide array of East Germanic legends for which there is practically no other evidence in Old English. Yet whether an Anglo-Saxon audience would actually have known of these figures, or whether the poet is here merely displaying his grasp of arcana, is debatable, since the poem also contains some decidedly literate lists, surely incomprehensible to anyone but a monkish bookworm. One such semi-biblical passage (82–7) begins with familiar Mediterranean nations (Israelites, Assyrians, Egyptians, and so forth) and ends with a series of mostly baffling non-Germanic names (Mofdings, Eolas, Ists, and Idumings, the latter two probably Balts or Slavs). Even very recently such passages have been regarded as interpolations, an idea prompted by the supposition that the poem is an early composition. Yet they need not be later additions for the poem to have been composed early. The Age of Bede is no less likely a time – indeed, perhaps an even likelier one – than the tenth century for a monkish poet to have compiled lists of names culled from familiar legends and Latin sources.

The prevalence even today of the view that *Widsith* (or at least the three *thulur* it contains) is one of the earliest compositions in Old English is due in part to the antiquity of its legendary material – the latest historically verifiable reference is to Ælfwine (Alboin), the Lombard conqueror of Italy, who died in 573 – in part because of some apparently archaic spellings (e.g. *Rūm-* 'Rome', elsewhere *Rōm-* in verse (see A. Campbell 1959: 203); and *Eatule* 'Italy', as opposed to *Ītalīa* in the *Meters of Boethius* 2.15), in part because of the improbability that such a rich fund of native lore should reflect late rather than early oral tradition, and in part because the *thula* form itself has been thought ancient, a survival of a verse type used in prehistory as a way to preserve tribal lore, under the scholarly assumption that the alliterative form was a mnemonic aid. Though the poem may well be old, the supposition that tribal lore was in prehistory commonly preserved and transmitted in the form of *thulur* seems to us improbable (though certainly not to all recent observers, e.g. Pasternack 1995: 72), and the listing of nations and kings in metrical form seems more likely a literate display of virtuosity than a common oral practice, despite some (limited) Icelandic parallels. Historically, the framework furnished by the character Widsith is entirely imaginary: a *glēoman* at the court of Eormenric (d. ca. 375) cannot have experienced the generoisty of Ælfwine (d. 573), and *Widsith* 'wide-journey' is obviously a fictitious name. The poem provoked intense interest when philology dominated Old English studies, most of the pertinent scholarship being devoted to identifying its allusions. It is no surprise, given the sharp turn away from philology in Old English studies, that relatively little has been written about it in the past half century. This is an unfortunate development, since much remains to be resolved about the poem's allusions.[42] The more salient questions in scholarship of the past half century have pertained to the poet's design and the poem's date. Is it a "begging poem," designed to earn material reward from the poet's patron(s) by highlighting the munificence of great lords of the heroic past, as some have argued?[43] Or does the poet express an ironic distance between Widsith's views and his own, implying a critique of the *glēoman*'s values?[44] As for the date, was the poem composed in the seventh century, as earlier scholarship typically held, or, in accordance with the postwar trend in Old English literary studies toward later dating, should the poet be placed in the tenth century?[45] Some of the reasons offered above militate against this last conjecture, though they do not demand a date as early as the seventh century.

The Battle of Maldon (*ASPR* 6.7–16) is best discussed here, for although it does not recount heroic legend, it is in the martial tradition of works like the Finnsburg Fragment and *Waldere*.[46] Like both, it is also a fragment, and like the former it is preserved only in a modern copy of the manuscript. The poem apparently was already a fragment when it was bound with a manuscript of Asser's life of Alfred and some Latin hagiographies (BL, Cotton Otho A. 12) in the seventeenth century. The fragment was destroyed in the Cottonian fire of 1731, and for the text we must rely on a transcript, made a few years before the fire, formerly attributed to John Elphinston (or Elphinstone), under-keeper of the library at Ashburnham House, but which is now known to have been made by his successor, David Casley.[47]

The poem describes a confrontation that occurred on August 10 or 11, 991, between a viking army encamped on an island in the estuary of the Blackwater (OE *Pante*) near Maldon, Essex, and a group of English defenders under the leadership of Byrhtnoth, *eorl* (i.e. *ealdormann*) of Essex, a nobleman of considerable influence and importance in the England of his day.[48] The engagement is mentioned as a viking victory in most versions of the Anglo-Saxon Chronicle; accounts of the battle are also given in some Latin sources, most notably in Byrhtferth of Ramsey's *Vita Oswaldi* (ca. 1000) and the *Liber Eliensis* (ca. 1170); but they add little to our knowledge that is trustworthy.[49] The real significance of the battle is that it represents the beginning, after roughly half a century of respite, of the renewed viking onslaught that was to lead ultimately to the placement of the Dane Cnut upon the English throne in 1016. The English defeat also prompted the first instance of Æthelred II's unpopular policy of paying off the vikings to stave off further attacks.

The poem, however, is concerned with none of these issues. At the start of the surviving fragment, on the shore opposite the island, Byrhtnoth rallies his troops and answers the vikings' demand to be bought off with the reply that the English will offer arms not in tribute but in battle. The tide goes out, but the vikings are prevented from crossing to the shore by Englishmen holding the narrow causeway. The vikings are then said to begin to practice deception (*lytegian*), asking for passage, and Byrhtnoth *for his ofermōde* 'on account of his pride' allows them to cross. In the battle that ensues, Byrhtnoth is killed almost immediately, prompting one Godric and his brothers to flee the battle, taking many with them. Perceiving these events, the remaining men steel themselves and each other to face the enemy nobly, and in a series of fine speeches, each in turn makes his "boast" – that is, his declaration that he will not flee the battle but will avenge his lord. As the situation grows ever more desperate, one more speech, the finest of all, is delivered by Byrhtwold, beginning, "Resolve must be the firmer, heart the keener, courage the greater, as our force diminishes" (312–13). The fragment breaks off shortly after this.

Though earlier scholarship often treated the poem as a factual account, it is now widely acknowledged to be an imaginative recreation of the battle.[50] Like the poems of heroic legend that it emulates, *Maldon* bestows mythic status on its heroes, putting into their mouths speeches that are at once splendid and impossible. Equally artificial is the ideal espoused by the men of dying by their lord rather than allowing him to lie unavenged. This may have been a requirement of warriors nearly a millennium earlier in the Germanic world described by Tacitus, but it does not seem to have been what was actually expected of Englishmen during the Viking Age.[51] Rather, just as the diction and attitudes of ancient heroic verse color all varieties of Old English versified narratives, including renderings of scripture and saints' lives, so do its conventions demand that the men at Maldon assume the traits of legendary heroes – in stark contrast to the prose entries in the Chronicle for the following years, which portray the English as cowardly and their commanders as corrupt (see Wilcox 1996). Very likely this is why heroic verse in Old English does not generally celebrate English heroes: being more familiar than the legendary figures of long ago and far away, they are less susceptible to being rendered larger than life with any plausibility, and so they are of inferior interest. (This, presumably, is the explanation for the still-unsolved question (see Shippey and Haarder 1998: 44) why there is no direct reference to anything English in *Beowulf*.) Comparably, we see a vagueness of location in time and space in the poems of the poetic edda. Englishmen can achieve such greatness only in a late poem like *Maldon*, which thus might very well have seemed to an earlier audience a violation of the tradition, and in that sense (though it hardly seems so to us) a

vulgarization. Certainly the form of the poem would not have satis-
fied the formal expectations of an audience even half a century earlier:
the text's many idiosyncrasies of alliteration and meter cannot all be
due to mistranscription.[52] Since the classical form was inaccessible to
the poet, it may very well be true, as argued by C. Davis (1999), that
the poem lacks the references to heroic tradition found in other heroic poems because that tradition was also no longer accessible. Yet it
may also be simply that that it would have seemed implausible to
compare familiar Englishmen to ancient heroes.

Aside from the question of the poem's fidelity to history and its oddly
Tacitean attitudes, the two issues that have engaged the most critical
interest in the postwar years are the poet's judgment of Byrhtnoth and
the date of composition. The former controversy is centered primarily
on the poet's remark that in allowing the Norsemen to cross the causeway, the English commander showed *ofermōd* 'pride'. Is this oppro-
brium, or is *ofermōd* something that might be admirable in a commander?
An exhaustive study by Gneuss (1976a) has shown that *ofermōd*, though
used more than 120 times in the Old English corpus, always means
'pride', and seemingly in a negative sense. Some have thus taken the
word to express criticism of the hero's moral state; others his capabilities as a commander – a position bolstered by reference to the vikings'
using guile (*lytegian*, 86) and Byrhtnoth's allowing the invaders too
much space (*landes tō fela*, 90), implying an unbecoming pliancy on
Byrhtnoth's part.[53] And yet despite a certain amount of exasperation on
the part of those who consider the matter closed, there persists among
some scholars a willingness to perceive *ofermōd* in this text as an admirable quality, an interpretation sanctioned by a passage in the Alfredian
Boethius.[54] Indeed, it has been argued that the treatment of Byrhtnoth
is hagiographical in nature, especially in connection with his dying prayer.
Yet the differences between *Maldon* and hagiography are perhaps more
remarkable than the similarities.[55] In any event, if it is true that the
virtue of dying by one's lord is an inauthentic ideal introduced from the
conventions of heroic verse in order to elevate the English to the ranks
of the heroes of old, it is more or less inevitable that any seeming criticism of Byrhtnoth on the poet's part should be suspect. As for the date
of the poem, it may be, as some have supposed, that it was composed a
considerable number of years, 30 or more, after the battle: the evidence
is chiefly linguistic and inconclusive. Probably most regard it as likelier
that the battle was in recent memory when the poem was composed,
since the poet's purpose in preserving the memory of such a wide array

of English participants grows more difficult to perceive, the greater the distance between the event and the poem.[56]

Lastly, *The Battle of Brunanburh* (*ASPR* 6.16–20) is another poem at the periphery of heroic literature, simultaneously evoking and altering heroic conventions.[57] It is one of the historical poems in the Chronicle, where it is preserved in four manuscripts as the sole entry for the year 937, a niche for which it was specifically composed, in all likelihood (see chapter 2). The poem was probably composed shortly after the event, but certainly no later than about 955, when it was copied into the Parker Chronicle. The location of the battle has not been identified conclusively, though it was probably near the west coast of England between Chester and Scotland. Even the name of the site cannot be determined with certainty, as the manuscripts allow either *Brūnanburh* or *Brunnanburh*. The battle was apparently an engagement of some consequence, as it was the climax of a protracted conflict memorialized in English, Norse, Welsh, Irish, Pictish, and Scottish sources (discussed by A. Campbell 1938: 43–80). It represented the culmination of a process by which the successors of Alfred the Great gradually regained control of all the areas of England seized by the vikings in the previous century. The Norseman Guthfrith, who claimed rule of the viking kingdom of York, established his rule in Dublin when he was driven out of England by King Athelstan. His son Anlaf (Óláfr) returned in 937 at the head of a viking army to claim his patrimony, an endeavor in which he was joined by Constantine III, king of the united Picts and Scots, with the support of Eugenius (Owen), king of the Strathclyde Welsh. The English under Athelstan and his brother Edmund Ætheling claimed a decisive victory, the poem telling us that five kings were killed that day. Having lost seven of his jarls, Anlaf fled the battle, as did Constantine, leaving his son dead on the field.

The poem is remarkable in several ways. It certainly employs conventions from heroic tradition, especially its poetic diction (including some classic kennings) and its use of the theme of the beasts of battle (60–5: see section 6 of the introduction). Yet unlike the Finnsburg Fragment, *Waldere*, and *Maldon*, it is unconcerned with individual encounters and heroic speeches. The poet identifies the invaders' losses and revels in their shame, but after the fact, with no attempt to portray the battle itself or identify participants other than the principals (as discussed by Klausner 1996). The tone of exultation is uncharacteristic of early Germanic heroic verse, which celebrates valor – on whichever side of a conflict – rather than the humiliation of the defeated. Moreover, it has

often been pointed out (e.g. by Phillpotts 1928) that this body of literature traditionally takes tragedies rather than victories as its theme,
since the measure of character – the chief interest of these works – is
how one acts in the face of grim duty and hopeless odds (see also Tolkien
1936). Even later Norse panegyric (skaldic court poetry) is not a very
close parallel to *Brunanburh*. The difference resides principally in
Brunanburh's unprecedented nationalism (see Thormann 1997), most
clearly expressed when the poet asserts that there had been no battle in
Britain producing greater casualties, according to records, "since the
Angles and the Saxons came up here from the east, approached Britain
over the broad surf, proud war-smiths, overcame the Britons; men keen
to gain glory took possession of the land" (69b–73). This sense of na-
tionhood and shared history springs, no doubt, particularly from the
recent reconquest of the Danelaw and the unification of England under
one monarch, Athelstan, the first king of all of England in both name
and actual authority. The new political structure, placing the multiple
centers of power of the independent Anglo-Saxon kingdoms in the past
and initiating the gradual centralization of power that was to fuel much
of the political conflict of the later Middle Ages, thus seems also to have
worked a transformative effect upon a literary tradition predicated on
an older conception of kingship and military structure. *Brunanburh*
and *Maldon* thus demonstrate that the heroic tradition in literature was
in decline in England – or at least had changed remarkably in nature –
long before the Conquest.

Conclusion

Making Old English New: Anglo-Saxonism and the Cultural Work of Old English Literature

It may not be obvious that the motives of scholars studying Old English literature are ideological. Yet nearly everyone will concede that the study of difficult texts from a remote period is unlikely to be undertaken by anyone for whom it serves no present purpose – that is, for whose benefit those texts are not perceived to perform some variety of "cultural work" in the present. And such cultural work can be performed only when those texts somehow engage the ideologies that inform, indeed constitute, the present and distinguish it from the past. We would not read Old English literature if it did not somehow touch on what we believe about ourselves. The aim of this conclusion, then, is to sketch briefly the history of Anglo-Saxonism – that is, the study of the Anglo-Saxons and their literature – and to highlight a few of the ways that each age after the Norman Conquest has appropriated Old English literature for its own ideological ends. In this way Old English literature has continually been remade into something new, something it never really was, but something relevant to present purposes.

Twenty-one years after the Norman Conquest, just one of the bishops in England, just two of the abbots, were English (James Campbell 1982b: 240). The displacement of English prelates naturally had a profound effect upon the production and transmission of English literature, activities that had been confined to religious houses. With rare exceptions (e.g. *A Prayer* and some copies of *Cædmon's Hymn*), after the Conquest, Old English verse ceased to be copied, and *Durham* – a poem that strays far from the formal standards of classical Old English verse – is the only poem in the *ASPR* standard collected edition of Old English verse known to have been composed after 1066. Poetry was an aristocratic genre, and its fate was therefore linked to the fortunes of the aristocracy, from which the ranks of bishops and abbots were drawn. Old English prose continued to be copied into manuscripts as late as the thirteenth century in the monastic cathedrals at Canterbury, Rochester, and Worcester (see Treharne 1998: 231) – not to mention the updating of the Peterborough Chronicle to 1154 – and some have taken this to evidence a certain monkish resistance to Norman hegemony (e.g. Clanchy 1993: 165–6 and Swanton 2000: xxvii). To be sure, a large portion of the copied texts comprises laws and charters (see Pelteret 1990), documents in which the Normans took considerable interest, the copying of which thus does not suggest anti-Norman sentiment. Yet there seems to have been more than a little antagonism between Saxon and Norman ecclesiastics, and a kind of national feeling, looking back nostalgically to an earlier age, is perceivable in some Latin and Middle English texts of the first two centuries after the Conquest.[1] Thus it is not entirely implausible that the copying of other Old English texts during this period, with relatively little modernization – including gospels, medical texts, the translation of the Benedictine Rule, and both Alfredian and Ælfrician texts – should reflect that same nostalgia. Just possibly this was the first manifestation of Anglo-Saxonism.

It is a matter of debate whether or not Old English texts were truly comprehensible in the later Middle Ages, though A. Cameron (1974) amasses an impressive body of evidence for the continuous use of Old English manuscripts into the sixteenth century.[2] By then, in any case, the language required careful study to be comprehended. Matthew Parker (1504–75), Elizabeth's first Archbishop of Canterbury, is the first person in post-medieval times known to have mastered the language, and he systematically engaged members of his household in its study, as well.[3] To do this he amassed a collection of Anglo-Saxon books, many of them set adrift from monastic libraries by the dissolution of the monasteries under Henry VIII – a collection that now resides at Cambridge. Parker's aim was baldly political: to prove with Old English evidence that the newly formed Church of England's differences with Rome did not represent an English discarding of immemorial practices and beliefs but a return to a more original state. Thus a homily by

Ælfric on the Eucharist, seemingly undercutting the Roman dogma of transubstantiation, appeared in the first fruit of the labors of Parker's circle, *A Testimonie of Antiquity* (1566–7), the first printed book to contain Old English. Old English translations of the Gospels offered precedent for the Protestant insistence on the legitimacy of translating Scripture into the vernacular, and accordingly Parker published an edition of them in 1571 under the name of John Foxe, the martyrologist. At about the same time, the antiquary Laurence Nowell published a collection of Anglo-Saxon laws titled *Archaionomia* (1568), with the assistance of his friend William Lambarde, under whose name the work appeared. The political significance of this edition was not fully realized until the Stuart era, when it was employed as a key to the interpretation of common law, and thus as an instrument for restoring rights and legal practices that were, in the view of Roundhead lawyers, immemorial, and which would have the effect of limiting royal authority. In the hands of Parker, Nowell, and their circles, then, Old English texts acquired remarkable political value by virtue of their originary status, reflecting the wellspring of English civilization.

It was in fact the political uses of Anglo-Saxon law that established study of the Old English language as an academic subject, for the Royalist jurist Sir Henry Spelman paid Abraham Wheelock, Professor of Arabic at Cambridge, to learn and teach the language, beginning in 1638. But it was at Queen's College, Oxford, that Anglo-Saxon studies really flourished, as there sprang up there a "profluvium of Saxonists" (Mores 1778: 26). There the first dictionary of the language, by William Somner, was published in 1659, and the first really substantial grammar by George Hickes in 1689, superseding the rather inadequate one by Wheelock that had appeared in Somner's dictionary. Hickes may be regarded as the first scholar to appreciate the comparative Germanic context of Old English studies, for when he published a revision of his grammar in 1703 it was in a much-expanded volume, his renowned *Thesaurus*, which included grammars of Old Icelandic and Gothic, along with an essay urging the utility of studying them, and studies of numismatics and diplomatics. It is the second volume of the *Thesaurus*, however, published in 1705, that is of great value even today, for in it, Hickes' assistant Humphrey Wanley catalogued all the Old English manuscripts that were known to reside in libraries in Britain. It was of fundamental importance at the time, since very few Old English texts had been edited and published, and students were obliged to consult the manuscripts. It is of great value today because it provides indispensable information about manuscripts that were subsequently lost, damaged or destroyed, particularly those in the Cotton Library, which was to suffer grievous damage when Ashburnham House in Westminster burned in 1731. What is remarkable about the efforts of Hickes and Wanley is not simply that they were made under the most difficult circumstances, and at great self-sacrifice for these men, but that these two seem to have been motivated chiefly by an intellectual passion for the subject itself. The study of Old English offered the two men no very obvious monetary rewards or political advantage.

The best-known writer to concern himself with Anglo-Saxon matters in the seventeenth century was John Milton, the last three books of whose *History of Britain* (1670, in six books, written probably in the 1650s) are devoted to the Anglo-Saxons. In this work his interests are as much literary as historical, for he lingers over incidents of narrative interest, revealing a "literary fascination with dramatic, tragic, or romantic events" (Glass 1982: 96). A similar romantic bent is evident in his commonplace book, containing a list (compiled after 1634) of nearly 30 Anglo-Saxon topics on which a drama might be based, including one on King Alfred, though naturally Milton never wrote any such play (see Scragg 2000: 8–9). It has often been speculated that his conception of Satan as a romantic anti-hero in *Paradise Lost* was inspired by the heroically individualized Satan of *Genesis B*. Indeed, the Old English poem was published in 1655 by Franciscus Junius, who was almost certainly an acquaintance of Milton's, if the testimony of Junius' nephew is to be credited (see Lever 1947). Yet Old English influence on Milton's epic remains impossible to prove.

The romantic strain in Milton's *History* is no doubt a consequence of the habit, as old as *The Battle of Brunanburh* in England, of seeking a concise national identity in a people's legendary past. Milton's choice of Alfred as the subject of a projected drama is unsurprising, then, given the extent to which Alfred's own circle seems to have conspired to confer upon him legendary status and the right to sole rule in Britain outside the Danelaw (see chapter 2). Indeed, although he was not styled "the Great" until the sixteenth century, he was clearly revered in the tenth and eleventh centuries, and a cult of the king seems to have been firmly established within a century of the Conquest, crediting him spuriously with such accomplishments as the founding of the University of Oxford and (according to a later age) of the Royal Navy (see Keynes and Lapidge 1983: 44–8). Thus when we find that Alfred throughout the eighteenth century formed the subject of dramas such as Milton had envisaged – no fewer than six between 1740 and the end of the century, a period crucial to the consolidation of empire – the intensely patriotic nature of such works should come as no surprise. The first of these, in fact, James Thomson and David Mallet's *Alfred: A Masque* (1740), commissioned by the Prince of Wales, is the source of the anthem *Rule, Britannia*.[4] The spectacle was a Drury Lane fixture for decades, attracting a steady stream of spectators and drawing on the greatest actors of the day. Alfred's cult, feeding on its basis in British national feeling, only intensified in the Romantic and Victorian Ages. It was endemic to high culture as well as low, from the comic opera *Alfred, or The Magic Banner* of John O'Keeffe (performed 1796) and Agnes M. Stewart's 1840 *Stories about Alfred the Great for Children* to Wordsworth's *Ecclesiastical Sonnets* (1822) and Antonin Dvorak's 1870 opera *Alfred* (which was not performed in the composer's lifetime).

Although the Anglo-Saxon period had acquired significant political, religious, and legal import for England as early as Elizabeth's reign, it was not until the rise of Romanticism that Old English poetry came to be a genuine focus of interest. Its obscure diction was an obstacle, and its form seemed barbaric to Englishmen, like Milton, whose literary models were all classical. Yet barbarousness was a quality that appealed to the Romantics. Thomas Percy's *Five Pieces of Runic Poetry* (1763) captured the imagination of English readers, seeming to offer Old Norse poems as a primitivist antidote to the conventions of neoclassicism, with the result that more than 50 translations and adaptations of Norse material appeared in the next half century (see Payne 1982: 151). Percy's *Reliques of Ancient English Poetry* (1765) proclaimed the oneness of Old English and Old Norse verse; but the truth is that very little Old English verse displaying the qualities that Percy's readers admired had been published, nor would most of it become available until well into the nineteenth century. When poems like *The Wanderer* and *The Seafarer* (first ed. Benjamin Thorpe, 1842) finally were made available, they would seem to invite readers to see in them the melancholic imagination, the individuality of expression, and the yearning for oneness with nature that were the Romantics' legacy.

Something of these qualities could be perceived already in *Beowulf*, which was first published in 1815; but the poem was so badly edited, and so poorly understood, that it was not until the appearance of J. M. Kemble's edition in 1833 that serious literary study of the poem could be undertaken. Yet the issues that fired the imaginations of early students of *Beowulf* were not literary in the modern sense of the word but ideological. As a record of Scandinavian history and legend earlier than any surviving from Scandinavia itself, the poem was eagerly seized upon by Danish scholars, and indeed the Danish reviews of the first edition tend to be unabashedly nationalist in tenor.[5] Both Danish and German scholars claimed the poem as a *völkisch* heirloom (see Bjork 1997b: 115–16). As a result, *Beowulf* became something of a surrogate battle-ground in the highly charged dispute between Denmark and Prussia over control of Schleswig-Holstein, a dispute that resulted in the mid-century Prusso-Danish Wars. In the scholarly journals as on the battle-field, it was the Germans who were victorious, for German philological methods dominated *Beowulf* scholarship – indeed, Old English schol-arship in general – throughout the nineteenth century, for good and ill. The nationalist basis for German fascination with *Beowulf* is nowhere clearer than in the dominance of *Liedertheorie*, with its obsessive drive to recover the "primitive" components out of which the poem was believed to have been constructed (see chapter 9). This fascination per-sisted long after *Liedertheorie* had grown passé, and to the extent that *Beowulf* scholarship contributed to national self-definition, it "provided a component for the creation of a racist ideology in Germany, as to a lesser extent in Britain."[6]

English scholars were by and large unresponsive to German philol-ogy, maintaining a belletristic approach to literary study that did not work to the benefit of texts valued popularly for their primitivism. Eng-lish hostility to German philology may have been fueled by the unifica-tion and rapid industrialization of Germany under the guidance of Bismarck, as the economic and military threat of the new German em-pire increasingly provoked rivalry with England. There was more than a little nationalist sentiment underlying the complaints of late nineteenth-century English linguists and literary scholars about the dominance of German schools (see Frantzen 1990: 71–3), and in the pointed English insistence on calling the language "Old English" rather than "Anglo-Saxon." When English scholars did finally turn their attention to the medieval texts that they had so badly neglected for most of the nine-teenth century, it was with characteristically Arnoldian attitudes. The greatest of the English critics to take up the subject of Old English literature was W. P. Ker, and in his discussion of *Beowulf* (1908) one finds nothing of the intense philological focus of German scholarship but rather a determined aestheticism, a set of judgments identifying the poem's sources of beauty and strength as well as its structural flaws.

It was to both German philology and English belletrism that Tolkien was reacting in his revolutionary lecture of 1936, but it was by no means aestheticism itself that he objected to in English scholarship – his lecture is itself profoundly invested in the rhetoric of artistic worth – but simply the notion that *Beowulf* should be understood on anything but what he perceived to be its own terms. That is, far from critiquing personal judgment as a basis for literary analysis, Tolkien wished merely to alter the basis on which such judgments are formed, segregating the autonomous text from any such interpretive context as the study of classical epic. The extent to which the fundamental tenets of the New Criticism are already embodied in Tolkien's lecture is remarkable (see above, chapter 9). Such formalist procedures dominated Old English criticism in the postwar years, and indeed they still represent the dominant mode for many. This is something of an anomaly, since New Criticism demands the assumption of an autonomous text deploying original effects. Yet Old English poetic texts are oral-derived (i.e. strongly characterized by oral features, even when they are literate compositions), and thus they are to be understood and appreciated within the historical context of Germanic oral tradition – while New Critics insist on the irrelevance of such contexts to the interpretation of works. The point was demonstrated above in regard to *Beowulf*: formalists are obliged to bracket the issue of the poet's originality and focus instead on the poet's inventive deployment of conventional devices. Yet in all likelihood it was the very conventionality of a poem's effects that made it most appealing, by invoking poetic tradition (see J. Foley 1991).

Residual orality also poses a challenge to poststructuralist approaches to Old English poetry. These are varied in nature, yet nearly all partake, to some degree, of the methods of deconstruction in their application of decentering strategies and in their critique of interpretive essentialism. Huisman (1997) argues convincingly that Old English poetry is narrated from a position of communal and locationless subjectivity that resists Derridean decentering, and that this state of narrative indeterminacy is a consequence ultimately of orality, which, being steeped in a communal tradition rather than in the cult of the author, cannot pretend to a univocal status. Huisman's point can in fact be generalized beyond the confines of narration: decentering strategies were devised to unsettle the seeming patness of modern texts, which might otherwise seem transparent in their meaning. Anglo-Saxonists require no demonstration of how meaning is continually deferred in the process of interpretation, since the meaning of an Old English poetic text is anything but transparent. The often painful gyrations of Old English scholars as they attempt to analyze texts without imposing just one of the many possible interpretations of the individual words is a paean to the radical undecidability that is inseparable from Old English textuality. The problem is fundamentally a historical one: the interpretation of Old English texts is profoundly dependent upon our ability to piece together the historical and cultural circumstances in which they were produced, while poststructuralist theory is almost uniformly developed in response to modern texts in which historical contextualization does not seem such a pressing issue – despite critical awareness that defamiliarizing the here and now is a prerequisite to analyzing it.

This presentism has been remarked particularly in feminist studies (see Lees 1997: 152), and indeed, it complicates the application of most recent gender theory to Old English literature. For example, when Gillian R. Overing, in her excellent study of the women in *Beowulf*, offers the poet's disinterest in heterosexual love and romance as evidence that marriage in the poem is a force for denying women agency (1995: 223), the perspective assumed would seem to be a modern Western one about what is normative behavior in the relations between the sexes, when of course modern Western views are historically anomalous. Indeed, the application of feminist theory derived from Lacanian psychoanalysis to premodern texts raises a raft of difficult issues, since it seems to demand transcendent gender characteristics (a charge that has been leveled, for example, at Hélène Cixous' Lacanian discourse, and a practice recapitulated in Overing's self-admittedly binaristic treatment of gender differences) that cultural historians must find questionable.

Clearly the cultural work that Old English literature has performed since the Elizabethan Age has been primarily to represent the ultimate source of English cultural and political institutions, satisfying a desire for identifying origins, as demonstrated forcefully by Frantzen (1990). Viewed this way, the literature has invited us since shortly after the Conquest to gauge the ways that contemporary institutions and practices either express or stray from their origins, and thus the extent to which those institutions and practices require either reverence or revision. The rhetoric of Anglo-Saxon origins persists even today in popular culture, in books of a patriotic nature (e.g. Phillips 1996, Linsell 2001), and in the tremendously popular genre of sword-and-sorcery novels, films, and fantasy games, which has created out of fragments of Anglo-Saxon, Norse, and Celtic cultures a pixilated version of the Dark Ages that is more congenial to feelings of nostalgia than the actual period could be. The rhetoric of origins is largely absent from current academic discourse, though perhaps its premise is recapitulated in Frantzen's own efforts to derive current ideologies in Old English scholarship from those that motivated its founders. Yet it would be naive to suppose that the general avoidance of such rhetoric in current scholarship means that the study of Old English has finally become objective and disinterested. The ideological motivation of feminist criticism and cultural materialism is self-proclaimed, and the topics that most interest poststructuralist Anglo-Saxonists of other sorts – particularly textuality, alterity, and power – are not by happenstance at the heart of the program that converted literary study over the course of the twentieth century from a gentleman's pastime to an instrument of cultural critique with unabashed political aims. Yet from the start, Old English texts have resisted and disrupted the constructions placed upon them. Ælfric's homily on the Holy Sacrament is not the refutation of transubstantiation that Matthew Parker and his circle wished it to be, nor are Anglo-Saxon legal codes a key to the interpretation of English common law. So, too, Old English texts have continuously unsettled the assumptions of the field of literary criticism that developed over the course of the twentieth century, for its residual orality challenges the tenets of twentieth-century formalism and its cultural remoteness resists the presentism of so many more recent hermeneutic trends.

It is by now a critical commonplace that Old English literary studies face a crisis of relevance – that they are marginalized in both academic and popular discourses.[7] Whether or not greater general regard for Old English studies would benefit the field, it would be a mistake to suppose that life on the margins is anything new for Anglo-Saxonists. Although the philological methods employed by some Anglo-Saxonists were at the forefront of critical theory in Germany and Scandinavia more than a century ago, there never was a time when Old English literature was central to the modern Anglophone tradition of academic literary studies. Even at the height of Anglo-American interest in Old English, in the first decades of the twentieth century, the proportion of articles devoted to Old English literature in the chief English and (to a lesser extent) American journals of general interest was small. Anglo-American literary scholarship never took its cue from Anglo-Saxon studies. Rather, the aestheticism on which the academic study of English literature was built, and the ahistorical approaches that it spawned, had the marginalization of Old English built into them. This is because Anglo-Saxon studies are in a broad sense an archaeological discipline, committed fundamentally to the recovery of a lost culture. The pervasive philological basis of Old English studies resembles nothing encountered in the study of later periods, and it demands methodologies that have remained relatively stable over time. It is for this reason, primarily, that Old English literary studies tend to resist conformity to changing trends in literary analysis, and thus to the homogenization of critical practices across fields. In our view, such difference is to be celebrated rather than lamented. The uncertainties inherent in the study of anonymous, undatable texts of unknown provenance in an imperfectly understood language promote a radical uncertainty to which there is nothing comparable in postmedieval studies. Especially at a time when indeterminacy plays such a vital role in the operation of literary hermeneutics, Old English offers valuable lessons on the mediation of language and culture. One trend that Anglo-Saxonists have pioneered is the development of electronic media for study (see Baker 1997), a direct result of the kinds of mainly philological needs of researchers in this field. Our difference has in this respect been our strength. Yet the greatest accomplishments in Anglo-Saxon literary studies of the past quarter century have been in recovering the contexts – material, liturgical, and intellectual – in which Old English texts were produced and received. Ultimately, then, this field's chief contribution to literary studies at large may be to serve as a model for dealing with the complexities of extreme textual alterities.

Notes

Introduction
Anglo-Saxon England and Its Literature: A Social History

1 Saenger 1982; but subsequently (1997: 98) he offers evidence for the beginnings of silent reading already in Aldhelm's day. Parkes (1997), who explains some of the occasions for different types of reading, would assign silent reading a more important role.

2 Among the excellent introductions and guides to the study of early English history, society, and culture, some of the more general ones of especial use to students are F. Stenton 1971, Hunter Blair 1977, Whitelock 1974, 1979, James Campbell 1982a, and Lapidge et al. 1999. For a handy select classified bibliography, see Keynes 1998.

3 For a well-balanced assessment of the obstacles to using the *Germania* as a historical source – particularly Tacitus' mixing of Germanic and non-Germanic groups, the influence of possibly dated sources, and the preconceptions of an established Greco-Roman ethnographic tradition – see Rives 1999: 56–66.

4 See James Campbell 1982a: 166; also 174.

5 For an overview of early Germanic feud and its conventions, see W. Miller 1983.

6 Overing (1995: 227–9) argues that such women are in fact annihilated, turned into something other than women, by their aggression, and Lees (1997: 159–67) similarly argues that Elene, despite her heroic role, lacks real agency. Whether or not this is true does not affect the accuracy of the observation that the treatment of such women in Old English literature is quite unlike that in later traditions.

7 Yet Wormald (1991a: 5) warns that the importance that Bede attaches to the date of Easter in his account of the council at Whitby may be exaggerated, given Bede's own particular interest in computus (see chapter 7).

8 See Fell 1984: 109–13, Robinson 1990, and Neuman de Vegvar 1996:

62–5. On women's Latin correspondence, particularly with Boniface, see Fell 1990, Sims-Williams 1990: 211–42, Wallace 1994–5, Cünnen 2000, and Horner 2001: 34–42.

9 Bede's reference to Æthelberht's laws is in his *Historia ecclesiastica* (ed. Plummer 1896, and Colgrave and Mynors 1969), II, 5. On Frankish influence on the early law codes, see Wormald 1999c: 96–101; and now Jurasinski (forthcoming) has uncovered linguistic evidence of direct borrowing.

10 The indispensable concise introduction to Anglo-Latin literature is Lapidge 1996a, to which the following discussion is deeply indebted; and, at greater scope, Lapidge 1993 and 1996b. For the earlier period (to 740), see also Bolton 1967.

11 For accounts of Theodore and his accomplishments, see Bischoff and Lapidge 1994: 5–81 and Lapidge 1995a.

12 Alhelm's life, works, and poetic style are described by Lapidge and Rosier (1985: 5–24), Orchard (1994b: 1–18), and Gwara (2001: 1.19–46).

13 For general discussion of Bede and his times, see A. Thompson 1935, Hunter Blair 1970, Bonner 1976, G. Brown 1987, and Lapidge 1994a.

14 Ed. and trans. Colgrave and Mynors (1969), though the commentary in the edition of Plummer (1896: 1.5–360) is superior. For other translations consult King 1930, Sherley-Price and Farmer 1990, and McClure and Collins 1994.

15 On Boniface's career, see Levison 1946: 70–93 and Reuter 1980.

16 On Alcuin's life and works, the only comprehensive treatments are Gaskoin 1904 and Duckett 1951.

17 Alfred's life and times are treated informatively by Keynes and Lapidge (1983), Frantzen (1986), Smyth (1995), and Abels (1998).

18 Morrish (1986) doubts that Latin literacy was as rare as Alfred claims; but Lapidge (1996d) finds that such Latin as late ninth-century scribes had was exceptionally poor.

19 Some have argued that there was a significant body of vernacular prose in existence before Alfred's day, likely of a Mercian nature: see Vleeskruyer 1953: 56, Schabram 1965: 75, and N. Chadwick 1963: 343. The evidence, though, is slender: see Gneuss 1986 and Bately 1988b. Certainly there was some Old English prose before Alfred: Æthelberht's laws were written in English at the beginning of the seventh century, and Bede's student Cuthbert tells us that at the time of his death Bede was working on translations of John 1.1–6.9 and Isidore's *De natura rerum* (*Epistola de obitu Bedae*, ed. and trans. Colgrave and Mynors 1969: 582–3).

20 We do know, however, from Asser's life of Alfred (cap. 75: see chapter 2), that Æthelweard, the younger of Alfred's two sons, was schooled in English and Latin together with the children of the court nobles, and that Alfred set aside tax revenues for the maintenance of this court school (cap. 102).

21 See Whitelock 1930: 14, line 23 (charter 1488 in the numeration of Sawyer 1968).

22 This is the chief obstacle to the arguments of Lowe (1998b) for lay literacy in the later period, an obstacle she admits (p. 178). The most influential studies of literacy in the period are those of Wormald (1977b) and Keynes (1990).

23 On the participation of persons we should call "illiterate" (by modern standards) in Anglo-Saxon reading communities, see M. Irvine 1991: 196–9 and Howe 1993.

24 The argument of Lutz (2000) that Æthelweard's style borrows from vernacular verse does not alter the judgment that his Latin is unskilled.

25 For a detailed description of the nature of the monks' duties and their way of life, see Knowles 1963: 448–71. For general introductions to the Reform, see F. Stenton 1971: 433–69 and Barlow 1979: 311–38; for a discussion of more recent studies, Cubitt 1997; and for further references, Keynes 1998: G115–95.

26 On the vocabulary of Late West Saxon see Gneuss 1972 and Hofstetter 1987, 1988.

27 Clemoes (1966), Hurt (1972), and Wilcox (1994: 1–65) furnish substantial introductions to Ælfric and his works; for bibliography see Reinsma 1987, supplemented by Kleist 2000.

28 On these and other of Ælfric's genuine and attributed Latin works, see Christopher Jones 1998b.

29 The best introductions to Wulfstan's life and writings are Bethurum 1957: 24–101 and 1966, and Whitelock 1967. He is not to be confused with Wulfstan II, bishop of Worcester (St. Wulfstan), the last of the Anglo-Saxon bishops, who died in 1095.

30 The best concise account of Byrhtferth's life, times, and *oeuvre* is to be found in Baker and Lapidge 1995: xv–xxxiv. For an overview of scholarship on Byrhtferth, with an annotated bibliography, see Hollis and Wright 1992: 147–84.

31 The standard edition of Old English poetry is Krapp and Dobbie 1931–53, which omits a few mostly irregular poems included in the database of the *Dictionary of Old English*. These are *Instructions for Christians* (ed. Rosier 1964–6), *Cnut's Song* (ed. E. Blake 1962: 153), *Godric's Prayer* (ed. Zupitza 1888: 415–16, 426), *The Grave* (ed. Schröer 1882), two distichs, on St. Kenelm and the sons of Ragnarr loðbrók, in Cambridge, Pembroke Coll, 82 (ed. Ker 1957: 124), and some fragments of psalms – though some of these texts might better be regarded as Middle English. There are also some brief metrical passages contained in prose texts, including some crude compositions in the Anglo-Saxon Chronicle and the verses identified by Trahern in a homily (see chapter 8, section 1) and by Kitson in a charter (1987). Throughout this book, verse citations derive

from Krapp and Dobbie's edition (abbr. *ASPR*, followed by volume and page), though macrons have been added to indicate vowel quantities. In the case of *Beowulf*, however, the edition referred to is that of Klaeber (1950); and the riddles of the Exeter book are cited from Williamson 1977. Translations of the greater part of Old English verse are available in R. Gordon 1954 and S. Bradley 1982; translations of Old English poetry are not referenced in this book except in discussions of poems not translated in either of those works. The indispensable guide to manuscripts containing Old English is N. Ker 1957; and for a list of the 1,000 and more manuscripts or fragments known to have been written or owned in England before the Conquest, see Gneuss 2001.

32   The facsimile is edited by Gollancz (1927); there is a detailed study by Raw (1984).

33   The best facsimile, with a careful study, is that of C. Sisam (1976); there is a valuable study of the manuscript by Scragg (1973).

34   Facsimile ed. Chambers, Förster, and Flower (1933). An electronic facsimile by Bernard J. Muir should appear in 2002. The construction of the manuscript was not long ago a matter of controversy: for discussion and references, see Muir 2000: 6–7.

35   Facsimiles by Malone (1963) and, of *Beowulf* only, Zupitza (1959). The digitized images of Kiernan 1999 serve as the best facsimile, though all interpretive matters in this electronic edition, especially Kiernan's conjectures about obscured readings, must be treated with caution – as Gerritsen (1999) has shown about some of Kiernan's earlier work. The manuscript was damaged in the Cottonian fire of 1731, and the two transcripts made in 1789 (facsimiles ed. Malone 1951 and Kiernan 1999) are of importance because apparently more was visible in the damaged portions then than now.

36   Except for some of the quasi-metrical passages mentioned in n. 31, this body of shorter verse is reproduced in facsimile from all known manuscripts by Robinson and Stanley 1991.

37   The most influential study of genres in Germanic oral tradition is Heusler 1941, though the assertion here of the predominance of heroic verse types in prehistory does not coincide with his views. See chapter 8 nn. 19–20.

38   For the most concise and accessible statement on Parry and Lord's findings, see Lord 1960. The volume of research into oral-formulaic theory is by now quite large. For an indispensable overview and annotated bibliography, see J. Foley 1985; also Olsen 1986–8; and for a concise history of oral-formulaic research in Old English, see Acker 1998: xiii–xvii.

39   On poetic diction, see Wyld 1925. For a survey of features of poetic style and rhetoric, as represented in *Beowulf*, see Schaefer 1997.

40   Nominal compounds are treated by Storch 1886; Brodeur (1959: 1–38) offers an enlightening discussion of compounding in *Beowulf*.

41 Kennings in Old English are treated by, among others, Marquardt 1938 and D. Collins 1959.

42 On variation in *Beowulf*, see Brodeur 1959: 39–70 (rpt. in Fulk 1991: 66–87) and Robinson 1985. Paetzel (1913) treats variation in Germanic verse generally.

43 Mandel 1971 studies contrast in verse.

44 See, among others, Bridges 1984.

45 Litotes is studied by Bracher 1937.

46 Some substantial studies of wisdom literature are Shippey 1976, Larrington 1993, and Cavill 1999a; and Deskis (1996) examines the gnomic content of *Beowulf*.

47 For discussion of this device and a list of examples, see Fulk 1996c: 77–8, 83 nn. 28–9.

48 For an extended discussion of dialect features in verse, see Fulk 1992: 269–347.

49 The metrical evidence is collected in Fulk 1992.

Chapter 1 The Chronology and Varieties of Old English Literature

1 Some have argued that there may have been a vernacular prose tradition before Alfred's day (see Vleeskruyer 1953: 18–22 and Turville-Petre 1963: 75; more cautious is Bately 1988b), but most find this implausible (e.g. Chambers 1925: 311, K. Sisam 1953b: 133 and n. 3, and Wormald 1977b: 102–4). See also the introduction, n. 19.

2 Much linguistic evidence is collected in Fulk 1992, particularly in regard to Saxonization (i.e. the rewriting of poetic texts into the West Saxon dialect). The issues, however, are complex, and given the evidence of O'Brien O'Keeffe (1990) and others for scribal rewriting of poetic texts, many doubt whether a Late West Saxon version may be regarded as "the same text" as a posited antecedent Anglian one.

3 An excellent concise introduction to the subject is Lendinara 1991: 273–5, to which the following account is indebted. There are also valuable essays on glossography in Derolez 1992 and Lendinara 1999.

4 For a list of continuous and occasional glosses, and of glossaries, see Quinn and Quinn 1990: 145–86. The most extensive edition (though it is far from comprehensive) is that of Wright and Wülcker (1884).

5 Ed. Pheifer 1974 and Lindsay 1921; both ed. in facsimile by Bischoff et al. (1988). On the date of the Épinal manuscript, see T. Brown 1982 and Malcolm Parkes in Bischoff et al. 1988: 16.

6 Three studies of fundamental importance are K. Sisam 1953a and Dumville 1976 and 1977; for more recent references, see Fulk forthcoming b.

7   For information on these and the royal lists mentioned above, see Quinn and Quinn 1990: 116–18.

8   For an extended study of the *Laterculus*, see J. Stevenson 1995a, and more briefly J. Stevenson 1995b.

9   Ed. Plummer 1896: 1.364–87; trans. Webb and Farmer 1983: 185–208.

10 Ed. and trans. A. Campbell 1967; studies by Lapidge (1990) and Orchard (1994b: 263–8).

11 *Vita Ædwardi*, ed. and trans. Barlow (1992).

12 Listed in Quinn and Quinn 1990: 132–4, 138–44; also N. Ker 1957: 520, 523; and for an annotated bibliography, see Hollis and Wright 1992: 257–310. There is a collection of prognostics edited in Cockayne 1864–6, vol. 3. For a fairly recent study of some Old English prognostics, see Epe 1995.

13 For collective editions and studies, see Cockayne 1864–6, vol. 3, Grendon 1909, and Storms 1948. Pettit (1999) edits a previously unprinted charm (or charms) in Oxford, Bodleian Library, Barlow 35. For bibliography on the charms, see Hollis and Wright 1992: 239–56 and 271–310; and for studies, Grattan and Singer 1952, B. Griffiths 1996, and Jolly 1996.

14 Hollis (1997) argues that cattle-theft charms may have had a legal function, since they are found in legal manuscripts.

15 *For a Sudden Stitch* 23–6 (*ASPR* 6.122). There is an illustration of elves afflicting a man with their "shot" in the Eadwine Psalter, reproduced as the frontispiece to Grattan and Singer 1952.

16 That clerics should have believed many of the same things about magic as the laity is argued by Meens (1998b), against the influential view of Flint (1991) that churchmen simply accommodated lay superstitions to their own purposes.

17 The "mysteries" of Tatwine and Eusebius are edited by Glorie (1968: 165–208 and 209–71), with translation.

18 Ed. Glorie (1968: 273–343), with German translation.

19 On Alcuin's enigmatic *carmina*, see Sorrell 1996; and on a riddle from the age of the monastic reform, see Porter 1996b, 1996c.

20 Some of the essays in Wilcox 2000a argue that there is humor to be found in other poems, but if that is the case, it is certainly humor of a different sort.

21 Rather than the *ASPR* edition, most scholarship on the riddles relies on the edition of Williamson (1977), whose numeration is followed here. In the latter, the former's Riddles 1–3 are treated as one, as are 68–9 (Williamson's 66), 75–6 (Williamson's 73), and 79–80 (Williamson's 76), while the former's 70 is divided in two (Williamson's 67, 68). For translations, see Williamson 1982 and Crossley-Holland 1993.

22 *ASPR* 6.109, but with corrections by Parkes (1972). Also ed. Smith (1978). For an explication of the vernacular rendering, see Klein 1997.

23 On runic inscriptions, see Elliott 1989 and Page 1999; on non-runic, Okasha 1971 and supplements.

24 As discovered by Ball (1966). For bibliography and illustrations, see Francovich Onesti 1998; also Elliott 1989: 138-39 and Plates XIX-XXIII.
25 For a synopsis of scholarship and an annotated bibliography, see Hollis and Wright 1992: 89–116. Goolden 1958 gives a Latin text *en face*, Archibald (1991: 112–79) a complete Latin text with translation.

Chapter 2 Literature of the Alfredian Period

1 In part because the sole manuscript was destroyed in the Cottonian fire of 1731, and the work is preserved only in early transcripts and extracts, there is a debate of long standing about its authenticity. Galbraith (1964: 88–128) raises doubts about Asser's authorship and suggests that Bishop Leofric of Exeter (once owner of the Exeter Book) forged the work. Whitelock (1968) answers Galbraith's reservations, and generally scholars accept the work's authenticity. Smyth (1995: 149–70; 271-324) revives the debate, but his arguments face significant obstacles: cf. James Campbell 1986, Keynes 1996b, Abels 1998: 318–26, and Prescott 1998.
2 On doubts about the veracity of this passage, see Lerer 1991: 64–70. The other most familiar anecdote about Alfred, how he was berated by a peasant for allowing her "cakes" (loaves of bread) to burn, is not found in Asser's life but is first narrated in the *Vita S. Neoti* (see Keynes and Lapidge 1983: 197–202).
3 For thorough introductions to Alfred's works, see Whitelock 1966 and Frantzen 1986. For bibliography see Quinn and Quinn 1990: 81–6 (table) and Discenza 2000.
4 Ed. Sweet 1871-2 (the edition employed here) and Carlson 1975–8 (Cotton MS only). N. Ker 1956 is a facsimile edition of three manuscripts.
5 Alfred's version is edited and translated by Sedgefield (1899, 1900). For bibliography, see Kaylor 1992: 33–69.
6 On the manuscripts, see Godden 1994b. The Cotton MS was severely damaged in the fire of 1731 (see Kiernan 1998), but substantive readings are recoverable from the partial collation that Franciscus Junius made in his transcript of the Bodley MS (now Oxford, Bodleian Library, Junius 12). There also existed in the Bodleian Library as late as 1886 a fragment, now lost, of a single leaf (ed. Napier 1887) containing prose from chapters 14 and 16 (see N. Ker 1957, item 337).
7 See S. Irvine 1996 and Benison 1998; and for references, Trahern 1991, esp. 170 n. 5.
8 See chapter 3. J. Nelson (1993), who calls this "the single best-known political idea with which Alfred has been credited" (p. 141), believes that it is not Alfred's creation but stems from Frankish sources. See also J. Nelson 1986.

9 See Donaghey 1964 and Gneuss 1986: 38, with the references there; Bately (1980a: 17) and Wittig (1983) cast doubt on this proposition.

10 For an edition, see Carnicelli 1969. There is also an edition by Endter (1922); and that of Hargrove (1902) places a Latin text at the bottom of the page through the first part of Book II. None of the editions is satisfactory: see Gatch 1986: 42 n. 29. The Old English is translated by Hargrove (1904).

11 Ed. O'Neill 2001. Note that for Old English purposes the numeration of the Psalter is that of the Vulgate. Thus, for example, Psalm 51 corresponds to 52 in the English Authorized Version.

12 For a recent study, see Scharer 1996.

13 Ælfric, *Catholic Homilies* II, 9 (ed. Godden 1979: 72); William, *De gestis regum Anglorum* (ed. Mynors, Thomson, and Winterbottom 1998, cap. 123.1).

14 For example, in Book II Bede states, "For they [the Britons] did not observe Easter at the proper time, but from the fourteenth until the twentieth day of the lunar month, a computation which is based on a cycle of eighty-four years" (Colgrave and Mynors 1969: II, 1). The Old English translator renders this simply "They would not listen to him, nor did they observe Easter at the proper time" (T. Miller 1890–8: 1.99). For other examples, see Whitelock 1962.

15 See Liggins 1970 and Bately 1970. The Old English Orosius provides very interesting evidence of having been dictated aloud by a Celtic speaker – presumably Asser, and presumably so that more than one scribe could copy it at once: see Bately 1966 and Kitson 1996.

16 For a useful study of the voyages of Ohthere and Wulfstan, see Lund and Fell 1984. The hypothesis of Odenstedt 1994 that Wulfstan was merely the interpreter, and the second voyage was also Ohthere's, requires a convoluted textual history to account for the Anglian verb forms of Wulfstan's account: see Fernández Cuestra and Senra Silva 2000.

17 The *terminus ad quem* for the Old English translation is 893, when Asser composed his *Life*; the *terminus post quem* is 871, when Alfred came to the throne. The Old English text is edited in Hecht 1900–7.

18 See in particular Yerkes 1982: 82–3. The revision also reflects the vocabulary of Æthelwold's Winchester school (see chapter 3), replacing thousands of words from Wærferth's translation (Yerkes 1979: xvi–xxvi). Yerkes 1982 examines inflectional morphology. For a succinct analysis of the linguistic differences between the two versions, see Yerkes 1986.

19 The most convenient edition remains that of Plummer and Earle 1892-99. But each chronicle is currently being edited on modern principles in a series under the general editorship of Dumville and Keynes (1983–). Of the seven versions, so far have appeared MSS A (vol. III, ed. Janet Bately, 1986), B (vol. IV, ed. Simon Taylor, 1983), C (vol. V, ed. Katherine O'Brien

O'Keeffe, 2001; also 956–1066 only, vol. x, ed. Patrick Conner, 1996), D (vol. vi, ed. G. P. Cubbin, 1996), and F (vol. viii, ed. Peter Baker, 2000; also a facsimile of F, vol. i, ed. David Dumville, 1995). Numerous translations are available. That of Whitelock (1961) is particularly authoritative; the most recent is that of Swanton (2000).

20   These five are the chief witnesses, as the others supply little new information: A² (also called G, in BL, Cotton Otho B. xi, mostly destroyed in the fire of 1731, but transcribed before that: see Lutz 1981) is a direct copy of A; F (BL Cotton Domitian viii, called the Domitian Bilingual because each entry is followed by a Latin translation) is a post-Conquest text based on an abridgment of the version that served as exemplar for E; and H (in BL, Cotton Domitian ix) is a single leaf. Swanton (2000: xxi–xxviv) briefly describes most of these texts and their relations. More distantly related texts are the *Annals of St. Neots* (ed. Dumville and Lapidge 1985), based on the pre-Alfredian source for all the Chronicles; Asser's life of Alfred; and the astonishing *Chronicle of Æthelweard* (ed. and trans. A. Campbell 1962a), written in densely hermeneutic Latin by a lay kinsman of Alfred, who was *ealdormann* of Wessex and patron to Abbot Ælfric. It is based on A's exemplar. There is an unrelated chronicle (designated I) in BL, Cotton Caligula A. xv, pertaining mostly to Christ Church, Canterbury. It is in English to the death of Archbishop Anselm in 1109; thereafter in Latin to 1193, subsequently extended to 1268.

21   For discussion and references, see Heinemann 1993 and Bremmer 1997. Scragg (1997b) argues that the annal is concerned less with heroic conduct than with loyalty and lawfulness, and John Hill (2000: 74–92) that it was designed during Alfred's reign to deal with the question of right and wrong treatment of kings rather than with the heroic code.

22   So Thormann 1997. Townend (2000) argues rather that the poems are inspired by skaldic panegyric.

23   With the exception of *The Rime of King William* (or *William the Conqueror*, ed. Fowler 1966: 14) and a few shorter but equally crude series of verses (see Plummer and Earle 1892–9: 1.187–8, 201, 210, 212, 239), as well as the two rhythmical passages discussed below, the Chronicle poems are edited in *ASPR* 6.16–26.

24   See Pope and Fulk 2001: 59 n. 26. The possibility that the beginnings of the poems have been modified (A. Campbell 1938: 36 n. 2) seems remote.

Chapter 3 Homilies

1   For an explanation, in particularly clear terms, of the nature and function of homilies, see Wilcox 1994: 15–22.

2 For a list of the anonymous homilies, with useful information about them (manuscripts, editions, criticism), see Quinn and Quinn 1990: 31–71. The lists of homilies in N. Ker 1957: 527–36 and Scragg 1979 are useful for different purposes, as the former is arranged by the liturgical calendar and the latter by manuscript.

3 Ed. Hurst 1955; trans. Martin and Hurst 1991. For studies, see Martin 1989, 1990.

4 See Gatch 1977: 122–8 and Charles Wright 1993. The indispensable guide to the sources of homilies, and indeed of all works in Old English, is the database of *Fontes Anglo-Saxonici*, now on the World Wide Web (Joyce Hill et al. 2001). Very useful information on sources is also available from the trial version of *Sources of Anglo-Saxon Literary Culture* (Biggs, Hill, and Szarmach 1990); further information on this project is available in Biggs et al. 1999.

5 Morris's edition contains 19 homilies, but his XVI is actually a detached leaf of IV. Thus his nos. XVII–XIX are here, as in most recent studies, referred to as XVI–XVIII.

6 See Clemoes 1962, and for a detailed study of the compilation of the manuscript, see Scragg 1985.

7 See Clayton 1985: 168–71. Gatch (1989, who does not refer to Clayton) argues that the use of sources addressed to ecclesiastics without thorough adaptation for a lay audience raises doubts about whom these homilies were intended for. Yet because this non-adaptation could be the result of carelessness, as evidence it is inconclusive.

8 That Latin sermons could in fact have been understood by Romance-speaking members of the laity in Carolingian Francia, if they were read with emergent Romance pronunciation, is argued by R. Wright (1982:112–22) and T. Amos (1989: 51–2).

9 Scragg (1973) and C. Sisam (1976: 37–44) offer exhaustive studies of the evidence of language and layout for such probable groupings within the manuscript.

10 For bibliography, see Bately 1993; and for the sources themselves, Joyce Hill et al. 2001.

11 See Jost 1950: 178–82, Whitbread 1963, Godden 1975, Scragg 1977, and Wilcox 1991.

12 On Ælfric's life, see Hurt 1972: 27–41. For bibliography, see Reinsma 1987, supplemented by Kleist 2000.

13 The first series is edited by Clemoes (1997), the second by Godden (1979), and for the combined commentary on the two series, see Godden 2000. Even now, some studies of these homilies rely upon the edition of Thorpe (1844–6), which includes a translation. On the dating of the two series, the latest examination of the evidence is by Godden (2000: xxix–xxxvi).

14 It is not impossible that Ælfric also expected an audience of clerics read-

ing the text for their own use, as argued by Godden (2000: xxii–xxiv). But since early medieval reading was not usually a silent activity (see section 1 of the introduction), the apparent references to such readers may actually be to those expected to preach the homilies.

15 The best introduction to Ælfric's prose styles remains that of Pope (1967–8: 1.105–36). Also valuable are Clemoes 1966: 193–206 and Wilcox 1994: 57–65.

16 *De gestis pontificum Anglorum*, ed. N. Hamilton (1870: 336).

17 N. Ker (1957: 511–15) provides a convenient table of homilies of the two series and the manuscripts containing them.

18 This suggestion, first made by Raynes (1957: 68), is supported by others listed by Reinsma (1987: 83). Godden (1985: 298), apparently independently, made a similar suggestion, critiqued by Leinbaugh (1994, esp. 197 n. 14). Christopher Jones (1998b: 12–13, 45–51) offers a careful reassessment of the evidence and finds it equivocal.

19 The standard edition is that of Bethurum (1957). Her treatment of the texts, however, is unsatisfactory, as the *apparatus criticus* is incomplete and often inaccurate, and she combines selections from different manuscripts to construct homilies in a way that is not currently acceptable to Anglo-Saxonists: see Wilcox 2000b: 396. Bethurum also excludes some genuine, undeveloped homiletic texts edited by Napier (1883), regarding them as non-homiletic: for a list, see Wilcox 1992: 200–1. A collection of Wulfstanian manuscripts is edited in facsimile by Wilcox (2000c).

20 For stylistic studies, see McIntosh 1949, Bethurum 1957: 87–98 (with further references at 97 n. 1), and Orchard 1992.

21 Homily xx; also in an informative edition by Whitelock 1967; trans. Whitelock 1979: 928–34; electronic text with translation, Bernstein 1997. Cross and Brown (1989) have pointed out some similarities between the opening of this homily and the *Sermo ad milites* of Abbo of Saint-Germain-des-Prés, preserved in a manuscript annotated by Wulfstan himself.

22 This is the view of both Bethurum (1957: 22-23) and Whitelock (1967: 2-5), challenged by Dien (1975).

23 See the discussion in Gatch 1977, esp. pp. 60–1 and 121–2.

Chapter 4 Saints' Legends

1 For an excellent account of these developments, see Peter Brown 1981, arguing that they are not the work of the ignorant and the superstitious, but that they involve the contributions of eminent churchmen.

2 For a concise overview of Anglo-Latin hagiography, excluding Alcuin's writings, see Lapidge and Love 2001, to which the following discussion is indebted.

3   Ed. Jaager 1935; for studies, see Lapidge 1989, Lutterkort 1996, and Eby 1997; and on the prose version, Cavill 1999b and W. Foley 1999.

4   The passage is quoted by Godman (1982: lxxxvi, n. 1) in the course of an informative history of *opera geminata*. The letter is edited by Dümmler (1895: no. 175).

5   The original is unprinted. On Theodore's possible authorship, see Franklin 1995. Bede's version is printed as the "Acta ex veteribus Latinis MSS" in the Bollandist *Acta Sanctorum* for Jan. 22 (see below, n. 34).

6   Ed. Plummer 1896: 2.388–404; trans. Boutflower 1912.

7   For a list, see Whatley 1996a: 18–21. Note may be made of a lost Latin life of St. Hildelith, the abbess of Barking to whom Aldhelm's *De virginitate* is dedicated, referred to by Bede (*Historia ecclesiastica* IV, 10).

8   See Colgrave 1958a and Rollason 1996.

9   Lantfred's hermeneutic prose *Translatio et miracula S. Swithuni* has never been printed entire; it will appear in Lapidge (forthcoming). Wulfstan's versification of this, *Narratio metrica de S. Swithuno*, is edited by A. Campbell (1950).

10 Political motives for the cults of saints must also be taken into account. For example, Æthelred the Unready seems to have promoted the cults of Edward the Martyr and Edith of Wilton because of their connections with the West Saxon royal house (Ridyard 1988). See also Rollason 1983, though Cubitt (2000) now argues for the popular nature of these cults.

11 Ed. Lapidge and Winterbottom 1991.

12 Ed. Stubbs 1874: 3–52.

13 The former is edited in Lapidge and Winterbottom 1991: 70–80; the latter in Lapidge (forthcoming).

14 Ed. Raine (1879–94: 1.399–475) and Giles (1854: 349–96), respectively. Lapidge (1979) first identified the latter as Byrhtferth's work.

15 For references, see Lapidge and Love 2001: 14, 18–19.

16 Lapide and Love 2001: 19–49. Ridyard (1988) and Rollason (1989) offer other evidence for the Normans' interest in Anglo-Saxon saints.

17 On the hybrid genre of such works, see Godden 1996.

18 Clemoes (1959: 222) conjectures that this was intended to be the first item in *LS*. Leinbaugh (1994) disputes this.

19 The lack of predicatory features, such as exhortations, self-reference, and mention of the feast itself, is natural enough, since it would be inappropriate to put a preacher's words into the mouth of a lay person reading them aloud.

20 On Ælfric's style, see chapter 3. Lees (1999: 34), to the contrary, assumes that such oral style may be a "calculated fiction."

21 The contents and layers of accretion are sifted by Jackson and Lapidge 1996.

22 On the changes that Ælfric has introduced to this text, see Joyce Hill 1989.

23 Third-century Alban of course was not technically English, but Ælfric apparently regarded him as such, since he places him in *Engla land*.

24 Scragg 1996: 224. For bibliographical information on anonymous lives, see Whatley 1996b: 452–9.

25 This situation shows some sign of change, however, as the legends of the Seven Sleepers and of St. Margaret have now been edited expertly by Magennis (1994) and Clayton and Magennis (1994) respectively, and Treharne (1997) has produced a fine edition of the legends of Ss. Nicholas and Giles, with translations and sources.

26 For an overview, see Pulsiano 1999.

27 For whomever the Exeter Book may have been compiled, it almost certainly was in the library of Bishop Leofric of Exeter (d. 1072), who is said in a list of benefactions to have left to his cathedral "one large English book on various subjects composed in verse" (N. Ker 1957: 153).

28 On devils in these works, see Dendle 2001.

29 For a summary of such views, see A. Cook 1900: lxxi–lxxvi.

30 The evidence is summarized by Fulk (1996a, especially 10–17 and n. 32 in response to Conner 1996).

31 'Finding of the Holy Cross'. On the identification of the exact form of the source, see Gradon 1996: 15–22 and Calder 1981: 104–5. Versions of the source are furnished in some editions of *Elene*, including those of Zupitza (1899) and Holthausen (1936); for a translation of the Latin, see Calder and Allen 1976: 60–8.

32 Certainly, however, Ælfric embellishes the Jews' guilt in his sermon on the Exaltation of the Holy Cross (*LS* xxvii): see Scheil 1999a: 69.

33 See particularly Calder 1981: 105–38, E. Anderson 1983: 103–25, Bridges 1984: 212–52, and Bjork 1985: 62–89.

34 For an account of the separate editions of this immense and incomplete collection of Latin saints' legends, see Whatley 1996a: 25 n. 49. The Bollandist text is reprinted in Strunk 1904: 33–49, trans. Calder and Allen 1976: 122–32.

35 No. xviii, ed. Morris (1874–80 as xix: 228–49, at 231). A complete but slightly abridged version of the same Old English homily is preserved in CCCC 198 (ed. Cassidy and Ringler 1971: 203–19), without the Latin sentence.

36 The Πράξεις and the Latin recensions are edited by Blatt (1930) and translated by Boenig (1991). The Bonnet fragment is also reprinted in K. Brooks 1961: 177–8. Calder and Allen, who regard the Latin version known as the *Recensio Casanatensis* as closer to the source, furnish a translation (1976: 15–34). For discussion of the relation of all these versions to the poem, see Schaar 1949: 12–24 and K. Brooks 1961: xv–xviii.

37 For references to the substantial literature, see D. Hamilton 1975: 81–2.
38 See esp. Lumiansky 1949 and Peters 1951.
39 Especially in view of such evidence it is difficult to credit the view of Conner (1993b) that the poem was composed later than ca. 960, on the basis of his belief that it expresses the ideals of reformed Benedictinism. The poet's four references to recent memory and the poem's lack of a verifiable written source on Guthlac's life have plausibly suggested an oral source to some (e.g. O'Brien O'Keeffe 1989).
40 Because the division is clear, the compromise proposed by Liuzza (1990), arguing that lines 1–29 were composed to link the two poems, seems kinder to the poem's editors and critics than to the scribal evidence.
41 This perhaps is not intended to value eremitism over cenobitism, since Christopher Jones (1995) argues that the poet intends the glory of the former to descend to the latter.
42 These works are referenced in Lapidge 1996a.

Chapter 5 Biblical Literature

1 On Anglo-Saxon bible manuscripts, see Remley 1996: 10–11 and Marsden 1995: 39–49.
2 For instance, the source for the *Canticum puerorum* in the Old English *Daniel* and *Azarias* has been variously identified as a Canticle version (*ASPR* 1.xxxiii), a version of the Vulgate that included both the *Canticum Azariae* and the *Canticum puerorum* (Farrell 1974: 24), and the Greek Septuagint (Muir 2000: 461).
3 We have no record of Theodore's early life to tell us where he studied, but it is likely that he visited Antioch (40 miles from his native Tarsus) and Edessa (an important center of Syriac education). For discussion of Theodore's education and the influence of Antioch and Edessa, see Bischoff and Lapidge 1994: 14–37, Lapidge 1995a: 3–8, and Brock 1995.
4 None of the manuscripts of the Canterbury biblical commentaries contains the entire text. The most complete manuscript was found in Milan in 1936 by Bernhard Bischoff (ed. Bischoff and Lapidge 1994).
5 Bede's commentaries are edited in CCSL 118–21. Much has been written about Bede as an exegete: for recent references, see DeGregorio 1999: 1–2 n. 2.
6 He authored commentaries on Genesis, Psalms, the Song of Songs, Ecclesiastes, John, three of Paul's epistles, and the Epistle to the Hebrews (all ed. in PL 100).
7 The text is edited by Crawford (1922), who combines material from the two most complete witnesses, the illustrated Hexateuch in BL, Cotton Claudius B. iv, with Ælfric's homily on Judges from Oxford, Bodleian

Library, Laud Misc. 509, to produce a "Heptateuch."

8   Contra Clemoes' identification of the anonymous translator with Byrhtferth, see Baker 1980.

9   Minkoff (1976) finds that the clarity of the Old English translation is undermined by obsessive adherence to the Latin syntax. Citing Minkoff, as well as Jerome's admonition against tampering with the language of Scripture, Greenfield and Calder (1986: 85) say, "Ælfric was so conservative on this point that he was willing to translate an occasionally incomprehensible passage from Jerome's Latin (itself based on an impenetrable Hebrew) into a 'nonsense' Old English in order to keep the deep spiritual meaning intact." Marsden (1991, 1995: 407–8), however, contends that the translators' literalness has been overstated. He shows that Ælfric and the anonymous translator(s) altered the syntax freely when differences in idiom required it. Barnhouse (2000) traces the omissions, alterations, and additions in both the Ælfrician and the non-Ælfrician portions of the Hexateuch to show how the translators exerted control over their audience's understanding of the text.

10   The only complete edition of the glosses on either the Lindisfarne or the Rushworth Gospels is Skeat 1871–87.

11   Ed. Liuzza (1994–2000), who prefers to call the text "The Old English Version of the Gospels" because three manuscripts are "strongly southeastern in character, and none of the other MSS can be said to be purely representative of the West-Saxon dialect" (1.xiii n. 1), and he posits a Kentish or southeastern origin for the translation (2.154). Yet the more usual title is not inappropriate, since the main features of the work in all manuscripts are undeniably West Saxon, and the conventional title is less likely to lead to confusion with gospel glosses in non-Saxon dialects.

12   The Old English *Gospel of Nicodemus* also survives in two twelfth-century manuscripts (BL, Cotton Vitellius A. xv, ff. 4–93, and BL, Cotton Vespasian D. xiv) and the *Vindicta Salvatoris* in an eleventh-century manuscript (CCCC 196) and a twelfth-century manuscript (BL Cotton Vespasian D. xiv).

13   Hall (1996: 45) notes that "a fundamental difficulty in documenting the early history of the *Descensus ad inferos* is that while a number of authors before the fourth century relate the story of Christ's descent into Hell, none is demonstrably indebted to the *Descensus*." See also Hall 1996: 37–47 for discussion of the textual history of the *Evangelium Nichodemi*.

14   Saint-Omer, Bibliothèque Municipale, 202, a book that seems to have been in the Exeter scriptorium in the day of Bishop Leofric (d. 1072), where the translations were thus very probably made (Cross 1996: 3–9).

15   The illustrations are reproduced by Ohlgren (1992: 526–76) and Karkov (2001: plates i–xliib).

16   Raw 1984: 135. For discussion of the manuscript illustrations, see Raw

1976, 1984, Broderick 1983, and Karkov 2001.

17　This is so in regard to the treatment of Genesis 3–5, 8–22, and the *Canticum trium puerorum*, according to Remley (1996:439).

18　For an overview of some major editions and studies of the relation between the Saxon and English poems, see Derolez 1995.

19　As argued by Lucas 1992 and McKill 1995–6. D. Johnson (1998) finds a parallel to the poet's conception of the fall of Lucifer in two Winchester charters.

20　As pointed out by Doane (1978: 63), who furnishes an overview of such alterations. The poem's relation to its sources has been studied in considerable detail: see particularly Remley 1988, 1996: 94–167, and Doane 1990. Indeed, most current scholarship on the poem is devoted to sources and analogues, e.g. Orchard 1994a and Charles Wright 1996. Exceptionally, Anlezark (2000: 189–91) studies how the poet deals with the problem of Abraham's deception in claiming that Sarah is his sister: he puts the problem entirely to one side. Much as with the poet of *Judith* (below), he instead highlights Sarah's beauty in order to focus attention on the purity of Abraham and Sarah in contrast to the lechery of Pharaoh and Abimelech. Battles (2000) also adopts an original approach, arguing that the poem evinces such a "migration myth" as Howe (1989) perceives the Anglo-Saxons to have maintained in regard to their own history.

21　On the possibility that Milton's *Paradise Lost* was influenced by *Genesis B*, see the conclusion.

22　For references, see Remley 1996: 153.

23　From a feminist standpoint, Overing (1991: 40–51) provides an overview and mordant critique of scholarly attitudes toward Eve, associating the two camps roughly with religious and secular (or "Germanic") approaches, respectively. The debate nonetheless continues, with Mintz (1997) arguing that Eve is an intelligent, responsible, and essentially admirable figure.

24　Haines (1999: 481) assumes, however, that at this point the poet is offering his own lesson rather than reporting Moses'.

25　See Lucas 1994: 30–3. Most studies of the past decade deal with the poem's typological aspects (e.g. Huisman 1992, Helder 1994, and Portnoy 2001). An exception is Wyly 1999, perceiving the poet's theme as legal in nature, laying particular emphasis on inheritance and judicial authority.

26　For references and discussion, see Farrell 1972, 1974: 22–9 and E. Anderson 1987: 2–3. Farrell's explanation for the appearance of the angel before the song of Azarias is less satisfying (essentially, there are other sorts of repetition in the corresponding passages in the Vulgate, and angels are used throughout for similar purposes).

27　Also ed. Farrell 1974. For bibliography, see Muir 2000: 461–7, where the poem is called *The Canticles of the Three Youths*.

28　Farrell (1972, 1974: 38–40) has suggested that *Azarias* concludes the poem immediately preceding it in the Exeter Book, *Guthlac B* – a hypothesis rebutted by Pope (1978: 37).

29 For the poem's manuscript context, see Lucas 1990. For bibliography, see Griffith 1997.

30 See Orchard 1995: 7–12 and Griffith 1997: 55–8. Much scholarship is devoted to comparison with the source. Thus, for example, Belanoff (1993) sees Judith as an amalgam of biblical and Germanic characteristics, and Fee (1997) finds that the poet has turned the Bethulians into competent warriors who require not a Judith who saves them but one who inspires them to save themselves. Garner (2001) argues that the changes made to the Hieronymian source reflect the poet's effort to bridge the gap between orality and literacy.

31 Huppé 1970: 114–88 exemplifies the latter position, de Lacy 1996 the former. Cf. Lochrie (1993), who deprecates both allegorical and political approaches (a critical opposition previously identified by Astell 1989), foregrounding instead the poet's juxtaposition of sexual violence and the politics of war. More literally, Kim (1999), like Hermann (1989: 181–98), reads the decapitation of Holofernes as symbolic of circumcision and/ or castration. By contrast, Dockray-Miller (1998, with a useful overview of approaches to gender in the poem) derives Iudith's heroism not from her appropriation of male violence but from the maternal bond that she forms with her handmaid.

32 For discussion and references, see Fulk 1992: 335–6 n. 147.

33 For an overview of arguments for and against the unity of the poem, see Sleeth 1982: 3–26. Portnoy (1994) argues for ordering on the basis of elements of the Paschal liturgy, and Stévanovitch (1996) on the basis of envelope patterns.

34 Thus Hasenfratz (1989) would emend *eisegan stefne* (36a) to give Satan an iron voice; Morey (1990) elucidates the syntax of lines 19–21; and Finnegan (1994) would identify the poem's narrator, who in his view can only be Christ. Glaeske (1999) focuses on the appearance of Eve in the Harrowing of Hell. The study by D. Johnson (below) is of this explicative sort, as well.

35 D. Johnson (1993) grapples with the problem of how Satan can be both a wandering exile and enchained, but this seems to be a Satanic convention (see Dendle 2001). In any case, the conventionality of Satan's rhetoric perhaps licenses a figurative reading.

36 For bibliography and sources, see Muir 2000: 677–83. See J. J. Campbell 1982 and Garde 1991: 113–30 on the Latin tradition of the Harrowing of Hell motif.

Chapter 6 Liturgical and Devotional Texts

1　For discussion of the interplay of Latin and Old English, see Brooks 1982, Bullough 1991, and G. Brown 1993.

2　See Mayr-Harting 1991: 173–4 for a brief overview of the books of the Roman mission.

3　On liturgical books, see Gneuss 1985 and Pfaff 1995.

4　*ASPR* 5.1–150. Another copy of some of the Psalms in this translation (90.16.1–95.2.1, ed. Baker 1984, not collated in *ASPR*) is to be found in Eadwine's Canterbury Psalter (Cambridge, Trinity Coll. R. 17. 1 (987)).

5　See Sisam and Sisam 1958: 17. For a detailed analysis of the style and its self-conscious distance from the heroic tradition of poetry, see Griffith 1991.

6　For an extended examination of *Psalm 50* and its relationship to Latin psalters, see Keefer 1991.

7　For a list, see Quinn and Quinn 1990: 95–104.

8　The most convenient list of Old English glosses on liturgical texts is in N. Ker 1957: 524–6; at 539–40 there is also a list of Latin forms of service found in manuscripts containing Old English.

9　A. Cook (1900: xvi–xxv) summarizes the controversy, though he advocates Cynewulf's authorship for all. On metrical and lexical differences, see Roberts 1994 and Fulk 1992: 396–9 and 1996a: 8–9. T. Hill (1986) contrasts the learned, orthodox, and eclectic *Christ I* with the relatively undemanding *Christ II* and the unorthodox *Christ III*.

10　For bibliography and sources, see Muir 2000: 384–400. For representative texts of the antiphons, see J. J. Campbell 1959: 6–8. Four of the lyrics in the sequence, VII (164–213), X (348–77), XI (378–415), and XII (416–39), lacked as clear a similarity as the others to any known Advent antiphon at the time of Cook's discovery, and later J. J. Campbell (1959) and Burlin (1968) discounted two of Cook's suggestions for antiphons, and they added an antiphonal source unknown to Cook for the twelfth lyric in the sequence. Later, Tugwell (1970: 34) and T. Hill (1977: 12-15) discovered antiphonal sources to lyrics X and VII, respectively. Rankin (1985) summarizes subsequent discoveries about the liturgical background of the 'O' antiphons. She also argues that although the order of the lyrics in *Christ I* has no liturgical precedent, it nonetheless shows a logical progression in accordance with the season, from lengthy anticipation to sudden joy and comprehension.

11　For a close reading of the lyrics on an aesthetic basis, see Irving 1996.

12　On the origins and development of penance and penitentials in Ireland, see Frantzen 1983a: 19–60. For discussion of recent views on the distinction between public and private penance, and when and how often penance was performed, see Meens 1998a.

13 Ed. Finsterwalder 1929: 239–52. For translations of this and some other of the Latin penitentials, see McNeill and Gamer 1938. The *Iudicia* are extant in two tenth-century Continental manuscripts in the Bibliothèque Nationale in Paris, Lat. 12021 and 3182. For a discussion of the chronology and textual history of the Theodoran penitential texts, see Charles-Edwards 1995.

14 Frantzen (1983a: 70–2) points to the lack of influence from the penitentials attributed to Bede in the Ecgberht text as evidence of the spuriousness of both attributions, considering the two men's relationship. The work ascribed to Ecgberht is likelier to contain a genuine core than that ascribed to Bede, though both may be pseudepigraphic. On this entire group of texts, see further Frantzen 1983b.

15 CCCC 190; Oxford, Bodleian Library, Junius 121; and Laud Misc. 482. The *Confessional* is edited by Spindler (1934) and the *Penitential* by Raith (1933).

16 Thus it is unfortunate that this shorter text is not included in the database of the *Dictionary of Old English*, as it contains some passages unparalleled in the longer one. The longer text (Brussels MS only) is edited by Mone (1830: 515–27), the shorter by Thorpe (1840: 2.228–30). R. D. Fulk has gathered materials for a new edition.

17 For a list of such texts, see N. Ker 1957: 522.

18 Christopher Jones (1998a) includes an edition and translation of the text as well as a thorough analysis of its sources, structure, and manuscript.

19 The bilingual texts are in CCCC 178; BL, Cotton Titus A. iv; CCCC 197; and Durham, Cathedral, B. iv. 24. The vernacular Rule is edited by Schröer (1885–8).

20 Ed. (unreliably) H. Norman 1849. It is much to be hoped that M. A. Locherbie-Cameron's 1998 University of Wales thesis, an edition, will be published.

21 BL, Cotton Titus D. xxvi and Paris, Bibliothèque Nationale, Lat. 943; ed. Brotanek 1913: 27–8.

22 See section 4 of the introduction, and for studies, see the references there. The works are edited by Ehwald (1919), trans. Lapidge and Herren (1979) and Lapidge and Rosier (1985).

23 See section 6 of the introduction. Orchard (1994b) points out other ways in which Aldhelm's poetic compositions (and those of his student Æthilwald) may reflect the influence of Old English verse; and by King Alfred's account (according to William of Malmesbury: ed. N. Hamilton 1870: 336), Aldhelm was an accomplished poet in the vernacular.

24 Modern editions of Alcuin's work are a pressing need. This text is edited by Dümmler (1895: 473–8, no. 309), and in PL 101, 639–50.

25 Ed. R. Warner 1917. For bibliography and backgrounds, see Hollis and Wright 1992: 76–86. On the dialogic form, see Förster 1901.

Augustodunum was once thought to be Autun, but the identification is now in doubt. Flint (1977) would place it in England.

26 *Epistola ad Ecgberhtum*, ed. Plummer 1896: 1.405–23; trans. Sherley-Price and Farmer 1990, and McClure and Collins 1994. On the *Epistola Cuthberti de obitu Bedae*, see chapter 8, n. 13. On other early letters, with references, see Lapidge 1996a.

27 These letters are summarized by Hurt (1972: 36–40).

28 The former are translated by Lapidge and Rosier (1985: 35–58). For the latter, which are poorly preserved, see Lapidge 1975.

29 Lapidge (1991a: 249–50) thinks the poem may have been composed for a king. Head (1999) observes that it balances stable, eternal, sacred time with the Chronicle's representation of continually open-ended human history.

30 BL, Harley 3271 and CCCC 422, ed. Henel 1934: 71–3.

31 Reconstructed by Quentin (1908: 17–119) from the later martyrologies into which it was incorporated; there is a preliminary edition by Dubois and Renaud (1976).

32 There is a series of articles by James Cross on the martyrologist's learning, e.g. Cross 1985, 1986, with references to other of his studies there.

33 It is thus necessary to retract the approval of Conner's argument expressed in Fulk 1996a.

34 Donoghue (1987: 113–16) argues that only the runic signature was composed *ab ovo* by Cynewulf, the rest being an anonymous composition that he adapted to his own use.

35 For bibliography, see Muir 2000: 401–17. Regrettably, no student's edition more recent than Cook's (1900) has been published. Studies in recent years have also been exceedingly sparse.

36 Letson 1980. Cynewulf makes use of a variety of other sources, as well (see Greenman 1992), most notably Bede's hymn on the Ascension (see Cook 1900: 116–18).

37 On the meter of the macaronic poems, see Cain 2001. The exception is ll. 3–4, both of which lack an off-verse. But *sāule þinre* (4) seems to be a translation of *anima tua*, which would make a perfect off-verse to *ā būtan ende* (3).

38 The attribution to Alcuin in one manuscript has been adequately explained by Whitbread (1944, 1967). Lapidge (1994b: n. 33) points out that the poem contains metrical faults uncharacteristic of Bede, but he nonetheless treats the poem as Bede's work.

39 For bibliography and sources, see Biggs 1986 and Muir 2000: 418–34. Calder and Allen (1976: 84–107) provide a wide selection of the poem's sources in translation.

40 Lactantius' poem is edited and translated by Duff and Duff (1954). Though it is less than satisfactory (see Frantzen 1993a), the best separate edition

of *The Phoenix* is that of N. Blake (1990).

41 Hoek 1997: 2. For Latin and Greek texts of the *Physiologus*, with translations, consult Squires 1988: 102–14, who also provides a bibliography of the poem (pp. 31–4). Tatwine, it should be noted, made use of the Latin *Physiologus* as the basis for some of his *enigmata* (see chapter 1).

42 See also Rossi-Reder 1999, arguing that the three poems form an Easter sequence on Christ's death, resurrection, and harrowing of hell, and that they celebrate baptism.

43 Bede's account and the poem *Cædmon's Hymn* are anthologized in numerous elementary textbooks, most recently in Pope and Fulk 2001: 3–4, 49–58, with a summary of recent scholarship.

44 For facsimiles, see Robinson and Stanley 1991: 2.1–21.

45 Most especially, it would seem an exceptional coincidence that a close rendering of Bede's Latin prose, with a few variations, happened to suggest to the supposed translator precisely the words he needed to fulfill the metrical and alliterative requirements of an Old English poem, if the form preserved differs from Cædmon's. Nonetheless, this old idea has been revived by a number of scholars in recent years: for references to studies pro and con, see Pope and Fulk 2001: 54–5, to which may be added Clemoes 1995: 242–3 n. 26 and E. Anderson 2000: 114.

46 That the inscription is later than the cross itself has been argued by several scholars: for discussion and references, see Fulk 1992: 342–3, n. 155. For a detailed study of the cross, see Cassidy 1992, with a convincing reconstruction of the inscription by D. Howlett, p. 83.

47 For bibliography, see Swanton 1996.

48 The homily on the Invention is edited and translated by Bodden (1987). For a list of legends of the cross, see Whatley 1996a: 5.

Chapter 7 Legal, Scientific, and Scholastic Works

1 The indispensable handbook is that of Sawyer (1968), whose numeration is now the standard. The chief collective editions are Kemble 1839–48, Birch 1885–99, Whitelock 1930 (wills), A. Robertson 1956, and Harmer 1989 (writs). There is also an ongoing series, Anglo-Saxon Charters, under various editorship, published by Oxford Univ. Press (1973–). For facsimiles, in addition to those listed in Sawyer's bibliography, see Keynes 1991. A valuable study is F. Stenton 1955; also Whitelock 1979: 369–84 and nos. 54–135; and N. Brooks 1974.

2 Sweet (1885: 421–60) offers a convenient edition of the linguistically relevant portions of the oldest reliable charters; for additions and deletions to his collection see Fulk 1992: 354 n. 9.

3 The existence of royal chanceries is a matter of contention: see Keynes

1980: 14–83, Chaplais 1985, and Keynes 1990.

4 See Pelteret 1986, 1995.

5 Ed. Harmer 1914: 17; trans. Whitelock 1979: no. 96, and with valuable commentary in Keynes and Lapidge 1983: 173–8, 313–26.

6 Lowe (1998a) supplies a handy catalogue of wills and their manuscript contexts, along with a sound overview of the relevant problems. Two other classic studies are Sheehan 1963 (chs. 1–3) and Vinogradoff 1906–7.

7 On the orality of wills, see Danet and Bogoch 1992, 1994.

8 For analysis of the manuscript contexts, see Richards 1986 and Wormald 1999c: 224–55.

9 The Anglo-Saxon laws are collected in the monumental edition of Liebermann (1903–16; for Æthelberht's code see 1.3–8). Many of the law codes can be found in translation in Attenborough 1963 and in Whitelock 1979: 357–439. A very useful reference work on early Germanic law is Brunner 1906–28; also Munske 1973, which is sadly neglected, due to the disgrace into which the early twentieth-century *Rechtsschule* has fallen. The profoundest influence on the study of Anglo-Saxon law has been exerted by Pollock and Maitland 1895. Indispensable to the study of the laws is now Wormald 1999c: see pp. 3–28 for a critical history of Old English legal scholarship. On the language of Æthelberht's and other early codes, see Oliver 1995 (with important insights from Jurasinski forthcoming); also Korte 1974 and Lendinara 1997. See Richards 1989 for a discussion of standardized language in the laws.

10 For a different account of Æthelberht's code, see Richardson and Sayles 1966, who see the provisions for clerics as later interpolations, and who explain the vernacular form as a legacy of Romano-British literate culture in Kent.

11 The laws of Alfred-Ine are preserved in complete form in two manuscripts: one is the Textus Roffensis, the other CCCC 173, containing also the Parker Chronicle.

12 That Alfred's reference, in the preface to his laws, to Offa's legislation does not necessarily point to a lost code is shown by Wormald (1991b, 1999c: 106–8).

13 For analysis of the political implications of the *Institutes*, see Loyn 1984: 86–90.

14 Ed. Liebermann (1903–16: 444–55). There is a synopsis of the provisions for free peasants in F. Stenton 1971: 472–6 and an important discussion of both texts in Harvey 1993.

15 All ed. Liebermann (1903–16).

16 See Wormald 1994. The author is now believed also to have compiled the *Leges Henrici Primi* (ca. 1114–118), which include much from the *Quadripartitus*. Cnut's laws were also translated into Latin in the twelfth

century, in the *Quadripartitus* and in the *Instituta Cnuti* (ca. 1103–20), which includes portions of the laws of Ine, Alfred, and Edgar, and in the *Consiliatio Cnuti* (ca. 1110–30). On early modern interest in Anglo-Saxon law, see the conclusion.

17 Bede's *De natura* is edited in CCSL 123A; Ælfric's *De temporibus* is edited by Henel 1942.

18 Ed. and trans. Baker and Lapidge 1995. For discussion of Byrhtferth, see Hart 1972, Baker 1980, 1982, Hollis and Wright 1992: 147–84, and Lapidge 1998. A fragment, very likely by Byrhtferth himself, of an Old English computus related to Byrhtferth's Latin *Computus* is edited by Baker and Lapidge (1995: 429–30).

19 For a discussion of scholarship on vernacular computus, along with an annotated bibliography, see Hollis and Wright 1992: 185–95.

20 For a history of scholarship on magico-medical texts, along with an annotated bibliography, see Hollis and Wright 1992: 211–383; also, for reference, Voigts and Kurtz 2001. For facsimiles of several texts, see Doane 1994.

21 See Weston 1995. Wilcox (1994: 52) similarly suggests that Ælfric's *Admonition to a Spiritual Son* (see chapter 6) may have been composed in English because its audience included nuns. Anglo-Latin medical treatises are more difficult to identify, naturally, than those in English. Two collections of medicinal recipes in Latin seem to have been produced at St. Augustine's, Canterbury, and Ramsey Abbey, found in Cambridge, University Library, Gg. 5.35 and Oxford, St. John's College 17, respectively: see M. Cameron 1993: 48–58.

22 BL, Royal 12. D. xvii; ed. Cockayne (1864–6: 2.2–358); facsimile ed. C. E. Wright (1955).

23 M. Cameron (1993: 42) says, "This separation of external and internal diseases may be unique in medieval medical texts; I know of no other quite like it." For cultural significance, see M. Cameron 1990.

24 On the compiler's sources, see M. Cameron 1983, 1993: 67–73, Meaney 1984, and Adams and Deegan 1992.

25 Ed. Cockayne (1864–6: 3.1–80), Grattan and Singer (1952), and Pettit 2001.

26 Ed. Cockayne (1864–6: 1.1–325) and de Vriend 1984.

27 See D'Aronco 1988 for a discussion of its botanical vocabulary. There are two Latin *Herbarium* complexes, and all four Old English manuscripts derive from a single translation, which is, on the whole, remarkably competent, given the difficulty of rendering Latin medical, botanical, and zoological terminology (in turn, often derived from Greek): see M. Cameron 1993: 61–4. Also see Hofstetter 1983.

28 Bede relied on an earlier anonymous Latin work composed in England on precious stones, the *Collectanea pseudo-Bedae*. Later, Frithegod used Bede's

work for his poem on the stones named in Revelation, *Cives celestis patrie*. On the early insular lapidary tradition, see Kitson 1983.

29 "Mocritum" is a misunderstanding of a reference to Democritus of Abdera in the lapidarist's source, Solinus' *Collectanea rerum memorabilium*: see Zettersten 1969.

30 Ed. and trans. Orchard 1995, with a study on pp. 86–115. The classic discussion of its Anglo-Saxon provenance is Lapidge 1982.

31 For an extended analysis of these connections, see Orchard 1995; and for an introduction and bibliography to both these texts, see Hollis and Wright 1992: 117–46.

32 BL, Cotton Tiberius B. v contains Latin and English descriptions with rich illustrations of 37 wonders (facsimile ed. McGurk, Dumville, and Godden 1983), while Cotton Vitellius A. xv omits the last five. Oxford, Bodleian Library, Bodley 614 is a later, expanded Latin description of 49 illustrated wonders. The two wonders texts in the *Beowulf* Manuscript have been edited several times, most recently by Orchard (1995: 183–203, 224–53, both with translations).

33 Tatwine's grammar is edited in CCSL 133, 1–141 and that of Boniface in CCSL 133B, 1–99.

34 Ed. in PL 101, 849–902.

35 Ed. Zupitza 1880. On its vernacular form, see Menzer 1999.

36 The *Colloquy* is edited by Garmonsway (1991). For a discussion of its influence, see Joyce Hill 1998.

37 See Gwara 1996, Porter 1996a, and Gwara and Porter 1997.

38 Bede's *De orthographia* and *De arte metrica* are edited in CCSL 123A; Alcuin's treatise on orthography is edited in PL 101, 901–20. Boniface's *Ars metrica* will be found in CCSL 133B.

39 Aldhelm's *Epistola* is printed in its entirety in MGH, Auctores Antiqq. 15; Lapidge and Herren (1979: 34–47) translate selections not dealing with meter.

40 Ed. in MGH, Auctores Antiqq. 15.

41 Ed. Guerreau-Jalabert 1982. On Abbo, see Biggs et al. 2001.

Chapter 8 Wisdom Literature and Lyric Poetry

1 Poole 1998 is a particularly useful bibliographical tool for the study of wisdom poetry.

2 Cavill (1999a: 41–59) demonstrates inadequacies in attempts to identify the difference between maxims (or gnomes) and proverbs. The distinction he draws is between "sententious generalisations" and the "linking of a thing with a defining characteristic," respectively. In addition, proverbs are metaphorical in nature (p. 107).

3 Ed. Cox 1972. For bibliography, see Hollis and Wright 1992: 15–33.

4 For an annotated bibliography on both *Solomon and Saturn* and *Adrian and Ritheus*, see Hollis and Wright 1992: 51–75.

5 On common authorship see Donoghue 1987: 91, 173–7 and O'Neill 1997. The latter argues that they were composed within Alfred's circle, and Larrington (1993: 152–6) assumes the poet's familiarity with Boethius' *Consolatio*. O'Neill's is a conclusion which, we believe, does not preclude the assumption that the poems were composed by an Anglian, as certain of their dialect features suggest. At the very least O'Neill's evidence shows that they passed through an Early West Saxon recension; and they are not likely to have been composed any earlier than Alfred's reign (Fulk 1992: 194–7).

6 On the Pater Noster as a canticle, see O'Neill 1997: 158–64.

7 Dendle (1999: 286–9) sees in the forms assumed by the devil a microcosm of Creation.

8 The poem forms the basis of a searching appraisal of the concept "source" in Old English studies by O'Brien O'Keeffe (1994).

9 On the difference between the two, see Larrington 1993: 6, but cf. Cavill 1999a: 45–50.

10 Jackson (1998) detects more local, rhetorical organizing principles in a variety of poetic lists.

11 McGillivray (1989) in fact argues that the unifying feature of Part B is its female perspective.

12 This is to be distinguished from eschatology in general, since its reference is upward-looking, being limited to heaven and the presence of God, and it is meant to exclude references to the horrors of death.

13 The letter ed. and trans. Colgrave and Mynors 1969: 580–7; facsimiles of the poem ed. Robinson and Stanley 1991. For a detailed study of the poem and its epistolary context, see Schopf 1996.

14 Ed. Étaix 1999: 57–64, 244–54; trans. Hurst 1990: 126–33, 226–35. The relevant portion of the latter is also translated by Calder and Allen (1976: 79–81).

15 This dual function suggests to Acker (1998: 55–7) that the poem has a pedagogical purpose.

16 For examples of studies of elegy that attempt to distinguish Christian and pagan elements, see Lawrence 1902b, Huppé 1943, and Timmer 1944.

17 Some examples are Smithers 1957–9, Cross 1959, and Galloway 1988.

18 For other criticisms, see Irving 1997: 184.

19 Klinck (1992: 230–1) nonetheless would reconstruct a Germanic type comparable to the Old English "elegies." On the other hand, although the standard view (that of Heusler 1941: 143–50, 183–9, and his many adherents, e.g. Erzgräber 1989) is that there was no common Germanic elegiac form, we agree with Mohr (1939–40: 211), Dronke (1969: 184)

and J. Harris (1982, 1988) that the lament in the form of "a dramatic monologue spoken by a figure from heroic story" (J. Harris 1988: 90), like Guðrún, Brynhildr, and Oddrún in the poetic edda, is likely to be an ancient literary type. The Old English "elegies," with their mostly anonymous speakers and often homiletic rhetoric, are generally far from this model.

20 In *Beowulf* several sad songs are sung, including that of the father who grieves for his hanged son (2460), of the unnamed Geatish woman who laments Beowulf's death (3150–2), and of Hrothgar, who sings a "true and sad" song on an unspecified topic (2108–9). Whether any of these songs resembled the Old English elegies is unknowable; possibly they were on heroic themes, given that when Hrothgar's *scop* sings a *Preislied* for Beowulf (867–915) it appears to be simply some selections of legendary material. Similarly, we have no clear idea of the content of the various Germanic songs mentioned in Latin sources from Tacitus to Venantius Fortunatus (as surveyed by Opland 1980: 40–60), or even whether some of them were not imitations of Mediterranean songs, as Opland (p. 61) does not think unlikely in the case of the celebrated lament of Gelimer, king of the Vandals, mentioned by Procopius (see Heusler 1941: 137).

21 On structure, see in particular Greenfield 1981, Leslie 1983, and Orton 1991.

22 Speech boundaries are discussed by Huppé 1943, Lumiansky 1950, Pope 1965, 1974, and Greenfield 1969.

23 See Dunning and Bliss 1969: 14–36 and Blockley 2001: 121–52. Such ambiguity is viewed as disjunction by Pasternack (1991) and taken as evidence that this poem and others like it were composed in a fluid process of eclectic recombination of conventional materials. This is the logical extreme to which the findings of O'Brien O'Keeffe about scribal participation in poetic production can be brought (see section 6 of the introduction). On linguistic and stylistic criteria it can be shown not to be true of some longer compositions (see chapter 9).

24 See Harbus 1996a: 174–5. Hasenfratz (1993b) understands the coalescence of birds and kin quite a bit more literally and derives it from the story of the transformation of Diomede's men into seabirds in *Aeneid* XI.

25 For readings of these sorts see Smithers 1957–9, Stanley 1955, and Henry 1966: 161–75.

26 The most prominent Latin instance is in Isidore of Seville's *Synonyma*, in a passage of which there is an extant Old English translation (Cross 1956: 27–8).

27 See Lumiansky 1950, Erzgräber 1961, Horgan 1987, and Pope and Fulk 2001: 98.

28 For other *de excidio* texts see Hume 1976: 344 and Zanna 1991.

29 For a convenient conspectus of studies of *The Ruin*, see Muir 2000: 699.

30 Synopses of these and other views of the speaker are offered by Lench 1970, Renoir 1975, and Klinck 1992: 49–54. Hardly worth mention now is the claim, on tortured linguistic grounds, that the grammatical endings in lines 1–2 do not prove the speaker to be female (see especially Stevens 1968). B. Mitchell (1972) identifies the syntactic obstacles to this view.

31 Bennett (1994) argues that the diction of the poem resists decisive interpretation because it is representative of women's metonymic language, as opposed to men's metaphoric. Some of Bennett's points (Anglo-Saxon women as cultural exiles, the poem as representing women's language) were anticipated by Belanoff (1990) and Desmond (1990).

32 Probably the least objectionable view is that of Kock (1921: 122–3), which, however, demands that the runes form noun compounds that must be interpreted metaphorically.

33 The fullest recent edition is that of Klinck (1992).

34 Baker (1981) gives thorough treatment to all of the poem's most baffling lexical ambiguities. Renoir (1965) adopts the opposite approach, reading the poem without attempting to resolve its ambiguities.

35 See chapter 9. On the possible connection of Odoacer to *Wulf and Eadwacer,* see Bouman 1949, Lehmann 1969, and J. Harris 1988, the last arguing briefly but forcefully that the poem is closely tied to the story told in *Hildebrandslied,* in which Odoacer is also mentioned.

36 This interpretation of *earne* was first proposed by H. Bradley 1888. It is also not improbable that *earne* should stand for *earmne* 'pitiable' (Holthausen 1893: 188 and others); but it is phonologically unlikely that it could represent *earone* 'swift' (*pace* Lawrence 1902a: 258). The parallel in *Vǫlsunga saga* was first remarked by Schofield (1902); recent advocates of this view include North (1994) and Hough (1995). Other analogues in heroic legend that have been proposed are a version of the Wolfdietrich story (Schücking 1919: 16–17) and the legend of the fifth-century Saxon Odoacer (Adovacrius, distinct from the Herulian: Imelmann 1907).

37 For bibliographic accounts of the history of scholarship on the poem, see Frese 1983, Klinck 1992, and Aertsen 1994.

38 See Frese 1983, Osborn 1983, Suzuki 1987, Pulsiano and Wolf 1991, and Tasioulas 1996.

Chapter 9 Germanic Legend and Heroic Lay

1 The letter is edited by Dümmler (1895: 181–4, no. 124); translated by Bullough (1993: 122–5). It was formerly *communis opinio* that the Speratus addressed in the letter in which this remark appears is Hygebald, bishop of Lindisfarne, and that Alcuin's reproof is of the monks' practices in the refectory there. Bullough (1993), however, has demonstrated what shift-

ing sands this opinion is based upon. His view is that the letter is more likely directed to a bishop unconnected to Lindisfarne, in reference to practices at his table in a secular Christian community. In connection with Alcuin's remark it is interesting to note that in Vercelli homily x (ed. Scragg 1992b: 200), sinners are portrayed as seduced by Satan's harp.

2   For a succinct discussion of heroic conventions, see O'Brien O'Keeffe 1991b.

3   The standard scholarly edition has for many years been that of Klaeber (1950), currently under revision by R. D. Fulk, Robert E. Bjork, and John D. Niles. Among the many translations, that of Donaldson (1966) is admired for its fidelity to the language of the poem, that of Heaney (1999) for its fidelity to the spirit. In addition to the bibliographical resources on Old English literature more generally, some of particular value for the study of *Beowulf* are Short 1980, Hasenfratz 1993a, and Bjork and Niles 1997; and for the earlier bibliography, Klaeber's edition and Chambers and Wrenn (1959) are most informative. Shippey and Haarder (1998) provide access to samples of a wide array of German and Scandinavian philological scholarship in translation, along with an excellent overview (pp. 1–74).

4   We believe, therefore, that the poem was perceived as analogous in form to the extended versified narratives of the Latin curriculum, or to the *Aeneid* itself, and may have been inspired (if not otherwise influenced) by them. If it was perceived as made in imitation of Latin models, it could claim the same right to manuscript preservation as, say, vernacular scriptural poetry, which was analogous to such curricular works as Alcimus Avitus' *Poema de Mosaicae historiae gestis* and Juvencus' *Evangelia*. There would be little point in recording a poem that might be recreated *ex tempore* by any *scop*.

5   For a fine account of the rise and fall of the *Liedertheorie*, and indeed of the entire history of views on the poem's structure, see Shippey 1997.

6   The effects of Tolkien's insistence that the poem is not an epic have been mixed. No one now refers to the poem as "the *Beowulf*," as they once did, and yet it is still very commonly referred to as an epic – even, due to the authors' oversight, in Fulk and Harris 2002: 98. Regardless, there have been some significant studies that flesh out Tolkien's premise by discerning organizing features in the poem that have nothing to do with classical ideas of structure: see in particular Niles 1983: 163–76 and Sorrell 1992. Tolkien's lecture was extracted from a book-length manuscript recently discovered, and currently being edited, by Michael Drout.

7   See particularly Magoun 1958, 1963, K. Sisam 1965, G. Jones 1972, and Frantzen 1990: 180.

8   For references to earlier stylistic studies bearing on the unity of the poem, see Bonjour 1950: 75–6. Irving (1984) finds differences in the incidence

of religious allusions in the two parts of the poem, but he himself offers several alternative explanations (1997: 185–6).

9   There are six examples in this section of 311 lines, at ll. 1906b, 1940a, 2046a, 2077a, 2108a, and 2120a – the same number found in all of *Andreas* (at 1,722 lines), and more than are found in any other Old English poem, including *Genesis A* (at 2,319 lines). For a full list of examples in *Beowulf*, see Bliss 1967: 27–9.

10   The most notable recent effort is Niles's compilation (1999a: 134–40) of a list of seven reasons to perceive the poem as a response to the cultural and political scene of the tenth century, as "a vehicle for political work in a time when the various peoples south of Hadrian's Wall were being assimilated into an emergent English nation" (p. 143).

11   A particularly forthright proponent of this view is Nicholas Howe: see his essay "The uses of uncertainty: On the dating of *Beowulf*," appended to the 1997 reprint of Chase 1981. For a fine overview of the current state of dating scholarship see Bjork and Obermeier 1997. The objections of Liuzza (1995) to linguistic arguments for dating are for the most part anticipated and answered in Fulk 1992, which he does not cite. A particular weakness in the objections of A. Amos (1980), duplicated by Liuzza, is the positivist importance she attaches to proof at the expense of more reliable probabilistic evidence.

12   For discussion, with references, see Bjork and Obermeier 1997: 31–3.

13   "Poetarum, citharistarum, musicorum, scurrorum": ed. Haddan and Stubbs 1871: 3.360–76 at 369. For a translation of the canons see Gee and Hardy 1896: 15–32.

14   Ready access to the Scandinavian analogues in translation is furnished by Garmonsway and Simpson (1968). Extensive discussion of the legendary and mythic analogues is offered by Chambers and Wrenn (1959), though the briefer consideration in Klaeber 1950: xii–xlviii is also most informative.

15   Lawrence (1930: 178–87) offers evidence that the version of the tale in *Grettis saga* is closer to the original form; but even if this is so, it is not impossible that the saga version should have been based on a folktale in circulation in England, rather than on the preserved version of *Beowulf*. For thorough reconsiderations of the relations between the Icelandic and English tales, with extensive bibliography, see Liberman 1986 and Fjalldal 1998, the former arguing that the resemblances are due to common inheritance of an ancient folktale, the latter that they are pure happenstance.

16   This consensus is challenged in Fulk and Harris 2002.

17   The classic examples are Ettmüller 1840 and Blackburn 1897, attempting to identify all Christian sentiments to be excised from the poem. For discussion, with references, see Irving 1997.

18   Mees is currently preparing his doctoral thesis at the University of Sydney

on collaboration and resistance among German philologists during the National Socialist era. We wish to express our gratitude to Mees and to Prof. Thomas Markey for much information they provided on this topic.

19 For bibliography and historical overview, see Bjork 1997a.

20 The essentials of this analysis were first set out by Schrøder 1875, and it is now the standard analysis, developed extensively in subsequent scholarship. K. Sisam 1965 is the most recent study to question the assumption of Hrothulf's treachery.

21 Overing 1990: 1–32 might be added here, for although her argument is that the literary mode of the poet is metonymic rather than metaphoric, her application of the principle pertains chiefly to style rather than diction. For a historical overview of studies of the poet's diction and use of variation, see O'Brien O'Keeffe 1997.

22 In this sense, then, "style" is not an inappropriate characterization of those presumably involuntary peculiarities of syntactic usage that differentiate poets, such as those studied by Andrew (1940) and Donoghue (1987). For a bibliographical survey of studies of Old English poetic style in this sense, see Calder 1979.

23 On irony in the poem, see Ringler 1966 and Irving 1968: 1–42.

24 See section 4 of the introduction. The general trend in studies of classical rhetoric in Old English verse has been to identify schemes and tropes without much attention to demonstrating Anglo-Saxon knowledge of progymnasmatic rhetoric: see, e.g., Bartlett 1935, Wine 1993, and E. Anderson 1998. Some important exceptions, in which the rhetorical content of the monastic curriculum has been studied in some detail, with the aim of demonstrating the plausibility of classical influence on native verse construction, are J. J. Campbell 1967 and Knappe 1994, 1998. See Schaefer 1997: 118–20 for discussion and further references.

25 Clark actually derives this view not from Tolkien's 1936 essay but from his 1953 study of *The Battle of Maldon*, in which his views on Beowulf's failings are explicit, as he finds *Beowulf* to be "a legend of 'excess' in a chief" (p. 15). Thus Clark argues that Tolkien's views changed: "After the war," he concludes, "Tolkien saw defeat as moral refutation" (1997: 280). The company of those who regard the hero as flawed is quite large. For some of the more significant contributions to the construction of this view, see, in addition to Tolkien and Goldsmith, Stanley 1963, Leyerle 1965, Robinson 1970, 1993b, Berger and Leicester 1974, Bolton 1978, Georgianna 1987, and Orchard 1995. For a forceful counterargument, portraying the poet's vision of the heroic world as an approving one, see John Hill 1995. In our view it is a mistaken assumption that the poem's somber tone evidences the poet's disapproval of the heroic ethos. Heroic literature outside of Old English is equally somber.

26 For a bibliographical overview of allegorical and exegetical approaches,

see Irving 1997.

27 Philologically this is improbable: see Fulk 1987, with the references there to views on Unferth. The belief – mistaken, in our view – is widespread in Beowulf criticism that personal names in the poem reflect, often ironically, on their bearers in a literary fashion, especially the names Hygelac, Hygd, Wealhtheow, and Thryth (see, e.g., Malone 1941, Kaske 1963, and Robinson 1968).

28 For a survey of approaches to the poem of this sort, see Lerer 1997; and in Old English studies in general, Pasternack 1997.

29 Substantial examples of the second phase are few, and not just in connection with *Beowulf,* as should be apparent from the very small number of references in the overview of Lees (1997). Lees remarks that "it is certainly premature to write the history of feminism in Anglo-Saxon studies because this history is even now only in the making" (p. 148). The most lucid and extensive application of feminist theory to *Beowulf* is certainly that of Overing (1990: 68–107; see also Overing 1995), who characterizes the women of the poem as hysterics who disrupt and subvert the dominant masculine desire that underlies the dynamics of the poem, and particularly its masculine discourse. Overing's distinction between violent masculine language, tending to resolution, and feminine language, maintaining ambiguity (deriving ultimately from French feminist theory), has been taken up by others, e.g. Bennett (1994). Psychoanalytic approaches, often with feminist import, have been most extensively practiced by Earl (1994).

30 The definitive statement of his views is Sievers 1893. For an introduction in English to Sievers' categories, see Pope and Fulk 2001: 129–58.

31 For bibliography see Gade and Fulk 2000.

32 For editions, see Klaeber 1950, Fry 1974, and Tolkien 1983, the last with translation. See also the important discussion in Chambers and Wrenn 1959: 245–89, 543–6.

33 North (1990), in agreement with Tolkien, argues that there are Jutes on both sides of the conflict.

34 Östman and Wårvik (1994) would make Garulf a Dane. This entails some improbabilities, including the assumption that it is one of the attackers rather than of the defenders who *duru hēolde* 'held the door' (22; cf. 42).

35 The most useful critical editions are those of F. Norman (1949) and Zettersten (1979), the latter with a complete facsimile.

36 Although Waldere's speech beginning in II, 14 is directed to Guthhere, and most scholars therefore assume that it is Guthhere who has just spoken, the first speaker's indication that his sword is sheathed suggests that he is Hagena (as first remarked by Wolff 1925), who in some of the analogues refuses to fight in the first attack (as implied also in II, 14–15), since he and Walter had sworn brotherhood at Attila's court.

37 For critical editions, see Malone 1933, Klinck 1992, and Pope and Fulk 2001.

38 Yet Malone (1933) ingeniously identifies the pair with the Gaute and Magnild of Scandinavian ballads, and some accept the connection, e.g. J. Foley (1999: 266).

39 Malone's identification (1933, 1939) of Theodric with the Frankish Wolfdietrich of Middle High German legend rather than with the Ostrogothic Dietrich von Bern has now rather generally been discarded. A legend, otherwise unknown to us, about Theodric's trials is hinted at in *Waldere*, where (as noted above) he is said to have been rescued from the grasp of monsters by Widia, son of Beadohild and Weland.

40 For editions, see Chambers 1912 and the more speculative Malone 1962b.

41 Joyce Hill (1984) asserts that some of the unidentified names in the Germanic sections are fictitious, inserted only to contribute to the overall effect of the catalogues. Whether or not the names are genuine is unprovable; yet the number of truly suspicious names is small, and given the relatively small amount of genuinely old heroic material that survives, it would be a rather extreme coincidence if all the names in *Widsith* had counterparts in other sources.

42 The latest scholarly edition, that of Malone (1962b), offers some daring and unorthodox views that have hardly been discussed outside of reviews of the book. Philological approaches have not died out altogether: examples are Bliss 1985 and Schramm 1998: 129–32.

43 See French 1945, Meindl 1964, and Eliason 1966. Note that this analysis demands the assumption of a secular setting for the poem's composition.

44 See Fry 1980 and R. Brown 1989.

45 See Reynolds 1953 and Langenfelt 1959. The hypothesis of Niles (1999b) that the poem represents a tenth-century "act of mythopoesis whereby a desired order of things is projected onto a formative period of the past" (p. 193) is as daring as any proposed by Malone. It rests upon the conjecture that the Myrgings would have been perceived as a branch of the Saxon nation and Widsith himself therefore as a "proto-Saxon."

46 The best editions are those of E. Gordon (1937) and Scragg (1981); more recent, but less elaborate, is that of Pope and Fulk (2001). For scholarly bibliography, consult Collier 1991, with updates to the electronic version. Some useful collections of essays on *Maldon* are Scragg 1991a, Niles 1991b, and Cooper 1993.

47 See Rogers 1985 for the evidence. In addition to the facsimile of the transcript in Robinson and Stanley 1991 there is an excellent one in Scragg 1991a. Robinson (1993a) finds reason to think another transcript may have been made before the fire, though it cannot now be located.

48 The identification of the site of the viking encampment (first made by Laborde 1925) as Northey Island, two miles downstream from Maldon,

is now consensus. It is an island of about a mile square, connected to the mainland by a causeway exposed at low tide. For a plan and views of the area, see Dodgson 1991. For discussion of Byrhtnoth's personal importance, see Scragg 1981: 14–20 and Locherbie-Cameron 1991.

49 The relevant portions of the Latin texts are edited and translated by Lapidge (1991a) and Kennedy (1991).

50 Much has been written on the historicity of the poem. See especially Macrae-Gibson 1970, Gneuss 1976b, and Scattergood 1984; for full bibliography of this topic, see Andersen 1991: 99–120, to whose list may be added Clark 1992 and Cooper 1993.

51 See in particular Woolf 1976, Frank 1991b, and John Hill 1991. J. Harris (1993) corrects Woolf's argument in important respects.

52 On the poem's formal deviations from classical standards of verse construction, see Scragg 1981: 28–35.

53 For a full bibliographical synopsis of the controversy, see Cavill 1995.

54 On the Alfredian evidence, see Clark 1979: 274. For examples of more recent studies finding a positive sense to *ofermōd*, see T. Hill 1997: 8 and C. Davis 1999: 157–63.

55 See N. Blake 1965. Dismissive of Blake's views are Cross 1965, Scragg 1981: 35, and Schwab 1990: 173–80.

56 For discussion and references see Fulk 1992: 415–18 and Scragg 1993.

57 The most thorough edition is that of A. Campbell (1938); see the simpler but more recent one in Pope and Fulk 2001.

Conclusion
Making Old English New: Anglo-Saxonism and the Cultural Work of Old English Literature

1 On Saxon–Norman antagonism and nationalist nostalgia in this period, see, e.g., James Campbell 1984: 131–3, Frankis 1995, Lerer 1999, S. Mitchell 2000, and Frederick 2000. Some of this anti-Norman feeling is evident in the Chronicle, e.g. in *The Rime of King William* and some of the later entries in the Laud manuscript. Franzen (1991: 183) finds evidence that the work of the prolific early thirteenth-century Worcester glossator known as the "Tremulous Hand" represents not a continuous tradition of interest in Old English manuscripts but a revival, perhaps associated with the canonization of St. Wulfstan in 1203. Collier (2000: 208) sees the Tremulous Hand's efforts as nostalgic and designed to help the language survive. For facsimiles of the Tremulous Hand's work, see Franzen 1998.

2 See also Pulsiano 2000. On the other hand, it is clear that the Tremulous Hand of Worcester (see the preceding note) was learning Old English as

he worked (Franzen 1991: 183).

3   On developments of the sixteenth and seventeenth centuries, see Murphy 1982, to which the following discussion is indebted; also Graham 2000.

4   On the history of drama and poetry devoted to Alfred, and indeed to all Anglo-Saxon themes in eighteenth- and early nineteenth-century English literature, see Scragg 2000. There is an exceptionally full study of Alfred's cult from his day to ours by Keynes (1999b).

5   For samples in translation see Shippey and Haarder 1998. Shippey's introduction to this collection includes a superb account of the political implications of *Beowulf* scholarship up to 1935, an account to which the following is indebted.

6   Shippey, in Shippey and Haarder 1998: 72. On parallels between German and English Teutonism of the nineteenth century, see Oergel 1998.

7   This, for example, is the premise of Frantzen (1990), whose concern is Anglo-Saxonism in the academy. Shippey (2000) laments the marginality of Anglo-Saxonism in popular culture, and he advocates the nationalist value of Old English for Englishmen in an age of devolution.

Works Cited

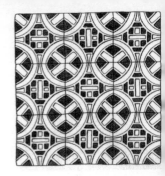

Diacritics are ignored for the purpose of alphabetization. Thus *ø* and *ö* are not differentiated alphabetically from *o*, nor *ä* or *å* from *a*, and so forth. The titles of journals and series are abbreviated as follows:

ANQ	*American Notes & Queries*
Archiv	*Archiv für das Studium der neueren Sprachen und Literaturen*
ASE	*Anglo-Saxon England*
ASPR	*Anglo-Saxon Poetic Records* (see Krapp and Dobbie 1931–53)
CCSL	Corpus Christianorum, Series Latina
CSASE	Cambridge Studies in Anglo-Saxon England
E&S	*Essays and Studies*
EEMF	Early English Manuscripts in Facsimile
EETS	Early English Text Society
ELN	*English Language Notes*
EME	*Early Medieval Europe*
ES	*English Studies*
JEGP	*Journal of English and Germanic Philology*
LSE	*Leeds Studies in English*
MÆ	*Medium Ævum*
MGH	Monumenta Germaniae Historica
MP	*Modern Philology*
MS	*Mediaeval Studies*
N&Q	*Notes and Queries*
NM	*Neuphilologische Mitteilungen*
OEN	*Old English Newsletter*
PBA	*Proceedings of the British Academy*
PL	Patrologia Latina (see Migne 1879–1974)
PMLA	*Publications of the Modern Language Association*
PQ	*Philological Quarterly*
RES	*Review of English Studies*

SN	*Studia Neophilologica*
SP	*Studies in Philology*
ZfdA	*Zeitschrift für deutsches Altertum und deutsche Literatur*

In addition, the following abbreviations are used:

A-S	Anglo-Saxon
OE	Old English

Abels, Richard. 1998. *Alfred the Great: War, Kingship and Culture in A-S England*. London: Longman.

Acker, Paul. 1998. *Revising Oral Theory: Formulaic Composition in OE and Old Icelandic Verse*. New York: Garland.

Adams, J. N., and Marilyn Deegan. 1992. *Bald's Leechbook* and the Physica Plinii. *ASE* 21.87–114.

Adams, John F. 1958. *Wulf and Eadwacer*: An interpretation. *MLN* 73.1–5.

Aertsen, Henk. 1994. *Wulf and Eadwacer*: A woman's *cri de coeur* — for whom, for what? In *Companion to OE Poetry*, ed. Henk Aertsen and Rolf H. Bremmer, 119–44. Amsterdam: VU University Press.

Ai, Low Soon. 1997. Mental cultivation in *Guthlac B. Neophilologus* 81.625–36.

Amos, Ashley Crandell. 1980. *Linguistic Means of Determining the Dates of OE Literary Texts*. Cambridge, Mass.: Medieval Academy of America.

Amos, Thomas L. 1989. Preaching and the sermon in the Carolingian world. In *De Ore Domini: Preacher and Word in the Middle Ages*, ed. T. Amos et al., 41–60. Studies in Medieval Culture 27. Kalamazoo: Medieval Institute Pubns.

Andersen, Hans Erik. 1991. *The Battle of Maldon: The Meaning, Dating and Historicity of an OE Poem*. Copenhagen: Department of English, University of Copenhagen.

Anderson, Earl R. 1983. *Cynewulf: Structure, Style, and Theme in His Poetry*. Rutherford, N.J.: Fairleigh Dickinson University Press.

—— 1987. Style and theme in the OE *Daniel. ES* 68.1–23.

—— 1989. Liturgical influence in *The Dream of the Rood. Neophilologus* 73.293–304.

—— 1998. *A Grammar of Iconism*. Madison, N.J.: Fairleigh Dickinson University Press.

—— 2000. OE poetic texts and their Latin sources: Iconicity in *Cædmon's Hymn* and *The Phoenix*. In *The Motivated Sign*, ed. Olga Fischer and Max Nänny, 109–32. Amsterdam: J. Benjamins.

Anderson, James E. 1983. *Deor, Wulf and Eadwacer, The Soul's Address*: How and where the OE Exeter Book riddles begin. In *The OE Elegies: New Essays in Criticism*, ed. M. Green, 204–30. Rutherford, N.J.: Fairleigh Dickinson University Press.

—— 1986. *Two Literary Riddles in the Exeter Book*. Norman: University of Oklahoma Press.

Andersson, Theodore M. 1980. Tradition and design in *Beowulf.* In *OE Literature in Context: Ten Essays*, ed. John D. Niles, 90–106 and 171–2. Cambridge: D.S. Brewer. Reprinted 1991 in *Interpretations of "Beowulf": A Critical Anthology*, ed. R. D. Fulk, 219–34. Bloomington: Indiana University Press.

—— 1988. Die oral-formulaic Poetry im Germanischen. In *Heldensage und Heldendichtung im Germanischen*, ed. Heinrich Beck, 1–14. Berlin: W. de Gruyter.

—— 1992. The speeches in the *Waldere* fragments. In *De Gustibus: Essays for Alain Renoir*, ed. John Miles Foley, 21–9. New York: Garland.

—— 1997. Sources and analogues. In *A "Beowulf" Handbook*, ed. Robert E. Bjork and John D. Niles, 125–48. Lincoln: University of Nebraska Press.

Andrew, Samuel O. 1940. *Syntax and Style in OE.* Cambridge: Cambridge University Press.

Anlezark, Daniel. 2000. An ideal marriage: Abraham and Sarah in OE literature. *MÆ* 69.187–210.

Archibald, Elizabeth. 1991. *Apollonius of Tyre: Medieval and Renaissance Themes and Variations.* Cambridge: D. S. Brewer.

Arngart, Olof, ed. 1979. *The Proverbs of Alfred: An Emended Text.* Studier utgivna av Kungl. Humanistiska Vetenskapssamfundet i Lund, Scripta Minora, 1979–80. Lund: C. Gleerup.

—— 1981. The Durham Proverbs. *Speculum* 56.288–300.

ASPR, see Krapp and Dobbie 1931-53.

Assmann, Bruno, ed. 1889. *Angelsächsische Homilien und Heiligenleben.* Bibliothek der angelsächsischen Prosa 3. Kassel: G. Wigand. Reprinted 1964 with a supplementary introduction by Peter Clemoes, Darmstadt: Wissenschaftliches Buchgesellschaft.

Astell, Ann. 1989. Holofernes' head: *tacen* and teaching in the OE *Judith. ASE* 18.117–33.

Attenborough, F. L., ed. and trans. 1963. *The Laws of the Earliest English Kings.* New York: Russell & Russell.

Baker, Peter S. 1980. The OE canon of Byrhtferth of Ramsey. *Speculum* 55.22–37.

—— 1981. The ambiguity of *Wulf and Eadwacer. SP* 78.5.39–51.

—— 1982. Byrhtferth's *Enchiridion* and the computus in Oxford, St. John's College 17. *ASE* 10.123–42.

—— 1984. A little-known variant text of the OE metrical psalms. *Speculum* 59.263–81.

—— ed. 1995. *Beowulf: Basic Readings.* New York: Garland (reprinted 2000 under the title *The "Beowulf" Reader*).

—— 1997. OE and computing: A guided tour. In *Reading OE Texts*, ed. Katherine O'Brien O'Keeffe, 192–215. Cambridge: Cambridge University Press.

—— 1999. Computus. In *The Blackwell Encyclopedia of A-S England*, ed. Michael Lapidge et al., 119–20. Oxford: Blackwell.

Baker, Peter S., and Michael Lapidge, eds. and transs. 1995. *Byrhtferth's Enchiridion*. EETS s.s. 15. Oxford: Oxford University Press.

Ball, C. J. E. 1966. The Franks Casket: Right side. *ES* 47.119–28.

Bambas, Rudolph C. 1963. Another view of the OE *Wife's Lament. JEGP* 62.303–9.

Barlow, Frank. 1979. *The English Church 1000–1066: A History of the Later A-S Church*. 2nd ed. London: Longman.

—— ed. and trans. 1992. *The Life of King Edward*. 2nd ed. Oxford: Clarendon.

Barnes, Daniel R. 1970. Folktale morphology and the structure of *Beowulf. Speculum* 45.416–34.

Barnhouse, Rebecca. 2000. Shaping the Hexateuch text for an A-S audience. In *The OE Hexateuch: Aspects and Approaches*, ed. Rebecca Barnhouse and Benjamin C. Withers, 91–108. Kalamazoo: Medieval Institute Pubns.

Bartlett, Adeline Courtney. 1935. *The Larger Rhetorical Patterns in A-S Poetry*. New York: Columbia University Press. Reprinted 1966, New York: AMS.

Bately, Janet. 1966. The OE Orosius: The question of dictation. *Anglia* 84.255–304.

—— 1970. King Alfred and the OE translation of Orosius. *Anglia* 88.433–60.

—— 1980a. The literary prose of King Alfred's reign: Translation or transformation? In *OE Prose: Basic Readings*, ed. Paul E. Szarmach, 3–27. New York: Garland. (Originally delivered as a 1980 lecture; subsequently published as OEN Subsidia 10 (1984).)

—— ed. 1980b. *The OE Orosius*. EETS s.s. 6. London: Oxford University Press.

—— 1982. Lexical evidence for the authorship of the prose psalms of the Paris Psalter. *ASE* 10.69–95.

—— 1985. Linguistic evidence as a guide to the authorship of OE verse: A reappraisal, with special reference to *Beowulf*. In *Learning and Literature in A-S England: Studies Presented to Peter Clemoes*, ed. Michael Lapidge and Helmut Gneuss, 409–31. Cambridge: Cambridge University Press.

—— 1988a. Manuscript layout and the A-S Chronicle. *Bulletin of the John Rylands University Library of Manchester* 70.1.21–43.

—— 1988b. OE prose before and during the reign of Alfred. *ASE* 17.93–138.

—— 1990. Those books that are most necessary for all men to know: The classics and late ninth-century England, a reappraisal. In *The Classics in the Middle Ages: Papers of the Twentieth Annual Conference of the Center for Medieval and Renaissance Studies*, ed. Aldo S. Bernardo and Saul Levin, 45–78. Binghamton: Center for Medieval and Early Renaissance Studies, State University of New York.

—— 1991a. *The A-S Chronicle: Texts and Textual Relationships*. Reading Medieval Studies Monographs 3. Reading: University of Reading Press.

—— 1991b. The nature of OE prose. In *The Cambridge Companion to OE Literature*, ed. Malcolm Godden and Michael Lapidge, 71–87. Cambridge: Cambridge University Press.

—— ed. 1992. *The Tanner Bede*. EEMF 24. Copenhagen: Rosenkilde & Bagger.

—— 1993. *Anonymous OE Homilies: A Preliminary Bibliography of Source Studies*. Binghamton: Center for Medieval and Early Renaissance Studies, State University of New York. 2nd electronic edition 1996 ‹http://www.wmich.edu/medieval/rawl/bately1/index.html›.

—— 1994a. Boethius and King Alfred. In *Platonism and the English Imagination*, ed. Anna Baldwin and Sarah Hutton, 38–44. Cambridge: Cambridge University Press.

—— 1994b. An Alfredian legacy? On the fortunes and fate of some items of Boethian vocabulary in OE. In *From A-S to Early Middle English: Studies Presented to E. G. Stanley*, ed. Douglas Gray, Malcolm Godden, and Terry Hoad, 8–32. Oxford: Clarendon.

Battles, Paul. 2000. *Genesis A* and the A-S "migration myth." *ASE* 29.43–66.

Bayless, Martha. 1993. *Beatus quid est* and the study of grammar in late A-S England. In *History of Linguistic Thought in the Early Middle Ages*, ed. Vivien Law, 67–110. Amsterdam: J. Benjamins.

Behr, Charlotte. 2000. The origins of kingship in early medieval Kent. *EME* 9.25–52.

Belanoff, Patricia A. 1989. The fall(?) of the OE female poetic image. *PMLA* 104.822–31.

—— 1990. Women's songs, women's language: *Wulf and Eadwacer* and *The Wife's Lament*. In *New Readings on Women in OE Literature*, ed. Helen Damico and Alexandra Hennessey Olsen, 193–203. Bloomington: Indiana University Press.

—— 1993. *Judith*: Sacred and secular heroine. In *Heroic Poetry in the A-S Period: Studies in Honor of Jess B. Bessinger, Jr.*, ed. Helen Damico and John Leyerle, 247–64. Studies in Medieval Culture 32. Kalamazoo: Medieval Institute Pubns.

Benison, Líam. 1998. Translation during King Alfred's reign: The politics of conversion and truth. *Medieval Translator* 6.82–100.

Bennett, Helen T. 1992. The female mourner at Beowulf's funeral: Filling in the blanks/hearing the spaces. *Exemplaria* 4.35–50.

—— 1994. Exile and semiosis of gender in OE elegies. In *Class and Gender in Early English Literature: Intersections*, ed. Britton J. Harwood and Gillian R. Overing, 43–58. Bloomington: Indiana University Press.

Benson, Larry D. 1966. The literary character of A-S formulaic poetry. *PMLA* 81.334–41. Reprinted 1995 in *Contradictions: From Beowulf to Chaucer: Selected Studies of Larry D. Benson*, ed. Theodore M. Andersson and Stephen

A. Barney, 1–14. Aldershot, Hants: Scolar.

—— 1970. The originality of *Beowulf.* In *The Interpretation of Narrative: Theory and Practice*, ed. Morton W. Bloomfield, 1–43. Cambridge, Mass.: Harvard University Press. Reprinted 1995 in *Contradictions: From Beowulf to Chaucer: Selected Studies of Larry D. Benson*, ed. Theodore M. Andersson and Stephen A. Barney, 32–69. Aldershot, Hants: Scolar.

Berger, Harry, Jr., and H. Marshall Leicester, Jr. 1974. Social structure as doom: The limits of heroism in *Beowulf.* In *OE Studies in Honour of John C. Pope*, ed. Robert B. Burlin and Edward B. Irving, Jr., 37–79. Toronto: University of Toronto Press.

Berkhout, Carl T., and Milton McC. Gatch, eds. 1982. *A-S Scholarship: The First Three Centuries.* Boston: G. K. Hall.

Bernstein, Melissa J., ed. 1997. *The Electronic "Sermo Lupi ad Anglos."* <http://www.cif.rochester.edu/~mjbernst/wulfstan/>.

Bethel, Patricia. 1991. Regnal and divine epithets in the metrical psalms and *Metres of Boethius. Parergon* n.s. 9.1.1–41.

Bethurum, Dorothy, ed. 1957. *The Homilies of Wulfstan.* Oxford: Clarendon.

—— 1966. Wulfstan. In *Continuations and Beginnings: Studies in OE Literature*, ed. E. G. Stanley, 210–46. London: Nelson.

Bieler, Ludwig, ed. 1984. *Anicii Manlii Severini Boethii philosophiae consolatio.* CCSL 94. Turnhout: Brepols.

Biggs, Frederick M. 1986. *The Sources of "Christ III": A Revision of Cook's Notes.* OEN Subsidia 12. Binghamton: Center for Medieval and Early Renaissance Studies, State University of New York.

—— 1989. The eschatalogical conclusion of the OE *Physiologus. MÆ* 58.286–97.

—— 1990. Unities in the OE *Guthlac B. JEGP* 89.155–65.

—— 1996. Ælfric as historian: His use of Alcuin's *Laudationes* and Sulpicius's *Dialogues* in his two lives of Martin. In *Holy Men and Holy Women: OE Prose Saints' Lives and Their Contexts*, ed. Paul E. Szarmach, 289–315. Albany: State University of New York Press.

Biggs, Frederick M., Thomas D. Hill, and Paul E. Szarmach, eds. 1990. *Sources of A-S Literary Culture: A Trial Version.* Binghamton: Center for Medieval and Early Renaissance Studies, State University of New York.

Biggs, Frederick M., et al. 1999. *SASLC: Sources of A-S Literary Culture.* <http://www.wmich.edu/medieval/saslc/>.

Biggs, Frederick M., et al. 2001. *Abbo of Fleury, Abbo of Saint-Germain-des-Prés, and Acta Sanctorum.* Kalamazoo: Medieval Institute Pubns.

Birch, W. de Gray. 1885–99. *Cartularium Saxonicum.* 3 vols. and index. London: Whiting/Phillimore. Reprinted 1964, New York: Johnson Rpt.

Bischoff, Bernhard, et al., eds. 1988. *The Épinal, Erfurt, Werden and Corpus Glossaries.* EEMF 22. Copenhagen: Rosenkilde & Bagger.

Bischoff, Bernhard, and Michael Lapidge, eds. 1994. *Biblical Commentaries from the Canterbury School of Theodore and Hadrian.* CSASE 10. Cambridge: Cambridge University Press.

Bjork, Robert E. 1980. Oppressed Hebrews and the song of Azarias in the OE *Daniel. SP* 77.213–26.

—— 1985. *The OE Verse Saints' Lives.* Toronto: University of Toronto Press.

—— 1989. *Sundor æt rune:* The voluntary exile of *The Wanderer. Neophilologus* 73.119–29.

—— 1997a. Digressions and episodes. In *A "Beowulf" Handbook,* ed. Robert E. Bjork and John D. Niles, 193–212. Lincoln: University of Nebraska Press.

—— 1997b. Nineteenth-century Scandinavia and the birth of A-S studies. In *Anglo-Saxonism and the Construction of Social Identity,* ed. Allen Frantzen and John D. Niles, 111–32. Gainesville: University Press of Florida.

Bjork, Robert E., and John D. Niles, eds. 1997. *A "Beowulf" Handbook.* Lincoln: University of Nebraska Press.

Bjork, Robert E., and Anita Obermeier. 1997. Date, provenance, author, audiences. In *A "Beowulf" Handbook,* ed. Robert E. Bjork and John D. Niles, 13–34. Lincoln: University of Nebraska Press.

Björkman, Erik. 1910. *Nordische Personennamen in England in alt- und frühmittel-englischer Zeit.* Studien zur englischen Philologie 37. Halle: M. Niemeyer.

Blackburn, F. A. 1897. The Christian coloring in the *Beowulf. PMLA* 12.205–25. Reprinted 1963 in *An Anthology of "Beowulf" Criticism,* ed. Lewis E. Nicholson, 1–21. Notre Dame: University of Notre Dame Press.

Blake, E. O., ed. 1962. *Liber Eliensis.* London: Royal Historical Society.

Blake, N. F. 1965. *The Battle of Maldon. Neophilologus* 49.332–45.

—— ed. 1990. *The Phoenix.* Rev. ed. Exeter: Exeter University Press.

Blatt, Franz, ed. 1930. *Die lateinischen Bearbeitungen der Acta Andreae et Matthiae apud anthropophagos.* Giezen: A. Topelmann.

Bliss, A. J. 1967. *The Metre of "Beowulf."* Rev. ed. Oxford: Blackwell.

—— 1985. The Aviones and *Widsith* 26a. *ASE* 14.97–106.

Bliss, A. J., and Allen J. Frantzen. 1976. The integrity of *Resignation. RES* 27.385–402.

Blockley, Mary. 2001. *Aspects of OE Syntax: Where Clauses Begin.* Urbana: University of Illinois Press.

Bloomfield, Morton W. 1949–51. *Beowulf* and Christian allegory: An interpretation of Unferth. *Traditio* 7.410–15. Reprinted 1963 in *An Anthology of "Beowulf" Criticism,* ed. Lewis E. Nicholson, 155–64. Notre Dame: University of Notre Dame Press.

Bodden, Mary Catherine, ed. and trans. 1987. *The OE Finding of the True Cross.* Woodbridge, Suffolk: D. S. Brewer.

—— 1988. Evidence for knowledge of Greek in A-S England. *ASE* 17.217–46.

Boenig, Robert E. 1980. *Andreas,* the eucharist, and Vercelli. *JEGP* 79.313–31.

—— trans. 1991. *The Acts of Andrew in the Country of the Cannibals: Translations from the Greek, Latin, and OE*. New York: Garland.

—— 1996. The A-S harp. *Speculum* 71.290–320.

Bolton, W. F. 1967. *A History of Anglo-Latin Literature 597–1066, Vol. 1: 597–740*. Princeton: Princeton University Press.

—— 1969. *The Wife's Lament* and *The Husband's Message*: A reconsideration revisited. *Archiv* 205.337–51.

—— 1978. *Alcuin and Beowulf: An Eighth-Century View*. New Brunswick: Rutgers University Press.

Bonjour, Adrien. 1950. *The Digressions in "Beowulf."* Medium Ævum Monographs 5. Oxford: Blackwell.

Bonner, Gerald, ed. 1976. *Famulus Christi: Essays in Commemoration of the Thirteenth Centenary of the Birth of the Venerable Bede*. London: Society for Promotion of Christian Knowledge.

Bostock, J. Knight, K. C. King, and D. R. McLintock. 1976. *A Handbook on Old High German Literature*. 2nd ed. Oxford: Clarendon.

Bouman, A. C. 1949. *Leodum is minum:* Beadohild's complaint. *Neophilologus* 33.103–13. Reprinted 1962 in *Patterns in OE and Old Icelandic Literature*, ed. A. C. Bouman, 93–106. Leidse Germanistische en Anglistische Reeks, Deel 1. Leiden: Universitaire.

—— 1962. *Patterns in OE and Old Icelandic Literature*. Leidse Germanistische en Anglistische Reeks, Deel 1. Leiden: Universitaire.

Boutflower, Douglas S., trans. 1912. *The Life of Ceolfrid*. Sunderland: Hills.

Bracher, Frederick. 1937. Understatement in OE poetry. *PMLA* 52.915–34. Reprinted 1968 in *Essential Articles for the Study of OE Poetry*, ed. J. B. Bessinger, Jr., and Stanley J. Kahrl, 228–54. Hamden, Conn.: Archon.

Bradley, Henry. 1888. The first riddle of the Exeter Book. *Academy* 33.197–8.

Bradley, S. A. J., trans. 1982. *A-S Poetry*. London: Dent.

Brandl, Alois. 1919. Venantius Fortunatus und die angelsächsischen Elegien *Wanderer* und *Ruine*. *Archiv* 139.84.

Brantley, Jessica. 1999. The iconography of the Utrecht Psalter and the OE *Descent into Hell*. *ASE* 28.43–63.

Braune, Wilhelm, and Ernst A. Ebbinghaus. 1994. *Althochdeutsches Lesebuch*. 17th ed. Tübingen: M. Niemeyer.

Bredehoft, Thomas. 1998. A note on Robinson's *Rewards of Piety*. *N&Q* n.s. 45.5–8.

—— 2001. *Textual Histories: Readings in the A-S Chronicle*. Toronto: University of Toronto Press.

Breeze, Andrew. 1992. *Finnsburh* and *Maldon: Celæs Bord, Cellod Bord*. *N&Q* n.s. 39.267–9.

Bremmer, Rolf H., Jr. 1997. The Germanic context of "Cynewulf and Cyneheard" revisited. *Neophilologus* 81.445–65.

Bridges, Margaret Enid. 1984. *Generic Contrast in OE Hagiographical Poetry*.

Anglistica 22. Copenhagen: Rosenkilde & Bagger.

Brock, Sebastian P. 1995. The Syriac background. In *Archbishop Theodore: Commemorative Studies on His Life and Influence*, ed. Michael Lapidge, 30–53. CSASE 11. Cambridge: Cambridge University Press.

Broderick, Herbert. 1983. Observations on the methods of illustration in MS Junius 11 and the relationship of the drawings to the text. *Scriptorium* 37.161–77.

Brodeur, Arthur Gilchrist. 1959. *The Art of "Beowulf."* Berkeley: University of California Press. Ch. 2 (pp. 39–70) reprinted 1991 in *Interpretations of "Beowulf": A Critical Anthology*, ed. R. D. Fulk, 66–87. Bloomington: Indiana University Press.

Brooks, Kenneth R., ed. 1961. *"Andreas" and "The Fates of the Apostles."* Oxford: Clarendon.

Brooks, Nicholas P. 1974. A-S charters: The work of the last twenty years. *ASE* 3.211–31.

—— 1982. *Latin and the Vernacular in Early Medieval Britain*. Leicester: Leicester University Press.

Brotanek, R. 1913. *Texte und Untersuchungen zur altenglischen Literatur und Kirchengeschichte*. Halle: M. Niemeyer.

Brown, Carleton. 1938. *Beowulf* and the *Blickling Homilies* and some textual notes. *PMLA* 53.905–16.

Brown, George Hardin. 1974. The descent-ascent motif in *Christ II* of Cynewulf. *JEGP* 73.1–12. Reprinted 1996 in *Cynewulf: Basic Readings*, ed. Robert E. Bjork, 133–46. New York: Garland (reissued 2001 as *The Cynewulf Reader*, New York: Routledge).

—— 1987. *Bede, the Venerable*. Boston: Twayne.

—— 1993. Latin writing and the OE vernacular. In *Schriftlichkeit im frühen Mittelalter*, ed. Ursula Schaefer, 36–57. Tübingen: G. Narr.

Brown, Peter. 1981. *The Cult of the Saints*. Chicago: University of Chicago Press.

Brown, Phyllis R. 1996. Beccel and the theme of death in *Guthlac B. Mediaevalia* 19.273–97.

Brown, Ray. 1989. The begging scop and the generous king in *Widsith. NM* 73. 281–92.

Brown, T. J. 1982. The Irish element in the insular system of scripts to circa A.D. 850. In *Die Iren und Europa im früheren Mittelalter*, ed. H. Lowe, 1.101–19. Stuttgart: Klett-Cota.

Brunner, Heinrich. 1906–28. *Deutsche Rechtsgeschichte*. 2 vols. Leipzig: Duncker & Humblot.

Buchholz, Richard. 1890. *Die Fragmente der Reden der Seele an den Leichnam*. Erlanger Beiträge zur englischen Philologie 6. Erlangen: A. Deichert. Reprinted 1970, Amsterdam: Rodopi.

Bullough, D. 1981. Hagiography as patriotism: Alcuin's "York Poem" and the early Northumbrian "Vitae sanctorum." In *Hagiographie, cultures et sociétés, IVe—XIIe siècles*, [n.e.], 339–59. Paris: Études augustiniennes.

—— 1991. The educational tradition in England from Alfred to Ælfric: Teaching *utriusque linguae*. In D. Bullough, *Carolingian Renewal: Sources and Heritage*, 297–334. Manchester: Manchester University Press.

—— 1993. What has Ingeld to do with Lindisfarne? *ASE* 22.93–125.

Bulst, Walther. 1938. Bedas Sterbelied. *ZfdA* 75.111–14.

Burchmore-Oldrieve, Susan. 1985. Traditional exegesis and the question of guilt in the OE *Genesis B. Traditio* 41.117–44.

Burlin, Robert. 1968. *The OE Advent Lyrics: A Typological Commentary*. Yale Studies in English 168. New Haven: Yale University Press.

Cabaniss, Allen. 1955. *Beowulf* and the liturgy. *JEGP* 54.195–201. Reprinted 1963 in *An Anthology of "Beowulf" Criticism*, ed. Lewis E. Nicholson, 223–32. Notre Dame: University of Notre Dame Press.

Cable, Thomas. 1974. *The Meter and Melody of "Beowulf."* Illinois Studies in Language and Literature 64. Urbana: University of Illinois Press.

—— 1991. *The English Alliterative Tradition*. Philadelphia: University of Pennsylvania Press.

Caie, Graham D. 1978. The OE *Daniel*: A warning against pride." *ES* 59.1–9.

—— 1994. Text and context in editing OE: The case of poetry in Cambridge, Corpus Christi College 201. In *The Editing of OE: Papers from the 1990 Manchester Conference*, ed. D. G. Scragg and Paul E. Szarmach, 155–62. Cambridge: D. S. Brewer.

—— ed. 2000. *The OE Poem "Judgement Day II."* Cambridge: D. S. Brewer.

Cain, Christopher M. 2001. Phonology and meter in the OE macaronic verses. *SP* 98: 273–91.

Calder, Daniel G. 1979. The study of style in OE poetry: A historical introduction. In *OE Poetry: Essays on Style*, ed. Daniel G. Calder, 1–65. Berkeley: University of California Press.

—— 1981. *Cynewulf*. Boston: Twayne.

—— 1986. Figurative language and its contexts in *Andreas*: A study in medieval expressionism. In *Modes of Interpretation in OE Literature: Essays in Honor of Stanley B. Greenfield*, ed. Phyllis R. Brown, Georgia R. Crampton, and Fred C. Robinson, 115–36. Toronto: University of Toronto Press.

Calder, Daniel G., and M. J. B. Allen, transs. 1976. *Sources and Analogues of OE Poetry: The Major Latin Sources in Translation*. Cambridge: D. S. Brewer.

Camargo, Martin. 1981. The Finn episode and the tragedy of revenge in *Beowulf*. In *Eight A-S Studies*, ed. Joseph S. Wittig. *SP* 78.5.120–34.

Cameron, Angus F. 1974. Middle English in OE manuscripts. In *Chaucer and Middle English Studies in Honour of Rossell Hope Robbins*, ed. Beryl Rowland, 218–29. London: Allen & Unwin.

Cameron, M. L. 1983. *Bald's Leechbook*: Its sources and their use in its compilation. *ASE* 12.153–82.

—— 1990. Bald's *Leechbook* and cultural interactions in A-S England. *ASE* 19.5–12.

—— 1993. *A-S Medicine.* CSASE 7. Cambridge: Cambridge University Press.

Campbell, A., ed. 1938. *The Battle of Brunanburh.* London: W. Heinemann.

—— ed. 1950. *Frithegodi monachi breuiloquium uitae beati Wilfredi et Wulfstani cantoris narratio metrica de Sancto Swithuno.* Zürich: Thesaurus Mundi.

—— ed. 1953. *The Tollemache Orosius.* EEMF 3. Copenhagen: Rosenkilde & Bagger.

—— 1959. *OE Grammar.* Oxford: Clarendon.

—— ed. and trans. 1962a. *The Chronicle of Æthelweard.* London: Nelson.

—— 1962b. The OE epic style. In *English and Medieval Studies Presented to J. R. R. Tolkien on the Occasion of His Seventieth Birthday,* ed. Norman Davis and C. L. Wrenn, 13–26. London: Allen & Unwin.

—— ed. and trans. 1967. *Aethelwulf: De abbatibus.* Oxford: Clarendon.

Campbell, A., and Simon Keynes, eds. 1998. *Encomium Emmae Reginae.* (Reprinted with introduction by Keynes.) Cambridge: Cambridge University Press.

Campbell, Jackson J. 1951. The dialect vocabulary of the OE Bede. *JEGP* 50.349–72.

—— 1959. *The Advent Lyrics of the Exeter Book.* Princeton: Princeton University Press.

—— 1967. Knowledge of rhetorical figures in A-S England. *JEGP* 66.1–20.

—— 1982. To hell and back: Latin tradition and literary use of the *Descensus ad inferos* in OE. *Viator* 13.107–58.

Campbell, James, ed. 1982a. *The Anglo-Saxons.* Ithaca: Cornell University Press.

—— 1982b. Epilogue. In J. Campbell, *The Anglo-Saxons,* 240–6. Ithaca: Cornell University Press.

—— 1984. Some twelfth-century views of the A-S past. *Peritia* 3.131–50.

—— 1986. Asser's *Life of Alfred.* In *The Inheritance of Historiography 360–900,* ed. Christopher Holdsworth and T. P. Wiseman, 115–35. Exeter: University of Exeter Press.

Carlson, Ingvar, ed. 1975–8. *The Pastoral Care, Edited from British Library MS. Cotton Otho B.ii.* 2 vols. Stockholm Studies in English 34, 48. Stockholm: Almqvist & Wiksell.

Carnicelli, Thomas A., ed. 1969. *King Alfred's Version of St. Augustine's Soliloquies.* Cambridge, Mass.: Harvard University Press.

Cassidy, Brendan, ed. 1992. *The Ruthwell Cross: Papers from a Colloquium.* Princeton: Princeton University Press.

Cassidy, F. G., and Richard N. Ringler, eds. 1971. *Bright's OE Grammar and Reader.* 3rd ed. New York: Holt, Rinehart.

Cavill, Paul. 1993. *Beowulf* and *Andreas:* Two maxims. *Neophilologus* 77.479–87.

—— 1995. Interpretation of *The Battle of Maldon,* lines 84–90: A review and reassessment. *SN* 67.149–64.

—— 1999a. *Maxims in OE Poetry.* Cambridge: D. S. Brewer.

—— 1999b. Some dynamics of story-telling: Animals in the early lives of St. Cuthbert. *Nottingham Medieval Studies* 43.1–20.

Chadwick, Henry. 1991. Gregory the Great and the mission to the Anglo-Saxons. In *Gregorio Magno e il suo tempo,* ed. Charles Pietri et al. Studia Ephemeridis "Augustinianum" 33. Rome: Institutum Patristicum.

Chadwick, Nora K. 1963. The Celtic background of early A-S England. In *Celt and Saxon: Studies in the Early British Border,* ed. Kenneth Jackson et al., 323–52. Cambridge: Cambridge University Press.

Chambers, R. W., ed. 1912. *Widsith: A Study in OE Heroic Legend.* Cambridge: Cambridge University Press.

—— 1925. The lost literature of mediaeval England. *The Library,* ser. 4, 5.293–321. Reprinted 1968 in *Essential Articles for the Study of OE Poetry,* ed. J. B. Bessinger, Jr., and Stanley J. Kahrl, 3–26. Hamden, Conn.: Archon..

Chambers, R. W., Max Förster, and Robin Flower, eds. 1933. *The Exeter Book of OE Poetry.* London: Humphries.

Chambers, R. W., and C. L. Wrenn. 1959. *Beowulf: An Introduction to the Study of the Poem.* 3rd ed. Cambridge: Cambridge University Press.

Chance, Jane. 1986. *Woman as Hero in OE Literature.* Syracuse: Syracuse University Press. Ch. 7 (pp. 95–108 and 131–5) reprinted 1991 in *Interpretations of "Beowulf": A Critical Anthology,* ed. R. D. Fulk, 251–63. Bloomington: Indiana University Press.

Chaplais, Pierre. 1985. The royal A-S "chancery" of the tenth century revisited. In *Studies in Medieval History Presented to R. H. C. Davis,* ed. Henry Mayr-Harting and R. I. Moore, 41–51. London: Hambledon.

Chapman, Don W. 2002. Germanic tradition and Latin learning in Wulfstan's echoic compounds. *JEGP* 101.1–18.

Charles-Edwards, Thomas. 1995. The penitential of Theodore and the *Iudicia Theodori.* In *Archbishop Theodore: Commemorative Studies on His Life and Influence,* ed. Michael Lapidge, 141–74. CSASE 11. Cambridge: Cambridge University Press.

Chase, Colin, ed. 1981. *The Dating of Beowulf.* Toronto: University of Toronto Press. Reissued 1997 with an afterword by Nicholas Howe.

Clanchy, M. T. 1993. *From Memory to Written Record: England 1066–1307.* 2nd ed. Oxford: Blackwell.

Clark, George. 1979. The hero of *Maldon:* Vir pius et strenuus. *Speculum* 54.257–82.

—— 1990. *Beowulf.* Boston: Twayne.

—— 1992. Maldon: History, poetry, and truth. In *De Gustibus: Essays for Alain Renoir,* ed. John Miles Foley, 66–84. New York: Garland.

—— 1997. The hero and the theme. In *A "Beowulf" Handbook,* ed. Robert E. Bjork and John D. Niles, 271–90. Lincoln: University of Nebraska Press.

Clayton, Mary. 1985. Homiliaries and preaching in A-S England. *Peritia*

4.207–42. Reprinted 2000 in *OE Prose: Basic Readings*, ed. Paul E. Szarmach, 151–98. New York: Garland.

—— 1994. Ælfric's Judith: Manipulative or manipulated? *ASE* 23.215–27.

Clayton, Mary, and Hugh Magennis, eds. 1994. *The OE Lives of St Margaret*. CSASE 9. Cambridge: Cambridge University Press.

Clemoes, Peter. 1959. The chronology of Ælfric's works. In *The Anglo-Saxons: Studies in Some Aspects of Their History and Culture Presented to Bruce Dickins*, ed. Peter Clemoes, 212–47. London: Bowes & Bowes. Reprinted 1980 as OEN Subsidia 10; also 2000 in *OE Prose: Basic Readings*, ed. Paul E. Szarmach, 29–72, New York: Garland.

—— 1962. Review of *The Blickling Homilies*, ed. Rudolph Willard, EEMF 10, Copenhagen: Rosenkilde & Bagger, 1960. *MÆ* 31.60–3.

—— 1966. Ælfric. In *Continuations and Beginnings: Studies in OE Literature*, ed. E. G. Stanley, 176–209. London: Nelson.

—— 1974. The composition of the OE text. In *The OE Illustrated Hexateuch. British Museum Cotton Claudius B.iv*, ed. C. R. Dodwell and Peter Clemoes, 42–53. EEMF 18. Copenhagen: Rosenkilde & Bagger.

—— 1992. King Alfred's debt to vernacular poetry: The evidence of *ellen* and *cræft*. In *Words, Texts, and Manuscripts: Studies in A-S Culture Presented to Helmut Gneuss*, ed. Michael Korhammer, 213–38. Woodbridge, Suffolk: D. S. Brewer.

—— 1994. King and creation at the crucifixion: The contribution of native tradition to *The Dream of the Rood*. In *Heroes and Heroines in Medieval English Literature: A Festschift Presented to André Crépin*, ed. Leo Carruthers, 31–43. Woodbridge, Suffolk: D. S. Brewer.

—— 1995. *Interactions of Thought and Language in OE Poetry*. CSASE 12. Cambridge: Cambridge University Press.

—— ed. 1997. *Ælfric's Catholic Homilies, the First Series*. EETS s.s. 17. Oxford: Oxford University Press.

Clunies Ross, Margaret. 1990. The A-S and Norse *Rune Poems:* A comparative study. *ASE* 19.23–39.

Cockayne, Thomas Oswald, ed. 1864–6. *Leechdoms, Wortcunning and Starcraft in Early England*. Rerum Britannicarum Medii Aevi Scriptores (Rolls Series) 35. 3 vols. London: Longman. Reprinted 1965, Wiesbaden: Kraus.

Colgrave, Bertram, ed. and trans. 1927. *The Life of Bishop Wilfrid by Eddius Stephanus*. Cambridge: Cambridge University Press.

—— ed. and trans. 1940. *Two "Lives" of Saint Cuthbert*. Cambridge: Cambridge University Press.

—— ed. and trans. 1956. *Felix's Life of Saint Guthlac*. Cambridge: Cambridge University Press.

—— 1958a. The earliest saints' lives written in England. *PBA* 44.35–60.

—— ed. 1958b. *The Paris Psalter*. EEMF 8. Copenhagen: Rosenkilde & Bagger.

—— ed. and trans. 1968. *The Earliest Life of Gregory the Great*. Lawrence: University of Kansas Press.

Colgrave, Bertram, and R. A. B. Mynors, eds. and transs. 1969. *Bede's Ecclesiastical History of the English People*. Corrected ed. 1991. Oxford: Clarendon.

Collier, Wendy E. J. 1991. A bibliography of the Battle of Maldon. In *The Battle of Maldon, AD 991*, ed. D. G. Scragg, 294–301. Oxford: Blackwell. (There is an electronic version on the World Wide Web at <http://www.wmich.edu/medieval/rawl/maldon/index.html>.)

—— 2000. The tremulous Worcester hand and Gregory's *Pastoral Care*. In *Rewriting OE in the Twelfth Century*, ed. Mary Swan and Elaine M. Treharne, 195–208. CSASE 30. Cambridge: Cambridge University Press.

Collins, Douglas C. 1959. Kenning in A-S poetry. *E&S* 12.1–17.

Collins, Rowland L. 1984. Blickling Homily XVI and the dating of *Beowulf*. In *Medieval Studies Conference, Aachen, 1983: Language and Literature*, ed. Wolf-Dietrich Bald and Horst Weinstock, 61–9. Frankfurt a.M.: P. Lang.

Conner, Patrick W. 1980. The liturgy and the OE "Descent into Hell." *JEGP* 79.179–91.

—— 1993a. *A-S Exeter: A Tenth-Century Cultural History*. Woodbridge, Suffolk: Boydell.

—— 1993b. Source studies, the OE *Guthlac A* and the English Benedictine Reformation. *Revue Bénédictine* 103.380–413.

—— 1996. On dating Cynewulf. In *Cynewulf: Basic Readings*, ed. Robert E. Bjork, 23–55. New York: Garland (reissued 2001 as *The Cynewulf Reader*, New York: Routledge).

Conybeare, J. J. 1826. *Illustrations of A-S Poetry*. Ed. W. D. Conybeare. London: Harding & Lepard.

Cook, Albert S., ed. 1900. *The Christ of Cynewulf*. Boston: Ginn.

Cook, Kimberly K. 1996. Philosophy's metamorphosis into wisdom: An explanation of King Alfred's re-creation of the central symbol in the *Consolation of Philosophy*. *Journal of Evolutionary Psychology* 17.177–85.

Cooper, Janet, ed. 1993. *The Battle of Maldon: Fiction and Fact*. London: Hambledon.

Cox, Robert S., Sr., ed. 1972. The OE *Dicts* of Cato. *Anglia* 90.1–42.

Crawford, S. J., ed. 1922. *The OE Version of the Heptateuch*. EETS o.s. 160. London: Oxford University Press.

Creed, Robert P. 1990. *Reconstructing the Rhythm of "Beowulf."* Columbia: University of Missouri Press.

Cross, James E. 1956. "Ubi sunt" passages in OE — sources and relationships. *Vetenskaps-Societetens i Lund Årsbok 1956*, 25–44.

—— 1959. On the allegory in *The Seafarer:* Illustrative notes. *MÆ* 28.104–6.

—— 1962. The OE poetic theme of "The Gifts of Men." *Neophilologus* 46.66–70.

—— 1963. Aspects of microcosm and macrocosm in OE literature. In *Studies in OE Literature in Honor of Arthur G. Brodeur*, ed. Stanley B. Greenfield, 1–22. Eugene: University of Oregon Books.

—— 1965. Oswald and Byrhtnoth: A Christian saint and a hero who is a Christian. *ES* 46.93–109.

—— 1985. On the library of the OE martyrologist. In *Learning and Literature in A-S England: Studies Presented to Peter Clemoes*, ed. Michael Lapidge and Helmut Gneuss, 227–49. Cambridge: Cambridge University Press.

—— 1986. The Latinity of the ninth-century OE martyrologist. In *Studies in Earlier OE Prose*, ed. Paul E. Szarmach, 275–99. Albany: State University of New York Press.

—— 1991. Wulfstan's *De Antichristo* in a twelfth-century Worcester manuscript. *ASE* 20.203–20.

—— ed. and trans. 1996. *Two OE Apocrypha and Their Latin Source: The Gospel of Nichodemus and the Avenging of the Saviour*. CSASE 19. Cambridge: Cambridge University Press.

Cross, James E., and A. Brown. 1989. Literary impetus for Wulfstan's *Sermo Lupi*. *LSE* n.s. 20.271–91.

Cross, James E., and Thomas D. Hill, eds. 1982. *The "Prose Solomon and Saturn" and "Adrian and Ritheus."* Toronto: University of Toronto Press.

Cross, James E., and Jennifer Morrish Tunberg, eds. 1993. *The Copenhagen Wulfstan Collection: Copenhagen Kongelige Bibliotek, Gl. Kgl. Sam. 1595.* EEMF 25. Copenhagen: Rosenkilde & Bagger.

Crossley-Holland, Kevin, trans. 1993. *The Exeter Book Riddles*. Rev. ed. Harmondsworth: Penguin.

Cubitt, Catherine. 1997. Review article: The tenth-century Benedictine Reform in England. *EME* 6.77–94.

—— 2000. Sites and sanctity: Revisiting the cult of the murdered and martyred A-S royal saints. *EME* 9.53–83.

Cünnen, Janina. 2000. *Fiktionale Nonnenwelten: Angelsächsische Frauenbriefe des 8. und 9. Jahrhunderts*. Heidelberg: C. Winter.

Dahlberg, Charles R. 1988. *The Literature of Unlikeness*. Hanover, N.H.: University Press of New England.

Dalbey, Marcia A. 1980. "Soul's Medicine": Religious psychology in the Blickling Rogation Homilies. *Neophilologus* 64.470–7.

Damico, Helen. 1984. *Beowulf's Wealhtheow and the Valkyrie Tradition*. Madison: University of Wisconsin Press.

Danet, Brenda, and Bryna Bogoch. 1992. From oral ceremony to written document: The transitional language of A-S wills. *Language and Communication* 12.95–122.

—— 1994. Orality, literacy, and performativity in A-S wills. In *Language and the Law*, ed. John Gibbons, 100–35. London: Longman.

D'Aronco, Maria Amalia. 1988. The botanical lexicon of the OE *Herbarium*. *ASE* 17.15–33.

D'Aronco, Maria Amalia, and M. L. Cameron, eds. 1998. *The OE Illustrated Pharmacopoeia*. EEMF 27. Copenhagen: Rosenkilde & Bagger.

Davidson, Clifford. 1975. Erotic "women's songs" in A-S England. *Neophilologus* 59.451–62.

Davis, Craig R. 1999. Cultural historicity in *The Battle of Maldon*. *PQ* 78.151–69.

Davis, Kathleen. 1998. National writing in the ninth century: A reminder for postcolonial thinking about the nation. *Journal of Medieval and Early Modern Studies* 28: 611–37.

—— 2000. The performance of translation theory in King Alfred's national literary program. In *Manuscript, Narrative, Lexicon: Essays on Literary and Cultural Transmission in Honor of Whitney F. Bolton*, ed. Robert Boenig and Kathleen Davis, 149–70. Lewisburg: Bucknell University Press.

Davis, R. H. C. 1971. Alfred the Great: Propaganda and truth. *History* 56.169–82.

Davis, Thomas M. 1965. Another view of *The Wife's Lament*. *Papers on Language and Literature* 1.291–305.

Deferrari, Roy J., trans. 1964. *Paulus Orosius, The Seven Books of History against the Pagans*. Washington: Catholic University of America Press.

de Gaiffier, Baudouin. 1961. De l'usage et de la lecture du martyrologe. *Analecta Bollandiana* 79.40–59.

DeGregorio, Scott. 1999. The Venerable Bede on prayer and contemplation. *Traditio* 54.1–39.

de Lacy, Paul. 1996. Aspects of Christianization and cultural adaptation in the OE *Judith*. *NM* 97.393–410.

de Looze, Laurence N. 1984. Frame narratives and fictionalization: Beowulf as narrator. *Texas Studies in Literature and Language* 26.145–56. Reprinted 1991 in *Interpretations of "Beowulf": A Critical Anthology*, ed. R. D. Fulk, 242–50. Bloomington: Indiana University Press.

Dendle, Peter J. 1999. The demonological landscape of the "Solomon and Saturn" cycle. *ES* 80.281–92.

—— 2001. *Satan Unbound: The Devil in OE Narrative Literature*. Toronto: University of Toronto Press.

Derolez, René, ed. 1992. *A-S Glossography: Papers Read at the International Conférence Held in the Koninklijke Academie voor Wetenschappen, Letteren en Schone Kunsten van België, Brussels, 8 and 9 September 1986*. Brussels: Paleis der Academiën.

—— 1995. Genesis: Old Saxon and OE. *ES* 76.409–23.

Deskis, Susan E. 1994. The gnomic woman in OE poetry. *PQ* 73.133–49.

—— 1996. *Beowulf and the Medieval Proverb Tradition*. Tempe, Ariz.: Medieval & Renaissance Texts & Studies.

—— 1998. Jonah and genre in *Resignation B*. *MÆ* 67.189–200.

Desmond, Marilynn. 1990. The voice of the exile: Feminist literary history and the anonymous A-S elegy. *Critical Inquiry* 16.572–90.

de Vriend, Hubert Jan, ed. 1984. *The OE Herbarium and Medicina de Quadrupedibus.* EETS o.s. 286. London: Oxford University Press.

Dien, S. 1975. *Sermo Lupi ad Anglos:* The order and date of the three versions. *NM* 76.561–70.

Dietrich, Sheila C. 1979. An introduction to women in A-S society (c.600–1066). In *The Women of England,* ed. B. Kanner, 32–56. Hamden, Conn.: Archon.

DiNapoli, Robert. 1998a. The heart of the visionary experience: *The Order of the World* and its place in the OE canon. *ES* 79.97–108.

—— 1998b. Poesis and authority: Traces of an A-S *Agon* in Cynewulf's *Elene. Neophilologus* 82.619–30.

Discenza, Nicole Guenther. 1997. Power, skill and virtue in the OE *Boethius. ASE* 26.81–108.

—— 2000. Alfred the Great: A bibliography with special reference to literature. In *OE Prose: Basic Readings,* ed. Paul E. Szarmach, 463–502. New York: Garland.

—— 2001. Alfred's verse preface to the *Pastoral Care* and the chain of authority. *Neophilologus* 85.625–33.

Doane, A. N. 1966. Heathen form and Christian function in *The Wife's Lament. MS* 28.77–91.

—— ed. 1978. *Genesis A: A New Edition.* Madison: University of Wisconsin Press.

—— 1990. The sources of *Genesis A* (Cameron A.1.1.1). In *Fontes Anglo-Saxonici: World Wide Web Register,* ed. Joyce Hill et al. 2001. <http://fontes.english.ox.ac.uk/>.

—— ed. 1991. *The Saxon Genesis: An Edition of the West Saxon Genesis B and the Old Saxon Vatican Genesis.* Madison: University of Wisconsin Press.

—— ed. 1994. *Books of Prayers and Healing.* Anglo-Saxon Manuscripts in Microfiche Facsimile 1. Tempe: Arizona Center for Medieval & Renaissance Studies.

Dockray-Miller, Mary. 1997. The feminized cross of *The Dream of the Rood. PQ* 76.1–18.

—— 1998. Female community in the OE *Judith. SN* 70.165–72.

—— 2000. *Motherhood and Mothering in A-S England.* New York: St. Martin's.

Dodgson, John McN. 1991. The site of the Battle of Maldon. In *The Battle of Maldon, AD 991,* ed. D. G. Scragg, 170–9. Oxford: Blackwell.

Dodwell, C. R., and Peter Clemoes, eds. 1974. *The OE Illustrated Hexateuch. British Museum Cotton Claudius B.iv.* EEMF 18. Copenhagen: Rosenkilde & Bagger.

Donaghey, Brian S. 1964. The sources of King Alfred's translation of Boethius' *De consolatione philosophiae. Anglia* 82.23–37.

Donahue, Charles. 1949–51. Beowulf, Ireland and the natural good. *Traditio* 7.263–77.

—— 1965. *Beowulf* and Christian tradition: A reconsideration from a Celtic stance. *Traditio* 21.55–116.

Donaldson, E. Talbot. 1966. *Beowulf: A New Prose Translation.* New York: W. W. Norton.

Donoghue, Daniel. 1987. *Style in OE Poetry: The Test of the Auxiliary.* New Haven: Yale University Press.

Donovan, Leslie A. 1999. *Women Saints' Lives in OE Prose.* Woodbridge, Suffolk: Boydell & Brewer.

Doubleday, James F. 1972. *The Ruin:* Structure and theme. *JEGP* 71.369–81.

Dronke, Ursula, ed. 1969. *The Poetic Edda, I: Heroic Poems.* Oxford: Clarendon.

Dubois, J., and G. Renaud, eds. 1976. *Edition pratique des martyrologes de Bède, de l'anonyme lyonnais et de Florus.* Paris: Centre national de la recherche scientifique.

Duby, Georges. 1980. *The Three Orders: Feudal Society Imagined.* Trans. Arthur Goldhammer. Chicago: University of Chicago Press.

Duckett, Eleanor S. 1951. *Alcuin, Friend of Charlemagne.* New York: Macmillan.

Duff, J. W., and A. M. Duff, eds. and transs. 1954. *Minor Latin Poets.* Loeb Classical Library 284. Cambridge, Mass.: Harvard University Press.

Dümmler, Ernst, ed. 1881. *Poetae Latini aevi Carolini, II.* MGH, Poetae Latini 1. Berlin: Weidmann.

—— ed. 1895. *Epistolae Karolini Aevi, II.* MGH, Epistolae 4. Berlin: Weidmann.

Dumville, David. 1976. The Anglian collection of royal genealogies and regnal lists. *ASE* 5.23–50.

—— 1977. Kingship, genealogies and regnal lists. In *Early Medieval Kingship,* ed. P. H. Sawyer and I. N. Wood, 72–104. Leeds: School of History, University of Leeds.

—— 1987. English square minuscule script: The background and earliest phases. *ASE* 16.147–79.

Dumville, David, and Simon Keynes, gen. eds. 1983–. *The A-S Chronicle: A Collaborative Edition.* Cambridge: D. S. Brewer.

Dumville, David, and Michael Lapidge, eds. 1985. *The Annals of St. Neots, with Vita Prima Sancti Neoti.* No. 17 in *The A-S Chronicle: A Collaborative Edition,* ed. David Dumville and Simon Keynes. Cambridge: D. S. Brewer.

Dunleavy, Gareth W. 1956. Possible Irish analogues for *The Wife's Lament. PQ* 35.208–13.

—— 1959. A "de excidio" tradition in the OE *Ruin? PQ* 38.112–18.

Dunning, T. P., and A. J. Bliss, eds. 1969. *The Wanderer.* London: Methuen.

Earl, James W. 1987. Hisperic style in the OE *Rhyming Poem. PMLA* 102.187–96.

—— 1989. King Alfred's talking poems. *Pacific Coast Philology* 24.49–61.

—— 1994. *Thinking about "Beowulf."* Stanford: Stanford University Press.

—— 1999. Prophecy and parable in medieval apocalyptic history. *Religion and Literature* 31.1.25–45.

Eby, John C. 1997. Bringing the vita to life: Bede's symbolic structure of the life of St. Cuthbert. *American Benedictine Review.* 48.316–38.

Ehwald, R., ed. 1919. *Aldhelmi opera.* MGH, Auctores Antiquissimi 15. Berlin: Weidmann.

Einar Ól. Sveinsson. 1962. *Íslenzkar bókmenntir í fornöld.* Reykjavík: Almenna bókafélagið.

Eliason, Norman E. 1966. Two OE scop poems. *PMLA* 81.185–92.

Eliason, Norman E., and Peter Clemoes, eds. 1966. *Ælfric's First Series of Catholic Homilies (British Museum Royal 7 C. xii, Fols. 4–218).* EEMF 13. Copenhagen: Rosenkilde & Bagger.

Elliott, Ralph W. V. 1989. *Runes: An Introduction.* 2nd ed. Manchester: Manchester University Press.

—— 1991. Coming back to Cynewulf. In *OE Runes and Their Continental Background,* ed. Alfred Bammesberger, 231–47. Anglistische Forschungen 217. Heidelberg: C. Winter.

Endter, Wilhelm, ed. 1922. *König Alfreds des grossen Bearbeitung der Soliloquien des Augustins.* Bibliothek der angelsächsischen Prosa 11. Hamburg: H. Grand. Reprinted 1964, Darmstadt: Wissenschaftliche Buchgesellschaft.

Epe, Andreas. 1995. *Wissensliteratur im angelsächsischen England: Das Fachschriftum der vergessenen "artes mechanicae" und "artes magicae." Mit besonderer Berücksichtigung des "Somniale Danielis": Edition der (lateinisch-) altenglischen Fassungen.* Münster (Westfalen): Tebbert.

Erickson, Jon. 1975. The *Deor* genitives. *Archivum Linguisticum* 6.77–84.

Erzgräber, Willi. 1961. *Der Wanderer:* Eine Interpretation von Aufbau und Gehalt. In *Festschrift zum 75. Geburtstag von Theodor Spira,* ed. H. Viebrock and W. Erzgräber, 57–85. Heidelberg: C. Winter.

—— 1989. The beginnings of a written literature in OE times. In *The Living Middle Ages: Studies in Mediaeval English Literature and Its Tradition: A Festschrift for Karl Heinz Göller,* ed. Uwe Böker et al., 25–43. Stuttgart: Belser.

Étaix, Raymond, ed. 1999. *Gregorius Magnus, Homiliae in evangelia.* CCSL 141. Turnhout: Brepols.

Ettmüller, Ernst Moritz Ludwig, trans. 1840. *Beowulf: Heldengedicht des achten Jahrhunderts, zum ersten Male aus dem Angelsächsischen in das Neuhochdeutsche übersetzt.* Zurich.

Evans, Joan, and Mary Serjeantson, eds. 1933. *English Medieval Lapidaries.* EETS o.s. 190. London: Oxford University Press.

Fanger, Claire. 1991. Miracle as prophetic gospel: Knowledge, power and the design of the narrative in *Daniel. ES* 72.123–35.

Faraci, Dora. 1991. *Navigatio Sancti Brendani* and its relationship with *Physiologus*. *Romanobarbarica* 11.149–73.

Farrell, R. T. 1972. Some remarks on the Exeter Book *Azarias*. *MÆ* 41.1–8.

—— ed. 1974. *Daniel and Azarias*. London: Methuen.

Faulkes, Anthony, ed. 1982. *Snorri Sturluson, Edda: Prologue and Gylfaginning*. Oxford: Clarendon.

—— trans. 1987. *Snorri Sturluson, Edda: New Complete Translation*. London: Dent.

Fee, Christopher. 1994. Productive destruction: Torture, text, and the body in the OE *Andreas*. *Essays in Medieval Studies* 11.51–62.

—— 1997. *Judith* and the rhetoric of heroism in A-S England. *ES* 78.401–6.

Fehr, Bernhard. 1914. *Die Hirtenbriefe Ælfrics*. Bibliothek der angelsächsischen Prosa 9. Hamburg: H. Grand. Reprinted 1966 with supplementary introduction by Peter Clemoes, Darmstadt: Wissenschaftliche Buchgesellschaft.

Fell, Christine. 1984. *Women in A-S England*. London: Colonnade.

—— 1990. Some implications of the Boniface correspondence. In *New Readings on Women in OE Literature*, ed. Helen Damico and Alexandra Hennessey Olsen, 29–43. Bloomington: Indiana University Press.

Fernández Cuestra, Julia, and Inmaculada Senra Silva. 2000. Ohthere and Wulfstan: One or two voyagers at the court of King Alfred? *SN* 72.18–23.

Finch, R. G., ed. and trans. 1965. *Vǫlsunga saga: The Saga of the Volsungs*. London: Nelson.

Finnegan, Robert E. 1994. Christ as narrator in the OE *Christ and Satan*. *ES* 75.2–16.

Finnur Jónsson, ed. 1912–15. *Den norsk-islandske skjaldedigtning*. 4 vols. in 2 parts. Copenhagen: Gyldendal.

Finsterwalder, Paul Willem, ed. 1929. *Die Canones Theodori Cantuariensis und ihre Überlieferungsformen*. Weimar: H. Böhlaus.

Fitzgerald, Robert P. 1963. *The Wife's Lament* and "The search for the lost husband." *JEGP* 62.769–77.

Fjalldal, Magnus. 1998. *The Long Arm of Coincidence: The Frustrated Connection between "Beowulf" and "Grettis saga."* Toronto: University of Toronto Press.

Flint, V. I. J. 1977. The plan and purpose of the works of Honorius Augustodunensis. *Revue Bénédictine* 87.97–127.

—— 1991. *The Rise of Magic in Early Medieval Europe*. Princeton: Princeton University Press.

Flower, Robin, and Hugh Smith, eds. 1941. *The Parker Chronicle and Laws* (*Corpus Christi College, Cambridge, MS. 173*). EETS o.s. 208. London: Oxford University Press.

Foley, John Miles. 1985. *Oral-Formulaic Theory and Research: An Introduction and Annotated Bibliography*. New York: Garland.

—— 1991. *Immanent Art: From Structure to Meaning in Traditional Oral*

Epic. Bloomington: Indiana University Press.

—— 1995. The poet's self-interruption in *Andreas*. In *Prosody and Poetics in the Early Middle Ages: Essays in Honour of C. B. Hieatt*, ed. M. J. Toswell, 42–59. Toronto: University of Toronto Press. Also in Foley's *Singer of Tales in Performance*, 181–207. Bloomington: Indiana University Press, 1995.

—— 1999. *Homer's Traditional Art*. University Park: Pennsylvania State University Press.

Foley, W. Trent. 1999. Suffering and sanctity in Bede's *Prose Life of St. Cuthbert*. *Journal of Theological Studies* 50.102–16.

Förster, Max. 1901. Two notes on OE dialogue literature. In *An English Miscellany Presented to Dr. Furnivall in Honour of His Seventy-Fifth Birthday*, ed. W. P. Ker et al., 86–106. Oxford: Clarendon.

—— 1902. Das latein-altenglische Fragment der Apokryphe von Jamnes und Mambres. *Archiv* 108.15–28.

—— 1942. Zur Liturgik der angelsächsischen Kirche. *Anglia* 66.1–51.

Fowler, Roger, ed. 1965. A late OE handbook for the use of a confessor. *Anglia* 83.1–34.

—— ed. 1966. *OE Prose and Verse*. London: Routledge.

—— ed. 1972. *Wulfstan's Canons of Edgar*. EETS o.s. 266. London: Oxford University Press.

Francovich Onesti, Nicoletta. 1998. Roman themes in the Franks Casket. In *L'Antichità nella cultura europea del Medioevo/L'Antiquité dans la culture européenne du Moyen Age*, ed. Rosanna Brusegan and Alessandro Zironi, 295–313. Greifswald: Reineke.

Frank, Roberta. 1988. What kind of poetry is *Exodus*? In *Germania: Comparative Studies in the Old Germanic Languages and Literatures*, ed. D. G. Calder and T. C. Christy, 191–205. Woodbridge, Suffolk: Boydell & Brewer.

—— 1991a. Germanic legend and OE literature. In *The Cambridge Companion to OE Literature*, ed. Malcolm Godden and Michael Lapidge, 88–106. Cambridge: Cambridge University Press.

—— 1991b. The ideal of men dying with their lord in *The Battle of Maldon*: Anachronism or *nouvelle vague*? In *People and Places in Northern Europe 500–1600: Studies Presented to Peter Hayes Sawyer*, ed. Ian Wood and Niels Lund, 95–106. Woodbridge, Suffolk: Boydell.

Frankis, John. 1995. Views of A-S England in post-Conquest vernacular writing. In *Orality and Literacy in Early Middle English*, ed. Herbert Pilch, 227–47. ScriptOralia 83. Tübingen: G. Narr.

Franklin, C. V. 1995. Theodore and the *Passio S. Anastasii*. In *Archbishop Theodore: Commemorative Studies on His Life and Influence*, ed. Michael Lapidge, 175–203. CSASE 11. Cambridge: Cambridge University Press.

Frantzen, Allen J. 1983a. *The Literature of Penance in A-S England*. New Brunswick, N.J.: Rutgers University Press.

—— 1983b. The penitentials attributed to Bede. *Speculum* 58.573–97.

—— 1986. *King Alfred*. Boston: Twayne.

—— 1990. *Desire for Origins: New Language, OE, and Teaching the Tradition*. New Brunswick, N.J.: Rutgers University Press.

—— ed. 1991. *Speaking Two Languages: Traditional Disciplines and Contemporary Theory in Medieval Studies*. Albany: State University of New York Press.

—— 1993a. Review of *The Phoenix*, ed. N. F. Blake, rev. ed., Exeter: Exeter University Press, 1990. *Speculum* 68.106–7.

—— 1993b. When women aren't enough. *Speculum* 68.445–71.

—— 1997. Bede and bawdy bale: Gregory the Great, angels, and the "Angli." In *Anglo-Saxonism and the Construction of Social Identity*, ed. Allen Frantzen and John D. Niles, 17–39. Gainesville: University Press of Florida.

—— 1998. *Before the Closet: Same-Sex Love from "Beowulf" to "Angels in America."* Chicago: University of Chicago Press.

Franzen, Christine. 1991. *The Tremulous Hand of Worcester: A Study of OE in the Thirteenth Century.* Oxford: Clarendon.

—— 1996. Late copies of A-S charters. In *Studies in English Language and Literature: "Doubt Wisely": Papers in Honour of E. G. Stanley*, ed. M. J. Toswell and E. M. Tyler, 42–70. London: Routledge.

—— ed. 1998. *Worcester Manuscripts*. A-S Manuscripts in Microfiche Facsimile 6. Tempe: Medieval & Renaissance Texts & Studies.

Frederick, Jill. 2000. The *South English Legendary*: A-S saints and national identity. In *Literary Appropriations of the Anglo-Saxons from the Thirteenth to the Twentieth Century*, ed. D. G. Scragg and Carole Weinberg, 57–73. CSASE 29. Cambridge: Cambridge University Press.

French, Walter H. 1945. *Widsith* and the scop. *PMLA* 60.623–30.

Frese, Dolores Warwick. 1983. *Wulf and Eadwacer*: The adulterous woman reconsidered. *Notre Dame English Journal* 15.1.1–22.

Fry, Donald K., ed. 1968. *The "Beowulf" Poet: A Collection of Critical Essays*. Englewood Cliffs, N.J.: Prentice-Hall.

—— ed. 1974. *Finnsburh: Fragment and Episode*. London: Methuen.

—— 1980. Two voices in *Widsith*. *Mediaevalia* 6 (1982 for 1980), 37–56.

—— 1992. A newly discovered version of the OE poem *Durham*. In *OE and New: Studies in Language and Linguistics in Honor of Frederic G. Cassidy*, ed. Joan H. Hall, Nick Doane, and Dick Ringler, 83–96. New York: Garland.

Fry, Timothy, et al., eds. and transs. 1980. *RB 1980: The Rule of St. Benedict in Latin and English*. Collegeville, Minn.: Liturgical Press.

Fulk, R. D. 1987. Unferth and his name. *MP* 85.113–27.

—— 1989. An eddic analogue to the Scyld Scefing story. *RES* n.s. 40.313–22.

—— ed. 1991. *Interpretations of "Beowulf": A Critical Anthology*. Bloomington: Indiana University Press.

—— 1992. *A History of OE Meter*. Philadelphia: University of Pennsylvania Press.

—— 1996a. Cynewulf: Canon, dialect, and date. In *Cynewulf: Basic Readings*, ed. Robert E. Bjork, 3–21. New York: Garland (reissued 2001 as *The Cynewulf Reader*, New York: Routledge).

—— 1996b. Inductive methods in the textual criticism of OE verse. *Medievalia et Humanistica* n.s. 23.1–24.

—— 1996c. Rhetoric, form, and linguistic structure in early Germanic verse: Toward a synthesis. *International Journal of Germanic Linguistics and Semiotic Analysis* 1.63–88.

—— 1997. Textual criticism. In *A "Beowulf" Handbook*, ed. Robert E. Bjork and John D. Niles, 35–53. Lincoln: University of Nebraska Press.

—— Forthcoming a. Male homoeroticism in the OE *Canons of Theodore*. To appear in *Sex and Sexuality in A-S England: Essays in Memory of Daniel G. Calder*, ed. Carol Braun Pasternack and Lisa M. Weston.

—— Forthcoming b. Myth in historical perspective. To appear in *Myth: A New Symposium*, ed. William F. Hansen and Gregory A. Schrempp. Bloomington: Indiana University Press.

Fulk, R. D., and Joseph Harris. 2002. Beowulf's name. In *Beowulf: A Verse Translation*, trans. Seamus Heaney, ed. Daniel Donoghue, 98–100. New York: W. W. Norton.

Funke, Otto. 1962. Studien zur alliterierenden und rhythmischen Prosa der älteren altenglischen Homiletik. *Anglia* 80.9–36.

Gade, Kari Ellen, and R. D. Fulk. 2000. *A Bibliography of Germanic Alliterative Meters*. OEN Subsidia 28. Kalamazoo: Medieval Institute, Western Michigan University. Also on the World Wide Web at <http://www.wmich.edu/medieval/saslc/fulk/>, and forthcoming in an updated edition in *Jahrbuch für Internationale Germanistik*.

Galbraith, V. H. 1964. *An Introduction to the Study of History*. London: C. Watts.

Galloway, Andrew. 1988. 1 Peter and *The Seafarer*. *ELN* 25.4.1–10.

Gang, T. M. 1952. Approaches to *Beowulf*. *RES* 33.1–12.

Garde, Judith N. 1991. *OE Poetry in Medieval Christian Perspective*. Woodbridge, Suffolk: Boydell & Brewer.

Garmonsway, G. N., ed. 1991. *Ælfric's Colloquy*. Rev. ed. Exeter: Exeter University Press.

Garmonsway, G. N., and Jacqueline Simpson. 1968. *"Beowulf" and Its Analogues*. Including "Archaeology and *Beowulf*," by Hilda Ellis Davidson. London: Dent. Reprinted 1971, New York: Dutton.

Garner, Lori Ann. 2001. The art of translation in the OE *Judith*. *SN* 73.171–83.

Gaskoin, C. J. B. 1904. *Alcuin: His Life and His Work*. London: C. Clay.

Gatch, Milton McC. 1965. Eschatology in the anonymous OE homilies. *Traditio* 21.117–65. Reprinted 2000 in Milton McC. Gatch, *Eschatology and Christian Nurture: Themes in A-S and Medieval Religious Life*. Aldershot, Hants: Ashgate.

—— 1977. *Preaching and Theology in A-S England*. Toronto: University of Toronto Press.

—— 1978. The achievement of Ælfric and his colleagues in European perspective. In *The OE Homily and Its Backgrounds*, ed. Paul E. Szarmach and Bernard F. Huppé, 43–73. Albany: State University of New York Press. Reprinted 2000 in Milton McC. Gatch, *Eschatology and Christian Nurture: Themes in A-S and Medieval Religious Life*. Aldershot, Hants: Ashgate.

—— 1986. King Alfred's version of the *Soliloquia*: Some suggestions on its rationale and unity. In *Studies in Earlier OE Prose*, ed. Paul E. Szarmach, 17–45. Albany: State University of New York Press. Reprinted 2000 in *OE Prose: Basic Readings*, ed. Paul E. Szarmach, 199–236. New York: Garland.

—— 1989. The unknowable audience of the Blickling Homilies. *ASE* 18.99–115. Reprinted 2000 in Milton McC. Gatch, *Eschatology and Christian Nurture: Themes in A-S and Medieval Religious Life*. Aldershot, Hants: Ashgate.

—— 1992. Piety and liturgy in the OE *Vision of Leofric*. In *Words, Texts, and Manuscripts: Studies in A-S Culture Presented to Helmut Gneuss*, ed. Michael Korhammer, 159–79. Woodbridge, Suffolk: D. S. Brewer. Reprinted 2000 in Milton McC. Gatch, *Eschatology and Christian Nurture: Themes in A-S and Medieval Religious Life*. Aldershot, Hants: Ashgate.

—— 1993. Miracles in architectural settings: Christ Church, Canterbury and St Clements, Sandwich, in the OE *Vision of Leofric*. *ASE* 22.227–52. Reprinted 2000 in Milton McC. Gatch, *Eschatology and Christian Nurture: Themes in A-S and Medieval Religious Life*. Aldershot, Hants: Ashgate.

Gee, Henry, and William John Hardy, transs. 1896. *Documents Illustrative of English Church History*. London: Macmillan.

Georgianna, Linda. 1987. King Hrethel's sorrow and the limits of heroic action in *Beowulf. Speculum* 62.829–50.

Gerritsen, Johan. 1999. What use are the Thorkelin transcripts of *Beowulf*? *ASE* 28.23–42.

Giles, J. A., ed. 1854. *Vita Quorundum Anglo-Saxonum*. London: J. Smith.

Gilles, Sealy. 1998. Territorial interpolations in the OE Orosius. In *Text and Territory: Geographical Imagination in the European Middle Ages*, ed. Sylvia Tomasch and Sealy Gilles, 79–96. Philadelphia: University of Pennsylvania Press.

Gilligan, Thomas F., ed. and trans. 1943. *The Soliloquies of Saint Augustine*. New York: Cosmopolitan.

Glaeske, Keith. 1999. Eve in A-S retellings of the Harrowing of Hell. *Traditio* 54.81–101.

Glass, Sandra A. 1982. The Saxonists' influence on seventeenth-century English literature. In *A-S Scholarship: The First Three Centuries*, ed. Carl T. Berkhout and Milton McC. Gatch, 91–105. Boston: G. K. Hall.

Glorie, Fr., ed. 1968. *Collectiones aenigmatum Merovingicae aetatis.* 2 vols. CCSL 133–133A. Turnhout: Brepols.

Gneuss, Helmut. 1972. The origin of standard OE and Æthelwold's school at Winchester. *ASE* 1.63–83.

—— 1976a. *The Battle of Maldon* 89: Byrhtnoð's *ofermod* once again. *SP* 73.117–37. Reprinted 1994 in *OE Shorter Poems: Basic Readings*, ed. Katherine O'Brien O'Keeffe, 149–72. New York: Garland.

—— 1976b. *Die Battle of Maldon als historisches und literarisches Zeugnis.* Munich: Bayerische Akademie der Wissenschaften.

—— 1985. Liturgical books in A-S England. In *Learning and Literature in A-S England: Studies Presented to Peter Clemoes*, ed. Michael Lapidge and Helmut Gneuss, 91–141. Cambridge: Cambridge University Press.

—— 1986. King Alfred and the history of the A-S libraries. In *Modes of Interpretation in OE Literature: Essays in Honor of Stanley B. Greenfield*, ed. Phyllis R. Brown, Georgia R. Crampton, and Fred C. Robinson, 29–49. Toronto: University of Toronto Press.

—— 2001. *Handlist of A-S Manuscripts: A List of Manuscripts and Manuscript Fragments Written or Owned in England up to 1100.* Tempe: Arizona Center for Medieval & Renaissance Studies.

Godden, Malcolm R. 1975. OE composite homilies from Winchester. *ASE* 4.57–65.

—— 1978. Ælfric and the vernacular prose tradition. In *The OE Homily and Its Backgrounds*, ed. Paul E. Szarmach and Bernard F. Huppé, 99–117. Albany: State University of New York Press.

—— ed. 1979. *Ælfric's Catholic Homilies, the Second Series: Text.* EETS s.s. 5. Oxford: Oxford University Press.

—— 1980. Ælfric's changing vocabulary. *ES* 61.206–23.

—— 1981. King Alfred's Boethius. In *Boethius: His Life, Thought and Influence*, ed. Margaret Gibson, 419–24. Oxford: Blackwell.

—— 1985. Anglo-Saxons on the mind. In *Learning and Literature in A-S England: Studies Presented to Peter Clemoes*, ed. Michael Lapidge and Helmut Gneuss, 271–98. Cambridge: Cambridge University Press.

—— 1991. Biblical literature: The Old Testament. In *The Cambridge Companion to OE Literature*, ed. Malcolm Godden and Michael Lapidge, 206–26. Cambridge: Cambridge University Press.

—— 1994a. Apocalypse and invasion in late A-S England In *From A-S to Early Middle English*, ed. Douglas Gray, Malcolm Godden, and Terry Hoad, 130–62. Oxford: Clarendon.

—— 1994b. Editing OE and the problem of Alfred's Boethius. In *The Editing of OE: Papers from the 1990 Manchester Conference*, ed. D. G. Scragg and Paul E. Szarmach, 163–76. Cambridge: D. S. Brewer.

—— 1996. Experiments in genre: The saints' lives in Ælfric's *Catholic Homilies*. In *Holy Men and Holy Women: OE Prose Saints' Lives and Their Contexts*, ed. Paul E. Szarmach, 261–87. Albany: State University of New York Press.

—— 1997. Wærferth and King Alfred: The fate of the OE dialogues. In *Alfred the Wise: Studies in Honor of Janet Bately on the Occasion of Her Sixty-Fifth Birthday*, ed. Jane Roberts, Janet L. Nelson, and Malcolm Godden, 35–51. Cambridge: D.S. Brewer.

—— 2000. *Ælfric's Catholic Homilies: Introduction, Commentary and Glossary*. EETS s.s. 18. Oxford: Oxford University Press.

Godman, Peter, ed. and trans. 1982. *Alcuin: The Bishops, Kings, and Saints of York*. Oxford: Clarendon.

—— ed. and trans. 1985. *The Poetry of the Carolingian Renaissance*. Norman: University of Oklahoma Press.

Goldsmith, Margaret E. 1962. The Christian perspective in *Beowulf*. *Comparative Literature* 14.71–90. Reprinted 1963 in *Studies in OE Literature in Honor of Arthur G. Brodeur*, ed. Stanley B. Greenfield, 71–90, Eugene: University of Oregon Books; 1991 in *Interpretations of "Beowulf": A Critical Anthology*, ed. R. D. Fulk, 103–19, Bloomington: Indiana University Press; and, partially, 1963 in *An Anthology of "Beowulf" Criticism*, ed. Lewis E. Nicholson, 373–86, Notre Dame: University of Notre Dame Press.

—— 1975. The enigma of *The Husband's Message*. In *A-S Poetry: Essays in Appreciation for John C. McGalliard*, ed. Lewis E. Nicholson and Dolores Warwick Frese, 242–63. Notre Dame: University of Notre Dame Press.

Gollancz, Israel, ed. 1927. *The Cædmon Manuscript*. Oxford: Oxford University Press.

Gonser, Paul, ed. 1909. *Das angelsächsische Prosa-Leben des hl. Guthlac*. Anglistische Forschungen 27. Heidelberg: C. Winter.

Goolden, Peter, ed. 1958. *The OE Apollonius of Tyre*. Oxford: Clarendon.

Gordon, E. V., ed. 1937. *The Battle of Maldon*. London: Methuen. Reprinted 1976, with a supplement by D. G. Scragg, Manchester: University of Manchester Press.

Gordon, I. L., ed. 1960. *The Seafarer*. London: Methuen. Reprinted 1996, with a bibliography by Mary Clayton, Exeter: University of Exeter Press.

Gordon, R. K., trans. 1954. *A-S Poetry*. 2nd ed. London: Dent.

Gradon, P. O. E., ed. 1996. *Cynewulf's "Elene."* Rev. ed. Exeter: University of Exeter Press.

Graham, Timothy, ed. 2000. *The Recovery of OE: A-S Studies in the Sixteenth and Seventeenth Centuries*. Kalamazoo: Medieval Institute Pubns.

Grant, Raymond J. S. 1989. *The B Text of the OE Bede: A Linguistic Commentary*. Amsterdam and Atlanta: Rodopi.

Grasso, Anthony R. 1991. Theology and structure in *The Dream of the Rood*. *Religion and Literature* 23.2.23–38.

Grattan, J. H. G., and Charles Singer. 1952. *A-S Magic and Medicine*. London: Oxford University Press.

Green, Eugene A. 1989. Ælfric the catechist. In *De Ore Domini: Preacher and Word in the Middle Ages*, ed. T. Amos et al., 61–74. Studies in Medieval

Culture 27. Kalamazoo: Medieval Institute Pubns.

Green, Richard, trans. 1962. *The Consolation of Philosophy: Boethius*. Indianapolis: Bobbs-Merrill.

Greenfield, Stanley B. 1966. The OE Elegies. In *Continuations and Beginnings: Studies in OE Literature*, ed. E. G. Stanley, 142–75. London: Nelson. Reprinted 1989 in *Hero and Exile: The Art of OE Poetry*, ed. George H. Brown, 93–123. London: Hambledon.

—— 1969. *Min, sylf,* and "dramatic voices" in *The Wanderer* and *The Seafarer. JEGP* 68.212–20. Reprinted 1989 in *Hero and Exile: The Art of OE Poetry*, ed. George H. Brown, 161–69. London: Hambledon.

—— 1972. *The Interpretation of OE Poems*. London: Routledge & Kegan Paul.

—— 1976. The authenticating voice in *Beowulf. ASE* 5.51–62. Reprinted 1995 in *Beowulf: Basic Readings*, ed. Peter S. Baker, 97–110. New York: Garland (reprinted 2000 under the title *The "Beowulf" Reader*).

—— 1981. *Sylf,* seasons, structure, and genre in *The Seafarer. ASE* 9.199–211. Reprinted 1989 in *Hero and Exile: The Art of OE Poetry*, ed. George H. Brown, 171–83. London: Hambledon.

—— 1986. *Wulf and Eadwacer:* All passion pent. *ASE* 15.5–14.

—— 1989. *Hero and Exile: The Art of OE Poetry*. Ed. George H. Brown. London: Hambledon.

Greenfield, Stanley B., and Daniel G. Calder. 1986. *A New Critical History of OE Literature*. New York: New York University Press.

Greenman, R. E. 1992. The sources of *Christ II* (Cameron A.3.1.2). In *Fontes Anglo-Saxonici: World Wide Web Register*, ed. Joyce Hill et al. 2001. ‹http://fontes.english.ox.ac.uk/›.

Grein, Christian W. M., ed. 1857–8. *Bibliothek der angelsächsischen Poesie*. 2 vols. Göttingen: G. Wigand.

—— trans. 1857–9. *Dichtungen der Angelsachsen stabreimend übersetzt*. 2 vols. Göttingen: G. Wigand.

—— 1865. Zur Textkritik der angelsächsischen Dichter. *Germania* 10.416–29.

Grendon, Felix, ed. 1909. The A-S charms. *Journal of American Folklore* 22.105–237.

Gretsch, Mechthild. 1992. The Benedictine rule in OE: A document of Bishop Æthelwold's reform politics. In *Words, Texts, and Manuscripts: Studies in A-S Culture Presented to Helmut Gneuss*, ed. Michael Korhammer, 131–58. Woodbridge, Suffolk: D. S. Brewer.

—— 1999. *The Intellectual Foundations of the English Benedictine Reform*. CSASE 25. Cambridge: Cambridge University Press.

Griffith, Mark S. 1991. Poetic language and the Paris Psalter: The decay of the OE tradition. *ASE* 20.167–86.

—— 1993. Convention and originality in the OE "beasts of battle" typescene. *ASE* 22.179–99.

—— 1995. Alliterative licence and the rhetorical use of proper names in *The Battle of Maldon*. In *Prosody and Poetics in the Early Middle Ages: Essays in Honour of C. B. Hieatt*, ed. M. J. Toswell, 60–79. Toronto: University of Toronto Press.

—— ed. 1997. *Judith*. Exeter: University of Exeter Press.

—— 2000. Ælfric's preface to Genesis: Genre, rhetoric and the origins of the *ars dictaminis*. *ASE* 29.215–34.

Griffiths, Bill, ed. and trans. 1991. *The Service of Prime from the OE Benedictine Office: Text and Translation*. Hockwold-cum-Wilton, Norfolk: Anglo-Saxon Books.

—— 1996. *Aspects of A-S Magic*. Hockwold-cum-Wilton, Norfolk: Anglo-Saxon Books.

Griffiths, Gwen. 1992. Reading Ælfric's Saint Æthelthryth as a woman. *Parergon* 10.35–49.

Grosz, Oliver J. H. 1970. Man's imitation of the ascension: The unity of *Christ II*. *Neophilologus* 54.398–408. Reprinted 1996 in *Cynewulf: Basic Readings*, ed. Robert E. Bjork, 95–108, New York: Garland (reissued 2001 as *The Cynewulf Reader*, New York: Routledge).

Guerreau-Jalabert, Anita, ed. and trans. 1982. *Abbo Floriacensis: Quaestiones grammaticales*. Paris: Belles Lettres.

Guðni Jónsson, ed. 1954. *Fornaldar sögur Norðurlanda*. 4 vols. Akureyri: Íslendingasagnaútgáfan.

Gulley, Alison. 1998. *Heo man ne wæs*: Cross-dressing, sex-change, and womanhood in Ælfric's life of Eugenia. *Mediaevalia* 22.1.113–31.

Gwara, Scott. 1996. *Latin Colloquies for Pre-Conquest Britain*. Toronto: Pontifical Institute of Mediaeval Studies.

—— ed. 2001. *Aldhelmi Malmesbiriensis Prosa de Virginitate, cum Glosa Latina atque Anglosaxonica*. 2 vols. CCSL 124–4A. Turnhout: Brepols.

Gwara, Scott, and David W. Porter. 1997. *A-S Conversations: The Colloquies of Ælfric Bata*. Woodbridge: Boydell.

Häcker, Martina. 1996. The original length of the OE *Judith*: More doubts on the "missing text." *LSE* n.s. 27.1–18.

Haddan, Arthur West, and William Stubbs, eds. 1869–71. *Councils and Ecclesiastical Documents Relating to Great Britain and Ireland*. 3 vols. Oxford: Clarendon.

Haines, Dorothy. 1999. Unlocking *Exodus* ll. 516–32. *JEGP* 98.481–98.

Hale, W. C. 1978. An edition and codicological study of CCCC MS. 214. Doctoral thesis, University of Pennsylvania.

Hall, Thomas N. 1996. The *Evangelium Nichodemi* and *Vindicta Salvatoris* in A-S England. In *Two OE Apocrypha and Their Latin Source: The Gospel of Nichodemus and the Avenging of the Saviour*, ed. James E. Cross, 36–81. CSASE 19. Cambridge: Cambridge University Press.

Halsall, Maureen, ed. 1981. *The OE Rune Poem: A Critical Edition*. Toronto:

University of Toronto Press.

Hamilton, David. 1975. *Andreas* and *Beowulf*: Placing the hero. In *A-S Poetry: Essays in Appreciation for John C. McGalliard*, ed. Lewis E. Nicholson and Dolores Warwick Frese, 81–98. Notre Dame: University of Notre Dame Press.

Hamilton, Marie P. 1946. The religious principle in *Beowulf*. *PMLA* 61.309–30. Reprinted 1963 in *An Anthology of "Beowulf" Criticism*, ed. Lewis E. Nicholson, 105–35. Notre Dame: University of Notre Dame Press.

Hamilton, N. E. S. A., ed. 1870. *Willelmi Malmesbiriensis monachi de gestibus pontifium Anglorum*. Rerum Britannicarum Medii Aevi Scriptores (Rolls Series) 52. London: Stationery Office. Reprinted 1964, Wiesbaden: Kraus Rpt.

Hansen, Elaine Tuttle. 1988. *The Solomon Complex*. Toronto: University of Toronto Press.

Harbus, Antonina. 1994a. Nebuchadnezzar's dreams in the OE *Daniel*. *ES* 75.489–508.

—— 1994b. Text as revelation: Constantine's dream in *Elene*. *Neophilologus* 78.645–53.

—— 1996a. Deceptive dreams in *The Wanderer*. *SP* 93.164–79.

—— 1996b. Dream and symbol in *The Dream of the Rood*. *Nottingham Medieval Studies* 40.1–15.

Hargrove, Henry L., ed. 1902. *King Alfred's OE Version of Saint Augustine's Soliloquies*. Yale Studies in English 13. New York: H. Holt.

—— trans. 1904. *King Alfred's OE Version of Saint Augustine's Soliloquies*. Yale Studies in English 22. New York: H. Holt.

Harmer, Florence E., ed. 1914. *Select English Historical Documents of the Ninth and Tenth Centuries*. Cambridge: Cambridge University Press.

—— 1989. *A-S Writs*. 2nd ed. by Paul Watkins. Stamford, Lincs: P. Watkins.

Harris, Joseph. 1982. Elegy in OE and Old Norse: A problem in literary history. In *The Vikings*, ed. Robert T. Farrell, 157–64. London: Phillimore. Reprinted 1983 in *The OE Elegies: New Essays in Criticism*, ed. M. Green, 46–56. Rutherford, N.J.: Fairleigh Dickinson University Press.

—— 1987. *Deor* and its refrain: Preliminaries to an interpretation. *Traditio* 43.23–53.

—— 1988. Hadubrand's lament: On the origin and age of elegy in Germanic. In *Heldensage und Heldendichtung im Germanischen*, ed. Heinrich Beck, 81–114. Berlin: W. de Gruyter.

—— 1993. Love and death in the *Männerbund*: An essay with special reference to the *Bjarkamál* and *The Battle of Maldon*. In *Heroic Poetry in the A-S Period: Studies in Honor of Jess B. Bessinger, Jr.*, ed. Helen Damico and John Leyerle, 77–114. Studies in Medieval Culture 32. Kalamazoo: Medieval Institute Pubns.

Harris, Stephen J. 2001. The Alfredian *World History* and A-S identity. *JEGP* 100.482–510.

Hart, Cyril. 1972. Byrhtferth and his manual. *MÆ* 41.95–109.

Harvey, P. D. A. 1993. Rectitudines singularum personarum and gerefa. *English Historical Review* 108.1–22.

Hasenfratz, Robert J. 1989. *Eisegan stefne* (*Christ and Satan* 36a), the *Visio Pauli*, and *ferrea vox* (*Aeneid* 6, 626). *MP* 86.398–403.

—— 1993a. *"Beowulf" Scholarship: An Annotated Bibliography, 1979–1990.* New York: Garland.

—— 1993b. *Wanderer,* lines 45–57 and the birds of Diomede. *JEGP* 92.309–24.

Hawkins, Emma. 1995. Gender, language, and power in *The Dream of the Rood. Women and Language* 18.2.33–6.

Head, Pauline. 1999. Perpetual history in the OE *Menologium.* In *The Medieval Chronicle,* ed. Erik Kooper, 155–62. Costerus n.s. 120. Amsterdam: Rodopi.

Healey, Antonette diPaolo, ed. 1978. *The OE Vision of St. Paul.* Cambridge, Mass.: Mediaeval Academy of America.

—— 1985. A-S use of the apocryphal gospel. In *The Anglo-Saxons: Synthesis and Achievement,* ed. J. Douglas Woods and David Pelteret, 93–104. Waterloo, Ont.: Wilfrid Laurier University Press.

Heaney, Seamus, trans. 1999. *Beowulf.* London: Faber & Faber.

Hecht, Hans, ed. 1900–7. *Bischof Waerferths von Worcester Übersetzung der Dialoge Gregors des Grossen.* 2 vols. Bibliothek der angelsächsischen Prosa 5. Leipzig: G. Wigand.

Heinemann, Fredrik J. 1993. "Cynewulf and Cyneheard" and *Landnámabók:* Another narrative tradition. *LSE* n.s. 24.57–89.

Helder, W. 1977. Beowulf and the plundered hoard. *NM* 78.317–25.

—— 1994. Abraham and the OE *Exodus.* In *Companion to OE Poetry,* ed. Henk Aertsen and Rolf H. Bremmer, 189–200. Amsterdam: VU University Press.

Henel, Heinrich. 1934. *Studien zum altenglischen Computus.* Beiträge zur englischen Philologie 26. Leipzig: B. Tauchnitz. Reprinted 1967, New York: Johnson Rpt.

—— ed. 1942. *Ælfric's De temporibus anni.* EETS o.s. 213. London: Oxford University Press.

Henry, P. L. 1961. Beowulf cruces. *Zeitschrift für vergleichende Sprachforschung* 77.140–59.

—— 1966. *The Early English and Celtic Lyric.* London: Allen & Unwin.

Hermann, John P. 1989. *Allegories of War: Language and Violence in OE Poetry.* Ann Arbor: University of Michigan Press.

Herzfeld, George, ed. 1900. *An OE Martyrology.* EETS o.s. 116. London: K. Paul, Trench, Trübner.

Heusler, Andreas. 1915. Sprichwörter in den eddischen Sittengedichten. *Zeitschrift des Vereins für Volkskunde* 25.108–15, 26.42–57. Here cited from

Andreas Heusler, *Kleine Schriften*, vol. 2, ed. Stefan Sonderegger, 292–313. Berlin: W. de Gruyter, 1969.

—— 1941. *Die altgermanische Dichtung*. 2nd ed. Potsdam: Athenaion.

Hickes, George. 1703–5. *Linguarum Veterum Septentrionalium Thesaurus Grammatico-Criticus et Archaeologicus*. Oxford. Reprinted. 1970, Hildesheim: G. Olms.

Hieatt, Constance B. 1975. Envelope patterns and the structure of *Beowulf*. *English Studies in Canada* 1.249–65.

Higley, S. L. 1993. *Between Languages: The Uncooperative Text in Early Welsh and OE Nature Poetry*. University Park: Pennsylvania State University Press.

Hill, John M. 1991. Transcendental loyalty in *The Battle of Maldon*. In Part I: History into literature, *Mediaevalia* 17.1–176, ed. John D. Niles, 67–88.

—— 1995. *The Cultural World in "Beowulf."* Toronto: University of Toronto Press.

—— 2000. *The A-S Warrior Ethic*. Gainesville: University Press of Florida.

Hill, Joyce. 1984. *Widsith* and the tenth century. *NM* 85.305–15. Reprinted 1994 in *OE Shorter Poems: Basic Readings*, ed. Katherine O'Brien O'Keeffe, 319–33. New York: Garland.

—— 1989. Ælfric, Gelasius, and St. George. *Mediaevalia* 11.1–17.

—— 1991. The *Regularis concordia* and its Latin and OE reflexes. *Revue Bénédictine* 101.299–315.

—— 1993. Reform and resistance: Preaching styles in late A-S England. In *De l'homélie au sermon: histoire de la prédication médiévale*, ed. Jacqueline Hamesse and Xavier Hermand, 15–46. Louvain-la-Neuve: Institut d'Etudes Médiévales de l'Université de Louvain.

—— 1996. The dissemination of Ælfric's *Lives of Saints*: A preliminary survey. In *Holy Men and Holy Women: OE Prose Saints' Lives and Their Contexts*, ed. Paul E. Szarmach, 235–59. Albany: State University of New York Press.

—— 1998. Winchester pedagogy and the *Colloquy* of Ælfric. *LSE* n.s. 29.137–52.

Hill, Joyce, et al. 2001. *Fontes Anglo-Saxonici: World Wide Web Register*. <http://fontes.english.ox.ac.uk/>.

Hill, Thomas D. 1977. A liturgical source for *Christ I* 164–213 (Advent Lyric VII). *MÆ* 46.12–15.

—— 1986. Literary history and OE poetry: The case of *Christ I, II*, and *III*. In *Sources of A-S Culture*, ed. Paul E. Szarmach, 3–22. Studies in Medieval Culture 20. Kalamazoo: Medieval Institute Pubns.

—— 1997. The *Liber Eliensis* "historical selections" and the OE *Battle of Maldon*. *JEGP* 96.1–12.

Hills, Catherine M. 1997. Beowulf and archaeology. In *A "Beowulf" Handbook*, ed. Robert E. Bjork and John D. Niles, 291–310. Lincoln: University of Nebraska Press.

Hilton, Chadwick B. 1986. The OE *Seasons for Fasting*: Its place in the vernacular tradition. *Neophilologus* 70.155–9.

Hinton, Rebecca. 1996. *The Dream of the Rood. The Explicator* 54.77–9.

Hitch, S. J. 1988. Alfred's reading of Augustine's *Soliloquies*. In *Sentences: Essays Presented to Alan Ward*, ed. D. M. Reeks, 21–9. Southampton: Bosphoros.

Hoek, Michelle C. 1997. A-S innovation and the use of the senses in the OE *Physiologus* poems. *SN* 69.110.

Hofstetter, Walter. 1983. Zur lateinischen Quelle des altenglischen Pseudo-Dioskurides. *Anglia* 101.315–60.

—— 1987. *Winchester und die spätaltenglische Sprachgebrauch*. Munich: W. Fink.

—— 1988. Winchester and the standardization of OE vocabulary. *ASE* 17.139–61.

Holder-Egger, O. 1887. *Vitae Willibaldi et Wynnebaldi*, MGH, Scriptores 15.1, 80–117. Hannover: Hahn.

Hollis, Stephanie. 1997. OE "cattle-theft charms": Manuscript contexts and social uses. *Anglia* 115.139–64.

Hollis, Stephanie, and Michael Wright. 1992. *OE Prose of Secular Learning*. Annotated Bibliographies of Old and Middle English Literature 4. Cambridge: D. S. Brewer.

Holthausen, Ferdinand. 1893. Zu alt- und mittelenglischen Denkmälern. *Anglia* 15.187–203.

—— ed. 1936. *Cynewulfs Elene*. 4th ed. Heidelberg: C. Winter.

Honegger, Thomas. 1998. Form and function: The beasts of battle revisited. *ES* 79.289–98.

Horgan, A. D. 1987. *The Wanderer:* A Boethian poem? *RES* n.s. 38.40–6.

Hörmann, Wolfgang, ed. 1987. *Sancti Aureli Augustini opera*. Sec. 1, part 4. Corpus Scriptorum Ecclesiasticorum Latinorum 89. Vienna: Hoelder-Pichler-Tempsky.

Horner, Shari. 2001. *The Discourse of Enclosure: Representing Women in OE Literature*. Albany: State University of New York Press.

Hough, Carole A. 1995. *Wulf and Eadwacer:* A note on *ungelic. ANQ* 8.3.3–6.

Houghton, John William. 1994. The OE *Benedictine Office* and its audience. *American Benedictine Review* 45.431–45.

Howe, Nicholas. 1985. *The OE Catalogue Poems*. Anglistica 23. Copenhagen: Rosenkilde & Bagger.

—— 1989. *Migration and Mythmaking in A-S England*. New Haven: Yale University Press.

—— 1993. The cultural construction of reading in A-S England. In *The Ethnography of Reading*, ed. Jonathan Boyarin, 58–79. Berkeley: University of California Press.

Howlett, David. 1978. *The Wife's Lament* and *The Husband's Message. NM* 79.7–10.

Huisman, Rosemary. 1992. A-S interpretative practices and the first seven lines of the OE poem *Exodus*: The benefits of close reading. *Parergon* 10.2.51–7.

—— 1997. Subjectivity/orality: How relevant are modern literary theories to the study of OE poetry? What light can the study of OE poetry cast on modern literary theory? In *The Preservation and Transmission of A-S Culture*, ed. Paul E. Szarmach and Joel T. Rosenthal, 313–31. Kalamazoo: Medieval Institute Pubns.

Hulme, William H., ed. 1903–4. The OE Gospel of Nicodemus. *MP* 1.579–614.

Hume, Kathryn. 1976. The "ruin motif" in OE poetry. *Anglia* 94.339–60.

Hunter Blair, Peter. 1970. *The World of Bede*. London: Secker & Warburg.

—— 1977. *An Introduction to A-S England*. 2nd ed. Cambridge: Cambridge University Press.

Huppé, B.F. 1943. *The Wanderer:* Theme and structure. *JEGP* 42.516–38.

—— 1970. *The Web of Words: Structural Analyses of the OE Poems "Vainglory," "The Wonder of Creation," "The Dream of the Rood," and "Judith."* Albany: State University of New York Press.

—— 1984. *The Hero in the Earthly City: A Reading of "Beowulf."* Binghamton: State University of New York Press.

Hurst, D., ed. 1955. *Bedae Venerabilis opera, III: opera homeletica.* CCSL 122. Turnhout: Brepols.

—— trans. 1990. *Gregory the Great, Forty Gospel Homilies.* Kalamazoo: Cistercian Pubns.

Hurt, James. 1972. *Ælfric*. Boston: Twayne.

Imelmann, Rudolf. 1907. *Die ae. Odoaker-Dichtung*. Berlin: Springer.

Ireland, Colin A. 1991. Some analogues of the OE *Seafarer* from Hiberno-Latin sources. *NM* 92.1–14.

Irvine, Martin. 1991. Medieval textuality and the archaeology of textual culture. In *Speaking Two Languages: Traditional Disciplines and Contemporary Theory in Medieval Studies*, ed. Allen J. Frantzen, 181–210. Albany: State University of New York Press.

Irvine, Susan. 1996. Ulysses and Circe in King Alfred's *Boethius*: A classical myth transformed. In *Studies in English Language and Literature: "Doubt Wisely": Papers in Honour of E. G. Stanley*, ed. M. J. Toswell and E. M. Tyler, 387–401. London: Routledge.

Irving, Edward B., Jr. 1968. *A Reading of "Beowulf."* New Haven: Yale University Press. Ch. 1 (pp. 1–42) reprinted 1991 in *Interpretations of "Beowulf": A Critical Anthology*, ed. R. D. Fulk, 168–93. Bloomington: Indiana University Press.

—— 1984. The nature of Christianity in *Beowulf. ASE* 13.7–21.

—— 1989. *Rereading "Beowulf."* Philadelphia: University of Pennsylvania Press.

—— 1996. The advent of poetry: *Christ I. ASE* 25.123–34.

—— 1997. Christian and pagan elements. In *A "Beowulf" Handbook*, ed. Robert

E. Bjork and John D. Niles, 175–92. Lincoln: University of Nebraska Press.

Jaager, W., ed. 1935. *Bedas metrische Vita Sancti Cuthberti*. Palaestra 198. Leipzig: Mayer & Müller.

Jackson, Elizabeth. 1998. "Not Simply Lists": An eddic perspective on short-item lists in OE poems. *Speculum* 73.338–71.

—— 2000. From the seat of the *þyle*? A reading of *Maxims I*, lines 138–40. *JEGP* 99.170–92.

Jackson, Peter, and Michael Lapidge. 1996. The contents of the Cotton-Corpus Legendary. In *Holy Men and Holy Women: OE Prose Saints' Lives and Their Contexts*, ed. Paul E. Szarmach, 131–46. Albany: State University of New York Press.

Jacobs, Nicholas. 1989. Syntactical connection and logical disconnection: The case of *The Seafarer*. *MÆ* 58.105–13.

—— 1990. Celtic saga and the contexts of OE elegiac poetry. *Études celtiques* 26.95–142.

Jager, Eric. 1990. Speech and the chest in OE poetry: Orality or pectorality? *Speculum* 65.845–59.

Jeffrey, J. Elizabeth. 1989. *Blickling Spirituality and the OE Vernacular Homily: A Textual Analysis*. Lewiston, N.Y.: E. Mellen.

Jennings, Margaret. 1994. *Rood* and Ruthwell: The power of paradox. *ELN* 31.6–12.

Johansen, John G. 1993. Language, structure, and theme in the "Cynewulf and Cyneheard" episode. *ELN* 31.3–8.

Johnson, David F. 1993. The Five Horrors of Hell: An insular homiletic motif. *ES* 74.414–31.

—— 1998. The fall of Lucifer in *Genesis A* and two A-S royal charters. *JEGP* 97.500–21.

Johnson, Richard F. 1998. Archangel in the margins: St. Michael in the homilies of Cambridge, Corpus Christi College 41. *Traditio* 53, 63–91.

Johnson, William C. 1983. *The Wife's Lament* as death-song. In *The OE Elegies: New Essays in Criticism*, ed. M. Green, 69–81. Rutherford, N.J.: Fairleigh Dickinson University Press.

Jolly, Karen Louise. 1996. *Popular Religion in Late Saxon England: Elf Charms in Context*. Chapel Hill: University of North Carolina Press.

Jonassen, Frederick B. 1988. The Pater Noster letters in the poetic *Solomon and Saturn*. *MLR* 83.1–9.

Jones, Charles W., ed. 1943. *Bedae opera de temporibus*. Cambridge, Mass.: Medieval Academy of America.

Jones, Christopher A. 1995. Envisioning the *cenobium* in the OE *Guthlac A*. *MS* 57.259–91.

—— ed. 1998a. *Ælfric's Letter to the Monks of Eynsham*. CSASE 24. Cambridge: Cambridge University Press.

—— 1998b. *Meatim sed et rustica*: Ælfric of Eynsham as a medieval Latin author. *Journal of Medieval Latin* 8.1–57.

Jones, Gwyn. 1972. *Kings, Beasts and Heroes.* London: Oxford University Press.

Jónsson, Finnur, see Finnur Jónsson.

Jónsson, Guðni, see Guðni Jónsson.

Jost, Karl. 1920. Zur Textkritik der altenglischen Soliloquienbearbeitung. *Anglia Beiblatt* 31.259–72.

—— 1923. Wulfstan und die Angelsächsische Chronik. *Anglia* 47.105–23.

—— 1932. Einige Wulfstantexte und ihre Quellen. *Anglia* 56.265–315, 448.

—— 1950. *Wulfstanstudien.* Schweizer anglistische Arbeiten 23. Bern: A. Francke.

—— ed. 1959. *Die Institutes of Polity, Civil and Ecclesiastical.* Swiss Studies in English 47. Bern: Francke.

Judic, Bruno, ed. 1992. *Gregoire le Grand: Regle pastorale.* Textual criticism by Floribert Rommel, French trans. by Charles Morel. Sources chrétiennes 381–2. Paris: Cerf.

Jurasinski, Stefan. Forthcoming. The continental origins of Aethelberht's code. To appear in *PQ.*

Kabir, Ananya Jahnara. 2001. *Paradise, Death and Doomsday in A-S Literature.* Cambridge: Cambridge University Press.

Kamphausen, Hans J. 1975. *Traum und Vision in der lateinischen Poesie der Karolingerzeit.* Bern: H. Lang.

Karkov, Catherine E. 2001. *Text and Picture in A-S England: Narrative Strategies in the Junius 11 Manuscript.* CSASE 31. Cambridge: Cambridge University Press.

Kaske, Robert E. 1958. *Sapientia et Fortitudo* as the controlling theme of *Beowulf. SP* 55.423–56. Reprinted in *An Anthology of "Beowulf" Criticism*, ed. Lewis E. Nicholson, 269–310. Notre Dame: University of Notre Dame Press.

—— 1963. "Hygelac" and "Hygd." In *Studies in OE Literature in Honor of Arthur G. Brodeur*, ed. Stanley B. Greenfield, 200–6. Eugene: University of Oregon Books.

—— 1967. A poem of the cross in the Exeter Book: *Riddle 60* and *The Husband's Message. Traditio* 23.41–71.

Kaylor, Noel Harold, Jr. 1992. *The Medieval "Consolation of Philosophy": An Annotated Bibliography.* New York: Garland.

Keefer, Sarah Larratt. 1979. *The OE Metrical Psalter: An Annotated Set of Collation Lists with the Psalter Glosses.* New York: Garland.

—— 1991. *Psalm-Poem and Psalter-Glosses.* New York: P. Lang.

—— 1998. Respect for the book: A reconsideration of "form," "content," and "context" in two vernacular poems. In *New Approaches to Editing OE Verse*, ed. Sarah Larratt Keefer and Katherine O'Brien O'Keeffe, 21–44. Cambridge: D. S. Brewer.

Kemble, John M. 1836. *Über die Stammtafel der Westsachsen.* Munich.

—— ed. 1839–48. *Codex Diplomaticus Aevi Saxonici.* 6 vols. London: Bentley. Reprinted 1964, Vaduz: Kraus Rpt.

Kendall, Calvin. 1988. Let us now praise a famous city: Wordplay in the OE *Durham* and the cult of St. Cuthbert. *JEGP* 87.507–21.

—— 1991. *The Metrical Grammar of "Beowulf."* Cambridge: Cambridge University Press.

Kennedy, Alan. 1991. Byrhtnoth's obits and twelfth-century accounts of the Battle of Maldon. In *The Battle of Maldon, AD 991*, ed. D. G. Scragg, 59–78. Oxford: Blackwell.

Ker, N. R. 1956. *The Pastoral Care: King Alfred's Translation of St. Gregory's Regula Pastoralis.* EEMF 6. Copenhagen: Rosenkilde & Bagger.

—— 1957. *Catalogue of Manuscripts Containing A-S.* Oxford: Clarendon. Reissued 1990, with a 1977 supplement from *ASE* 5, 121–31.

Ker, W. P. 1908. *Epic and Romance: Essays on Medieval Literature.* 2nd ed. London: Macmillan.

Kershaw, Paul. 2001. Illness, power and prayer in Asser's *Life of King Alfred. EME* 10.201–224.

Keynes, Simon. 1980. *The Diplomas of King Æthelred the Unready, 978–1016.* Cambridge: Cambridge University Press.

—— 1990. Royal government and the written word in late A-S England. In *The Uses of Literacy in Early Mediaeval Europe*, ed. Rosamund McKitterick, 226–57. Cambridge: Cambridge University Press.

—— ed. 1991. *Facsimiles of A-S Charters.* A-S Charters Suppl. Vol. 1. Oxford: Oxford University Press.

—— ed. 1996a. *The Liber Vitae of the New Minster and Hyde Abbey, Winchester.* EEMF 26. Copenhagen: Rosenkilde & Bagger.

—— 1996b. On the authenticity of Asser's Life of King Alfred. *Journal of Ecclesiastical History* 47: 529–51.

—— 1998. *A-S History: A Select Bibliography.* 2nd online ed. ‹http://www.wmich.edu/medieval/rawl/keynes1/home.htm›.

—— 1999a. Charters and writs. In *The Blackwell Encyclopedia of A-S England*, ed. Michael Lapidge et al., 99–100. Oxford: Blackwell.

—— 1999b. The cult of King Alfred the Great. *ASE* 28.225–356.

Keynes, Simon, and Michael Lapidge. 1983. *Alfred the Great: Asser's "Life of King Alfred" and other Contemporary Sources.* Harmondsworth: Penguin.

Kieckhefer, Richard. 1989. *Magic in the Middle Ages.* Cambridge: Cambridge University Press.

Kiernan, Kevin S. 1981a. *"Beowulf" and the "Beowulf" Manuscript.* New Brunswick: Rutgers University Press. Reissued 1996, with a new preface, an appendix (a reprint of a 1983 article) by Kevin S. Kiernan, and a foreword by Katherine O'Brien O'Keeffe. Ann Arbor: University of Michigan Press.

—— 1981b. The eleventh-century origin of *Beowulf* and the *Beowulf* manuscript. In *The Dating of Beowulf*, ed. Colin Chase, 9–22 Toronto: University of Toronto Press (reissued 1997 with an afterword by Nicholas Howe). Reprinted 1994 in *A-S Manuscripts: Basic Readings*, ed. Mary P. Richards, 277–99. New York: Garland.

—— 1998. Alfred the Great's burnt Boethius. In *The Iconic Page in Manuscript, Print, and Digital Culture*, ed. George Bornstein and Teresa Tinkle, 7–32. Ann Arbor: University of Michigan Press.

—— 1999. *Electronic "Beowulf."* 2 CD-ROMs. London: British Library; Ann Arbor: University of Michigan Press.

Kim, Susan. 1999. Bloody signs: Circumcision and pregnancy in the OE *Judith*. *Exemplaria* 11.285–307.

King, J. E., ed. and trans 1930. *Bede: Historical Works*. 2 vols. Loeb Classical Library 246, 248. London: Heinemann.

Kitson, Peter. 1978. Lapidary traditions in A-S England: Part I, the background: The OE *Lapidary*. *ASE* 7.9–60.

—— 1983. Lapidary traditions in A-S England: Part II, Bede's *Explanatio apocalypsis* and related works. *ASE* 12.72–123.

—— 1987. Some unrecognized OE and Anglo-Latin verse. *N&Q* 232, n.s. 34.147–51.

—— 1996. The dialect position of the OE Orosius. *Studia Anglica Posnaniensia* 30.3–35

Klaeber, Friedrich. 1911–12. Die christlichen Elemente im Beowulf. *Anglia* 35.111–36, 249–70, 453–82; 36.169–99. Trans. 1996 by Paul Battles as *The Christian Elements in "Beowulf."* OEN Subsidia 24. Kalamazoo: Medieval Institute, Western Michigan University.

—— 1923. Zu König Alfreds Vorrede zu seiner Übersetzung der Cura Pastoralis. *Anglia* 47.53–65.

—— ed. 1950. *Beowulf and the Fight at Finnsburg*. 3rd ed. with 1st and 2nd supplements. Lexington, Mass.: D. C. Heath.

Klausner, David N. 1996. Aspects of time in the battle poetry of early Britain. In *The Middle Ages in the North-West*, ed. Tom Scott and Pat Starkey, 85–107. Oxford: Leopard's Head.

Klein, Thomas. 1997. The OE translation of Aldhelm's riddle *Lorica*. *RES* n.s. 48.345–9.

Kleist, Aaron J. 2000. An annotated bibliography of Ælfrician studies: 1983–1996. In *OE Prose: Basic Readings*, ed. Paul E. Szarmach, 503–52. New York: Garland.

Klinck, Anne L. 1987. *Resignation*: Exile's lament or penitent's prayer? *Neophilologus* 71.423–30.

—— 1992. *The OE Elegies: A Critical Edition and Genre Study*. Montreal: McGill-Queen's University Press.

Kluge, F. 1885. Zu altenglischen Dichtungen. *Englische Studien* 8.472–9.

Knappe, Gabrielle. 1994. *Traditionen der klassischen Rhetorik im angelsächsischen England*. Anglistische Forschungen 236. Heidelberg: Winter.

—— 1998. Classical rhetoric in A-S England. *ASE* 27.5–29.

Knowles, David. 1963. *The Monastic Order in England*. 2nd ed. Cambridge: Cambridge University Press.

Kock, E. A. 1921. Interpretations and emendations of early English texts, VIII. *Anglia* 45.122–3.

Kornexl, Lucia. 1995. The *Regularis concordia* and its OE gloss. *ASE* 24.95–130.

Korte, Dirk. 1974. *Untersuchungen zu Inhalt, Stil und Technik angelsächsischer Gesetze und Rechtsbücher des. 6. bis 12. Jahrhunderts*. Meisenheim: A. Hain.

Kotzor, Günther, ed. 1981. *Das altenglische Marytologium*. Abhandlungen der Bayerische Akademie der Wissenschaften, phil.-hist. Klasse, n.s. 88. 2 vols. Munich: C. Beck.

—— 1986. The Latin tradition of martyrologies and the *OE Martyrology*. In *Studies in Earlier OE Prose*, ed. Paul E. Szarmach, 301–333. Albany: State University of New York Press.

Krapp, George Philip, and Elliott Van Kirk Dobbie, eds. 1931–53. *The A-S Poetic Records*. 6 vols. New York: Columbia University Press. Contents of the individual volumes: I, *The Junius Manuscript* (Krapp, 1931); II, *The Vercelli Book* (Krapp, 1932); III, *The Exeter Book* (Krapp and Dobbie, 1936); IV, *Beowulf and Judith* (Dobbie, 1953); V, *The Paris Psalter and the Meters of Boethius* (Krapp, 1932); VI, *The A-S Minor Poems* (Dobbie, 1942).

Kratz, Dennis M., ed. and trans. 1984. *"Waltharius" and "Ruodlieb."* New York: Garland.

Kretzschmar, William A., Jr. 1987. Adaptation and *anweald* in the OE Orosius. *ASE* 16.127–45.

Kruger, Steven F. 1994. Oppositions and their opposition in the OE *Exodus*. *Neophilologus* 78.165–70.

Laborde, E. D. 1925. The site of the Battle of Maldon. *English Historical Review* 40.161–73.

Langefeld, Brigitte. 1996. *Regula canonicorum* or *Regula monasterialis vitae?* The rule of Chrodegang and Archbishop Wulfred's reforms at Canterbury. *ASE* 25.21–36.

Langenfelt, Gösta. 1959. Studies on *Widsith*. *Namn och Bygd* 47.70–111.

Lapidge, Michael. 1975. Some remnants of Bede's lost *Liber epigrammatum*. *English Historical Review* 90.798–820. Reprinted 1996 in Michael Lapidge, *Anglo-Latin Literature 600–899*, 357–79. London: Hambledon.

—— 1979. Byrhtferth and the *Vita S. Ecgwini*. *MS* 41.331–53. Reprinted 1993 in Michael Lapidge, *Anglo-Latin Literature 900–1066*, 293–315. London: Hambledon.

—— 1981. Byrhtferth of Ramsey and the early sections of the *Historia regum* attributed to Symeon of Durham. *ASE* 10.97–122. Reprinted 1993 in Michael Lapidge, *Anglo-Latin Literature 900–1066*, 317–42. London: Hambledon.

—— 1982. *Beowulf,* Aldhelm, the *Liber monstrorum* and Wessex. *Studi medievali.* 3rd ser. 23.151–92. Reprinted 1996 in Michael Lapidge, *Anglo-Latin Literature 600–899,* 271–311. London: Hambledon.

—— 1984. A tenth-century metrical calendar from Ramsey. *Revue Bénédictine* 94.326–69. Reprinted 1993 in Michael Lapidge, *Anglo-Latin Literature 900–1066,* 343–86. London: Hambledon.

—— 1986a. The Anglo-Latin background. In *A New Critical History of OE Literature,* ed. Stanley B. Greenfield and Daniel G. Calder, 5–37. New York: New York University Press.

—— 1986b. The school of Theodore and Hadrian. *ASE* 15.45–72. Reprinted 1996 in Michael Lapidge, *Anglo-Latin Literature 600–899,* 141–68. London: Hambledon.

—— 1988. A Frankish scholar in tenth-century England: Frithegod of Canterbury/Fredegaud of Brioude. *ASE* 17.45–65. Reprinted 1993 in Michael Lapidge, *Anglo-Latin Literature 900–1066,* 157–81. London: Hambledon.

—— 1989. Bede's metrical *Vita S. Cuthberti.* In *St. Cuthbert, His Cult and His Community to AD 1200,* ed. Gerald Bonner et al., 77–93. Woodbridge, Suffolk: Boydell. Reprinted 1996 in Michael Lapidge, *Anglo-Latin Literature 600–899,* 339–55. London: Hambledon.

—— 1990. Aediluulf and the school of York. In *Lateinische Kultur im VIII. Jahrhundert: Traube-Gedenkschrift,* ed. A. Lehner and W. Berschin, 161–78. St. Ottilien: EOS. Reprinted 1996 in Michael Lapidge, *Anglo-Latin Literature 600–899,* 381–98. London: Hambledon.

—— 1991a. The *Life of St Oswald.* In *The Battle of Maldon, AD 991,* ed. D. G. Scragg, 51–8. Oxford: Blackwell.

—— 1991b. The saintly life in A-S England. In *The Cambridge Companion to OE Literature,* ed. Malcolm Godden and Michael Lapidge, 243–63. Cambridge: Cambridge University Press.

—— 1991c. Schools, learning and literature in tenth-century England. *Settimane di studio del Centro italiano di Studi sull'alto medioevo* 38.951–98. Reprinted 1996 in Michael Lapidge, *Anglo-Latin Literature 600–899,* 1–48. London: Hambledon.

—— 1993. *Anglo-Latin Literature 900–1066.* London: Hambledon.

—— ed. 1994a. *Bede and His World: The Jarrow Lectures.* 2 vols. Aldershot, Hants: Variorum.

—— 1994b. Bede the poet. *The Jarrow Lecture 1993.* Jarrow: St. Paul's Church. Reprinted 1996 in Michael Lapidge, *Anglo-Latin Literature 600–899,* 313–38. London: Hambledon.

—— 1994c. On the emendation of OE texts. In *The Editing of OE: Papers from the 1990 Manchester Conference,* ed. D. G. Scragg and Paul E. Szarmach, 53–67. Cambridge: D. S. Brewer.

—— 1994d. Stoic cosmology and the source of the first OE riddle. *Anglia* 112.1–25.

—— 1995a. The career of Archbishop Theodore. In *Archbishop Theodore: Commemorative Studies on His Life and Influence*, ed. Michael Lapidge, 1–29. CSASE 11. Cambridge: Cambridge University Press.

—— 1995b. Theodore and Anglo-Latin octosyllabic verse. In *Archbishop Theodore: Commemorative Studies on His Life and Influence*, ed. Michael Lapidge, 260–80. CSASE 11. Cambridge: Cambridge University Press. Reprinted 1996 in Michael Lapidge, *Anglo-Latin Literature 600–899*, 225–45. London: Hambledon.

—— 1996a. Anglo-Latin literature. In Michael Lapidge, *Anglo-Latin Literature 600–899*, 1–35. London: Hambledon. (Revision of "The Anglo-Latin background," in *A New Critical History of OE Literature*, ed. Stanley B. Greenfield and Daniel G. Calder, 5–37. New York: New York University Press, 1986.)

—— 1996b *Anglo-Latin Literature 600–899*. London: Hambledon.

—— 1996c. Artistic and literary patronage in A-S England. In Michael Lapidge, *Anglo-Latin Literature 600–899*, 37–91. London: Hambledon. (Originally appeared in *Settimane di studio del Centro italiano di Studi sull'alto medioevo* 39 (1992), 137–91.)

—— 1996d. Latin learning in ninth-century England. In Michael Lapidge, *Anglo-Latin Literature 600–899*, 409–54. London: Hambledon.

—— 1998. Byrhtferth at work. In *Words and Works: Studies in Medieval English Language and Literature in Honour of Fred C. Robinson*, ed. Peter S. Baker and Nicholas Howe, 25–43. Toronto: University of Toronto Press.

—— 2000. The archetype of *Beowulf*. *ASE* 29.5–41.

—— Forthcoming. *The Cult of St. Swithun*.

Lapidge, Michael, and Michael Herren, transs. 1979. *Aldhelm: The Prose Works*. Cambridge: D. S. Brewer.

Lapidge, Michael, and R. C. Love. 2001. England and Wales (600–1550). In *Hagiographies: histoire internationale de la literature hagiographique latine et vernaculaire en Occident des origins à 1550*, 3 vols, ed. Guy Philippart, 3.1–120. Turnhout: Brepols, 1994–2001.

Lapidge, Michael, and James L. Rosier, transs. 1985. *Aldhelm: The Poetic Works*. Cambridge: D. S. Brewer.

Lapidge, Michael, and Michael Winterbottom, eds. and transs. 1991. *Wulfstan of Winchester, The Life of St. Æthelwold*. Oxford: Clarendon.

Lapidge, Michael, et al., eds. 1999. *The Blackwell Encyclopedia of A-S England*. Oxford: Blackwell.

Larrington, Carolyne. 1993. *A Store of Common Sense: Gnomic Theme and Style in Old Icelandic and OE Wisdom Poetry*. Oxford: Clarendon.

Laszlo, Renate. 1996. *Das mystische Weinfass: Ein altenglisches Rätsel des Vercellibuches*. Marburg: Tectum.

Law, Vivien. 1982. *The Insular Latin Grammarians*. Woodbridge, Suffolk: Boydell.

Lawrence, W. W. 1902a. The first riddle of Cynewulf. *PMLA* 17.247–61.

—— 1902b. *The Wanderer* and *The Seafarer. JEGP* 4.460–80.

—— 1930. *"Beowulf" and Epic Tradition.* Cambridge, Mass.: Harvard University Press.

Lee, Alvin A. 1997. Symbolism and allegory. In *A "Beowulf" Handbook*, ed. Robert E. Bjork and John D. Niles, 233–54. Lincoln: University of Nebraska Press.

Lees, Clare A. 1994. Men and *Beowulf.* In *Medieval Masculinities: Regarding Men in the Middle Ages*, ed. Clare A. Lees, 129–48. Minneapolis: University of Minnesota Press.

—— 1997. At a crossroads: OE and feminist criticism. In *Reading OE Texts*, ed. Katherine O'Brien O'Keeffe, 146–69. Cambridge: Cambridge University Press.

—— 1999. *Tradition and Belief: Religious Writing in Late A-S England.* Minneapolis: University of Minnesota Press.

Lees, Clare A., and Gillian R. Overing. 2001. *Double Agents: Women and Clerical Culture in A-S England.* Philadelphia: University of Pennsylvania Press.

Lehmann, Ruth P. M. 1969. The metrics and structure of *Wulf and Eadwacer. PQ* 48.151–65.

Leinbaugh, T. H. 1994. Ælfric's *Lives of Saints* I and the Boulogne Sermon: Editorial, authorial, and textual problems. In *The Editing of OE: Papers from the 1990 Manchester Conference*, ed. D. G. Scragg and Paul E. Szarmach, 191–211. Cambridge: D. S. Brewer.

Leinenweber, John, trans. 1998. *Pastoral Practice: Books 3 and 4 of the Regula pastoralis, by Gregory the Great.* Harrisburg, Pa.: Trinity.

Lench, Elinor. 1970. *The Wife's Lament:* A poem of the living dead. *Comitatus* 1.3–23.

Lendinara, Patrizia. 1991. The world of A-S learning. In *The Cambridge Companion to OE Literature*, ed. Malcolm Godden and Michael Lapidge, 264–81. Cambridge: Cambridge University Press.

—— 1997. The Kentish laws. In *The Anglo-Saxons, from the Migration Period to the Eighth Century*, ed. J. Hines, 211–43. Woodbridge, Suffolk: Boydell.

—— 1999. *A-S Glosses and Glossaries.* Aldershot, Hampshire: Ashgate.

Lenker, Ursula. 1999. The *West Saxon Gospels* and the gospel-lectionary in A-S England: Manuscript evidence and liturgical practice. *ASE* 28.141–74.

Leo, Friedrich, ed. 1881. *Venanti Fortunati opera poetica.* MGH, Auctores Antiquissimi 4.1. Berlin: Weidmann.

Lerer, Seth. 1991. *Literacy and Power in A-S Literature.* Lincoln: University of Nebraska Press.

—— 1997. *Beowulf* and contemporary critical theory. In *A "Beowulf" Handbook*, ed. Robert E. Bjork and John D. Niles, 325–39. Lincoln: University of Nebraska Press.

—— 1999. OE and its afterlife. In *The Cambridge History of Medieval English*

Literature, ed. David Wallace, 7–34. Cambridge: Cambridge University Press.

Leslie, R. F. 1983. The meaning and structure of *The Seafarer*. In *The OE Elegies: New Essays in Criticism*, ed. M. Green, 96–122. Rutherford, N.J.: Fairleigh Dickinson University Press.

—— ed. 1985. *The Wanderer*. Rev. ed. Exeter: University of Exeter Press.

—— ed. 1988. *Three OE Elegies: The Wife's Lament, The Husband's Message, The Ruin*. Rev. ed. Exeter: University of Exeter Press.

Letson, D. R. 1979. The OE *Physiologus* and the homiletic tradition. *Florilegium* 1.15–41.96–122.

—— 1980. The homiletic nature of Cynewulf's ascension poem. *Florilegium* 2.192–216.

Lever, Julius W. 1947. *Paradise Lost* and the A-S tradition. *RES* 23.97–106.

Levison, Wilhelm. 1946. *England and the Continent in the Eighth Century*. Oxford: Clarendon.

Leyerle, John. 1965. Beowulf the hero and the king. *MÆ* 34.89–102.

—— 1967. The interlace structure of *Beowulf*. *University of Toronto Quarterly* 37.1–17. Reprinted 1991 in *Interpretations of "Beowulf": A Critical Anthology*, ed. R. D. Fulk, 146–67, Bloomington: Indiana University Press; and 2002 in *Beowulf: A Verse Translation*, trans. Seamus Heany, ed. Daniel Donoghue, 130–52, New York: W. W. Norton.

Liberman, Anatoly. 1986. Beowulf-Grettir. In *Germanic Dialects: Linguistic and Philological Investigations*, ed. Bela Brogyanyi and Thomas Krömmelbein, 353–401. Amsterdam: Benjamins.

Liebermann, Felix, ed. 1903–16. *Die Gesetze der Angelsachsen*. 3 vols. Halle: M. Niemeyer.

Liggins, Elizabeth M. 1970. The authorship of the OE Orosius. *Anglia* 88.289–322.

Lindsay, W. M., ed. 1921. *The Corpus Glossary*. Cambridge: Cambridge University Press.

Lindström, Bengt. 1988. The OE translation of Alcuin's *Liber de virtutibus et vitiis*. *SN* 60.23–35.

Linsell, Tony. 2001. *Our Englishness*. Hockwold-cum-Wilton, Norfolk: Anglo-Saxon Books.

Lionarons, Joyce Tally. 1998. Cultural syncretism and the construction of gender in Cynewulf's *Elene*. *Exemplaria* 10.51–68.

Liuzza, Roy M. 1990. The OE *Christ* and *Guthlac*: Texts, manuscripts, and critics. *RES* n.s. 41.1–11.

—— 1995. On the dating of *Beowulf*. In *Beowulf: Basic Readings*, ed. Peter S. Baker, 281–302. New York: Garland (reprinted 2000 under the title *The "Beowulf" Reader*).

—— 1994–2000. *The OE Version of the Gospels*. 2 vols. EETS o.s. 304, 314. Oxford: Oxford University Press.

Locherbie-Cameron, Margaret A. L. 1991. Byrhtnoth and his family. In *The*

Battle of Maldon, AD 991, ed. D. G. Scragg, 253–62. Oxford: Blackwell.

Lochrie, Karma. 1993. Gender, sexual violence, and the politics of war in the OE "Judith." In *Class and Gender in Early English Literature: Intersections*, ed. Britton J. Harwood and Gillian R. Overing, 1–20. Bloomington: Indiana University Press.

Loewe, Raphael. 1969. The medieval history of the Latin vulgate. In *The Cambridge History of the Bible, II: The West from the Fathers to the Reformation*, ed. G. Lampe, 102–54. Cambridge: Cambridge University Press.

Lord, Albert Bates. 1960. *The Singer of Tales*. Cambridge, Mass.: Harvard University Press.

—— 1993. Cædmon revisited. In *Heroic Poetry in the A-S Period: Studies in Honor of Jess B. Bessinger, Jr.*, ed. Helen Damico and John Leyerle, 121–37. Studies in Medieval Culture 32. Kalamazoo: Medieval Institute Pubns.

Lowe, Kathryn A. 1998a. The nature and effect of the A-S vernacular will. *Journal of Legal History* 19.23–61.

—— 1998b. Lay literacy in A-S England and the development of the chirograph. In *A-S Manuscripts and Their Heritage*, ed. Phillip Pulsiano and Elaine M. Treharne, 161–204. Aldershot, Hants: Ashgate.

Loyn, H. R. 1984. *The Governance of A-S England, 500–1087*. Stanford: Stanford University Press.

Lucas, Peter J. 1979. On the incomplete ending of *Daniel* and the addition of *Christ and Satan* to MS. Junius 11. *Anglia* 97.46–59.

—— 1990. The place of *Judith* in the *Beowulf*-Manuscript. *RES* n.s. 41.463–78.

—— 1992. Loyalty and obedience in the OE *Genesis* and the interpolation of *Genesis B* into *Genesis A*. *Neophilologus* 76.121–35.

—— ed. 1994. *Exodus*. Rev. ed. Exeter: University of Exeter Press.

—— ed. 2000. *Franciscus Junius, Cædmonis Monachi Paraphrasis Poetica Genesios ac Præcipuarum Sacræ Paginæ Historiarum*. Amsterdam and Atlanta: Rodopi.

Lumiansky, Robert M. 1949. The contexts of the OE "ealuscerwen" and "meoduscerwen." *JEGP* 48.116–26.

—— 1950. The dramatic structure of the OE *Wanderer*. *Neophilologus* 34.104–12.

Lund, Niels, ed., and Christine E. Fell, trans. 1984. *Two Voyagers at the Court of King Alfred*. York: W. Sessions.

Lutterkort, Karl. 1996. Beda Hagiographicus: Meaning and function of miracle stories in the *Vita Cuthberti* and the *Historia ecclesiastica*. In *Beda Venerabilis*, ed. L. A. J. R. Houwen and Alasdair MacDonald, 81–106. Gronigen: E. Forsten.

Lutz, Angelika. 1981. *Die Version G der Angelsächsischen Chronik: Rekonstruktion und Edition*. Munich: W. Fink.

—— 2000. Æthelweard's *Chronicon* and OE poetry. *ASE* 29.177–214.

Luyster, Robert. 1998. *The Wife's Lament* in the context of Scandinavian myth and ritual. *PQ* 77.243–70.

MacKay, T. W. 1976. Bede's hagiographical method: His knowledge and use of Paulinus of Nola. In *Famulus Christi: Essays in Commemoration of the Thirteenth Centenary of the Birth of the Venerable Bede*, ed. Gerald Bonner, 77–92. London: Society for Promotion of Christian Knowledge.

MacLean, George E., ed. 1883–4. Ælfric's version of *Alcuini Interrogationes Sigeuulfi in Genesin*. *Anglia* 6.425–73, 7.1–59.

Macrae-Gibson, O. D. 1970. How historical is *The Battle of Maldon*? *MÆ* 39.89–105.

—— ed. and trans. 1983. *The OE Riming Poem*. Corrected reprint 1987. Cambridge: D. S. Brewer.

Magennis, Hugh, ed. 1994. *The Anonymous OE Legend of the Seven Sleepers*. Durham Medieval Texts 7. New Elvet, Durham: Department of English Studies.

—— 1995. Contrasting narrative emphases in the OE poem *Judith* and Ælfric's paraphrase of the Book of Judith. *NM* 96.61–6.

—— 1996. St. Mary of Egypt and Ælfric: Unlikely bedfellows in Cotton Junius E. vii? In *The Legend of Mary of Egypt*, ed. Erich Poppe and Bianca Ross, 99–112. Blackrock, Co. Dublin: Four Courts.

Magoun, Francis P., Jr. 1953. The oral-formulaic character of A-S narrative poetry. *Speculum* 28.446–67. Reprinted in *An Anthology of "Beowulf" Criticism*, ed. Lewis E. Nicholson, 189–221, Notre Dame: University of Notre Dame Press; 1968 in *The "Beowulf" Poet: A Collection of Critical Essays*, ed. Donald K. Fry, 83–113, Englewood Cliffs, N.J.: Prentice-Hall; 1968 in *Essential Articles for the Study of OE Poetry*, ed. J. B. Bessinger, Jr., and Stanley J. Kahrl, 319–51, Hamden, Conn.: Archon; and 1991 in *Interpretations of "Beowulf": A Critical Anthology*, ed. R. D. Fulk, 45–65, Bloomington: Indiana University Press.

—— 1955. Bede's story of Cædman: The case history of an A-S oral singer. *Speculum* 30.49–63.

—— 1958. *Béowulf A'*: A folk-variant. *Arv: Journal of Scandinavian Folklore* 14.95–101.

—— 1963. *Béowulf B*: A folk-poem on Beowulf's death. In *Early English and Norse Studies presented to Hugh Smith in Honour of His Sixtieth Birthday*, ed. Arthur Brown and Peter Foote, 127–40. London: Methuen.

Malone, Kemp. 1931. Ealhhild. *Anglia* 55.266–72.

—— ed. 1933. *Deor*. London: Methuen. Rev. ed. 1977, Exeter: University of Exeter Press.

—— 1939. Becca and Seafola. *Englische Studien* 73.180–4. Reprinted in Kemp Malone, *Studies in Heroic Legend and in Current Speech*, ed. Stefán Einarsson and Norman E. Eliason, 164–7. Copenhagen: Rosenkilde & Bagger.

—— 1941. Hygd. *MLN* 56.356–8.

—— ed. 1951. *The Thorkelin Transcripts of "Beowulf."* EEMF 1. Copenhagen: Rosenkilde & Bagger.

—— 1961. Cædmon and English poetry. *MLN* 76.193–5.

—— 1962a. Two English *Frauenlieder*. *Comparative Literature* 14.106–17. Reprinted in *Studies in OE Literature in Honor of Arthur G. Brodeur*, ed. Stanley B. Greenfield, 106–117. Eugene: University of Oregon Books.

—— ed. 1962b. *Widsith*. 2nd ed. Copenhagen: Rosenkilde & Bagger.

—— ed. 1963. *The Nowell Codex (British Museum Cotton Vitellius A. xv, Second MS)*. EEMF 12. Copenhagen: Rosenkilde & Bagger.

—— 1969. The OE calendar poem. In *Studies in Language, Literature, and Culture of the Middle Ages and Later*, ed. E. Bagby Atwood and Archibald A. Hill, 193–9. Austin: University of Texas Press.

Mandel, Jerome. 1971. Contrast in OE poetry. *Chaucer Review* 6.1–13.

Marchand, James W. 1991. The *Partridge*? An OE multiquote. *Neophilologus* 75.603–11.

Marquardt, Hertha. 1938. *Die altenglische Kenningar*. Halle: M. Niemeyer.

Marsden, Richard. 1991. Ælfric as translator: The OE prose Genesis. *Anglia* 109.319–58.

—— 1994. Old Latin intervention in the OE *Hexateuch*. *ASE* 23.229–64.

—— 1995. *The Text of the Old Testament in A-S England*. CSASE 15. Cambridge: Cambridge University Press.

—— 2000. Translation by committee? The "anonymous" text of the OE Hexateuch. In *The OE Hexateuch: Aspects and Approaches*, ed. Rebecca Barnhouse and Benjamin C. Withers, 41–89. Kalamazoo: Medieval Institute Pubns.

Martin, Lawrence T. 1989. The two worlds in Bede's homilies. In *De Ore Domini: Preacher and Word in the Middle Ages*, ed. T. Amos et al., 27–40. Studies in Medieval Culture 27. Kalamazoo: Medieval Institute Pubns.

—— 1990. Augustine's influence on Bede's *Homeliae euangelii*. In *Collectanea Augustiniana: Augustine: "Second Founder of the Faith,"* ed. Joseph C. Schnaubelt and Frederick Van Fleteren, 357–69. New York: P. Lang.

Martin, Lawrence T., and David Hurst, transs. 1991. *Homilies on the Gospels/ Bede the Venerable*. 2 vols. Kalamazoo: Cistercian Pubns.

Mayr-Harting, Henry. 1991. *The Coming of Christianity to A-S England*. 3rd ed. London: B. Batsford.

McClure, Judith, and Roger Collins, transs. 1994. *Bede: The Ecclesiastical History of the English People, The Greater Chronicle, Bede's Letter to Egbert*. Oxford: Oxford University Press.

McCulloh, John M. 2000. Did Cynewulf use a martyrology? Reconsidering the sources of *The Fates of the Apostles*. *ASE* 29.67–83.

McEnerney, J. I. 1988. The dream of Aedilvulf. *Mitellateinisches Jahrbuch* 23.28–36.

McEntire, Sandra. 1990. The monastic context of OE. *Precepts*. *NM* 91.243–9.

McGillivray, Murray. 1989. The Exeter Book *Maxims I B:* An A-S woman's view of marriage. *English Studies in Canada* 15.383–97.

McGurk, Patrick, D. N. Dumville, and M. R. Godden, eds. 1983. *An Eleventh-Century A-S Illustrated Miscellany (British Library Cotton Tiberius B.V Part I.)* EEMF 21. Copenhagen: Rosenkilde & Bagger.

McIntosh, Angus. 1949. Wulfstan's prose. *PBA* 35.109–42.

McKill, Larry N. 1995–6. Patterns of the fall: Adam and Eve in the OE *Genesis A. Florilegium* 14.25–41.

McNamee, Maurice B. 1960. *Beowulf*— An allegory of salvation? *JEGP* 59.190–207. Reprinted 1963 in *An Anthology of "Beowulf" Criticism*, ed. Lewis E. Nicholson, 331–52, Notre Dame: University of Notre Dame Press; and 1991 in *Interpretations of "Beowulf": A Critical Anthology*, ed. R. D. Fulk, 88–102, Bloomington: Indiana University Press.

McNeill, John T., and Helena M. Gamer. 1938. *Medieval Handbooks of Penance: A Translation of the Principal "libri poenitentiales" and Selections from Related Documents.* New York: Columbia University Press.

Meaney, Audrey L. 1984. Variant versions of OE medical remedies and the compilation of *Bald's Leechbook. ASE* 13.235–68.

Meens, Rob. 1994. A background to Augustine's mission to A-S England. *ASE* 23.5–17.

—— 1998a. The frequency and nature of early medieval penance. In *Handling Sin: Confession in the Middle Ages*, ed. Peter Biller and A. J. Minnis, 35–61. York: York Medieval Press.

—— 1998b. Magic and the early medieval world view. In *The Community, the Family and the Saint: Patterns of Power in Early Medieval Europe*, ed. Joyce Hill and Mary Swan, 285–95. International Medieval Research 4. Turnhout: Brepols.

Mees, Bernard. 2000. Völkische Altnordistik: The politics of Nordic studies in the German-speaking countries, 1926–45. Paper presented at the 11th International Saga Conference, University of Sydney, 2000. Proceedings on the Web at <http://www.arts.usyd.edu.au/Arts/departs/medieval/saga/pdf/>.

Meindl, Robert J. 1964. The artistic unity of *Widsith. Xavier University Studies* 3.19–28.

Menner, Robert J., ed. 1941. *The Poetical Dialogues of Solomon and Saturn.* New York: Modern Language Assn.; London: Oxford University Press.

—— 1949. The Anglian vocabulary of the Blickling Homilies. In *Philologica: The Malone Anniversary Studies*, ed. Thomas Austin Kirby and Henry Bosley Woolf, 56–64. Baltimore: Johns Hopkins Press.

Menzer, Melinda. 1999. Ælfric's *Grammar:* Solving the problem of the English-language text. *Neophilologus* 83.637–52.

—— 2000. The preface as admonition: Ælfric's Preface to Genesis. In *The OE Hexateuch: Aspects and Approaches*, ed. Rebecca Barnhouse and Benjamin

C. Withers, 15–39. Kalamazoo: Medieval Institute Pubns.

Migne, J.-P., ed. 1879–1974. *Patrologia Latina Cursus Completus*. Paris: Garnier.

Milfull, Inge B. 1996. *The Hymns of the A-S Church*. CSASE 17. Cambridge: Cambridge University Press.

Miller, Thomas, ed. 1890–8. *The OE Version of Bede's Ecclesiastical History of the English People*. EETS o.s. 95, 96, 110, and 111. London: N. Trübner.

Miller, William Ian. 1983. Choosing the avenger: Some aspects of the bloodfeud in medieval Iceland and England. *Law and History Review* 1.159–204.

Minkoff, Harvey. 1976. Some stylistic consequences of Ælfric's theory of translation. *SP* 73.29–41.

Mintz, Susannah B. 1997. Words devilish and divine: Eve as speaker in *Genesis B*. *Neophilologus* 81.609–23.

Mitchell, Bruce. 1972. The narrator of the *Wife's Lament*: Some syntactical problems reconsidered. *NM* 73.222–34. Reprinted 1988 in Bruce Mitchell, *On Old English*, 134–45. Oxford: Blackwell.

Mitchell, Sarah. 2000. Kings, constitution and crisis: "Robert of Gloucester" and the A-S remedy. In *Literary Appropriations of the Anglo-Saxons from the Thirteenth to the Twentieth Century*, ed. D. G. Scragg and Carole Weinberg, 39–56. CSASE 29. Cambridge: Cambridge University Press.

Moffat, Douglas. 1983. The MS transmission of the OE *Soul and Body*. *MÆ* 52.300–2.

—— ed. 1987. *The Soul's Address to the Body: The Worcester Fragments*. East Lansing: Colleagues.

—— ed. and trans. 1990. *The OE "Soul and Body."* Woodbridge, Suffolk: D. S. Brewer.

—— 1992. A-S Scribes and OE verse. *Speculum* 67.805–27.

Mohr, Wolfgang. 1939-40. Wortschatz und Motive der jüngeren Eddalieder mit südgermanischem Stoff. *ZfdA* 76.149–217.

Mone, Franz J., ed. 1830. *Quellen und Forschungen zur Geschichte der teutschen Literatur und Sprache*. Aachen and Leipzig: J. Mayer.

Mores, Edward Rowe. 1778. *A Dissertation upon English Typographical Founders and Founderies*. Ed. Harry Carter and Christopher Ricks. London: Oxford University Press, 1961.

Morey, James H. 1990. Adam and Judas in the OE *Christ and Satan*. *SP* 87.397–409.

Morrell, Minnie Cate. 1965. *A Manual of OE Biblical Materials*. Knoxville: University of Tennessee Press.

Morris, R., ed. and trans. 1874–80. *The Blickling Homilies*. EETS o.s. 58, 63, and 73. London: N. Trübner. Reprinted 1967 as one vol. London: Oxford University Press.

Morrish (Tunberg), Jennifer. 1986. King Alfred's letter as a source on learning in England. In *Studies in Earlier OE Prose*, ed. Paul E. Szarmach, 87–107.

Albany: State University of New York Press.

Muir, Bernard J., ed. 2000. *The Exeter Anthology of OE Poetry*. Rev. ed. 2 vols. Exeter: University of Exeter Press.

Müllenhoff, Karl. 1869. Die innere Geschichte des Beowulfs. *ZfdA* 14.193–244. (Incorporated into Karl Müllenhoff, *Beovulf: Untersuchungen über das angelsächsische Epos und die älteste Geschichte der germanischen Seevolker*, 110–65. Berlin: Weidmann, 1889.)

—— 1889. *Beovulf: Untersuchungen über das angelsächsische Epos und die älteste Geschichte der germanischen Seevolker*. Berlin: Weidmann.

Munske, Horst Haider. 1973. *Der germanische Rechtswortschatz im Bereich der Missetaten*. Berlin: de Gruyter.

Murphy, Michael. 1982. Antiquary to academic: The progress of A-S scholarship. In *A-S Scholarship: The First Three Centuries*, ed. Carl T. Berkhout and Milton McC. Gatch, 1–17. Boston: G. K. Hall.

Mynors, R. A. B., R. M. Thomson, and M. Winterbottom, eds. and transs. 1998. *William of Malmesbury, Gesta regum Anglorum*. 2 vols. Oxford: Clarendon.

Napier, Arthur S., ed. 1883. *Wulfstan: Sammlung der ihm zugeschriebenen Homilien nebst Untersuchungen über ihre Echtheit*. Berlin: Weidmann.

—— 1887. Bruchstück einer altenglischen Boetiushandschrift. *ZfdA* 31.52–4.

—— ed. 1894. *History of the Holy Rood-Tree*. EETS o.s. 103. London: N. Trübner.

—— ed. 1908. An OE vision of Leofric, Earl of Mercia. *Transactions of the Philological Society* 1907–10.180–8.

—— ed. 1916. *The OE Version of the Enlarged Rule of Chrodegang; An OE Version of the Capitula of Theodulf; An Interlinear OE Rendering of the Epitome of Benedict of Aniane*. EETS o.s. 150. London: Kegan Paul, Trench, Trübner.

Near, Michael. 1993. Anticipating alienation: *Beowulf* and the intrusion of literacy. *PMLA* 108.320–2.

Neckel, Gustav, and Hans Kuhn, eds. 1983. *Edda: Die Lieder des Codex regius, nebst verwandten Denkmälern*. 5th ed. Heidelberg: M. Niemeyer.

Nelson, Janet. 1986. Wealth and wisdom: The politics of Alfred the Great. In *Kings and Kingship*, ed. Joel T. Rosenthal, 31–52. Binghamton: State University of New York Press.

—— 1993. The political ideas of Alfred of Wessex. In *Kings and Kingship in Medieval Europe*, ed. Anne J. Duggan, 125–58. London: King's College London Centre for Late Antique and Medieval Studies.

Nelson, Marie. 1990. King Solomon's magic: The power of a written text. *Oral Tradition* 5.20–36.

Neuman de Vegvar, Carol. 1996. Saints and companions to saints: A-S royal women in context. In *Holy Men and Holy Women: OE Prose Saints' Lives and Their Contexts*, ed. Paul E. Szarmach, 51–93. Albany: State University of

New York Press.

Neville, Jennifer. 1999. *Representations of the Natural World in OE Poetry.* CSASE 27. Cambridge: Cambridge University Press.

Nicholls, Alex. 1994. The corpus of prose saints' lives and hagiographic pieces in OE and its manuscript distribution. *Reading Medieval Studies* 20.51–87.

Nicholson Lewis E., ed. 1963. *An Anthology of "Beowulf" Criticism.* Notre Dame: University of Notre Dame Press.

—— ed. 1991. *The Vercelli Book Homilies: Translations from the A-S.* Lanham, Md.: University Press of America.

Niles, John D. 1983. *Beowulf: The Poem and Its Tradition.* Cambridge: Harvard University Press.

—— 1991a. Pagan survivals and popular belief. In *The Cambridge Companion to OE Literature*, ed. Malcolm Godden and Michael Lapidge, 126–41. Cambridge: Cambridge University Press.

—— ed. 1991b. Part I: History into literature. *Mediaevalia* 17.1–176.

—— 1999a. *Homo Narrans: The Poetics and Anthropology of Oral Literature.* Philadelphia: University of Pennsylvania Press.

—— 1999b. *Widsith* and the anthropology of the past. *PQ* 78.171–213.

Norman, F., ed. 1949. *Waldere.* London: Methuen.

Norman, Henry W., ed. 1849. *The A-S Version of the Hexameron of St. Basil.* 2nd ed. London: J. Smith.

North, Richard. 1990. Tribal loyalties in the *Finnsburh Fragment* and episode. *LSE* n.s. 21.13–43.

—— 1994. Metre and meaning in *Wulf and Eadwacer:* Signy reconsidered. In *Loyal Letters: Studies on Mediaeval Alliterative Poetry and Prose*, ed. L. A. J. R. Houwen and A. A. MacDonald, 29–54. Groningen: Forsten.

O'Brien O'Keeffe, Katherine. 1989. Review of Jane Roberts, *Guthlac A*: Sources and source hunting (*Medieval English Studies Presented to George Kane*, ed. Edward D. Kennedy et al., 1–18, Woodbridge, Suffolk: Boydell, 1988), *OEN* 23.1.59–60.

—— 1990. *Visible Song: Transitional Literacy in OE Verse.* CSASE 4. Cambridge: Cambridge University Press.

—— 1991a. The geographic list of *Solomon and Saturn II. ASE* 20.123–41.

—— 1991b. Heroic values and Christian ethics. In *The Cambridge Companion to OE Literature*, ed. Malcolm Godden and Michael Lapidge, 107–25. Cambridge: Cambridge University Press.

—— 1994. Source, method, theory, practice: On reading two OE verse texts. *Bulletin of the John Rylands University Library of Manchester* 76.1.51–73.

—— 1997. Diction, variation, the formula. In *A "Beowulf" Handbook*, ed. Robert E. Bjork and John D. Niles, 85–104. Lincoln: University of Nebraska Press.

Obst, Wolfgang. 1987. *Der Rhythmus des "Beowulf": Eine Akzent- und Takttheorie.* Anglistische Forschungen 187. Heidelberg: C. Winter.

Obst, Wolfgang, and Florian Schleburg, eds. 1998. *Lieder aus König Alfreds Trostbuch: Die Stabreimverse der altenglischen Boethius-Übertragung.* Anglistische Forschungen 259. Heidelberg: Winter.

Ó Carragáin, Éamonn. 1981. How did the Vercelli collector interpret "The Dream of the Rood"? In *Studies in English Language and Early Literature in Honour of Paul Cristophersen*, ed. P. M. Tilling, 63–104. [Coleraine]: New University of Ulster.

Odenstedt, Bengt. 1994. Who was Wulfstan? A new theory of "Ohthere's and Wulfstan's voyages." *SN* 66.147–57.

Oergel, Maike. 1998. The redeeming Teuton: Nineteenth-century notions of the "Germanic" in England and Germany. In *Imagining Nations*, ed. Geoffrey Cubitt, 75–91. Manchester: Manchester University Press.

Ohlgren, Thomas H. 1992. *A-S Textual Illustration.* Kalamazoo: Medieval Institute Pubns.

Okasha, Elisabeth. 1971. *Hand-List of A-S Non-Runic Inscriptions.* Cambridge: Cambridge University Press. Supplements in *ASE* 11 (1983), 83–118, and 21 (1992), 37–85.

Oliver, Lisi. 1995. The language of the early English laws. Doctoral thesis, Harvard University.

Olsan, Lea. 1992. Latin charms of medieval England: Verbal healing in a Christian oral tradition. *Oral Tradition* 7.116–42.

Olsen, Alexandra Hennessey. 1986–8. Oral-formulaic research in OE studies. *Oral Tradition* 1.548–606, 3.138–90.

—— 1990. Cynewulf's autonomous women: A reconsideration of Elene and Juliana. In *New Readings on Women in OE Literature*, ed. Helen Damico and Alexandra Hennessey Olsen, 222–32. Bloomington: Indiana University Press.

—— 1993. Formulaic tradition and the Latin *Waltharius*. In *Heroic Poetry in the A-S Period: Studies in Honor of Jess B. Bessinger, Jr.*, ed. Helen Damico and John Leyerle, 265–82. Kalamazoo: Medieval Institute Pubns.

—— 1994. OE women, OE men: A reconsideration of "minor" characters. In *OE Shorter Poems: Basic Readings*, ed. Katherine O'Brien O'Keeffe, 65–83. New York: Garland.

—— 1997. Gender roles. In *A "Beowulf" Handbook*, ed. Robert E. Bjork and John D. Niles, 311–24. Lincoln: University of Nebraska Press.

O'Neill, Patrick P. 1981. The OE introductions to the prose psalms of the Paris Psalter: Sources, structure, and composition. In *Eight A-S Studies*, ed. Joseph S. Wittig. *SP* 78: 20–38.

—— 1997. On the date, provenance, and relationship of the "Solomon and Saturn" dialogues. *ASE* 26.139–68.

—— 2001. *King Alfred's OE Prose Translation of the First Fifty Psalms.* Cambridge, Mass.: Medieval Academy of America.

Opland, Jeff. 1980. *A-S Oral Poetry: A Study of the Traditions.* New Haven:

Yale University Press.

Orchard, Andy P. McD. 1992. Crying wolf: Oral style and the *Sermones Lupi*. *ASE* 21.239–64.

—— 1994a. Conspicuous heroism: Abraham, Prudentius, and the OE Verse *Genesis*. In *Heroes and Heroines in Medieval English Literature: A Festschift Presented to André Crépin*, ed. Leo Carruthers, 45–58. Woodbridge, Suffolk: D. S. Brewer.

—— 1994b. *The Poetic Art of Aldhelm*. CSASE 8. Cambridge: Cambridge University Press.

—— 1995. *Pride and Prodigies: Studies in the Monsters of the "Beowulf"-Manuscript*. Cambridge: D. S. Brewer.

—— 1996. Poetic inspiration and prosaic translation: The making of *Cædmon's Hymn*. In *Studies in English Language and Literature: "Doubt Wisely": Papers in Honour of E. G. Stanley*, ed. M. J. Toswell and E. M. Tyler, 402–22. London: Routledge.

—— 1997. Oral tradition. In *Reading OE Texts*, ed. Katherine O'Brien O'Keeffe, 101–23. Cambridge: Cambridge University Press.

Orton, Peter. 1985. An approach to *Wulf and Eadwacer*. *Proceedings of the Royal Irish Academy*, Sec. C, 85.223–58.

—— 1989. *The Wife's Lament* and *Skírnismál*: Some parallels. In *Úr dölum til dala: Guðbrandur Vigfússon Centenary Essays*, ed. R. McTurk and A. Wawn, 205–37. Leeds Texts and Monographs, n.s. 11. Leeds: Leeds Studies in English.

—— 1991. The form and structure of *The Seafarer*. *SN* 63.37–55.

Osborn, Marijane. 1983. The text and context of *Wulf and Eadwacer*. In *The OE Elegies: New Essays in Criticism*, ed. M. Green, 174–89. Rutherford, N.J.: Fairleigh Dickinson University Press.

—— 1989. Translation, translocation, and the native context of *Cædmon's Hymn*. *New Comparison* 8.13–23.

Östman, Jan-Ola, and Brita Wårvik. 1994. *The Fight at Finnsburh*: Pragmatic aspects of a narrative fragment. *NM* 95. 207–27.

Overing, Gillian R. 1990. *Language, Sign and Gender in "Beowulf."* Carbondale: Southern Illinois University Press.

—— 1991. On reading Eve: *Genesis B* and the readers' desire. In *Speaking Two Languages: Traditional Disciplines and Contemporary Theory in Medieval Studies*, ed. Allen J. Frantzen, 35–63. Albany: State University of New York Press.

—— 1995. The women of *Beowulf*: A context for interpretation. In *Beowulf: Basic Readings*, ed. Peter S. Baker, 219–60. New York: Garland (reprinted 2000 under the title *The "Beowulf" Reader*). A revision of Gillian R. Overing, *Language, Sign, and Gender in "Beowulf,"* 68–112, Carbondale: Southern Illinois University Press.

Paetzel, Walther. 1913. *Die Variationen in der altgermanischen Alliteration-*

spoesie. Palaestra 48. Berlin: Mayer & Müller.

Page, R. I. 1999. *An Introduction to English Runes*. 2nd ed. Woodbridge, Suffolk: Boydell.

Panzer, Friedrich. 1910. *Studien zur germanischen Sagengeschichte, I: Beowulf*. Munich: C. Beck.

Parkes, M.B. 1972. The manuscript of the Leiden Riddle. *ASE* 1.207–17 and pl. 1.

—— 1997. *Rædan, areccan, smeagan*: How the Anglo-Saxons read. *ASE* 26.1–22.

Parks, Ward. 1988. Ring structure and narrative embedding in Homer and *Beowulf*. *NM* 89.237–51.

Parsons, Wilfrid, trans. 1953. *Saint Augustine, Letters*. Vol. 3. New York: Fathers of the Church.

Pasternack, Carol Braun. 1991. Anonymous polyphony and *The Wanderer*'s textuality. *ASE* 20.99–122.

—— 1995. *The Textuality of OE Poetry*. CSASE 13. Cambridge: Cambridge University Press.

—— 1997. Post-structuralist theories: The subject and the text. In *Reading OE Texts*, ed. Katherine O'Brien O'Keeffe, 170–91. Cambridge: Cambridge University Press.

Payer, Pierre. 1984. *Sex and the Penitentials: The Development of a Sexual Code 550–1150*. Toronto: University of Toronto Press.

Payne, Richard C. 1982. The rediscovery of OE poetry in the English literary tradition. In *A-S Scholarship: The First Three Centuries*, ed. Carl T. Berkhout and Milton McC. Gatch, 149–66. Boston: G. K. Hall.

Pelteret, David. 1986. Two OE lists of serfs. *MS* 48.470–513.

—— 1990. *Catalogue of English Post-Conquest Vernacular Documents*. Woodbridge, Suffolk: Boydell.

—— 1995. *Slavery in Early Mediaeval England from the Reign of Alfred until the Twelfth Century*. Woodbridge, Suffolk: Boydell.

—— 1998. Saint Wilfrid: Tribal bishop, civic bishop or Germanic lord? In *The Community, the Family and the Saint: Patterns of Power in Early Medieval Europe*, ed. Joyce Hill and Mary Swan, 159–80. International Medieval Research 4. Turnhout: Brepols.

Peters, L. J. 1951. The relationship of the OE *Andreas* to *Beowulf*. *PMLA* 66.844–63.

Pettit, Edward. 1999. A-S charms in Oxford, Bodleian Library MS Barlow 35. *Nottingham Medieval Studies* 43.33–46.

—— ed. 2001. *A-S Remedies, Charms, and Prayers from British Library Ms Harley 585: The Lacnunga*, I: *Introduction, Text, Translation and Appendices*. Lewiston, N.Y.: E. Mellen.

Pfaff, Richard W. 1995. *The Liturgical Books of A-S England*. OEN Subsidia 23. Kalamazoo: Medieval Institute, Western Michigan University.

Pheifer, J. D., ed. 1974. *OE Glosses in the Épinal-Erfurt Glossary*. Oxford: Clarendon.

—— 1987. Early A-S glossaries and the school of Canterbury. *ASE* 16.17–44.

Phillips, Andrew. 1996. *The Rebirth of England and the English: The Vision of William Barnes*. Hockwold-cum-Wilton, Norfolk: Anglo-Saxon Books.

Phillpotts, Bertha S. 1928. Wyrd and providence in A-S thought. *E&S* 13.7–27. Reprinted 1991 in *Interpretations of "Beowulf": A Critical Anthology*, ed. R. D. Fulk, 1–13. Bloomington: Indiana University Press.

Pigg, Daniel F. 1992. *The Dream of the Rood* in its discursive context: Apocalypticism as a determinant of form and treatment. *ELN* 29.13–22.

PL, see Migne 1879-1974.

Plummer, Charles, ed. 1896. *Venerabilis Bedae opera historica*. 2 vols. Oxford: Clarendon.

Plummer, Charles, and John Earle, eds. 1892–9. *Two of the Saxon Chronicles Parallel*. 2 vols. Oxford: Clarendon. Reprinted 1952 with two notes by D. Whitelock.

Pollock, Frederick, and Fredric W. Maitland. 1895. *History of English Law before the Time of Edward I*. Cambridge: Cambridge University Press.

Poole, Russell. 1998. *OE Wisdom Poetry*. Annotated Bibliographies of Old and Middle English Literature 5. Woodbridge, Suffolk: D. S. Brewer.

Pope, John C. 1942. *The Rhythm of "Beowulf."* (2nd ed. 1966.) New Haven: Yale University Press.

—— 1965. Dramatic voices in *The Wanderer* and *The Seafarer*. In *Franciplegius: Medieval and Linguistic Studies in Honor of Francis Peabody Magoun, Jr.*, ed. Jess B. Bessinger and Robert P. Creed, 164–93. New York: New York University Press. Reprinted 1968 in *Essential Articles for the Study of OE Poetry*, ed. J. B. Bessinger, Jr., and Stanley J. Kahrl, 533–70, Hamden, Conn.: Archon; and 1968 in *OE Literature: Twenty-Two Analytical Essays*, ed. Martin Stevens and Jerome Mandel, 163–97, Lincoln: University of Nebraska Press.

—— ed. 1967–8. *Homilies of Ælfric: A Supplementary Collection*. EETS o.s. 259–60. London: Oxford University Press.

—— 1974. Second thoughts on the interpretation of *The Seafarer*. *ASE* 3.75–86. Reprinted 1994 in *OE Shorter Poems: Basic Readings*, ed. Katherine O'Brien O'Keeffe, 213–29. New York: Garland.

—— 1978. Palaeography and poetry: Some solved and unsolved problems of the Exeter Book. In *Medieval Scribes, Manuscripts, and Libraries: Essays Presented to N. R. Ker*, ed. M. B. Parkes and Andrew G. Watson, 25–65. London: Scolar.

Pope, John C., and R. D. Fulk, eds. 2001. *Eight OE Poems*. 3rd ed. New York: W. W. Norton.

Porter, David W. 1996a. Ælfric's *Colloquy* and Ælfric Bata. *Neophilologus* 80.639–60.

—— 1996b. "Æthelwold's bowl" and the "Chronicle of Abingdon." *NM* 97.163–67.

—— 1996c. A double solution to the Latin riddle in MS. Antwerp, Plantin-Moretus Museum, M16.2. *ANQ* 9.2.3–9.

Portnoy, Phyllis. 1994. "Remnant" and ritual: The place of *Daniel* and *Christ and Satan* in the Junius epic. *ES* 75.408–22.

—— 2001. Ring composition and the digressions of *Exodus:* The "legacy" of the "remnant." *ES* 82.289–307.

Powell, Stephen D. 1998. The journey forth: Elegiac consolation in *Guthlac B. ES* 79.489–500.

Powell, T. E. 1994. The "thee orders" of society in A-S England. *ASE* 23.103–32.

Prescott, Andrew. 1998. The ghost of Asser. In *A-S Manuscripts and Their Heritage*, ed. Phillip Pulsiano and Elaine M. Treharne, 255–91. Aldershot, Hants: Ashgate.

Pulsiano, Phillip. 1983. The sea of life and the ending of *Christ II. In Geardagum* 5.1–12.

—— 1999. Blessed bodies: The vitae of A-S female saints. *Parergon* 16.2.1–42.

—— 2000. The OE gloss of the *Eadwine Psalter*. In *Rewriting OE in the Twelfth Century*, ed. Mary Swan and Elaine M. Treharne, 166–94. CSASE 30. Cambridge: Cambridge University Press.

Pulsiano, Phillip, and Kirsten Wolf. 1991. The "hwelp" in *Wulf and Eadwacer. ELN* 28.3.1–9.

Quentin, H. 1908. *Les martyrologes historiques du moyen âge.* Paris: V. Lecoffre.

Quinn, Karen J., and Kenneth P. Quinn. 1990. *A Manual of OE Prose.* New York: Garland.

Raine, James, ed. 1879–94. *The Historians of the Church of York and Its Archbishops.* 3 vols. London: Longman.

Raith, Josef, ed. 1933. *Die altenglische Version des Halitgar'schen Bussbuches* (*sog. Poenitentiale Pseudo-Ecgberti*). Bibliothek der angelsächsischen Prosa 13. Hamburg: H. Grand.

Rankin, Susan. 1985. The liturgical background of the OE *Advent Lyrics.* A reappraisal. In *Learning and Literature in A-S England: Studies Presented to Peter Clemoes*, ed. Michael Lapidge and Helmut Gneuss, 317–40. Cambridge: Cambridge Univ. Press.

Raw, Barbara C. 1976. The probable derivation of most of the illustrations in Junius 11 from an illustrated Old Saxon Genesis. *ASE* 5.133–48.

—— 1984. The construction of Oxford, Bodleian Library, Junius 11. *ASE* 13.187–207. Reprinted 1994 in *A-S Manuscripts: Basic Readings*, ed. Mary P. Richards, 251–75. New York: Garland.

Raynes, Enid M. 1957. MS. Boulogne-sur-Mer 63 and Ælfric. *MÆ* 26.65–73.

Reichl, Karl. 2000. *Singing the Past: Turkic and Medieval Heroic Poetry.* Ithaca:

Cornell University Press.

Reinsma, Luke M. 1987. *Ælfric: An Annotated Bibliography*. New York: Garland.

Remley, Paul G. 1988. The Latin textual basis of *Genesis A. ASE* 17.163–89.

—— 1996. *OE Biblical Verse: Studies in Genesis, Exodus, and Daniel*. CSASE 16. Cambridge: Cambridge University Press.

Renoir, Alain. 1965. *Wulf and Eadwacer:* A non-interpretation. In *Franciplegius: Medieval and Linguistic Studies in Honor of Francis Peabody Magoun, Jr.*, ed. Jess B. Bessinger and Robert P. Creed, 147–63. New York: New York University Press.

—— 1975. A reading context for *The Wife's Lament*. In *A-S Poetry: Essays in Appreciation for John C. McGalliard*, ed. Lewis E. Nicholson and Dolores Warwick Frese, 224–41. Notre Dame: University of Notre Dame Press.

—— 1990. Eve's I.Q. rating: Two sexist views of *Genesis B*. In *New Readings on Women in OE Literature*, ed. Helen Damico and Alexandra Hennessey Olsen, 262–72. Bloomington: Indiana University Press.

Reuter, Timothy. 1980. *The Greatest Englishman: Essays on St. Boniface and the Church at Crediton*. Greenwood, S.C.: Attic.

Reynolds, Robert L. 1953. Le poème a-s *Widsith:* réalité et fiction. *Le Moyen Âge* 59.299–324.

Richards, Mary P. 1986. The manuscript contexts of the OE laws: Tradition and innovation. In *Studies in Earlier OE Prose*, ed. Paul E. Szarmach, 171–92. Albany: State University of New York Press.

—— 1989. Elements of a written standard in the OE laws. In *Standardizing English: Essays in the History of Language Change in Honor of John Hurt Fisher*, ed. Joseph B. Trahern, Jr., 1–22. Knoxville: University of Tennessee Press.

—— 1992. Prosaic poetry: Late OE poetic composition. In *OE and New: Studies in Language and Linguistics in Honor of Frederic G. Cassidy*, ed. Joan H. Hall, Nick Doane, and Dick Ringler, 63–75. New York: Garland.

—— 1997. Anglo-Saxonism in the OE laws. In *Anglo-Saxonism and the Construction of Social Identity*, ed. Allen Frantzen and John D. Niles, 40–59. Gainesville: University Press of Florida.

Richardson, H. G., and G. O. Sayles. 1966. *Law and Legislation from Æthelberht to Magna Carta*. Edinburgh: Edinburgh University Press.

Richman, Gerald. 1982. Speaker and speech boundaries in *The Wanderer. JEGP* 81.469–79. Reprinted 1994 in *OE Shorter Poems: Basic Readings*, ed. Katherine O'Brien O'Keeffe, 303–18. New York: Garland.

Rickert, Edith. 1904–5. The OE Offa Saga. *MP* 2.29–76, 321–76.

Ridyard, Susan J. 1988. *The Royal Saints of A-S England*. Cambridge: Cambridge University Press.

Riedinger. Anita. 1989. *Andreas* and the formula in transition. In *Hermeneutics and Medieval Culture*, ed. Patrick J. Gallacher and Helen Damico, 183–91.

Albany: State University of New York Press.

—— 1993. The formulaic relationship between *Beowulf* and *Andreas*. In *Heroic Poetry in the A-S Period: Studies in Honor of Jess B. Bessinger, Jr.*, ed. Helen Damico and John Leyerle, 283–312. Studies in Medieval Culture 32. Kalamazoo: Medieval Institute Pubns.

Rieger, Max. 1869. Der *Seefahrer* als Dialog hergestellt. *Zeitschrift für deutsche Philologie* 1.334–9.

Ringler, Richard N. 1966. *Him sēo wēn gelē ah:* The design for irony in Grendel's last visit to Heorot. *Speculum* 41.49–67. Reprinted 1991 in *Interpretations of "Beowulf": A Critical Anthology*, ed. R. D. Fulk, 127–45. Bloomington: Indiana University Press.

Rives, J. B., trans. 1999. *Tacitus: Germania*. Oxford: Clarendon.

Roberts, Jane, ed. 1979. *The Guthlac Poems of the Exeter Book*. Oxford: Clarendon.

—— 1986. The OE prose translation of Felix's *Vita sancti Guthlaci*. In *Studies in Earlier OE Prose*, ed. Paul E. Szarmach, 363–79. Albany: State University of New York Press.

—— 1988. *Guthlac A*: Sources and source hunting. In *Medieval English Studies Presented to George Kane*, ed. Edward D. Kennedy et al., 1–18. Woodbridge, Suffolk: Boydell.

—— 1994. Some reflections on the metre of *Christ III*. In *From A-S to Early Middle English: Studies Presented to E. G. Stanley*, ed. Douglas Gray, Malcolm Godden, and Terry Hoad, 33–59. Oxford: Clarendon.

Robertson, A. J., ed. 1956. *A-S Charters*. 2nd ed. Cambridge: Cambridge University Press.

Robertson, Durant W., Jr. 1951. The doctrine of charity in mediaeval literary gardens: A topical approach through symbolism and allegory. *Speculum* 26.24–49. Reprinted 1963 in *An Anthology of "Beowulf" Criticism*, ed. Lewis E. Nicholson, 165–88. Notre Dame: University of Notre Dame Press.

Robinson, Fred C. 1968. The significance of names in OE literature. *Anglia* 86.14–58. Reprinted 1993 in Fred C. Robinson, *The Tomb of Beowulf and Other Essays on OE*, 185–218. Oxford: Blackwell.

—— 1970. Lexicography and literary criticism: A caveat. In *Philological Essays: Studies in Old and Middle English Language and Literature in Honor of Herbert Dean Merrit*, ed. James L. Rosier, 99–110. The Hague: Mouton. Reprinted 1993 in Fred C. Robinson, *The Tomb of Beowulf and Other Essays on OE*, 140–52. Oxford: Blackwell.

—— 1980. OE literature in its most immediate context. In *OE Literature in Context*, ed. John D. Niles, 11–29, 157–61. Cambridge: D. S. Brewer; Totowa, N.J.: Rowman & Littlefield. Reprinted 1994 in Fred C. Robinson, *The Editing of OE*, 3–24, Oxford: Blackwell.

—— 1985. *Beowulf and the Appositive Style*. Knoxville: University of Tennessee Press.

—— 1989. "The rewards of piety": "Two" OE poems in their manuscript context. In *Hermeneutics and Medieval Culture*, ed. Patrick J. Gallacher and Helen Damico, 193–200. Albany: State University of New York Press. Reprinted 1994 in Fred C. Robinson, *The Editing of OE*, 180–95, Oxford: Blackwell.

—— 1990. OE poetry: The question of authorship. *ANQ* n.s. 3.74–9.

—— 1993a. Another eighteenth-century transcription of *Maldon*? In *The Centre and Its Compass: Studies in Medieval Literature in Honor of Professor John Leyerle*, ed. Robert A. Taylor et al., 407–15. Studies in Medieval Culture 33. Kalamazoo: Medieval Institute Pubns.

—— 1993b. The tomb of Beowulf. In Fred C. Robinson, *The Tomb of Beowulf and Other Essays on OE*, 3–19. Oxford: Blackwell. Reprinted 2002 (partially) in *Beowulf: A Verse Translation*, trans. Seamus Heany, ed. Daniel Donoghue, 181–97, New York: W. W. Norton

—— 1994. Eve's "weaker" mind in *Genesis B*, line 590. In Fred C. Robinson, *The Editing of OE*, 124–7, Oxford: Blackwell.

Robinson, Fred C., and E. G. Stanley, eds. 1991. *OE Verse Texts from Many Sources*. EEMF 23. Copenhagen: Rosenkilde & Bagger.

Rogers, H. L. 1985. *The Battle of Maldon*: David Casley's Transcript. *N&Q* 230 (n.s. 32), 147–55.

Rollason, David. 1983. The cults of murdered royal saints in A-S England. *ASE* 11.1–22.

—— 1989. *Saints and Relics in A-S England*. Oxford: Blackwell.

—— 1996. Hagiography and politics in early Northumbria. In *Holy Men and Holy Women: OE Prose Saints' Lives and Their Contexts*, ed. Paul E. Szarmach, 95–114. Albany: State University of New York Press.

Ronalds, Craig, and Margaret Clunies Ross. 2001. *Thureth*: A neglected OE poem and its history in A-S scholarship. *N&Q* 246 (n.s. 48), 359–70.

Rosier, J. L. 1964–6. Instructions for Christians. *Anglia* 82.4–22 and 84.74.

Rossi-Reder, Andrea. 1999. Beasts and baptism: A new perspective on the OE *Physiologus*. *Neophilologus* 83.461–77.

Rowland, Jenny. 1990. OE *ealuscerwen/meoduscerwen* and the concept of "paying for mead." *LSE* n.s. 21.1–12.

Roy, Gopa. 1992. A virgin acts manfully: Ælfric's *Life of St. Eugenia* and the Latin versions. *LSE* n.s. 23.1–27.

Russom, Geoffrey. 1987. *OE Meter and Linguistic Theory*. Cambridge: Cambridge University Press.

—— 1998. *"Beowulf" and Old Germanic Meter*. Cambridge: Cambridge University Press.

Saenger, Paul. 1982. Silent reading: Its impact on late medieval script and society. *Viator* 13.367–414.

—— 1997. *Space between Words: The Origins of Silent Reading*. Stanford: Stanford University Press.

Sarrazin, Gregor. 1888. *Beowulf-Studien: Ein Beitrag zur Geschichte altgermanischer Sage und Dichtung.* Berlin: Mayer & Müller.

Sauer, Hans, ed. 1978. *Theodulfi Capitula in England: Die altenglischen Übersetzung zusammen mit lateinischen Texte.* Texte und Untersuchungen zur englische Philologie 8. Munich: W. Fink.

—— 1996. König Alfreds Boethius und seine Rhetorik. *Anglistik* 7.2.57–89.

Sawyer, Peter. 1957–62. *Textus Roffensis.* 2 vols. EEMF 7, 11. Copenhagen: Rosenkilde & Bagger.

—— 1968. *A-S Charters: An Annotated List and Bibliography.* London: Royal Historical Society.

Scattergood, J. 1984. *The Battle of Maldon* and history. In *Literature and Learning in Medieval and Renaissance England: Essays Presented to Fitzroy Pyle*, ed. J. Scattergood, 11–24. Blackrock, Co. Dublin: Irish Academic.

Schaar, Claes. 1949. *Critical Studies in the Cynewulf Group.* Lund: C. Gleerup.

Schabram, Hans. 1965. *Superbia: Studien zum altenglischen Wortschatz.* Vol. 1. Munich: W. Fink.

Schaefer, Ursula. 1986. Two women in need of a friend: A comparison of *The Wife's Lament* and Eangyth's letter to Boniface. In *Germanic Dialects: Linguistic and Philological Investigations*, ed. Bela Brogyanyi and Thomas Krömmelbein, 491–524. Amsterdam: Benjamins.

—— 1997. Rhetoric and style. In *A "Beowulf" Handbook*, ed. Robert E. Bjork and John D. Niles, 105–24. Lincoln: University of Nebraska Press.

Scharer, Anton. 1996. The writing of history at King Alfred's court. *EME* 5.177–206.

Scheil, Andrew P. 1999a. Anti-Judaism in Ælfric's *Lives of Saints. ASE* 28.65–86.

—— 1999b. Somatic ambiguity and masculine desire in the OE Life of Euphrosyne. *Exemplaria* 11.345–61.

—— 2000. Bodies and boundaries in the OE *Life of St. Mary of Egypt. Neophilologus* 84.137–56.

Schlauch, Margaret. 1941. An OE *encomium urbis. JEGP* 40.14–28.

Schofield, W. H. 1902. Signy's Lament. *PMLA* 17.262–95.

Schopf, Alfred. 1996. Bedas Sterbelied. *Literaturwissenschaftliches Jahrbuch* 37.9–30.

Schramm, Gottfried. 1998. Wanderwege des Hunnenschlachstoffes und das Schicksal seiner osteuropäischen Szenerie. *Skandinavistik* 28.118–38.

Schrøder, Ludvig Peter. 1875. *Om Bjovulfs-drapen.* Copenhagen: Schønberg.

Schröer, Arnold, ed. 1882. The grave. *Anglia* 5.289–90.

—— ed. 1885-88. *Die angelsächsische Prosabearbeitungen der Benediktinerregel.* Bibliothek der angelsächsischen Prosa 2. Kassel: G. Wigand. Reprinted 1964 with an addendum by Helmut Gneuss, Darmstadt: Wissenschaftliches Buchgesellschaft.

—— ed. 1888. *Die Winteney-Version der Regula S. Benedicti.* Halle: M.

Niemeyer. Reprinted 1978 with an addendum by Mechthild Gretsch, Tübingen: M. Niemeyer.

Schücking, Levin L. 1905. *Beowulfs Rückkehr: Eine kritische Studie.* Studien zur englischen Philologie 21. Halle: M. Niemeyer.

—— ed. 1919. *Kleines ags. Dichterbuch: Lyrik und Heldenepos.* Cöthen: O. Schulze.

—— 1929. Das Königsideal im Beowulf. *Bulletin of the Modern Humanities Research Association* 3.143–54. Trans. as "The ideal of kingship in *Beowulf*," in *An Anthology of "Beowulf" Criticism*, ed. Lewis E. Nicholson, 35–49. Notre Dame: University of Notre Dame Press.

Schwab, Ute. 1990. *Servire il Signore morto. Funzione e trasformazione di riti funebri germanici nell'epica medievale inglese e tedesca.* Università di Catania, Facoltà di Lettere e Filosofia, Collana di studi di filologia moderna 5. Soveria Manelli: Rubbettino.

Scragg, D. G. 1973. The compilation of the Vercelli Book. *ASE* 2.189–207. Reprinted 1994, with a postscript, in *A-S Manuscripts: Basic Readings*, ed. Mary P. Richards, 317–43. New York: Garland.

—— 1977. Napier's "Wulfstan" Homily xxx: Its sources, its relationship to the Vercelli Book and its style. *ASE* 6.197–211.

—— 1979. The corpus of vernacular homilies and prose saints' lives before Ælfric. *ASE* 8.223–77. Reprinted 2000 in *OE Prose: Basic Readings*, ed. Paul E. Szarmach, 73–150, with additions 147–50. New York: Garland.

—— ed. 1981. *The Battle of Maldon.* Manchester: Manchester University Press.

—— 1985. The homilies of the Blickling manuscript. In *Learning and Literature in A-S England: Studies Presented to Peter Clemoes*, ed. Michael Lapidge and Helmut Gneuss, 299–316. Cambridge: Cambridge University Press.

—— ed. 1991a. *The Battle of Maldon, AD 991.* Oxford: Blackwell.

—— 1991b. *The Battle of Maldon.* In *The Battle of Maldon, AD 991*, ed. D. G. Scragg, 1–36. Oxford: Blackwell.

—— 1992a. An OE homilist of Archbishop Dunstan's day. In *Words, Texts, and Manuscripts: Studies in A-S Culture Presented to Helmut Gneuss*, ed. Michael Korhammer, 181–92. Woodbridge, Suffolk: D. S. Brewer.

—— ed. 1992b. *The Vercelli Homilies and Related Texts.* EETS o.s. 300. Oxford: Oxford University Press.

—— 1993. *The Battle of Maldon:* Fact or fiction? In *The Battle of Maldon: Fiction and Fact*, ed. Janet Cooper, 19–31. London: Hambledon.

—— 1996. The corpus of anonymous lives and their manuscript context. In *Holy Men and Holy Women: OE Prose Saints' Lives and Their Contexts*, ed. Paul E. Szarmach, 209–30. Albany: State University of New York Press.

—— 1997a. Source study. In *Reading OE Texts*, ed. Katherine O'Brien O'Keeffe, 39–58. Cambridge: Cambridge University Press.

—— 1997b. *Wifcyþþe* and the morality of the Cynewulf and Cyneheard episode in the A-S Chronicle. In *Alfred the Wise: Studies in Honor of Janet*

Bately on the Occasion of Her Sixty-Fifth Birthday, ed. Jane Roberts, Janet L. Nelson, and Malcolm Godden, 179–85. Cambridge: D. S. Brewer.

—— 2000. Introduction. The Anglo-Saxons: Fact and fiction. In *Literary Appropriations of the Anglo-Saxons from the Thirteenth to the Twentieth Century*, ed. D. G. Scragg and Carole Weinberg, 1–21. CSASE 29. Cambridge: Cambridge University Press.

Sedgefield, Walter J. 1899. *King Alfred's OE Version of Boethius.* Oxford: Clarendon. Reprinted 1968, Darmstadt: Wissenschaftliche Buchgesellschaft.

—— trans. 1900. *King Alfred's Version of the Consolations of Boethius, Done into Modern English.* Oxford: Clarendon.

Sheehan, Michael M. 1963. *The Will in Medieval England.* Toronto: Pontifical Institute of Medieval Studies.

Sherley-Price, Leo, and D. H. Farmer, transs. 1990. *Bede: A History of the English People, with Bede's Letter to Egbert and Cuthbert's Letter on the Death of Bede.* Rev. ed. London: Penguin.

Shippey, T. A. 1969. The fairy-tale structure of *Beowulf. N&Q* 214.2–11.

—— 1972. *OE Verse.* London: Hutchinson University Library.

—— 1976. *Poems of Wisdom and Learning in OE.* Cambridge: D. S. Brewer.

—— 1993a. OE poetry: The prospects for literary history. In *Segundo Congreso Internacional de la Sociedad Española de Lengua y Literatura Inglesa Medieval*, ed. Antonio León Sendra et al., 164–79. Oviedo.

—— 1993b. Recent writing on OE: A response. *Æstel* 1.111–34.

—— 1994a. Miscomprehension and re-interpretation in Old and early Middle English proverb collections. In *Text und Zeittiefe*, ed. Hildegard L. C. Tristram, 293–311. ScriptOralia 58. Tübingen: G. Narr.

—— 1994b. *The Wanderer* and *The Seafarer* as wisdom poetry. In *Companion to OE Poetry*, ed. Henk Aertsen and Rolf H. Bremmer, 145–58. Amsterdam: VU University Press.

—— 1997. Structure and unity. In *A "Beowulf" Handbook*, ed. Robert E. Bjork and John D. Niles, 149–74. Lincoln: University of Nebraska Press.

—— 2000. The undeveloped image: A-S in popular consciousness from Turner to Tolkien. In *Literary Appropriations of the Anglo-Saxons from the Thirteenth to the Twentieth Century*, ed. D. G. Scragg and Carole Weinberg, 215–36. CSASE 29. Cambridge: Cambridge University Press.

Shippey, T. A., and Andreas Haarder, eds. 1998. *"Beowulf": The Critical Heritage.* London: Routledge.

Short, Douglas D. 1976. The OE *Gifts of Men* and the pedagogic theory of the *Pastoral Care. ES* 57.497–501.

—— 1980. *"Beowulf" Scholarship: An Annotated Bibliography.* New York: Garland.

Sievers, Eduard, ed. 1875. *Der Heliand und die angelsächsische Genesis.* Halle: M. Niemeyer.

—— 1885. Zur Rhythmik des germanischen Alliterationsverses. *PBB* 10.209–

314, 451–545.

—— 1893. *Altgermanische Metrik*. Halle: M. Niemeyer.

Sims-Williams, Patrick. 1976–8. "Is it fog or smoke or warriors fighting?": Irish and Welsh parallels to the *Finnsburg* fragment. *Bulletin of the Board of Celtic Studies* 27.505–14.

—— 1990. *Religion and Literature in Western England 600–800*. CSASE 3. Cambridge: Cambridge University Press.

Sisam, Celia, ed. 1976. *The Vercelli Book*. EEMF 19. Copenhagen: Rosenkilde & Bagger.

Sisam, Kenneth. 1953a. A-S royal genealogies. *PBA* 39.287–348.

—— 1953b. *Studies in the History of OE Literature*. Oxford: Clarendon.

—— 1965. *The Structure of "Beowulf."* Oxford: Clarendon.

Sisam, Kenneth, and Celia Sisam. 1958. The psalm texts. In *The Paris Psalter*, ed. Bertram Colgrave, 15–17, EEMF 8. Copenhagen: Rosenkilde & Bagger.

Skeat, Walter W., ed. 1871-87. *The Holy Gospels in A-S, Northumbrian, and Old Mercian Versions*. 4 vols. Cambridge: Cambridge University Press.

—— ed. and trans. 1881–1900. *Ælfric's Lives of Saints*. EETS o.s. 76, 82, 94, and 114. Oxford: Oxford University Press. Reprinted in two vols. 1966.

Sleeth, Charles R. 1982. *Studies in Christ and Satan*. Toronto: University of Toronto Press.

Smith, A. H. 1956. *English Place-Name Elements*. English Place-Name Soc. 25–6. Cambridge: Cambridge University Press.

—— ed. 1978. *Three Northumbrian Poems*. Rev. ed. Exeter: University of Exeter Press.

Smithers, G. V. 1957–9. The meaning of *The Seafarer* and *The Wanderer*. *MÆ* 26.137–53; 28.1–22, 99–104.

Smyth, Alfred P. 1995. *King Alfred the Great*. Oxford: Oxford University Press.

—— 1998. The emergence of English identity, 700–1000. In *Medieval Europeans: Studies in Ethnic Identity and National Perspectives in Medieval Europe*, ed. Alfred P. Smyth, 24–52. New York: St. Martin's.

Sorrell, Paul. 1992. Oral poetry and the world of *Beowulf*. *Oral Tradition* 7.28–65.

—— 1996. Alcuin's "comb" riddle. *Neophilologus* 80.311–18.

Spindler, Robert. 1934. *Das altenglische Bussbuch (sog. Confessionale Pseudo-Egberti)*. Leipzig: B. Tauchnitz.

Squires, Ann, ed. 1988. *The OE "Physiologus."* Durham Medieval Texts 5. New Elvet, Durham: Department of English Studies.

Standop, Ewald. 1969. Formen der Variation im Beowulf. In *Festschrift für Edgar Mertner*, ed. Bernhard Fabian and Ulrich Suerbaum, 55–63. Munich: W. Fink.

Stanley, E. G. 1955. OE poetic diction and the interpretation of *The Wanderer*, *The Seafarer*, and *The Penitent's Prayer*. *Anglia* 73.413–66. Reprinted

1968 in *Essential Articles for the Study of OE Poetry*, ed. J. B. Bessinger, Jr., and Stanley J. Kahrl, 458–514. Hamden, Conn.: Archon.

—— 1963. Hæþenra hyht in *Beowulf*. In *Studies in OE Literature in Honor of Arthur G. Brodeur*, ed. Stanley B. Greenfield, 192–208. Eugene: University of Oregon Books.

—— 1971. Studies in the prosaic vocabulary of OE verse. *NM* 72.385–418.

—— 1988. King Alfred's prefaces. *RES* n.s. 39.349–64.

Stefanovíc, Svetislav. 1909. Das angelsächsische Gedicht *Die Klage der Frau*. *Anglia* 32.399–433.

Stenton, Doris Mary. 1957. *The English Woman in History*. London: Allen & Unwin.

Stenton, F. M. 1955. *The Latin Charters of the A-S Period*. Oxford: Clarendon.

—— 1971. *A-S England*. 3rd ed. Oxford: Clarendon.

Stévanovitch, Colette. 1996. Envelope patterns and the unity of the OE *Christ and Satan*. *Archiv* 233.260–7.

Stevens, Martin. 1968. The narrator of the *Wife's Lament*. *NM* 69.72–90.

Stevenson, Jane. 1995a. *The "Laterculus Malalianus" and the School of Archbishop Theodore*. CSASE 14. Cambridge: Cambridge University Press.

—— 1995b. Theodore and the *Laterculus Malalianus*. In *Archbishop Theodore: Commemorative Studies on His Life and Influence*, ed. Michael Lapidge, 204–21. CSASE 11. Cambridge: Cambridge University Press.

Stevenson, William Henry, ed. 1904. *Asser's Life of King Alfred*. Oxford: Clarendon.

Stitt, J. Michael. 1992. *Beowulf and the Bear's Son: Epic, Saga and Fairytale in Northern Germanic Tradition*. New York: Garland.

Stockwell, Robert P., and Donka Minkova. 1997. Prosody. In *A "Beowulf" Handbook*, ed. Robert E. Bjork and John D. Niles, 55–83. Lincoln: University of Nebraska Press.

Storch, Theodor. 1886. *Angelsächsische Nominalcomposita*. Strassburg: K. Trübner.

Stork, Nancy Porter. 1990. *Through a Gloss Darkly: Aldhelm's Riddles in the British Library MS Royal 12. C. xxiii*. Toronto: Pontifical Institute of Medieval Studies.

Storms, G. 1948. *A-S Magic*. The Hague: M. Nijhoff.

Strunk, William, Jr., ed. 1904. *The "Juliana" of Cynewulf*. Boston: D. C. Heath.

Stubbs, W., ed. 1874. *Memorials of St. Dunstan*. London: Longman.

Sundquist, John D. Forthcoming. Relative clause variation and the unity of *Beowulf*. To appear in the *Journal of Germanic Linguistics*.

Suzuki, Seiichi. 1987. *Wulf and Eadwacer*: A reinterpretation and some conjectures. *NM* 88.175–85.

—— 1996. *The Metrical Organization of "Beowulf": Prototype and Isomophism*. Berlin: Mouton de Gruyter.

Sveinsson, Einar Ól., see Einar Ól. Sveinsson.

Swan, Mary. 1996. Holiness remodelled: Theme and technique in OE composite homilies. In *Models of Holiness in Medieval Sermons*, ed. Beverly M. Kienzle, 35–46. Louvain-la-Neuve: Fédération Internationale des Instituts d'Études Médiévales.

Swanton, Michael J. 1964. *The Wife's Lament* and *The Husband's Message:* A reconsideration. *Anglia* 82.269–90.

—— ed. 1996. *The Dream of the Rood*. Rev. ed. Exeter: University of Exeter Press.

—— trans. 2000. *The A-S Chronicle*. Rev. ed. London: Phoenix.

Sweet, Henry, ed. 1871–2. *King Alfred's West-Saxon Version of Gregory's Pastoral Care*. EETS o.s. 45 and 50. London.

—— ed. 1885. *The Oldest English Texts*. EETS o.s. 83. London: N. Trübner.

Symons, Thomas, ed. and trans. 1953. *Regularis Concordia*. New York: Nelson & Sons.

Szarmach, Paul E. 1978. The Vercelli Homilies: Style and structure. In *The OE Homily and Its Backgrounds*, ed. Paul E. Szarmach and Bernard F. Huppé, 241–67. Albany: State University of New York Press.

—— 1986. The Latin tradition of Alcuin's *Liber de virtutibus et vitiis*, cap. xxvii—xxxv, with special reference to Vercelli Homily xx. *Medievalia* 12.13–41.

——1990. Ælfric's women saints: Eugenia. In *New Readings on Women in OE Literature*, ed. Helen Damico and Alexandra Hennessey Olsen, 146–57. Bloomington: Indiana University Press.

—— 1996. St. Euphrosyne: Holy transvestite. In *Holy Men and Holy Women: OE Prose Saints' Lives and Their Contexts*, ed. Paul E. Szarmach, 353–65. Albany: State University of New York Press.

—— 1997. Alfred's Boethius and the four cardinal virtues. In *Alfred the Wise: Studies in Honor of Janet Bately on the Occasion of Her Sixty-Fifth Birthday*, ed. Jane Roberts, Janet L. Nelson, and Malcolm Godden, 223–35. Cambridge: D. S. Brewer.

Szarmach, Paul E., and Bernard F. Huppé, eds. 1978. *The OE Homily and Its Backgrounds*. Albany: State University of New York Press.

Talbot, C. H. 1954. *The A-S Missionaries in Germany*. London: Sheed & Ward.

Tangl, M., ed. 1916. *Die Briefe des heiligen Bonifatius und Lullus*. MGH, Epistolae Selectae 1. Berlin: Weidmann.

Tanke, John W. 1994. *Wonfeax wale:* Ideology and figuration in the sexual riddles of the Exeter Book. In *Class and Gender in Early English Literature: Intersections*, ed. Britton J. Harwood and Gillian R. Overing, 21–42. Bloomington: Indiana University Press.

Tasioulas, J. A. 1996. The mother's lament: *Wulf and Eadwacer* reconsidered. *MÆ* 65.1–18.

Taylor, Simon, ed. 1983. *MS B*. Vol. 4 of *The A-S Chronicle: A Collaborative Edition*, ed. David Dumville and Simon Keynes. Cambridge: D. S. Brewer.

ten Brink, Bernhard. 1888. *Beowulf: Untersuchungen.* Quellen und Forschungen 62. Strassburg: N. Trübner.

Terry, Patricia, trans. 1990. *Poems of the Elder Edda.* Philadelphia: University of Pennsylvania Press.

Thompson, A. H., ed. 1923. *Liber Vitae Dunelmensis.* Surtees Society Publications 136. Durham and London: B. Quaritch.

—— ed. 1935. *Bede: His Life, Times and Writings.* Oxford: Clarendon.

Thompson, Stith. 1966. *Motif-Index of Folk Literature.* 6 vols. 2nd printing. Bloomington: Indiana University Press.

Thormann, Janet. 1997. The A-S Chronicle poems and the making of the English nation. In *Anglo-Saxonism and the Construction of Social Identity,* ed. Allen Frantzen and John D. Niles, 60–85. Gainesville: University Press of Florida.

Thorpe, Benjamin, ed. 1840. *Ancient Laws and Institutes of England.* 2 vols. London: Commissioners of the Public Records of the Kingdom. (Also issued in a one-vol. folio ed.)

—— ed. 1844–6. *Ælfric, Sermones Catholici, in the Original A-S, with an English Version.* 2 vols. London: Ælfric Society. Reprinted 1983 Hildesheim: G. Olms.

—— ed. 1865. *Diplomatarium Anglicum Ævi Saxonici.* London: Macmillan.

Timmer, B. J. 1942. The elegiac mood in OE poetry. *ES* 24.33–44.

—— 1944. Heathen and Christian elements in OE poetry. *Neophilologus* 29.180–5.

Tolkien, J. R. R. 1936. *Beowulf:* The monsters and the critics. *PBA* 22.245–95. Reprinted 1963 in *An Anthology of "Beowulf" Criticism,* ed. Lewis E. Nicholson, 51–103, Notre Dame: University of Notre Dame Press; 1968 in *The "Beowulf" Poet: A Collection of Critical Essays,* ed. Donald K. Fry, 8–56, Englewood Cliffs, N.J.: Prentice-Hall 1968; 1991 in *Interpretations of "Beowulf": A Critical Anthology,* ed. R. D. Fulk, 14–44, Bloomington: Indiana University Press; and 2002 (partially) in *Beowulf: A Verse Translation,* trans. Seamus Heany, ed. Daniel Donoghue, 103–30, New York: W. W. Norton.

—— 1953. The homecoming of Beorhtnoth Beorhthelm's son. *E&S* n.s. 6.1–18.

—— 1983. *Finn and Hengest: The Fragment and the Episode.* Ed. Alan Bliss. Boston: Houghton Mifflin.

Tonsfeldt, H. Ward. 1977. Ring structure in *Beowulf. Neophilologus* 61.443–52.

Toswell, M. Jane. 1997. The relationship of the Metrical Psalter to the OE glossed psalters. *ES* 78.297–315.

—— 2000. Bede's sparrow and the psalter in A-S England. *ANQ* 13.1.7–12.

Townend, Matthew. 2000. Pre-Cnut praise-poetry in viking age England. *RES* n.s. 51.349–70.

Trahern, Joseph B., Jr. 1970. The *Ioca Monachorum* and the OE *Pharaoh*. *ELN* 7 (1969–70), 165–8.

—— 1975. Caesarius, Chrodegang, and the OE *Vainglory*. In *Gesellschaft, Kultur, Literatur: Rezeption und Originalität im Wachsen einer europäischen Literatur und Geistigkeit*, ed. Karl Bosl, 167–78. Stuttgart: Hiersemann.

—— 1982. An OE metrical proverb in the Junius 121 *De descensu Christi*. *Anglia* 100.419–21.

—— 1991. Fatalism and the millennium. In *The Cambridge Companion to OE Literature*, ed. Malcolm Godden and Michael Lapidge, 160–71. Cambridge: Cambridge University Press.

Treharne, Elaine M., ed. and trans. 1997. *The OE Life of St. Nicholas, with the OE Life of St. Giles*. Leeds Texts and Monographs, n.s. 15. Leeds: Leeds Studies in English.

—— 1998. The dates and origins of three twelfth-century OE manuscripts. In *A-S Manuscripts and Their Heritage*, ed. Phillip Pulsiano and Elaine M. Treharne, 227–53. Aldershot, Hants: Ashgate.

Tripp, Raymond P. 1972. The narrator as revenant: A reconsideration of three OE elegies. *Papers on Language and Literature* 8.339–61.

Tugwell, Simon. 1970. Advent lyrics 348–77 (Lyric No. x). *MÆ* 39.34.

Tupper, Frederick, Jr., ed. 1910. *The Riddles of the Exeter Book*. Boston: Ginn. Reprinted 1968, Darmstadt: Wissenschaftliches Buchgesellschaft.

Turville-Petre, Joan. 1963. Translations of a lost penitential homily. *Traditio* 19.51–78.

Ure, James M., ed. 1957. *The Benedictine Office*. Edinburgh University Pubns. in Language and Literature 11. Edinburgh: Edinburgh University Press.

VanderBilt, Deborah. 1996. Cædmon and the translated word: Orality, textuality, and authority. *Mediaevalia* 19.299–317.

van Meurs, Jan. 1955. *Beowulf* and literary criticism. *Neophilologus* 39.114–30.

Vinogradoff, Paul. 1906–7. Transfer of land in OE law. *Harvard Law Review* 20.532–48.

Vleeskruyer, Rudolf, ed. 1953. *The Life of St. Chad: An OE Homily*. Amsterdam: North-Holland.

Voigts, Linda E., and Patricia D. Kurtz. 2001. *Scientific and Medical Writings in Old and Middle English: An Electronic Reference*. CD-ROM. Ann Arbor: University of Michigan Press.

Wainwright, F. T. 1959. Æthelflæd, Lady of the Mercians. In *The Anglo-Saxons: Studies in Some Aspects of Their History and Culture Presented to Bruce Dickins*, ed. Peter Clemoes, 53–70. London: Bowes & Bowes. Reprinted 1975 in *Scandinavian England: Collected Papers by F. T. Wainwright*, ed. H. P. R. Finberg, 305–24, Chichester: Phillimore; and 1990 in *New Readings on Women in OE Literature*, ed. Helen Damico and Alexandra Hennessey Olsen, 44–55, Bloomington: Indiana University Press.

Walker-Pelkey, Faye. 1992. *Frige hwæt ic hatte: The Wife's Lament* as riddle.

Papers on Language and Literature 28.242–66.

Wallace, D. Patricia. 1994–5. Feminine rhetoric and the epistolary tradition: The Boniface correspondence. *Women's Studies* 24.229–46.

Ward, Benedicta. 1991. Preface. In *Homilies on the Gospels/Bede the Venerable*, trans. Lawrence T. Martin and David Hurst, iii–ix. Kalamazoo: Cistercian Pubns.

Warner, G. F., ed. 1928. *The Guthlac Roll*. Oxford: Roxburghe Club.

Warner, Rubie D-N. ed. 1917. *Early English Homilies from the Twelfth Century MS. Vesp. D. xiv*. EETS o.s. 152. London: Keegan Paul, Trench, & Trübner.

Wasserschleben, F. W. H., ed. 1851. *Die Bußordnungen der abendländischen Kirche*. Halle: Graeger. Reprinted 1958, Graz: Akademische Druck- und Verlagsanstalt.

Watson, Gerard, ed. and trans. 1990. *Saint Augustine, Soliloquies and Immortality of the Soul*. Warminster: Aris & Phillips.

Waugh, Robin. 1997. The characteristic moment as a motif in *The Finnsburg Fragment* and *Deor*. *English Studies in Canada* 23.249–61.

Webb, J. F., and D. H. Farmer, eds. and transs. 1983. *The Age of Bede*. Rev. ed. Harmondsworth: Penguin.

Wehlau, Ruth. 1997. *"The Riddle of Creation": Metaphor Structures in OE Poetry*. New York: P. Lang.

—— 1998. The power of knowledge and the location of the reader in *Christ and Satan*. *JEGP* 97.1–12.

Wentersdorf, Karl P. 1981. The situation of the narrator in the OE *Wife's Lament*. *Speculum* 56.492–516.

—— 1985. The OE *Rhyming Poem*: A ruler's lament. *SP* 82.265–94.

Weston, L. M. C. 1995. Women's medicine, women's magic: The OE metrical childbirth charms. *MP* 92.279–93.

Whatley, E. Gordon. 1996a. An introduction to the study of OE prose hagiography: Sources and resources. In *Holy Men and Holy Women: OE Prose Saints' Lives and Their Contexts*, ed. Paul E. Szarmach, 3–32. Albany: State University of New York Press.

—— 1996b. Late OE hagiography ca. 950–1150. In *Hagiographies: histoire internationale de la literature hagiographique latine et vernaculaire en Occident des origins à 1550*, 3 vols, ed. Guy Philippart, 2.429–99. Turnhout: Brepols, 1994–2001.

—— 1997. Lost in translation: Omission of episodes in some OE prose saints' legends. *ASE* 26.187–208.

Whitbread, Leslie. 1944. A study of Bede's *Versus de die iudicii*. *PQ* 23.193–221.

—— 1945. The OE poem *Alms-Giving*. *N&Q* 189.2–4.

—— 1946. The OE poem *Pharaoh*. *N&Q* 190.52–4.

—— 1963. "Wulfstan" Homilies xxix, xxx and some related texts. *Anglia*

81.347–64.

—— 1967. After Bede: The influence and dissemination of his Dommsday verses. *Archiv* 204.250–66.

White, Stephen D. 1989. Kinship and lordship in early medieval England: The story of Sigeberht, Cynewulf, and Cyneheard. *Viator* 20.1–18.

Whitelock, Dorothy, ed. 1930. *A-S Wills.* Cambridge: Cambridge University Press.

—— 1950. The interpretation of *The Seafarer.* In *The Early Cultures of North-West Europe* (*H. M. Chadwick Memorial Studies*), ed. Cyril Fox and Bruce Dickins, 261–72. Reprinted 1968 in *Essential Articles for the Study of OE Poetry*, ed. J. B. Bessinger, Jr., and Stanley J. Kahrl, 442–57. Hamden, Conn.: Archon; and 1969 in *OE Literature: Twenty-Two Analytical Essays*, ed. Martin Stevens and Jerome Mandel, 198–211, Lincoln: University of Nebraska Press.

—— 1951. *The Audience of "Beowulf."* Oxford: Clarendon.

—— ed. 1954. *The Peterborough Chronicle.* EEMF 4. Copenhagen: Rosenkilde & Bagger.

—— trans. and ed. 1961. *The A-S Chronicle, A Revised Translation.* London: Eyre & Spottiswoode; New Brunswick, N.J.: Rutgers University Press.

—— 1962. The OE Bede. *PBA* 48.57–90.

—— 1966. The prose of Alfred's reign. In *Continuations and Beginnings: Studies in OE Literature*, ed. E. G. Stanley, 67–103. London: Nelson.

—— ed. 1967. *Sermo Lupi ad Anglos.* 3rd ed. London: Methuen.

—— 1968. *The Genuine Asser.* Reading: University of Reading Press.

—— 1969. William of Malmesbury on the works of King Alfred. In *Medieval Literature and Civilization: Studies in Memory of G. N. Garmonsway*, ed. D. A. Pearsall and R. A. Waldron, 78–93. London: Athlone.

—— 1970. Fact and fiction in the legend of St. Edmund. *Proceedings of the Suffolk Institute of Archaeology* 31.217–33.

—— 1974. *The Beginnings of English Society.* Harmondsworth: Penguin.

—— ed. 1979. *English Historical Documents I, c.500–1042.* 2nd ed. London: Eyre Methuen.

Whitelock, D., M. Brett, and C. N. L. Brooke. 1981. *Councils & Synods with Other Documents Relating to the English Church, I: A.D. 871–1204.* Oxford: Clarendon.

Whobrey, William T. 1991. King Alfred's metrical epilogue to the *Pastoral Care. JEGP* 90.175–86.

Wieland, Gernot. 1988. *Manna mildost:* Moses and Beowulf. *Pacific Coast Philology* 23.86–93.

Wiesenekker, Evert. 2000. Translation procedures in the West-Saxon Prose Psalter. *Amsterdamer Beiträge zur älteren Germanistik* 53.41–85.

Wilcox, Jonathan. 1991. Napier's "Wulfstan" Homilies XL and XLII: Two anonymous works from Winchester. *JEGP* 90.1–19.

—— 1992. The dissemination of Wulfstan's homilies: The Wulfstan tradition in eleventh-century vernacular preaching. In *England in the Eleventh Century: Proceedings of the 1990 Harlaxton Symposium*, ed. Carola Hicks, 199–217. Stamford: P. Watkins.

—— ed. 1994. *Ælfric's Prefaces*. Durham Medieval Texts 9. New Elvet, Durham: Department of English Studies.

—— 1996. *The Battle of Maldon* and the A-S Chronicle, 979–1016: A winning combination. *Proceedings of the Medieval Association of the Midwest* 3 (1996 for 1995), 31–50.

—— ed. 2000a. *Humour in A-S Literature*. Cambridge, D. S. Brewer.

—— 2000b. The wolf on shepherds: Wulfstan, bishops, and the context of the *Sermo Lupi ad Anglos*. In *OE Prose: Basic Readings*, ed. Paul E. Szarmach, 395–418. New York: Garland.

—— ed. 2000c. *Wulfstan Texts and Other Homiletic Materials*. Anglo-Saxon Manuscripts in Microfiche Facsimile 8. Tempe: Arizona Center for Medieval & Renassiance Studies.

Willard, Rudolph, ed. 1960. *The Blickling Homilies*. EEMF 10. Copenhagen: Rosenkilde & Bagger.

Williamson, Craig, ed. 1977. *The OE Riddles of the Exeter Book*. Chapel Hill: University of North Carolina Press.

—— trans. 1982. *A Feast of Creatures: A-S Riddle-Songs*. Philadelphia: University of Pennsylvania Press.

Wine, Joseph D. 1993. *Figurative Language in Cynewulf: Defining Aspects of a Poetic Style*. New York: P. Lang.

Winterbottom, Michael. 1967. The style of Æthelweard. *MÆ* 36.109–18.

—— ed. 1975. *Cornelii Taciti opera minora*. Oxford: Clarendon.

Wittig, Joseph S. 1983. King Alfred's *Boethius* and its Latin sources: A reconsideration. *ASE* 11.157–98.

Wolff, Ludwig. 1925. Zu den Waldere-Bruchstücken. *ZfdA* 62.81–6.

Woolf, Rosemary. 1975. *The Wanderer, The Seafarer*, and the genre of planctus. In *A-S Poetry: Essays in Appreciation for John C. McGalliard*, ed. Lewis E. Nicholson and Dolores Warwick Frese, 192–207. Notre Dame: University of Notre Dame Press.

—— 1976. The ideal of men dying with their lord in the *Germania* and in *The Battle of Maldon*. *ASE* 5.63–81.

—— ed. 1993. *Cynewulf's "Juliana."* Rev. ed. Exeter: University of Exeter Press.

Wormald, Patrick. 1977a. *Lex Scripta* and *Verbum Regis*: Legislation and Germanic kingship from Euric to Cnut. In *Early Medieval Kingship*, ed. P. H. Sawyer and I. N. Wood, 105–38. Leeds: School of History, University of Leeds. Reprinted 1999, with an additional note, in Patrick Wormald, *Legal Culture in the Early Medieval West: Law as Text, Image and Experience*, 1–44. London: Hambledon.

—— 1977b. The uses of literacy in A-S England and its neighbors. *Transactions of the Royal Historical Society*, 5th ser., 95–114.

—— 1978. Bede, *Beowulf*, and the conversion of the A-S aristocracy. In *Bede and A-S England*, ed. Robert T. Farrell, 32–95. Oxford: British Archaeological Reports.

—— 1991a. A-S society and its literature. In *The Cambridge Companion to OE Literature*, ed. Malcolm Godden and Michael Lapidge, 1–22. Cambridge: Cambridge University Press.

—— 1991b. In search of King Offa's "law-code." In *People and Places in Northern Europe 500–1600: Studies Presented to Peter Hayes Sawyer*, ed. Ian Wood and Niels Lund, 25–45. Woodbridge, Suffolk: Boydell. Reprinted 1999 in Patrick Wormald, *Legal Culture in the Early Medieval West: Law as Text, Image and Experience*, 201–23. London: Hambledon.

—— 1994. *Quadripartitus*. In *Law and Government in Medieval England and Normandy: Studies Presented to Sir James Holt*, ed. A. Rumble and D. Hill, 111–47. Cambridge: Cambridge University Press. Reprinted 1999 in Patrick Wormald, *Legal Culture in the Early Medieval West: Law as Text, Image and Experience*, 81–114. London: Hambledon.

—— 1999a. Archbishop Wulfstan and the holiness of society. In Patrick Wormald, *Legal Culture in the Early Medieval West: Law as Text, Image and Experience*, 225–51. London: Hambledon. Also in *A-S History: Basic Readings*, ed. David Pelteret. New York: Garland, 2000.

—— 1999b. Laws. In *The Blackwell Encyclopedia of A-S England*, ed. Michael Lapidge et al., 279–80. Oxford: Blackwell.

—— 1999c. *The Making of English Law: King Alfred to the Twelfth Century, I: Legislation and Its Limits*. Oxford: Blackwell.

Wrenn, C. L. 1946. The poetry of Cædmon. *PBA* 32.277–95.

Wright, C. E., ed. 1955. *Bald's Leechbook*. EEMF 5. Copenhagen: Rosenkilde & Bagger.

Wright, Charles. 1993. *The Irish Tradition in OE Literature*. CSASE 6. Cambridge: Cambridge University Press.

—— 1996. The blood of Abel and the branches of sin: *Genesis A, Maxims I* and Aldhelm's *Carmen de Uirginitate*. *ASE* 25.7–19.

Wright, Roger. 1982. *Late Latin and Early Romance in Spain and Carolingian France*. ARCA Classical and Medieval Texts, Papers and Monographs 8. Liverpool: F. Cairns.

Wright, Thomas, ed. 1850. *The Anglo-Norman Metrical Chronicle of Geoffrey Gaimar*. London: Caxton Society. Reprinted 1967, New York: B. Franklin.

Wright, Thomas, and R. P. Wülcker, eds. 1884. *A-S and OE Vocabularies*. 2nd ed. 2 vols. London: Trübner. Reprinted 1968, Darmstadt: Wissenschaftliches Buchgesellschaft.

Wyld, Henry Cecil. 1925. Diction and imagery in A-S poetry. *E&S* 11.49–91.

Wyly, Bryan Weston. 1999. *Figures of Authority in the OE "Exodus."* Anglistische

Forschungen 262. Heidelberg: C. Winter.

Yerkes, David, ed. 1979. *The Two Versions of Waerferth's Translation of Gregory's Dialogues: An OE Thesaurus*. Toronto: University of Toronto Press.

—— 1982. *Syntax and Style in OE: A Comparison of the Two Versions of Waerferth's Translation of Gregory's Dialogues*. Binghamton: Center for Medieval and Early Renaissance Studies, State University of New York.

—— 1986. The translation of Gregory's *Dialogues* and its revision: Textual history, provenance, authorship. In *Studies in Earlier OE Prose*, ed. Paul E. Szarmach, 335–43. Albany: State University of New York Press.

Zangemeister, C., ed. 1889. *Pauli Orosii historiarum adversum paganos*. Leipzig: Teubner.

Zanna, Paolo. 1991. "Descriptiones urbium" and elegy in Latin and vernaculars, in the early Middle Ages. *Studi medievali*, 3rd ser. 32.523–96.

Zettel, Patrick H. 1982. Saints' lives in OE: Latin manuscripts and vernacular accounts: Ælfric. *Peritia* 1.17–37.

Zettersten, Arne. 1969. The source of **mocritum* in OE. *SN* 41.375–7.

—— ed. 1979. *Waldere*. Manchester: University of Manchester Press.

Zupitza, Julius, ed. 1880. *Ælfrics Grammatik und Glossar*. Berlin: Weidmann. Reprinted 1966, with preface by Helmut Gneuss.

—— ed. 1888. Cantus Beati Godrici. *Englische Studien* 11.401–32.

—— ed. 1899. *Elene*. 4th ed. Berlin: Weidmann.

—— ed. 1959. *"Beowulf" Reproduced in Facsimile from the Unique Manuscript, British Museum MS. Cotton Vitellius A. xv*. 2nd ed. rev. by Norman Davis. EETS o.s. 245. London: Oxford University Press.

Index

Works are listed by author if the author is known, otherwise by title.